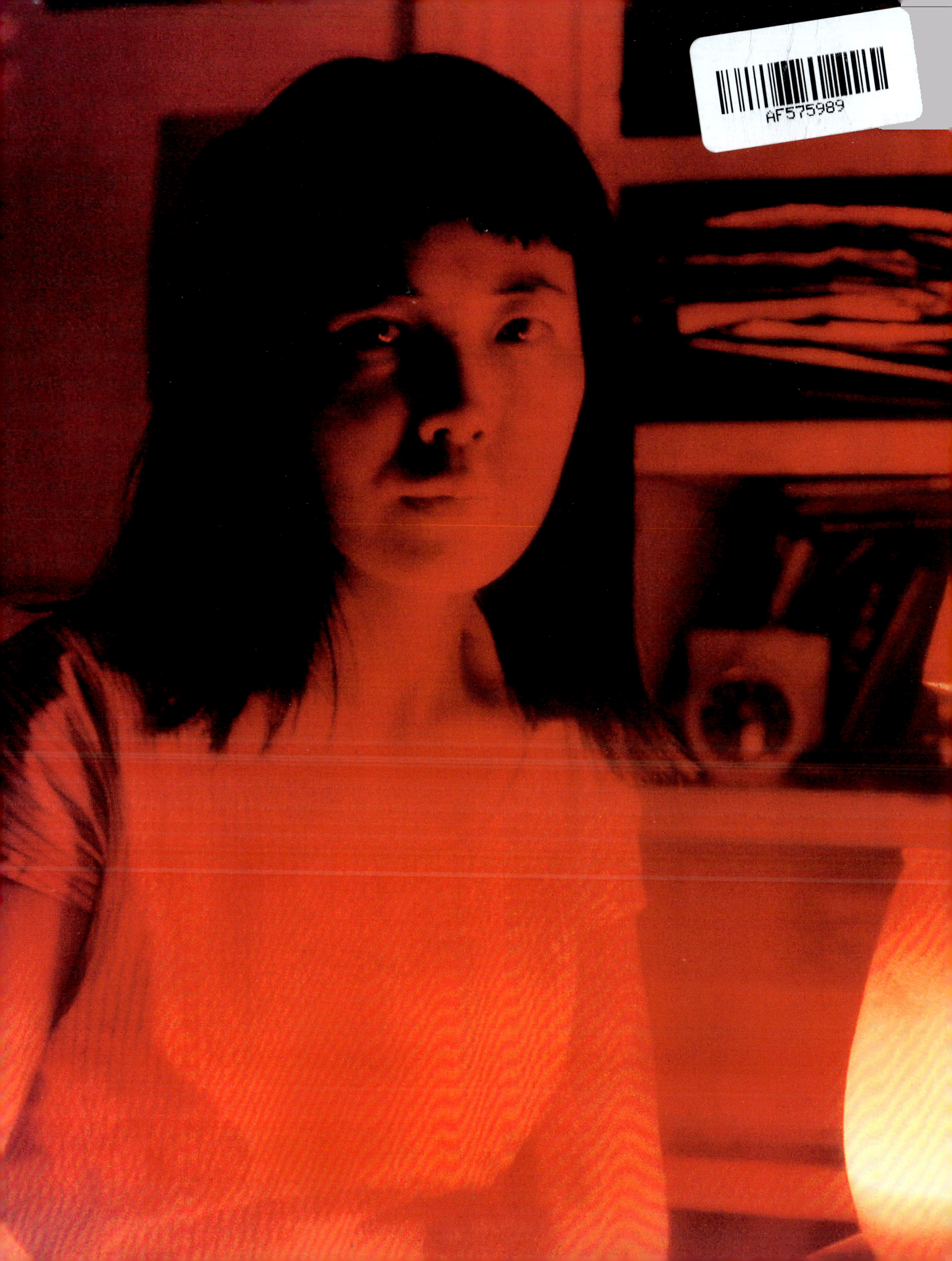

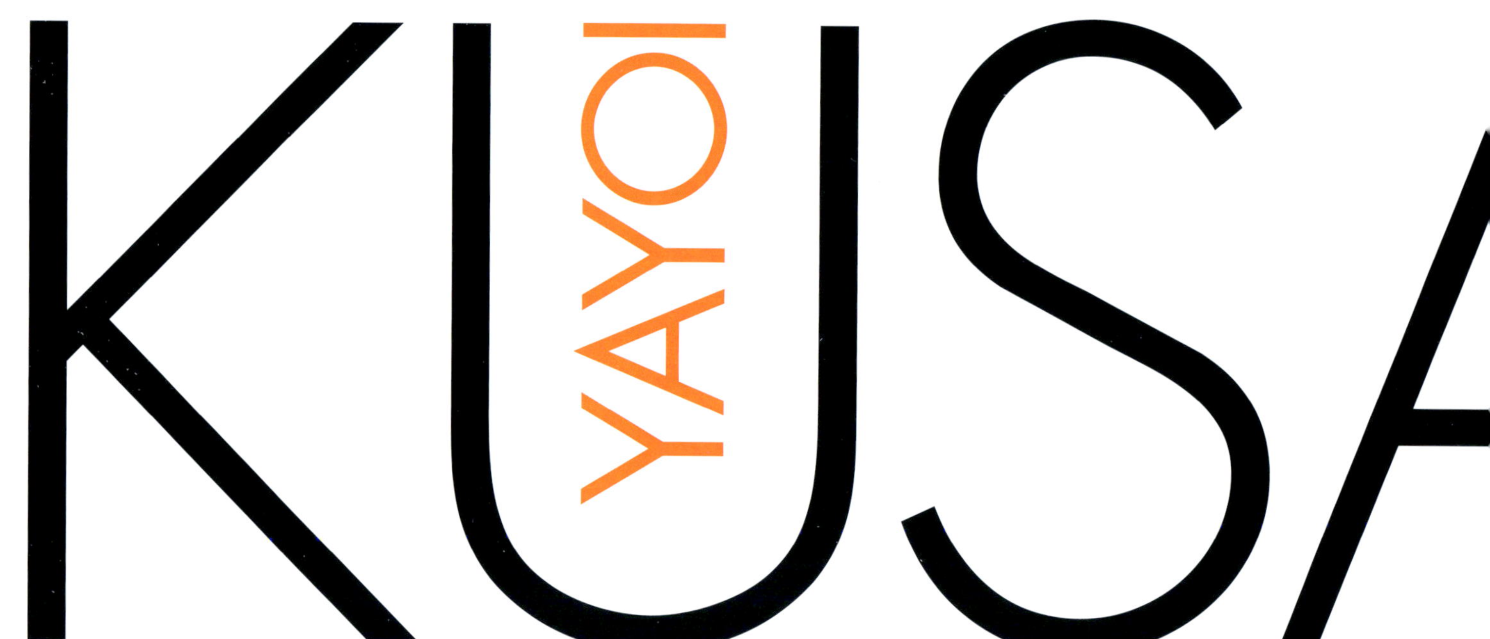

With contributions by

Jo Applin
Juliet Mitchell
Frances Morris
Mignon Nixon
Rachel Taylor
Midori Yamamura

Edited by Frances Morris

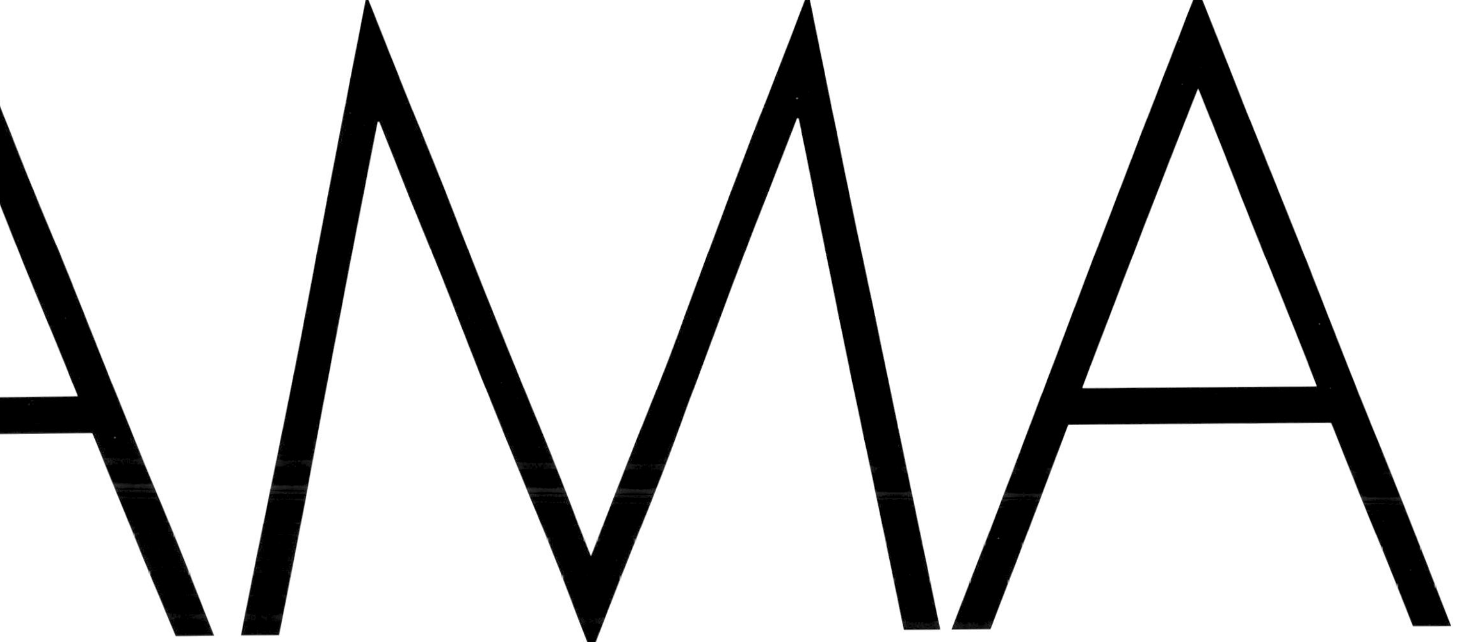

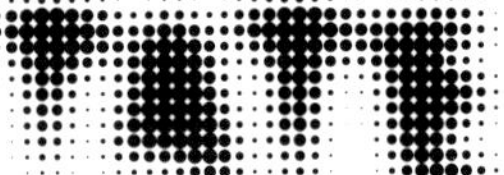

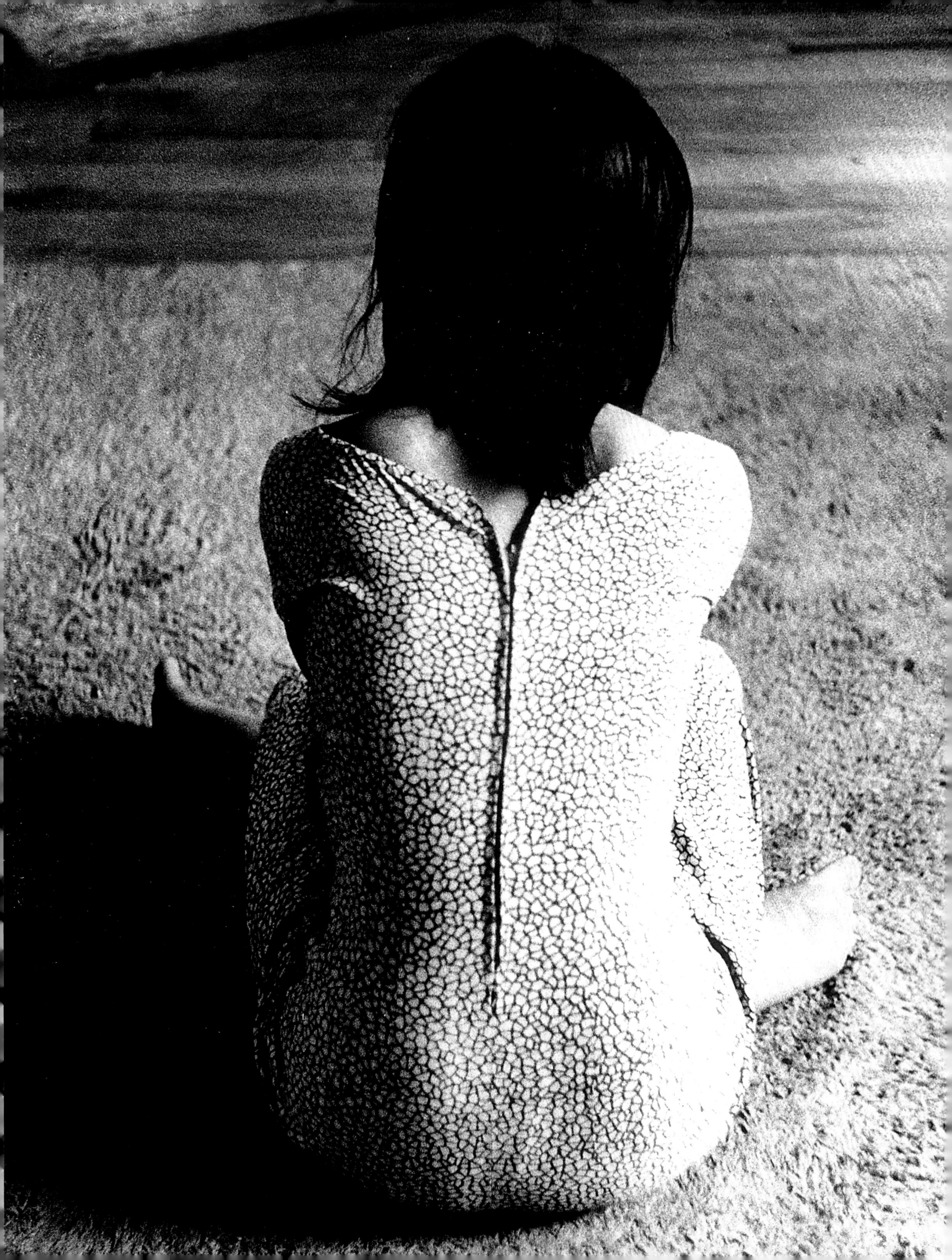

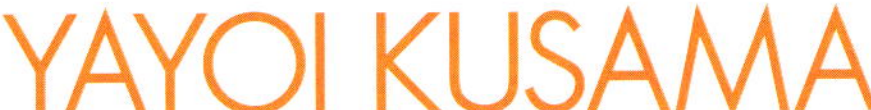

a privilege to have the opportunity to revisit her extraordinary career for this survey.

This exhibition and publication would not have been possible without the close collaboration of Yayoi Kusama and her splendid studio team in Tokyo who have given their support throughout. Ota Fine Arts, Kusama's gallery in Tokyo, has been enormously helpful and we would particularly like to thank Director Hidenori Ota as well as Yoriko Tsuruta who has provided exceptional assistance to the curators at all stages of this long project. In London, Victoria Miro Gallery have been closely involved – Victoria, Glenn Scott Wright, Kathy Stephenson and Mary Taylor have been greatly supportive. We are also especially grateful to the Kusama Studio, Victoria Miro Gallery and Ota Fine Arts for their generous support of the exhibition tour.

The exhibition draws on loans from private and public collections. We have been touched by the readiness of so many individuals to lend their treasured works by Kusama for such an extended period and we offer them our heartfelt thanks. A number of public collections have also gone to remarkable lengths in agreeing to lend and we are indebted to them for their willingness to collaborate with us so readily.

The exhibition has been realised with support from our exhibition tour partners, and we have been lucky to work with such extraordinary individuals and exemplary institutions: Manuel J. Borja-Villel, Director, and Teresa Velazquez Cortés, Head of Exhibitions, at the Museo Nacional Centro de Arte Reina Sofía; Alfred Pacquement, Director, and Chantal Beret, Curator at the Centre Georges Pompidou; and Adam D. Weinberg, the Alice Pratt Brown Director, and David Kiehl, Curator of Prints and Special Collections, at the Whitney Museum of American Art. Each institution has sensitively shaped the exhibition for their own galleries and audiences and we are grateful to them and to all their colleagues at their respective museums for enabling the exhibition to reach a broader international audience.

Preparation for an exhibition of this scale and ambition inevitably begins long before the opening date and involves the input of key individuals along the way. Of the many individuals consulted we would especially like to thank Hart Perry, Caroline de Westenholz, Christopher D'Amelio, Ryutaro Takahashi and Daisuke Miyatsu, who, in different ways, have each been especially helpful to the project. We have also learnt a huge amount from the contributors to the catalogue Jo Applin, Juliet Mitchell, Mignon Nixon and Midori Yamamura and we are grateful to them for their thoughtful, original and fascinating texts. Special thanks are also due to Adam Brown for his elegant design of the catalogue.

The exhibition is supported by Louis Vuitton and we owe them a huge debt of thanks for enabling us to bring Kusama's work to a larger public. We would particularly like to extend our thanks to Yves Carcelle, Tom Meggle, and Eleonore de Boysson for their creative collaboration. We would also like to thank the committed group of individuals and charitable foundations that have supported the staging of the exhibition at Tate as part of The Yayoi Kusama Exhibition Supporters Group.

This exhibition has been made possible by the provision of insurance through the Government Indemnity Scheme. Tate Modern would like to thank HM Government for providing Government Indemnity and the Department for Culture, Media and Sport and the Arts Council England for arranging the indemnity.

Yayoi Kusama has been curated by Frances Morris, Head of Collections, International Art at Tate. Her remarkable vision, creativity and commitment have driven the project from its outset, shaping the content and form of the exhibition and ensuring its visual and conceptual rigour. Frances worked very closely with her colleague Rachel Taylor, who has also contributed the documentary display of archival material and worked tirelessly towards the exhibition's realisation. Roanne Hathaway, Ted McDonald-Toone, Mary McNicholas and Felicity Hartfield have provided admirable back-up throughout, as did Exhibition Intern Sayoko Nakahara. The curatorial team has been exceptionally complemented by Exhibition Registrars Stephanie Bush and, in the early stages of the project, Susan Thompson. Phil Monk has led the art installation team at Tate Modern with support from Kerstin Doble, while Sam Clarke has ably overseen the Tate Modern art handling team. As ever we are indebted to Tate's exceptional conservators who have contributed their expertise to the installation and care of vulnerable loans. Sheena Wagstaff, Chief Curator; Helen Sainsbury, Head of Exhibitions Programme Management and Rachel Kent, Exhibition Touring Manager have provided invaluable senior support, as did Stephen Mellor, Tate's former Exhibitions Co-ordinator. Other teams at Tate Modern are owed a debt of thanks including our colleagues in Tate Learning, including Simon Bolitho and Minnie Driver, who assisted with the preparation of interpretation texts. Development colleagues Sarah Robinson, Marina Busse, Emelia Fellows, Silaja Suntharalingam and Clare Walton have been instrumental in securing financial support for the exhibition. The exhibition's marketing has been masterminded by Pete Gomori, Sarah Briggs and Livia Ratcliffe, while Daisy Mallabar, Duncan Holden and Rose Dahlsen have supervised press coverage. We are grateful to those who worked on the catalogue: Nicola Bion, Roanne Marner, Richard Mason, Roz Young, and Tate Photographers Andrew Dunkley, Marcus Leith and Dave Lambert.

Finally we would like to emphasise our deep gratitude to Yayoi Kusama herself for responding so readily to our invitation to make this exhibition and for her commitment to and interest in all aspects of the project, from the selection of work to the catalogue essays, throughout the long period of its development.

Chris Dercon
Director, Tate Modern, 2011–2016

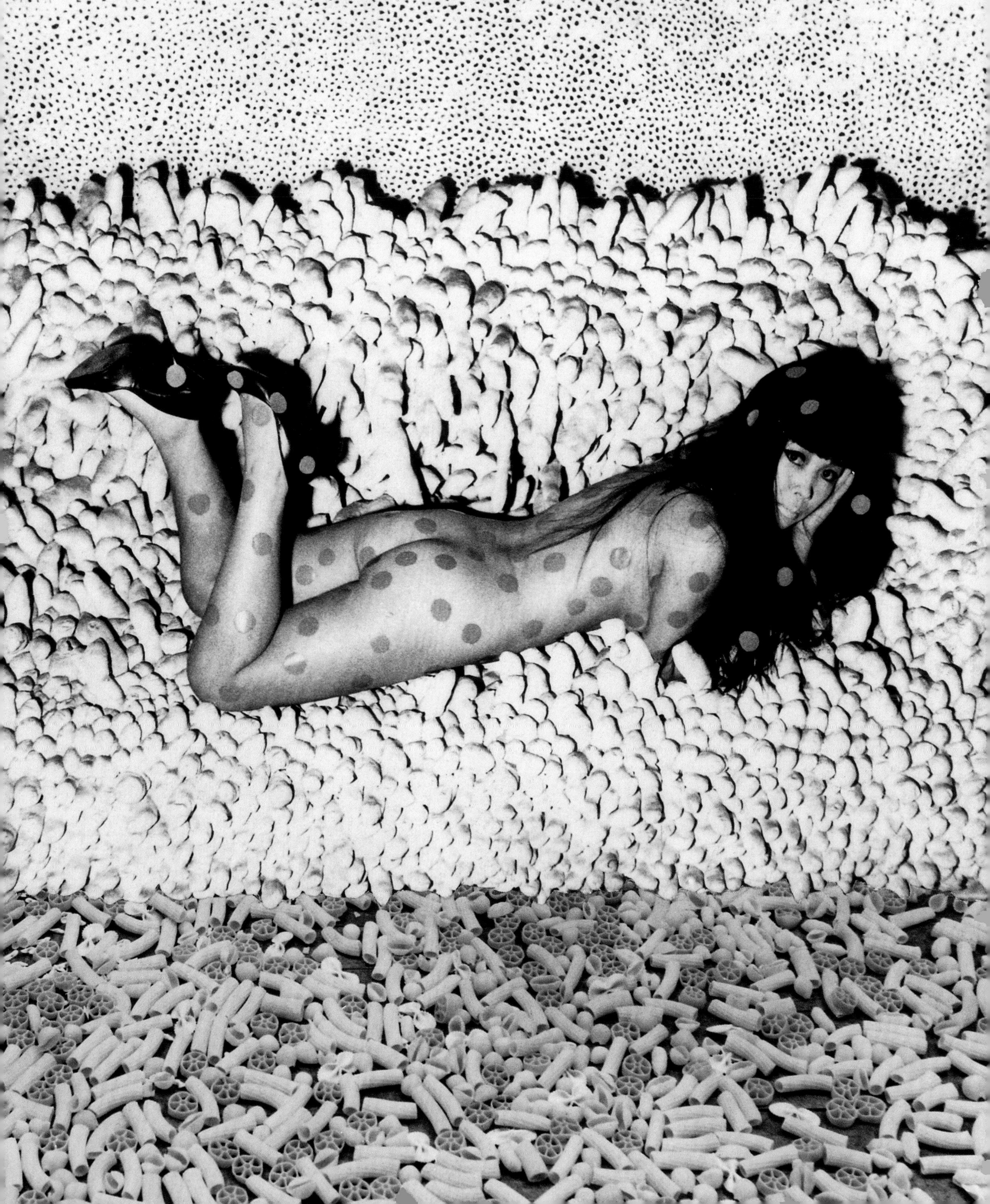

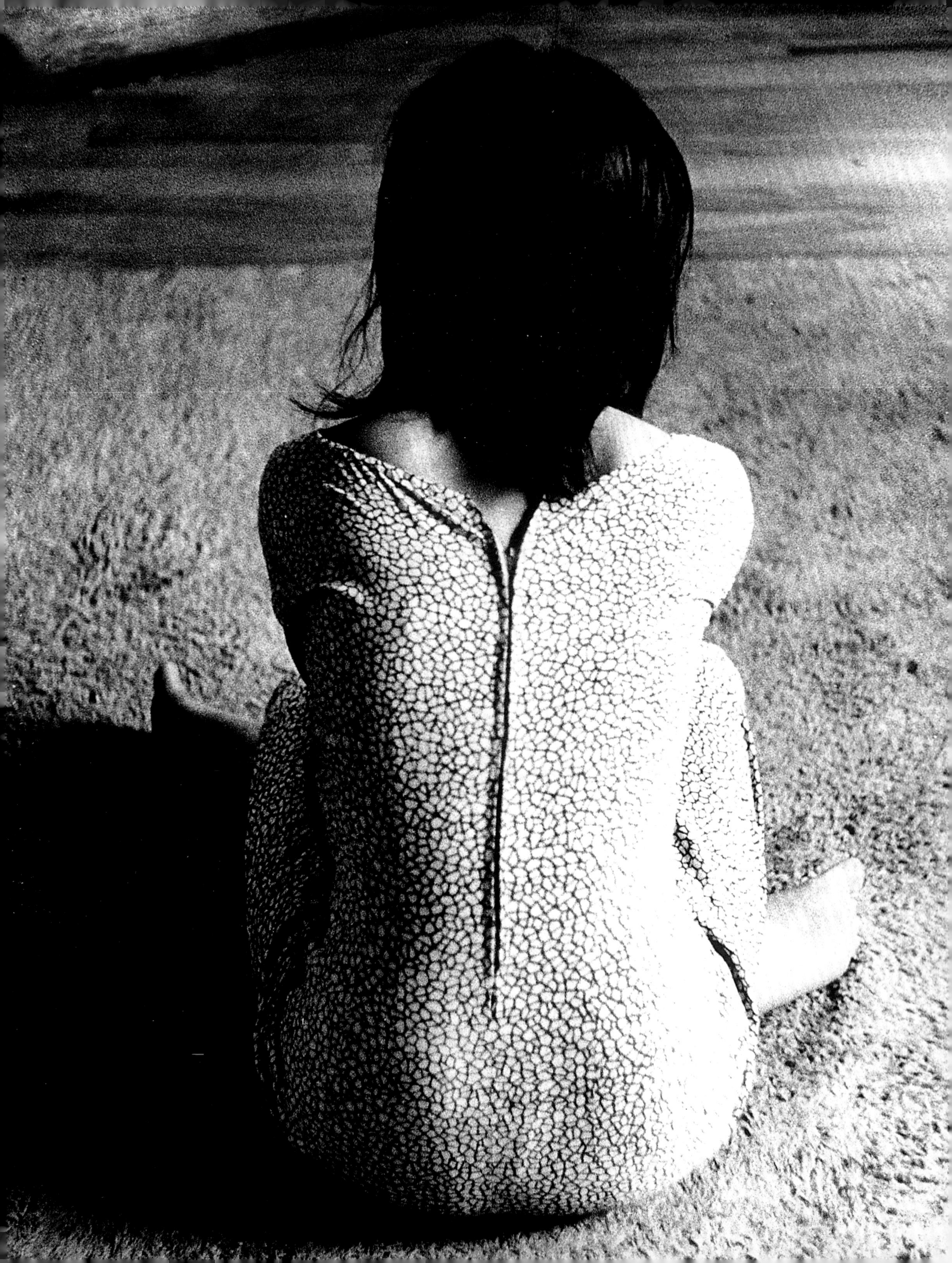

Kusama, 1959

Frances Morris

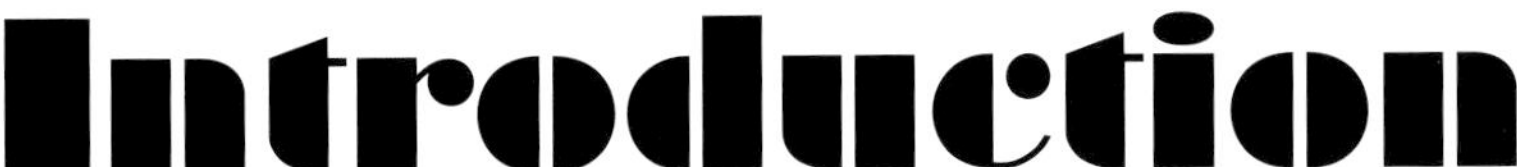

For a Japanese artist in the late 1950s to journey to the US was not an unprecedented act, but it *was* unusual, and especially so for a young female artist from the provinces. Neither exile nor émigré, Yayoi Kusama's adventure was nomadic, her residence in America punctuated by extended visits to Europe over the course of a decade. Her return in 1973 to Japan, where she has remained to this day, marks Kusama's experience as fundamentally different to the majority of her contemporaries in Europe and America. Many of the great artists we associate with the flowering of American art gave their careers to the histories of their adopted homeland. Not so Kusama who briefly, if brilliantly, *lent* her name to American art for a decade, during which time she evolved for herself a singular position on the New York alternative scene. This was, however, already a second chapter in a long career: Japan – New York – Japan. The division of her creative life into three distinct phases has naturally encouraged a compartmentalised thinking about her history that tends to overlook important questions about how individual creative identities are formed and reformed by different contexts over time. Rebuilding this narrative highlights the shifts that characterised Kusama's development, while also signalling the continuities that underpin her multifaceted history.

The narrative of Kusama's career is of necessity, therefore, one of ebb and flow between east and west, of dialogue, exchange and rupture. The artist was schooled in the traditional manner of Japanese *Nihonga* painting – itself a blend of east and west. She then, as Midori Yamamura argues in her catalogue essay, rejected a tradition tainted by association with Nationalist rule – *Nihonga* realism was the preferred style of the wartime dictatorship – and began avidly to absorb the influence of 'Western' cubism and surrealism, through magazines and especially through her friendship with the Japanese surrealist poet and critic Takiguchi Shūzō, who also wrote about her work at the time. Kusama's early experiments in watercolour were extensive, ambitious and highly original. She evolved an intensely coloured and animated manner, with spontaneous lyrical gestures and distinctive types of patterning – Kusama's trademark dots originate in these works on paper – and developed a vocabulary of biomorphic and microscopic organic forms, essentially abstract but evocative of stellar, aquatic or subterranean worlds. These watercolours demonstrate how far and how fast Kusama had travelled from her early grounding in Japanese tradition.

In turning to art Kusama displayed audacity as well as ambition: she faced obstacles from all sides, near and far – social, cultural and familial – in the masculine and deeply conservative Japan of the 1950s. Although she forged the beginnings of a promising career in Japan with exhibitions in Tokyo and her home town of Matsumoto, she soon turned her attention further afield: Kusama chose her destination because she believed the 'future lay in New York' and aspired 'to grab everything that went on in the city and become a star'.[1] Arriving in America, Kusama consciously traded on her Eastern persona, an image encapsulated in photographs and performances of herself – kimono clad – taken throughout her stay. While thus asserting her Japanese identity in a foreign land, in her art she assimilated new influences rapidly: the speed with which she located and then penetrated the epicentre of the New York avant-garde was remarkable. She immersed herself in the community of Greenwich Village, and her work progressively absorbed and then began to challenge the most advanced studio practices of the time, first in painting, and later in more radical forms, as a critical response to the heady mix of commercial excess and rampant 1960s counter-culture. The climate of dissent that embraced the interlocking themes of Vietnam, gender and race provides 'contexts' for understanding Kusama's practice in the USA. So total was her immersion that when she returned to Japan in 1973 – to a country radically changed through its post-war 'economic miracle' – she found herself, perversely, a 'Western' artist, without coordinates in the Tokyo scene. For a period she withdrew – mental instability necessitating periods of hospitalisation – and focused on poetry, fiction and fashioning smaller-scale, more 'private' work in ceramic and collage. By the 1980s she had returned to public view, her confidence and ambition restored. The huge paintings she made in these years are covered, from edge to edge, with fantastic biomorphic patterns in psychedelic colours that generate dazzling optical sensations. Their billboard scale and their smooth, flat finish, their almost mass-produced feel, reveal Kusama's response to aspects of Japanese commercial art with its embrace of 'pop' culture and spectacle. This ability to adapt to and reconcile contrasting cultural contexts links Kusama to a much younger generation of 'international' artists who now move routinely between cities in today's more globalised world, and whose practices transcend their locales.

Another of the distinctive features of today's international art scene is artists' refusal to confine themselves to a 'signature' style or medium; instead they tend to select their tools and materials on a project by project basis, seeking out the most appropriate means for their message or taking an idea through a number of different material manifestations. Kusama's manner of radically recasting her strategy in different guises appears prescient in this respect. While her move from realist *Nihonga* painting to a Miróesque abstract mode in the late 1940s marked a fundamental shift in direction, in the longer view it represented simply the first of many such reorientations. In just one decade, from 1958 to 1968, she moved from painting to sculpture and collage and on to installations, films, performances and 'happenings', political actions and counter-cultural events; she extended her practice through published magazines and newspapers, designed clothes and ran a boutique. Along the way Kusama's work was co-opted by different, sometimes irreconcilable tendencies – Donald Judd, for example, cited her practice in 'Specific Objects', first published in 1965, his defining text on emerging minimalism, while the critic Lucy Lippard enlisted the work in her exploration of post-minimalist 'eccentric abstraction' only the following year – but in truth Kusama never stood still long enough for labels to stick, and she seems anyway to have eschewed groups and associations. She was not alone at the time in moving her forum from studio and gallery to street and newspaper, but even amongst those seeking a wider and more expansive modus operandi, few experimented over such a wide stage and only Andy Warhol comes close to Kusama in his expansive and totalising practice, his disregard for distinctions between high and low art. In today's more diversified cultural context, with the erasure of borders between private and public, commercial and independent, and the near universal access to technology, the selection of a particular medium, technique and audience is, for artists, rarely a commitment for life; it is rather the result of strategic decision-making over time. Kusama's precocious development anticipates this way of working.

Kusama launched her New York career in a solo show she herself organised at the Tenth Street Cooperative Gallery in October 1959. The five very large white monochrome canvases that she exhibited represented a radical shift from the works on paper she had brought with her from Japan. They matched – indeed surpassed – the scale of most abstract expressionist artworks, but with their distinctive, almost formulaic looping brushstrokes, appearing as if lace or netting, they challenged the gestural spontaneity of Jackson Pollock and Willem de Kooning. We know this to be a change of style – achieved only through intense experimentation, as period studio photographs of many now-lost paintings attest – in which Kusama set out to do something radical and new. Writing to a Japanese magazine just four months before the show, she declared 'I am planning to create a revolutionary new work that will stun the international art world … [and will] show the New York art world a decisive direction for the future'.[2] For a brief and intense period Kusama produced 'Infinity Net paintings', as they came to be known, on an almost industrial scale. They were well received, and taken seriously by critics such as Dore Ashton of *The New York Times*, but just as they (and the artist) were gaining recognition across America and Europe, Kusama presented herself in an entirely new guise. In June 1962, at the Green Gallery, she exhibited the first of her 'accumulations', a sofa and a chair covered in hundreds of hand-made and white-painted phallic protuberances. In many ways this was an astonishing development. In place of the formal vocabulary of aesthetic abstraction, the language here was an aberrant take on realism, its evocation of male sexuality vivid, shocking and at the same time comic. It was also a move brilliantly in tune with, even anticipatory of, the most advanced avant-garde developments: a shift across disciplines, from two to three dimensions – from painting to sculpture – but also a step from art towards life, from high culture to low, incorporating as it did elements from the studio, found objects of domestic use. It was an innovation that one might expect would attract attention, debate, even derision. Kusama's two works in the show were exhibited alongside ones by Claes Oldenburg, Andy Warhol, James

Rosenquist and George Segal, indisputably linking Kusama to the birth of American pop art.

Subsequent reinventions were equally unexpected and historically significant, but while they garnered publicity – which she sought assiduously – they led Kusama increasingly away from the mainstream. Her 1968 film *Kusama's Self-Obliteration* (no.82) was made by Kusama with assistance from the young experimental filmmaker Jud Yalkut. The film presents a collage of images of her early paintings and dream sequences of Kusama painting the landscape with spots, with mantra-like music by The CIA Change with Paul Kilb and Ted Bork and a chorus of amplified frogs; into this is interwoven footage of the radical participatory art form Kusama called 'Audio-Visual Light Performance', which she had organised as the self-appointed director of a cluster of New York-based hippie and alternative scene organisations such as the Happening Poster-Corporation.

Kusama managed these projects largely on her own. Unlike so many other successful artists of her generation, whose careers were shrewdly managed and financed by dealers almost as celebrated as the artists they represented, Kusama 'made' herself in these seminal early years. There were gallerists, critics, artists and curators who provided crucial encouragement and support along the way – amongst them Donald Judd, Joseph Cornell and the gallerist Beatrice Perry in the USA, the young German curator Udo Kultermann, and fellow artists such as Henk Peeters in the Netherlands and Lucio Fontana in Italy – but ultimately Kusama pursued, essentially alone, a high-risk entrepreneurial strategy. Half a century before websites and blogs were available, she had taken on the business of exhibiting, advertising and documenting her own work: she was an avid self-publicist, writer of manifestos and frequent correspondent to the papers.

When, during the 1980s, Kusama re-established her studio practice, she steadily regained a foothold in the marketplace as well as garnering the critical support of a new generation of admirers. In 1993 she represented Japan at the Venice Biennale, creating a new environmental installation for the first time since the 1960s. Since then, although her career has been increasingly supported by successful commercial gallerists in Tokyo, New York and London, Kusama has eagerly embraced risk-taking in other forms. These have included initiating a series of artist-curated touring shows across Europe and Asia from 2000, and taking up the challenge to show work, often new commissions, alongside much younger artists, in unfamiliar contexts and to unknown, potentially hostile audiences, on the circuit of biennials and triennials that characterise the contemporary international art scene.

To visit Kusama in her Tokyo studio today is to visit an artist in full control of her world and emphatically living in the present. She presides, by day, over a team of dedicated assistants, conceiving and directing site-specific installations and major public sculptures for institutions and individuals across the world. Much of her recent work is an extension of ideas first explored in the 1960s. Her sensational and immersive mirror rooms with their twinkling pinpricks of light, and her zany other-worldly installations filled by vinyl balloons in biomorphic forms covered in her polka dots, can be seen as originating in her early environmental piece, *Infinity Mirror Room – Phalli's Field* 1966, carpeted in red and white phalli,

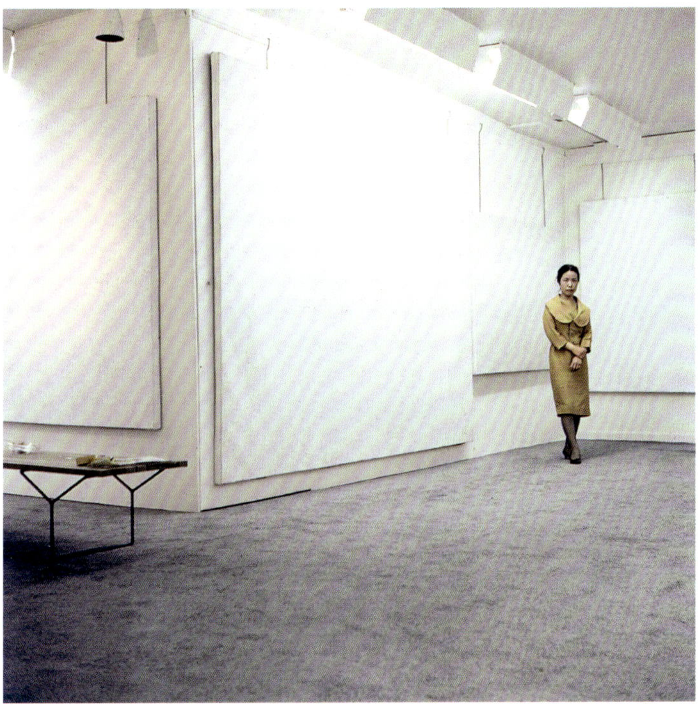

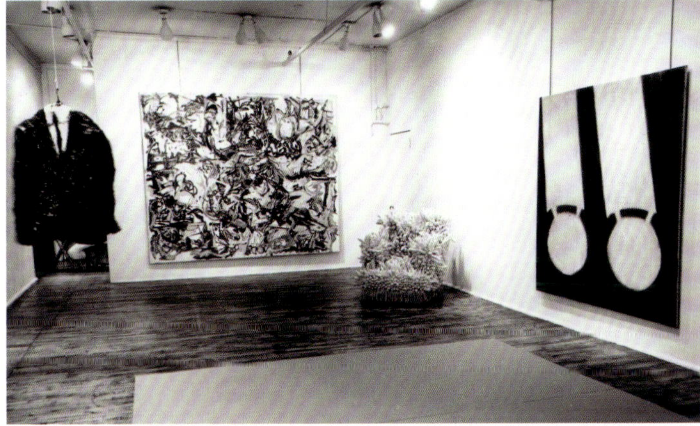

Top: Kusama at the Stephen Radich Gallery, New York, 1961
Above: *Accumulation No.1*, soft sculpture exhibited in a group show at Green Gallery, New York, 1962

in which the phalli and the viewer were endlessly reflected (see p.186). Other aspects of her recent work are without precedent and demonstrate an insatiable need to explore new realms. Beginning in 1992 with her first pumpkin sculptures, Kusama has evolved a whole vocabulary of image-forms: plants, flowers, animals and people, especially children. Although fully volumetric these objects and characters have a flat, graphic quality and decorative naivety which arguably relate them to the recent tradition of 'cute' cartoon-like characters or 'kawaii' that are such a distinctive feature of Japanese commercial and popular culture. This fantasy style evolved in the post-war era as part of the explosion of 'manga' and 'anime' comic-book art, and Kusama's appropriation of its essence demonstrates again her continuing ability to keep pace with, exploit and reconcile seemingly opposite ends of the cultural spectrum, even as she enters her eighties. Most recently she has produced a series of over one hundred acrylic paintings on canvas, brilliantly coloured and hand-painted in a spontaneous and continuous process. In animating their surfaces Kusama deploys a limited range of unmixed colours – orange, green, red and purple – and draws on a vocabulary of decorative and iconographic motifs, with extensive 'quotations' from earlier graphic work, combined on each canvas in unique and infinite variations.

In the studio's small reception area, the visitor is surrounded by hundreds of books, catalogues and magazines devoted to Kusama's art, and by dozens of branded products carrying her now famous designs: a small spotted dog, pigtailed country girls, voluptuous yellow pumpkins and, everywhere, her brightly coloured dots. As Kusama works, and when meetings take place, a filmmaker is present, calmly recording the day's events and interviewing visitors as they come and go, capturing it all for posterity.

Almost from the start visual documentation of her activity was an integral part of Kusama's practice: her face, like Warhol's, fast became inseparable from her creations. She had herself photographed before her works – in her studio and at exhibitions, at every opportunity – presenting herself in many guises, from vulnerable outsider to predatory temptress. Although these images were made for different reasons – documentation, publicity and artistic experimentation (in a series of collages) – they share a common focus on the artist in the role of author, mistress and controller of her environment, signifying the environment *as* the work, creating a kind of Kusama-world with its own internal logic, and with the persona of the artist at its centre.

By the time Kusama began to write her autobiography, in the mid-1970s back in Japan, she had come to understand and explain her own work and obsessions as intrinsically linked to hallucinatory episodes during her childhood that resurfaced in later recurrent mental breakdowns. There is now a growing literature around the role of mental illness in art as well as pathological interpretations of creativity. Much of the writing on Kusama's work has followed the artist's lead in linking her motivation, her manner of working, the style of the work itself and its subject matter – such as the focus on food and sex – to a psychological disorder dating from childhood and related to memorable traumatic incidents in her early years, from her father's philandering to her mother's alleged violence towards her daughter. Since 1977 Kusama has chosen to live within a psychiatric hospital close to her studio, and this context has

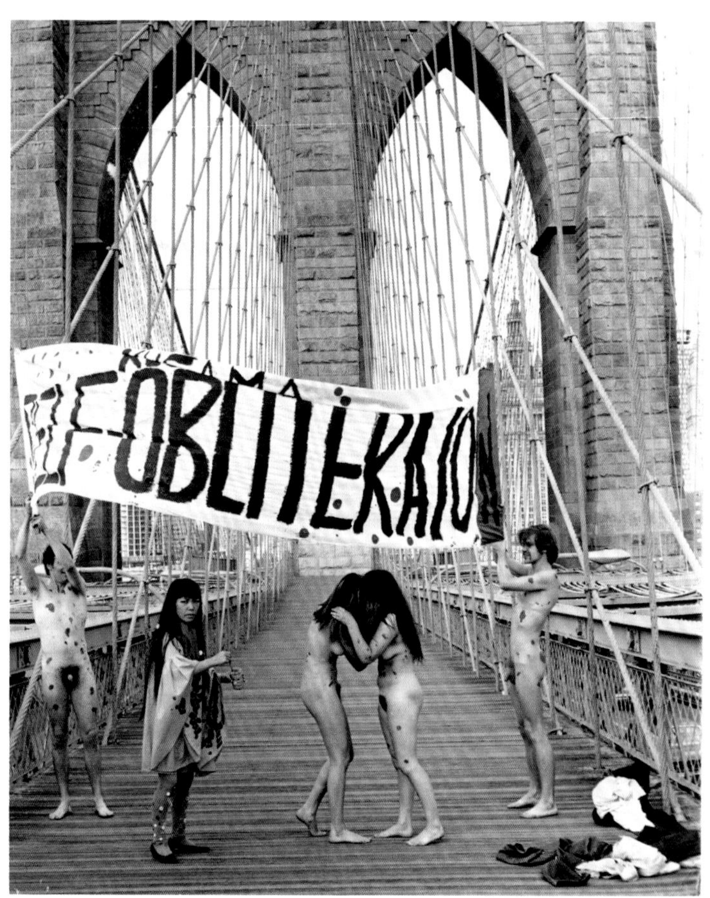

Above: Anti-war naked happening, New York, 1968
Opposite, top: *Hi, Konnichiwa (Hello)*, 2004, installation view, KUSAMATRIX at Mori Art Museum, Tokyo
Opposite, bottom: Kusama in her studio, Tokyo, 2010

framed much of the speculation around her work. Consideration of her working process as an artist is frequently diagnostic in character, particularly in relation to notions of proliferation, accumulation, repetition and obliteration within the work, all of which are signalled in the titles she has given her works. Kusama's mental health is undoubtedly one of the most fascinating aspects of the artist's life and art. However, rather than repeating a narrative well told by Kusama and echoed by others, psychoanalyst Juliet Mitchell offers a fresh analysis, examining how this artist has put the experience of hallucinosis at the heart of her work, and focusing on the traumatic conditions that underpin the construction of 'Kusama's World' and on what Kusama herself makes of her history.

This publication seeks to extend the view of Kusama's art beyond the lens of mental illness. While the artist's personal biography and circumstances are fully set out in Rachel Taylor's introductions to each plate section, the catalogue also examines the cultural and political background of the places and times from which her startlingly original work emerged. Midori Yamamura sheds light on Kusama's formative years in wartime and post-war Japan, as well as the affinities between her work and that of the Seattle School abstractionists who first welcomed her to the US. Mignon Nixon excavates the more familiar history of Kusama's New York years, connecting her successive innovations to the local context and reinvesting Kusama's various adventures with a sense of the work's transgressive political agency. Finally, in looking at Kusama's more recent work, and in particular her large-scale environmental installations such as *I'm Here, but Nothing* 2000 (no.96), Jo Applin re-examines these sites of 'psychic fragmentation' as relational, social spaces, closely connected to Kusama's participatory happenings of the late 1960s.

While this exhibition spans over sixty years of endeavour, it constitutes only a representative selection from a lifetime's work. It is staged as a series of rooms, discrete encounters with aspects of Kusama's practice, unfolding over time. Although Kusama has continued, in some cases repeatedly, to return to and re-engage with particular idioms, such as the Infinity Net paintings that she first made in the 1960s, the focus here is on the moment of genesis of each idiom, showing them as they emerged and while they absorbed the artist's full creative energies. Some of these rooms show self-contained installations or experiential environments, while others include selected individual pieces that evoke the ways in which Kusama arranged her work in her studio and in exhibitions, partial reconstructions following the evidence of documentary images. They follow and attempt to echo the artist's preference for dense, wall-to-wall display and an excess of content, evident in the crowded double-height hang of her early watercolours shown in Matsumoto, October 1952, the expansive horizontality of her white Infinity Net paintings at Brata Gallery, October 1959, and the massed accumulation sculptures in her East 19th studio around 1963. The aim has been to demonstrate both the intensity of Kusama's engagement at any given moment, and the way in which she deliberately constructed and documented evidence of her obsessional activity in retrospect.

Writing about her art in May 1961, Kusama spoke of her monochrome net paintings as the maturation of a long-anticipated desire to release a semi-cosmic vision of nature, which she had first tried to visualise in ink drawings as a teenager.[3] Subsequent statements by the artist have implied a kind of immanence, a sense of her work developing in a context shaped by inner compulsion, one thing begetting the next. It seems unlikely, however, that her work would have followed the course it did had she not struck out from, and later returned to, her native Japan, or that it would have been so precisely in tune with, even in advance of, so many avant-garde innovations (monochrome painting, the ready-made, environmental installation) had she not been so open to influences from near and far, high and low, east and west. Her declared independence from any group or association allowed her to respond fully, freely and immediately to the most diverse positions and influences – from cool minimalism to manga kitsch – at different times. Kusama's art is presented here as a journey of personal discovery as well as a sequence of striking positions, strongly rooted in the various moments and contexts of its making.

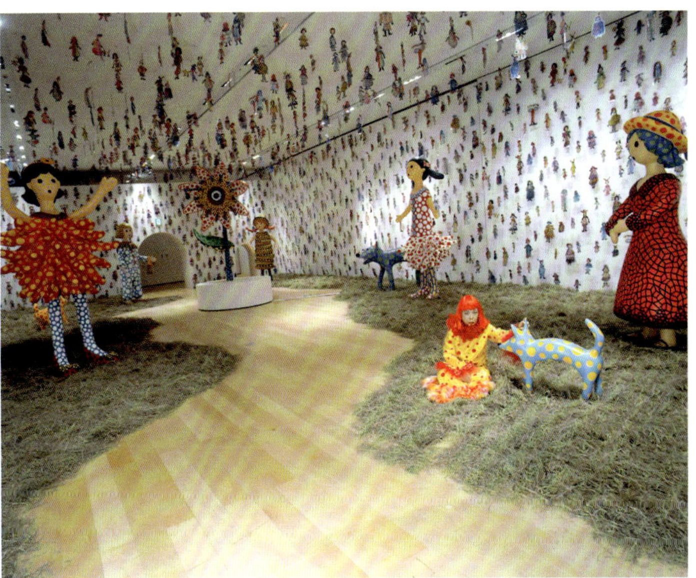

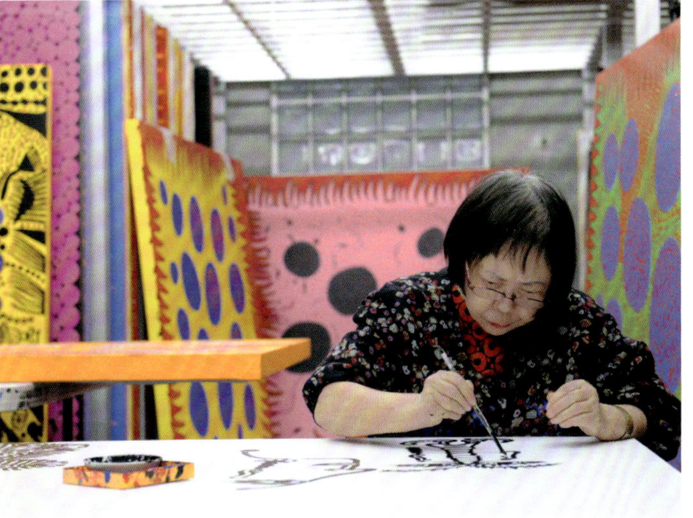

Early Years 1929–1957

Yayoi Kusama was born on 22 March 1929 in Matsumoto City, a provincial town in the mountainous region of Nagano Prefecture about 130 miles west of Tokyo. She was the youngest of four children in an upper middle-class family whose wealth was derived from the management of wholesale seed nurseries. Kusama developed her passion for art making from a very young age, taking her sketchbooks to her family's seed-harvesting grounds and drawing the budding flowers for hours on end.

Kusama was educated at the Kamata Elementary School and the Matsumoto First Girls' High School in her home town. On 7 December 1941 the Japanese attack on Pearl Harbor heralded the outset of the Pacific War. Along with other school-age children in Japan, Kusama was drafted into working to support the war effort, forced to endure long hours in the Kureha Textile factory assisting in the production of parachutes and military uniforms. Despite these difficult conditions she continued to draw and paint whenever she could, using the few materials available to her. Kusama began publicly exhibiting her work while still in her teens, successfully submitting works to the open-competition Zen-Shinshū Regional Art Exhibitions in 1945 and 1946.

In 1948, overcoming her parents' objections to her ongoing quest to forge a career as a professional artist, Kusama enrolled for a year at the Kyoto Municipal Hiyoshigaoka Upper Secondary School to study painting in the modern Japanese *Nihonga* style. Pursuing an artistic career was an extremely unusual step for a young woman in conservative post-war Japan, but Kusama displayed a single-minded determination in pursuing her goal. After the end of her studies in Kyoto, she briefly studied with *Nihonga* master Maeda Seison at his studio in Kamakura City. As she states in her autobiography, Kusama soon became disillusioned by the strict hierarchical approach of the master-student dynamic, however, and by the restrictions of *Nihonga* painting itself. The largest of Kusama's extant *Nihonga* works is *Lingering Dream*, an otherworldly vision of a war-scarred landscape with crimson sunflowers (no.1).

Her frustration with conventional teaching methods at art school and in her short-lived apprenticeship was matched, if not exceeded, by Kusama's autodidactic enthusiasms. She immersed herself in magazines detailing the latest artistic tendencies in Europe and America. Journals including *Mizue* and *Atelier* exposed her to symbolism and surrealism as well as contemporary Japanese avant-garde movements.

Fiercely independent and with a seemingly insatiable desire to develop her practice, Kusama began to experiment with materials and techniques. She set out to teach herself Western-style oil painting, in the process mixing elements of Japanese and Western approaches to painterly media. In *Accumulation of the Corpses (Prisoner Surrounded by the Curtain of Depersonalization)* (no.3) and *Earth of Accumulation* (no.5), for instance, she combined oil paint with enamel; the characteristic grainy impasto of *On the Table* (no.4) results from mixing sand with animal-glue (a medium used as a binding agent in Japanese *kōsai* painting).

Kusama continued to develop her techniques on works on paper, which she produced in the hundreds in the early 1950s. Executed in a variety of media including ink, pastel, watercolour, gouache and tempera, her early works on paper testify to the artist's constant exploration of form and colour. These works vary in content, but often feature abstracted forms that suggest natural phenomena. Kusama's subjects include eggs, seeds, trees and flowers. Hinting

1945

Zen-Shinshū Regional Art Exhibition, Nagano Prefectural Normal School, Nagano City, 16–18 November, touring to Ueda City, 21–3 November; Matsumoto City, 27–9 November; Iida City, 3–5 December

1946

The Second Zen-Shinshū Art Exhibition, Nagano City Shiroyama Merchandise Exhibition Hall, 23–7 October, touring to Matsumoto City, Sakurabashi, Municipal Women's High School, 2–6 November

1949

The Second Nagano Prefectural Art Exhibition, Nagano Community Centre, 21 September – 8 October, touring to Matsumoto Community Centre, Matsumoto Municipal Museum, 11–17 November; Suwa Art Museum, 20–3 November; Okaya City Hall, 25–7 November; Komuro Junior High School, 2–6 December

The Second Sōzō Bijutsu Exhibition, Tokyo Municipal Art Museum, 21 September – 8 October, touring to Matsuzakaya Nagoya, 15–21 October; Osaka Daimaru, 1–6 November; Kyoto Daimaru, 8–13 November

1952

**Yayoi Kusama*, The First Community Centre, Matsumoto, 18–19 March

**Yayoi Kusama: New Works*, The First Community Centre, 31 October – 2 November

1954

**Yayoi Kusama*, Shiroki-ya Department Store, Tokyo, 27 February – 3 March

1955

The International Watercolor Exhibition Preview, Bridgestone Museum of Art, Tokyo, 19–21 January

**Yayoi Kusama*, Takemiya Gallery, Tokyo, 21–31 January

**Yayoi Kusama*, Kyuryu-do Gallery, Tokyo, 28 March – 2 April

The International Watercolor Exhibition: 18th Biennial, Brooklyn Museum, New York, 4–13 June

at growth and decay, these drawings and paintings suggest microscopic or cosmological topographies and have been read in the context of surrealism. The surfaces are carefully worked, often featuring tiny hieroglyphic details that have become part of the artist's recurring personal vocabulary of forms: eyes, dots, spiky networks of cilia and tadpole-like forms that suggest spermatozoa.

In March 1952, shortly before her twenty-third birthday, Kusama staged her first solo exhibition at the First Community Centre in Matsumoto. This was quickly followed by another solo show at the same venue seven months later. Each of these exhibitions contained more than two hundred and fifty works. Spurred on by her pursuit of artistic success, in February 1954 Kusama accepted the offer of a solo exhibition at the Shiroki-ya Department Store in Tokyo, forgoing her planned enrolment at the Académie de la Grande Chaumière in Paris for a chance to display her work at the centre of the Japanese art world. She staged three subsequent solo exhibitions in Tokyo in the next thirteen months, and her work began to garner critical attention. In May 1954 Kusama's *Flower Bud No.6* 1952 (no.16) was featured on the cover of *Mizue*, accompanying a review by painter Masao Tsuruoka of her Shiroki-ya exhibition, in which he praised Kusama's 'microcosmic worlds'.[1] The following year critic Kenjirō Okamoto applauded Kusama's exhibition at Tokyo's Kyuryudo Gallery:

> She combines various techniques from Cubism and Surrealism, such as décalcomanie and frottage, and makes them her own, getting unforeseen results from such juxtapositions. Her work has no connection to the doctrines of Cubism or Surrealism but seems to operate directly through the senses, linking technique to physiology without conflict or contradiction. It's a very feminine painterly sensibility, and the works done some years ago with traditional Japanese materials are masterfully evocative.[2]

Despite this acclaim, by the mid-1950s Kusama was determined to find a way to leave Japan to broaden her artistic horizons. Her heart was set on travelling to the United States and forging her career there.

In 1955 three of Kusama's works were chosen by the Japan Art Critics Association for inclusion in the *International Watercolor Exhibition: 18th Biennial* at New York's Brooklyn Museum. This exhibition signalled a growing American interest in contemporary Japanese art and enhanced Kusama's enthusiasm to make her name in the United States. She has written:

> For art like mine – art that does battle at the border of life and death, questioning what we are and what it means to live and die – [Japan] was too small, too servile, too feudalistic, and too scornful of women. My art needed a more unlimited freedom, and a wider world.[3]

From the perspective of the early twenty-first century it is easy to underestimate the exceptional achievement of Kusama's early successes. It was extraordinary for a woman from a relatively small town in the Japanese hinterland to achieve the degree of artistic attention she garnered at such a young age, and during a period in which Japanese women were bound by the strictures of feudal, patriarchal conventions. Kusama's achievement is even more astonishing when seen in the context of the artist's psychological history.

Kusama's early years have been the subject of much discussion and speculation. Although it would not have been evident to viewers of her earliest exhibitions, from the vantage point of the 1960s and later Kusama described her early, compulsive art-making as a refuge from the external pressures of her fraught familial relationships, and from the oppressive, imperialist zeal indoctrinated during the war years. She has also spoken of how losing herself in her art was a retreat from psychological symptoms she began experiencing at an early age. A sensitive and anxious child, she describes suffering from frightening hallucinations in which her field of vision was overtaken by repeated forms: the pattern on a tablecloth bleeding into and beyond the surrounding room, for instance, or an endless sea of violets that 'spoke' to her. These disturbing visions have frequently been cited as a driving force in the artist's extraordinarily prolific output. For Kusama, productivity is crucial to her mental health: she has said, 'I am pursuing art in order to correct the disability which began in my childhood.'[4]

1929–1957

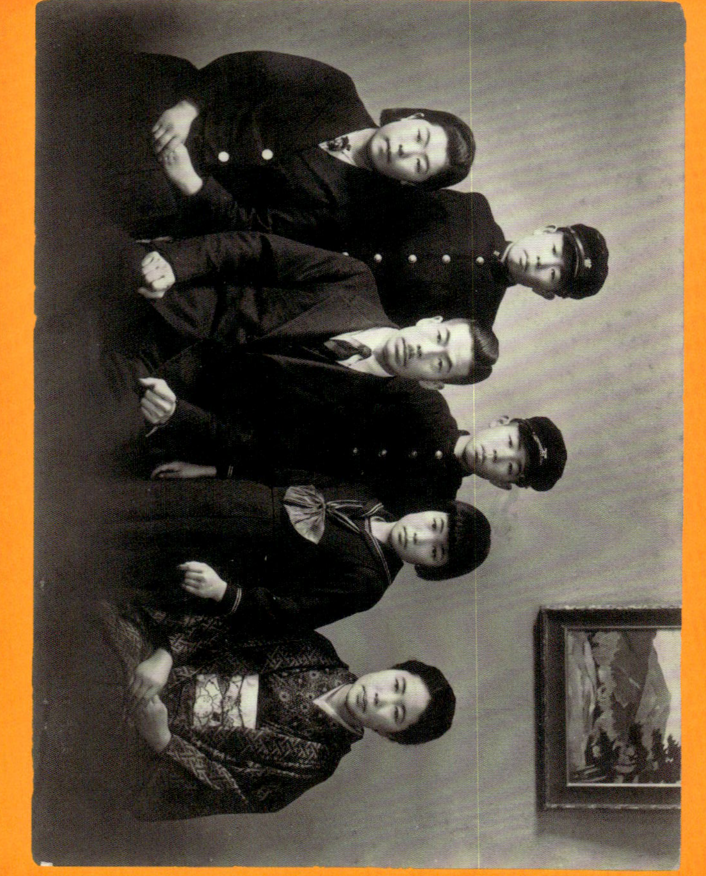

Kusama's family (Yayoi is second from the right)

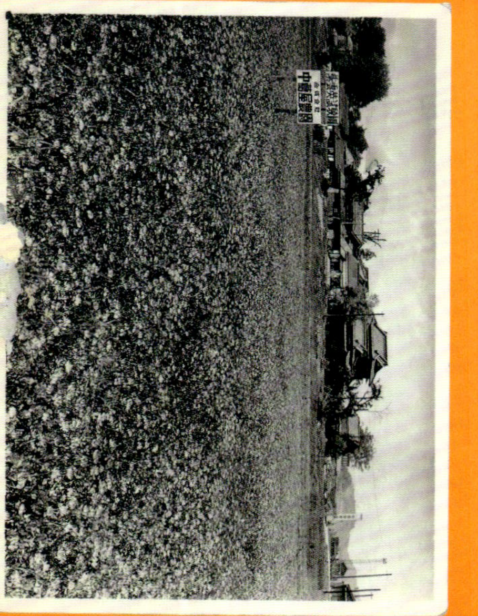

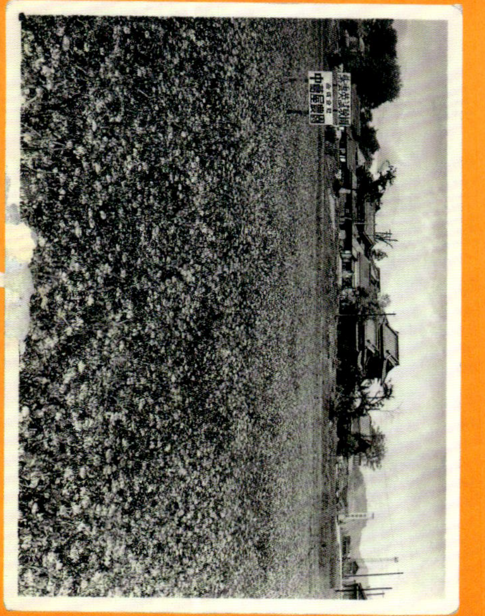

Kusama's parents' house and nursery business, with a field of Chinese milk vetch in the foreground. Kusama's studio was on the first floor.

Kusama aged about fourteen, c.1943

Kusama in her studio at her parents' home in Matsumoto, c.1951

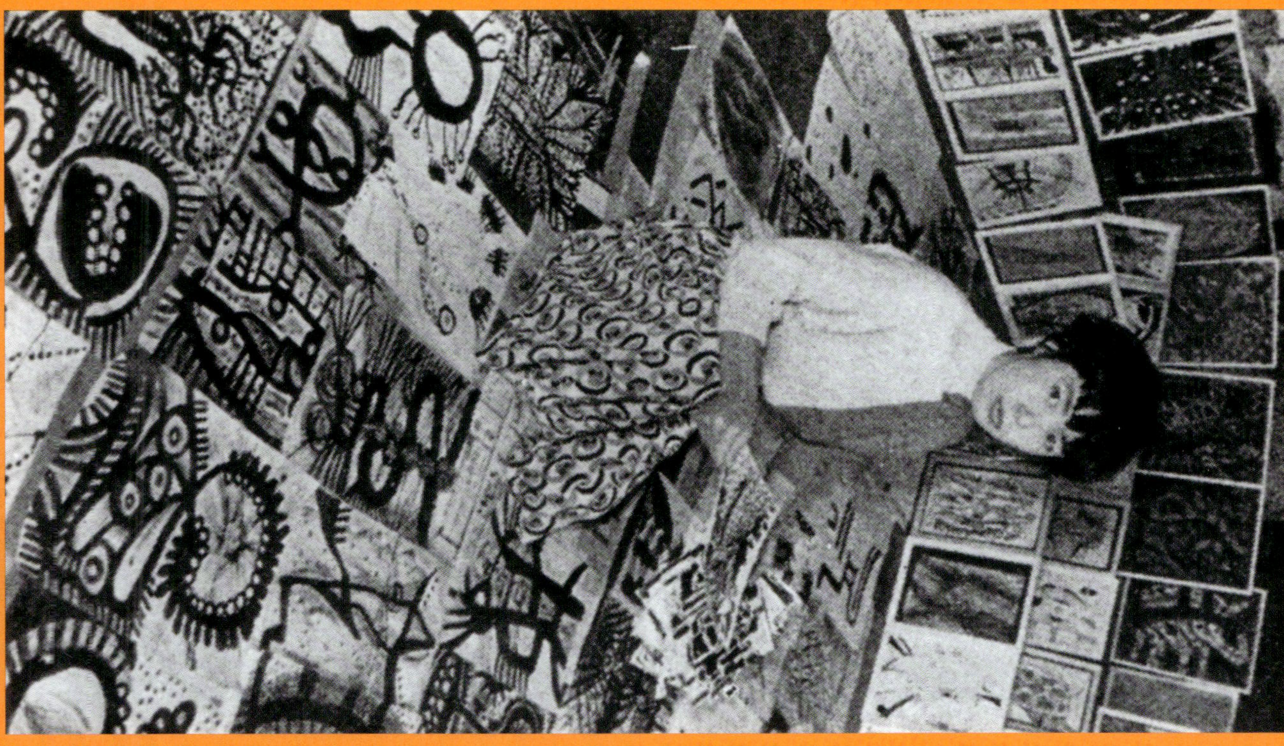

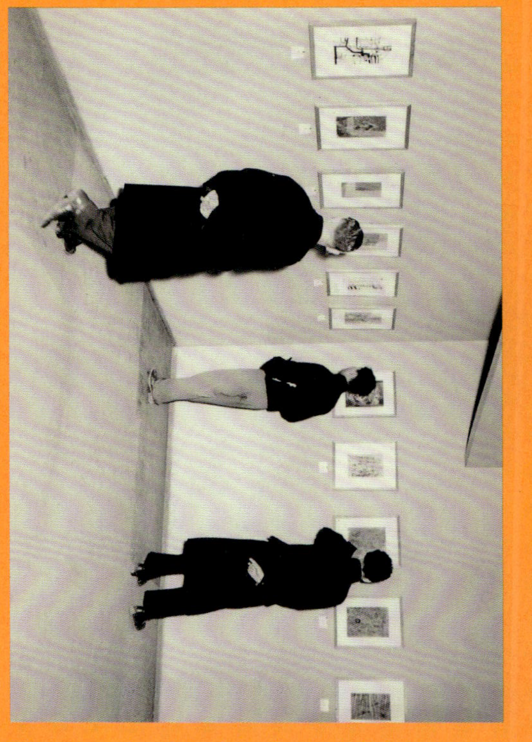

Kusama's third solo exhibition, the first in Tokyo, Shiroki-ya department store in Tokyo, 1954

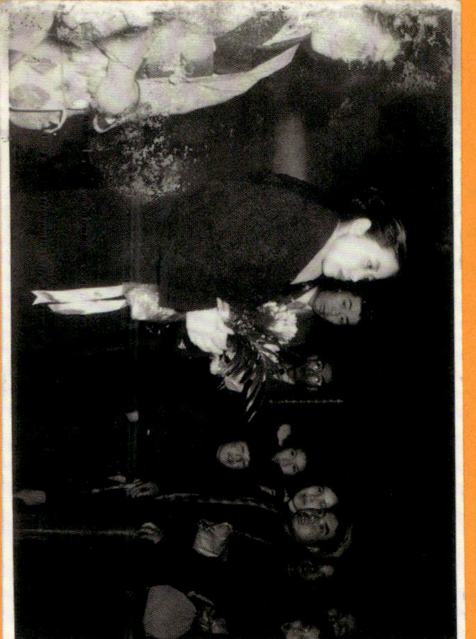

Farewell moment at Matsumoto station, before Kusama's departure for the US, 1957

20.21

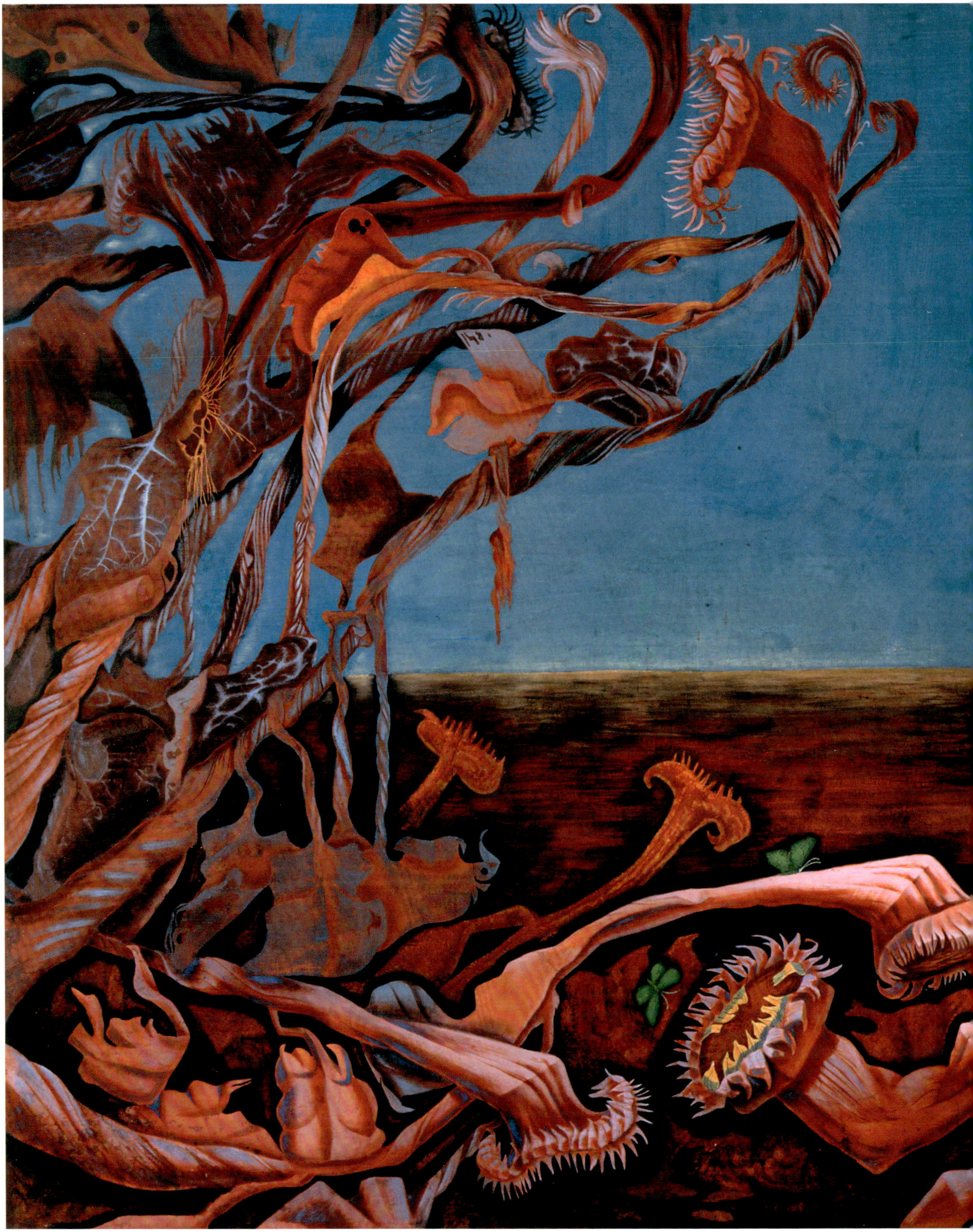

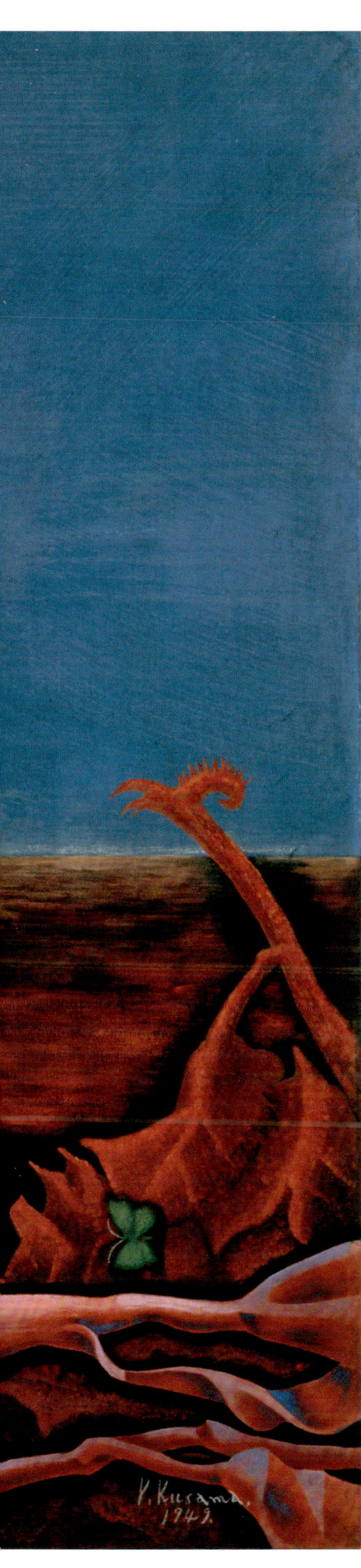

1 | **Lingering Dream** 1949

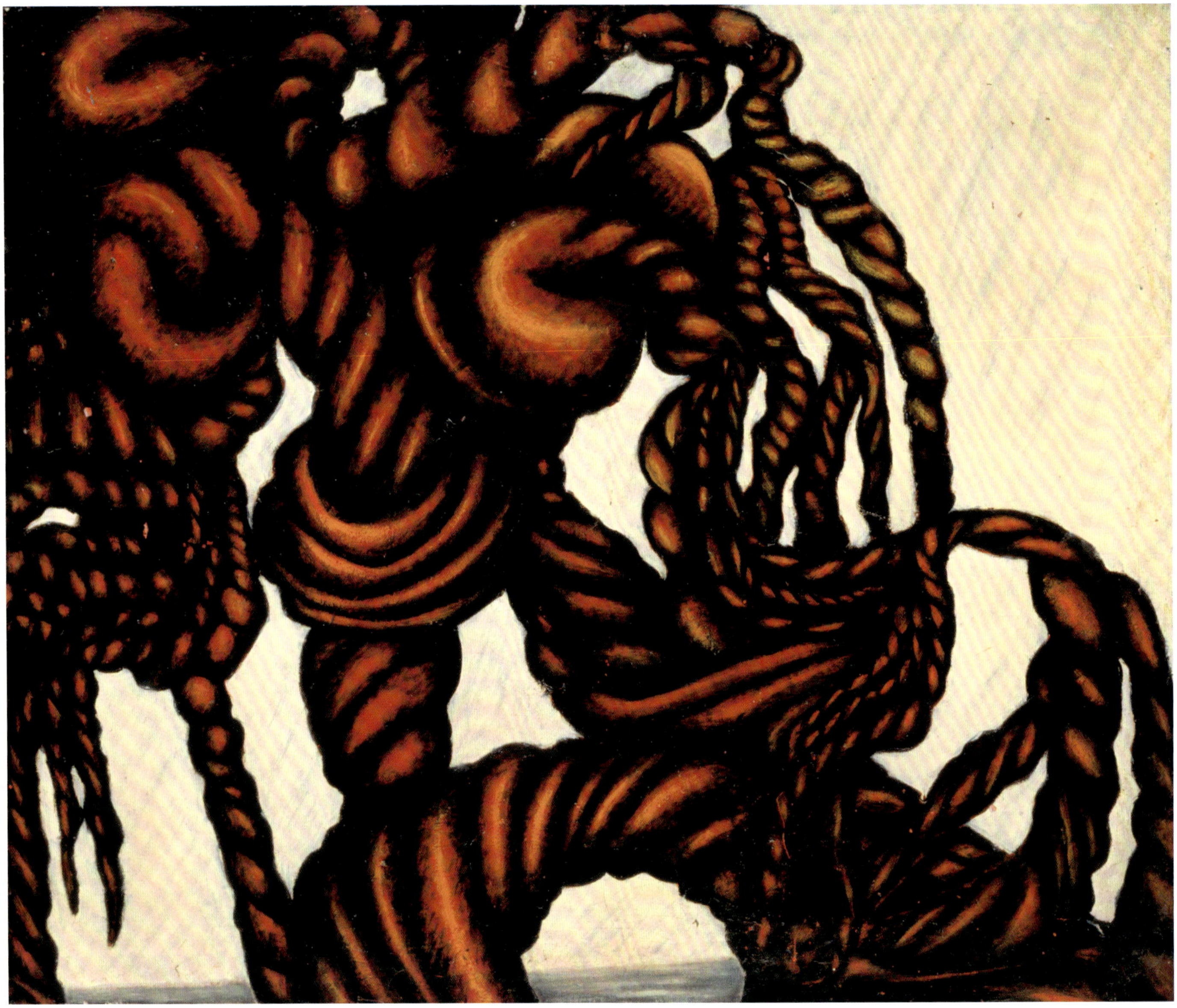

2 | **Corpses** 1950

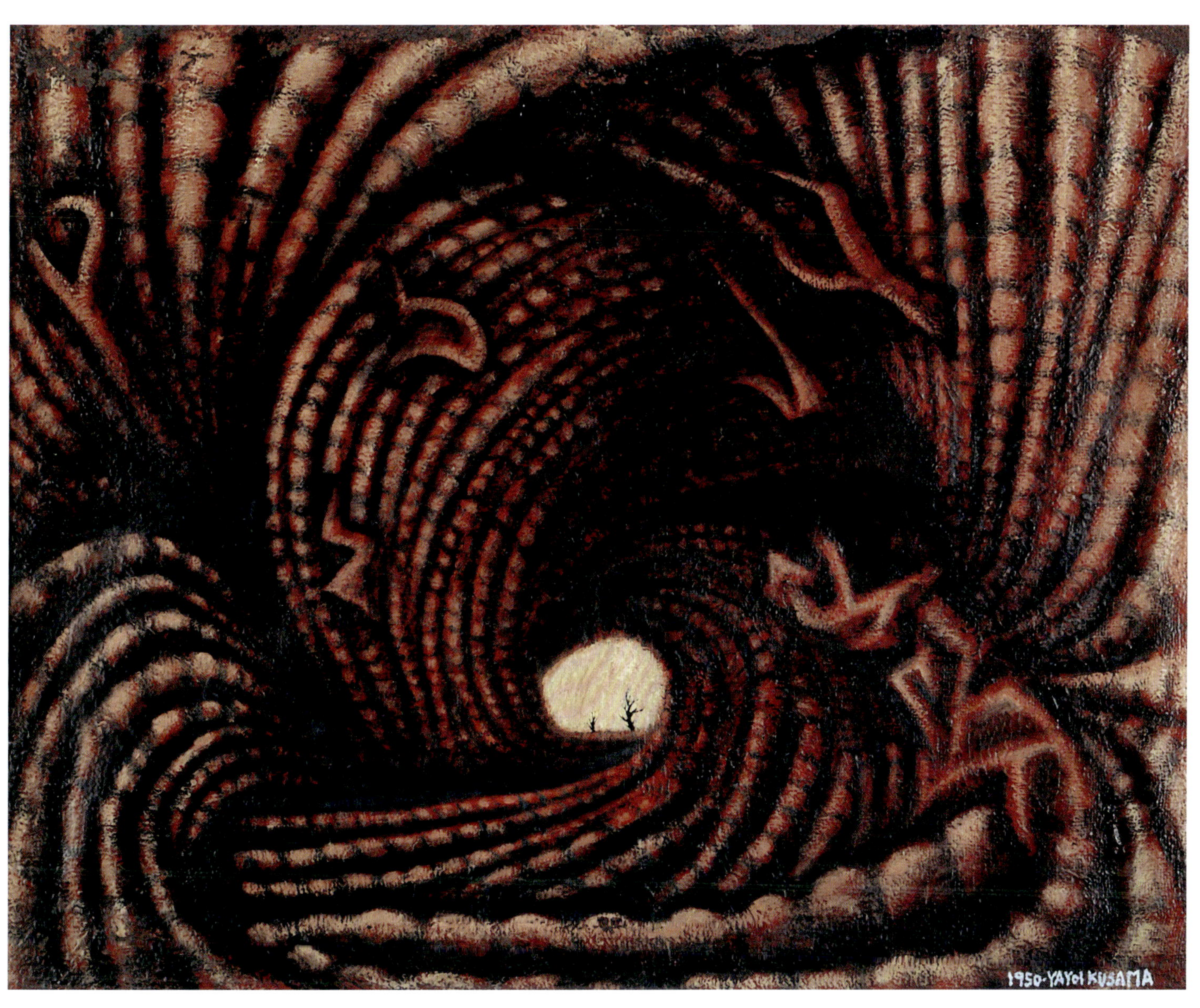

3 | **Accumulation of the Corpses (Prisoner Surrounded by the Curtain of Depersonalization)** 1950

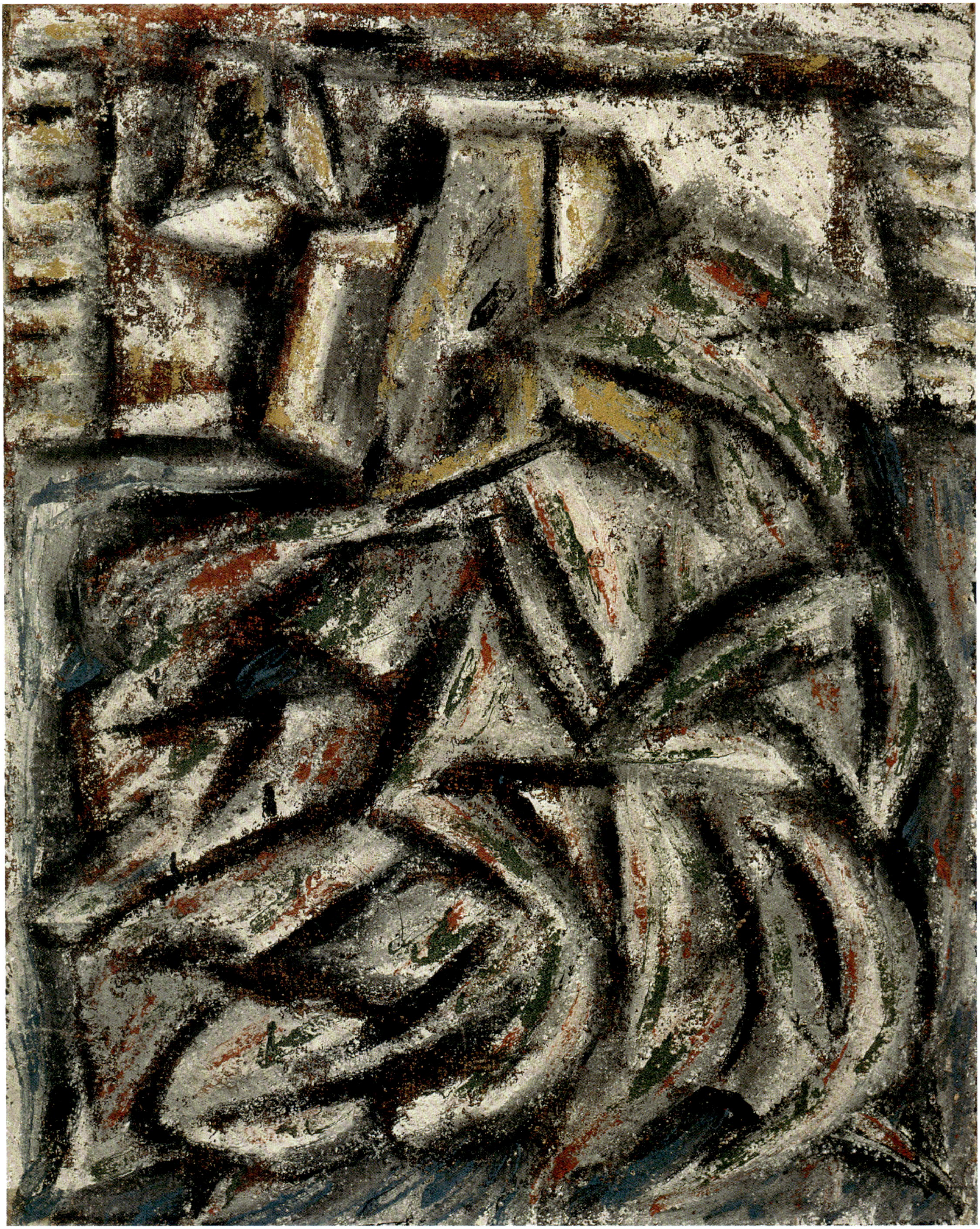

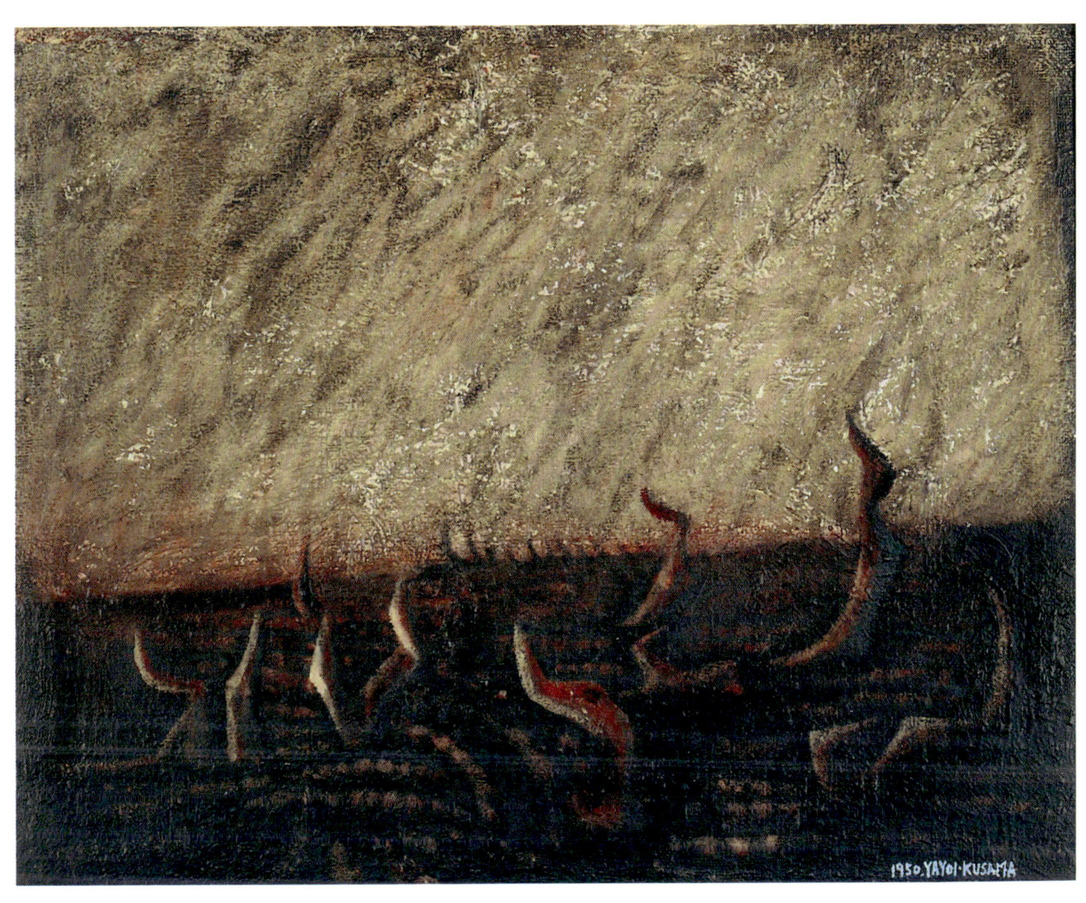

4 | **On the Table** 1950

5 | **Earth of Accumulation** 1950

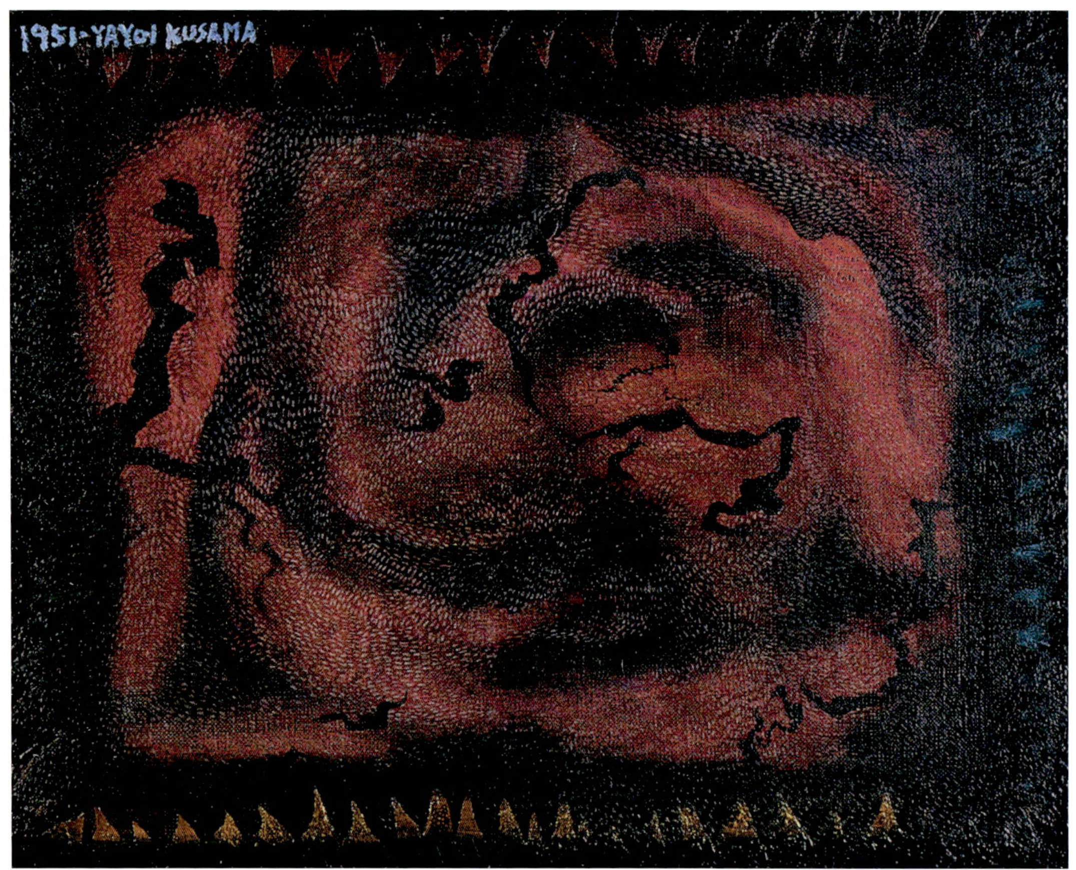

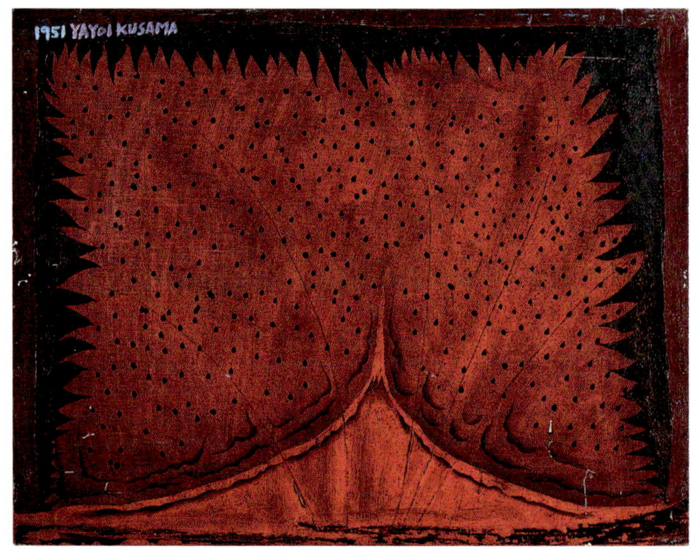

6 | **Inside the Forest** 1951

7 | **Heart** 1951

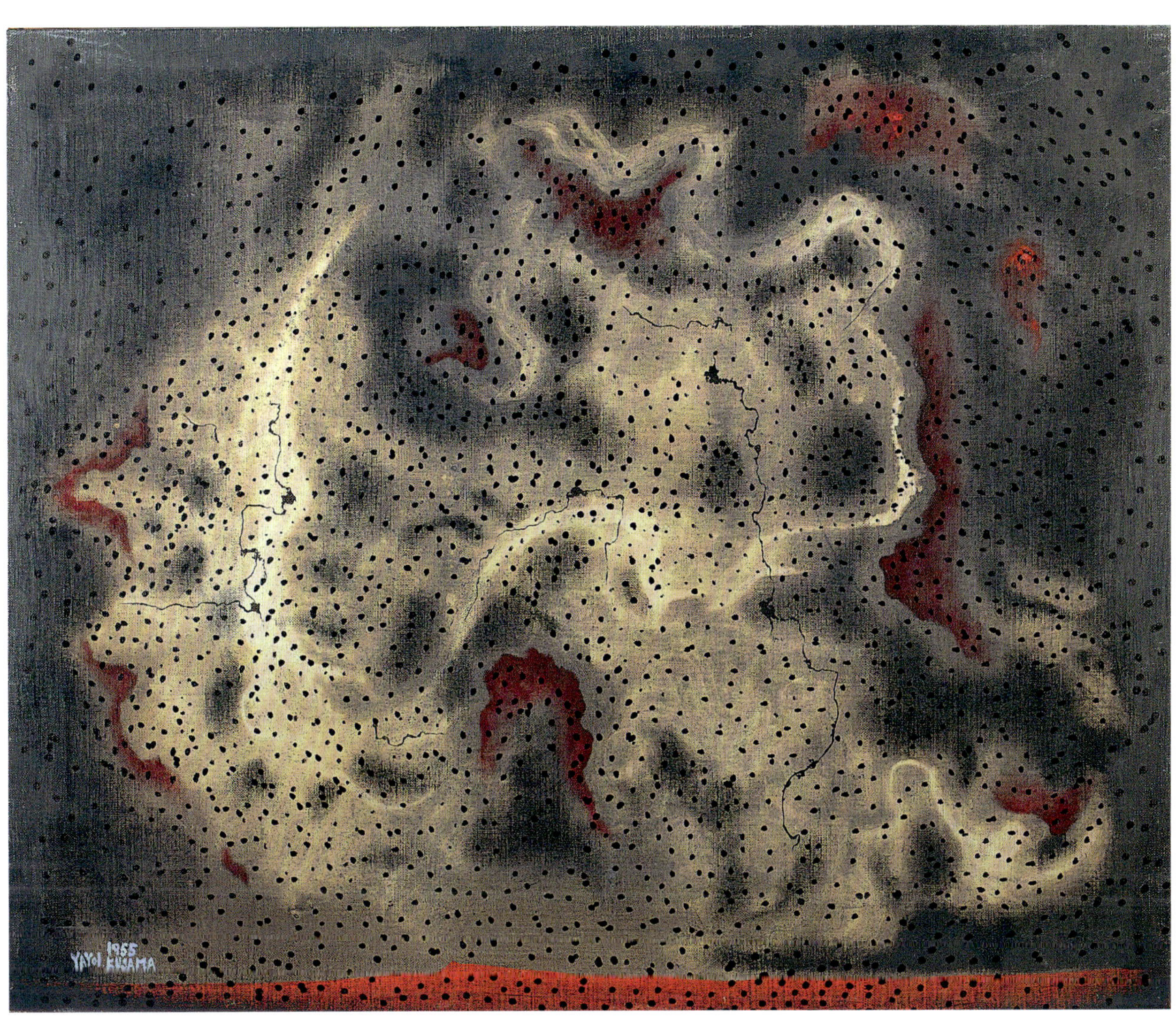

 God of the Wind 1955

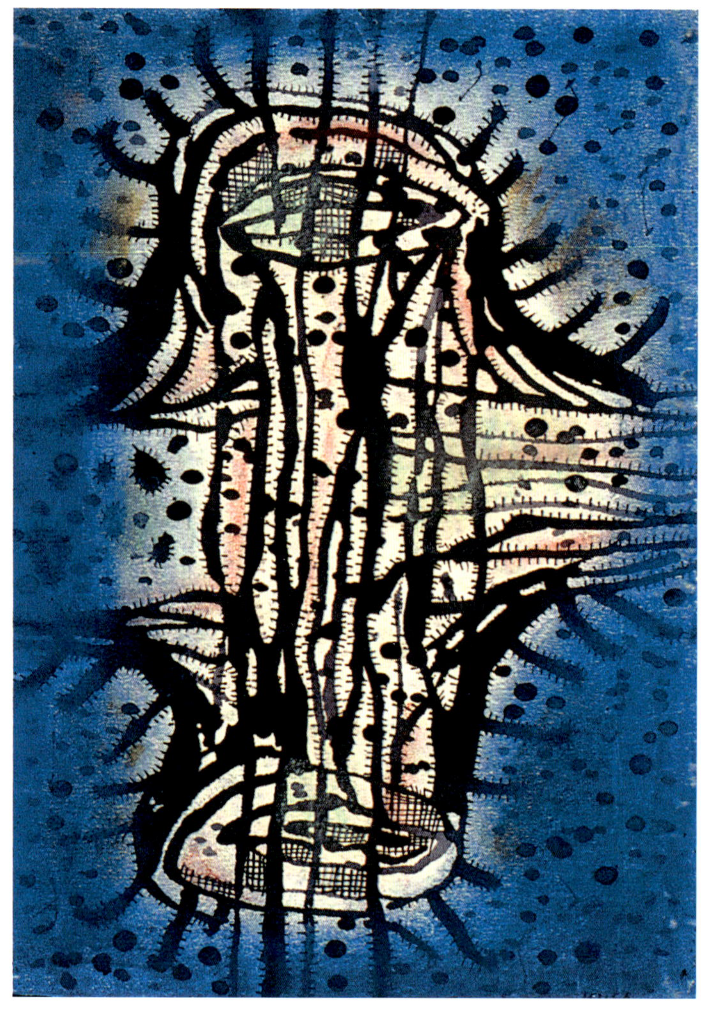

28.29

9 | **The Germ** 1952

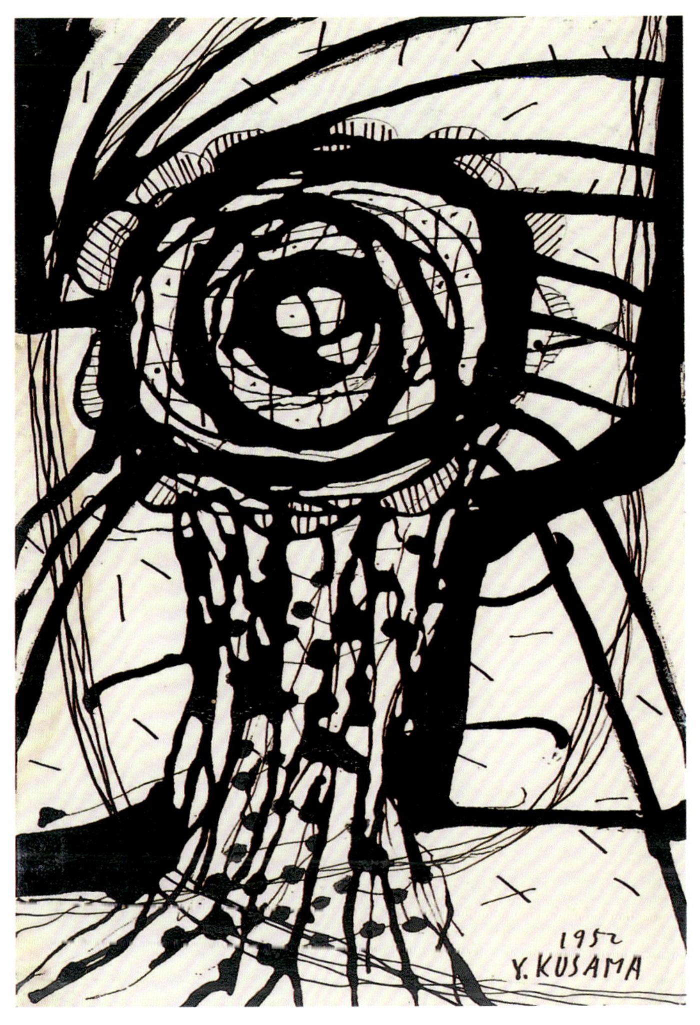

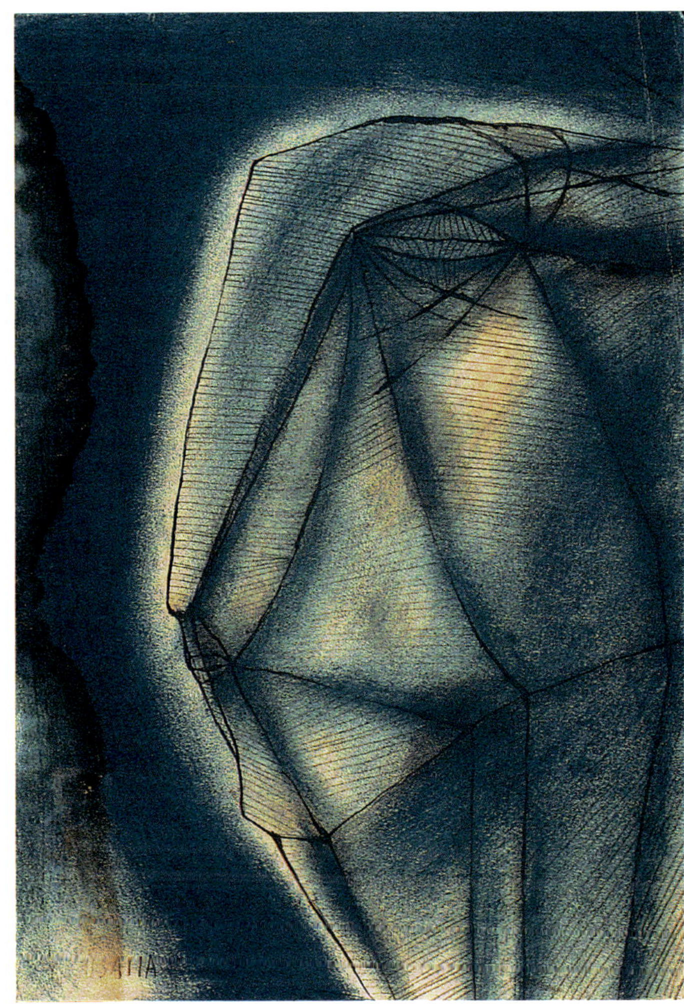

10 | **A Flower** 1952

11 | **Untitled** 1952

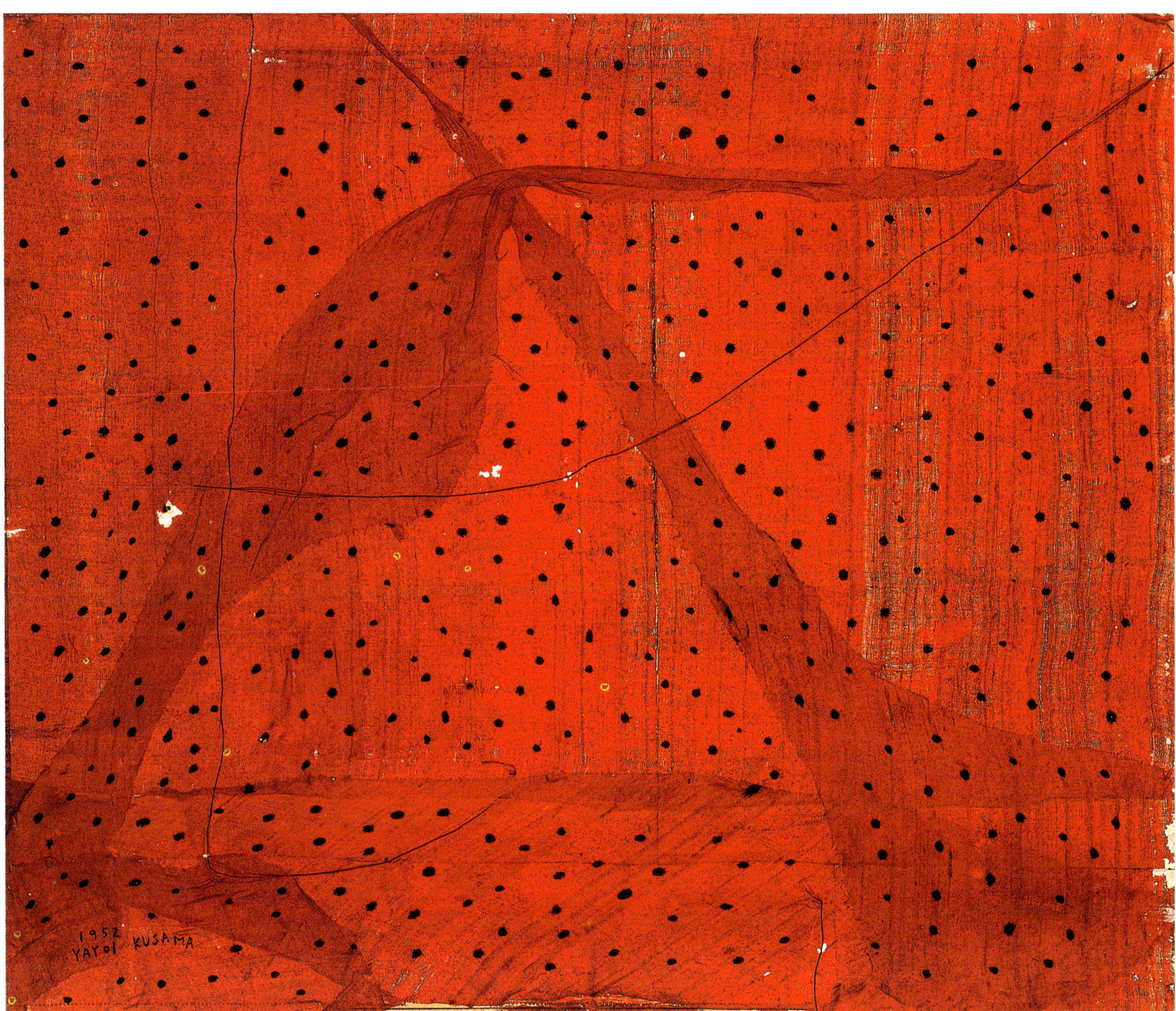

30.31

12 | **The Parting** 1952

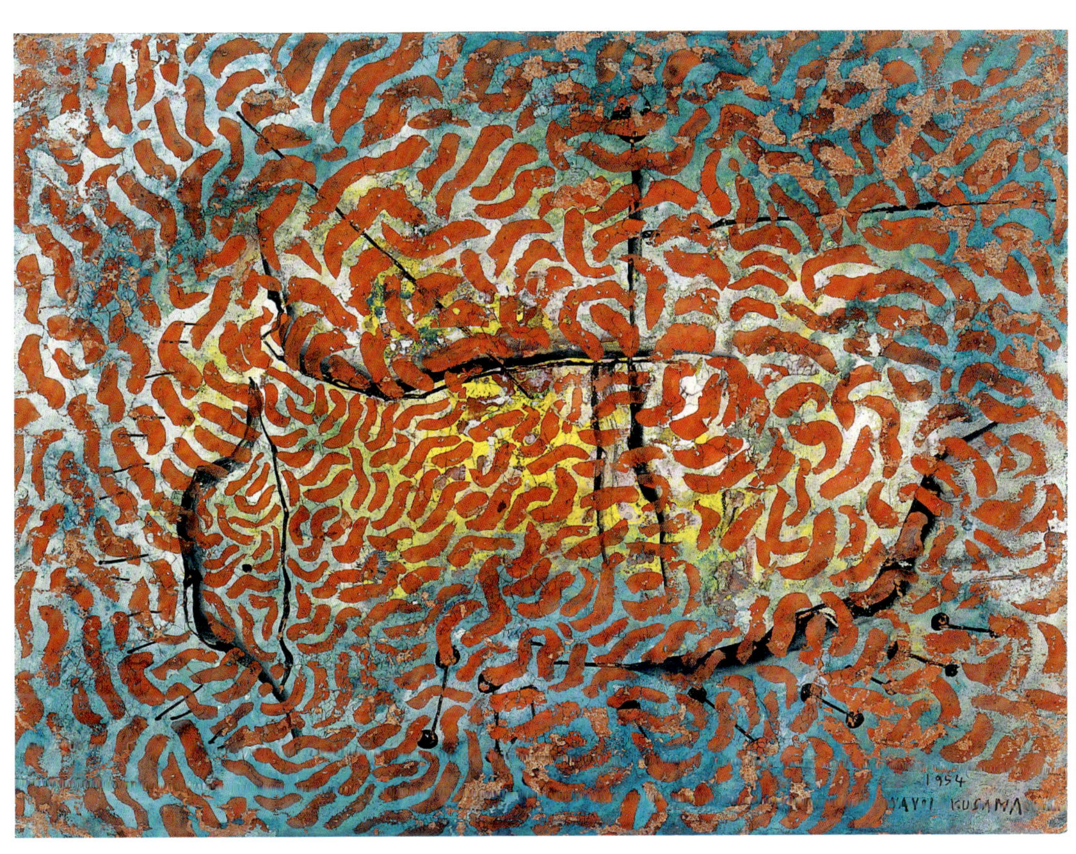

13 | **Leaves** 1954

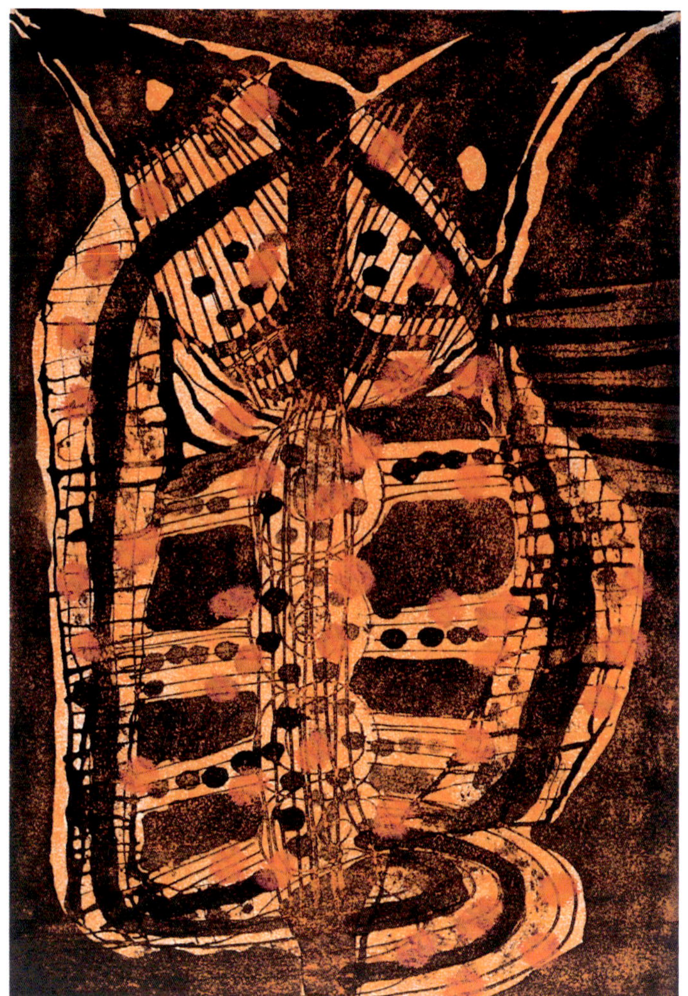

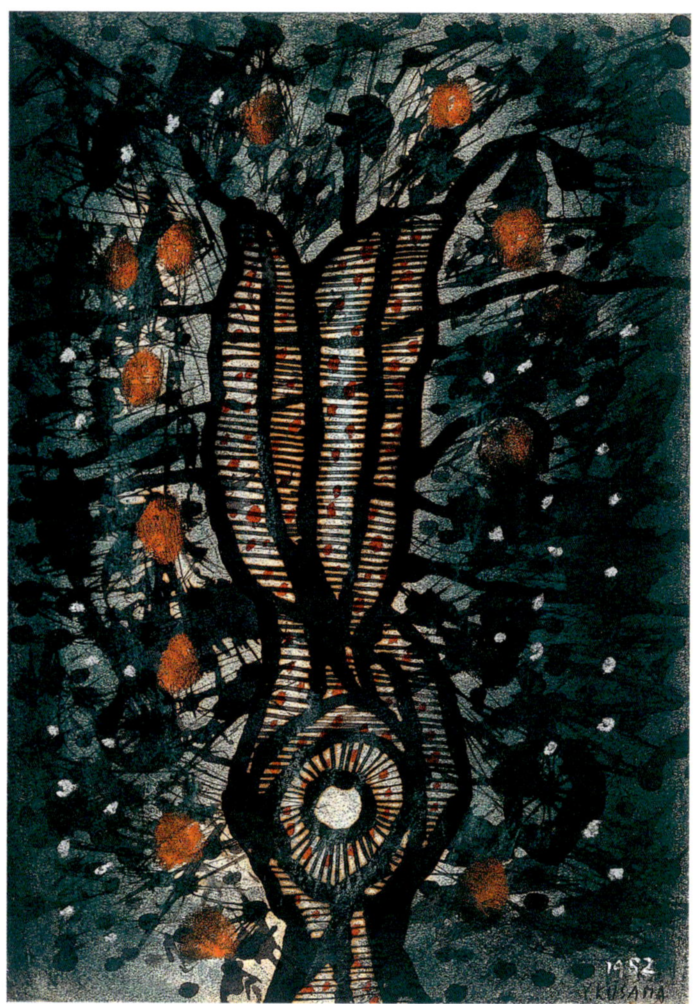

14 | **An Animal** 1952

15 | **Tree** 1952

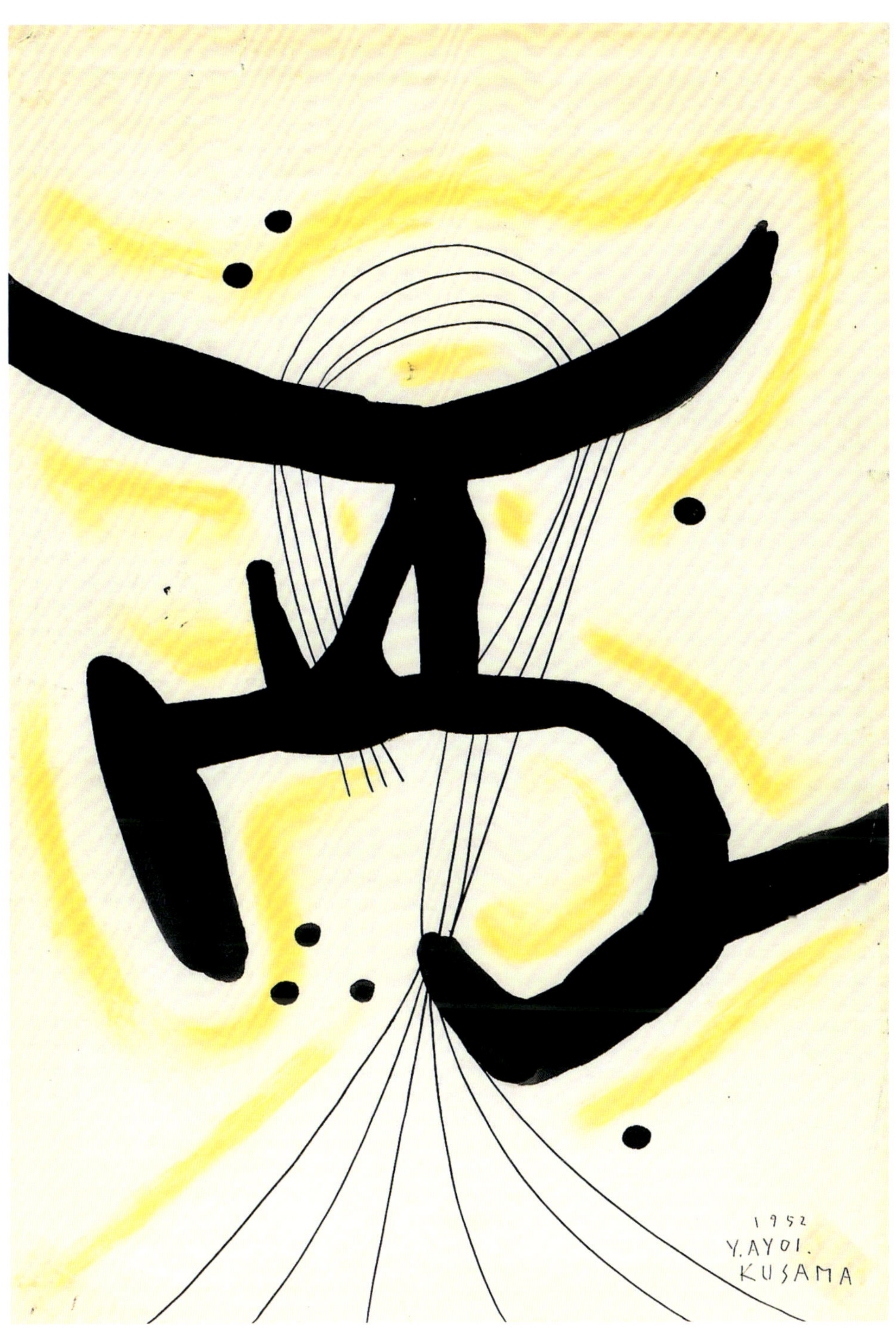

 Flower Bud No.6 1952

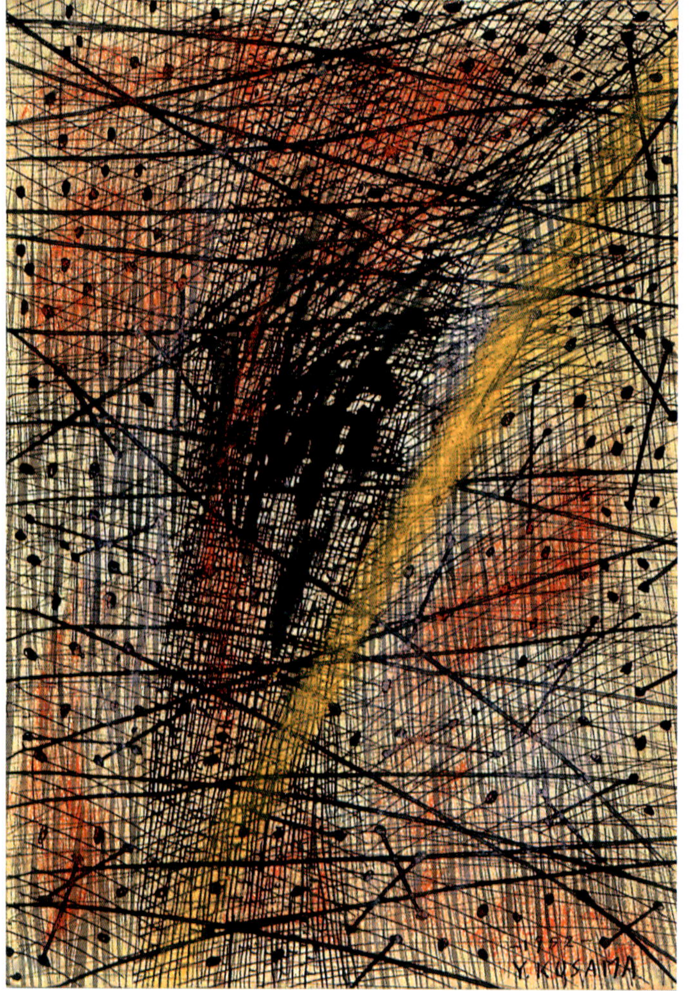

17 | **The Stem** 1952

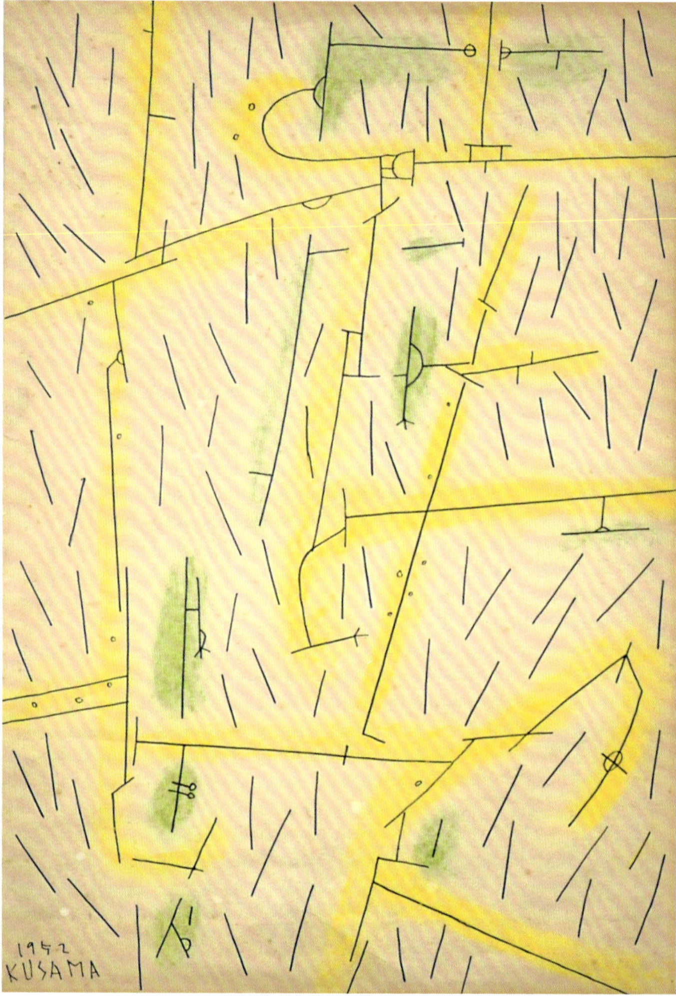

18 | **Rain in a City** 1952

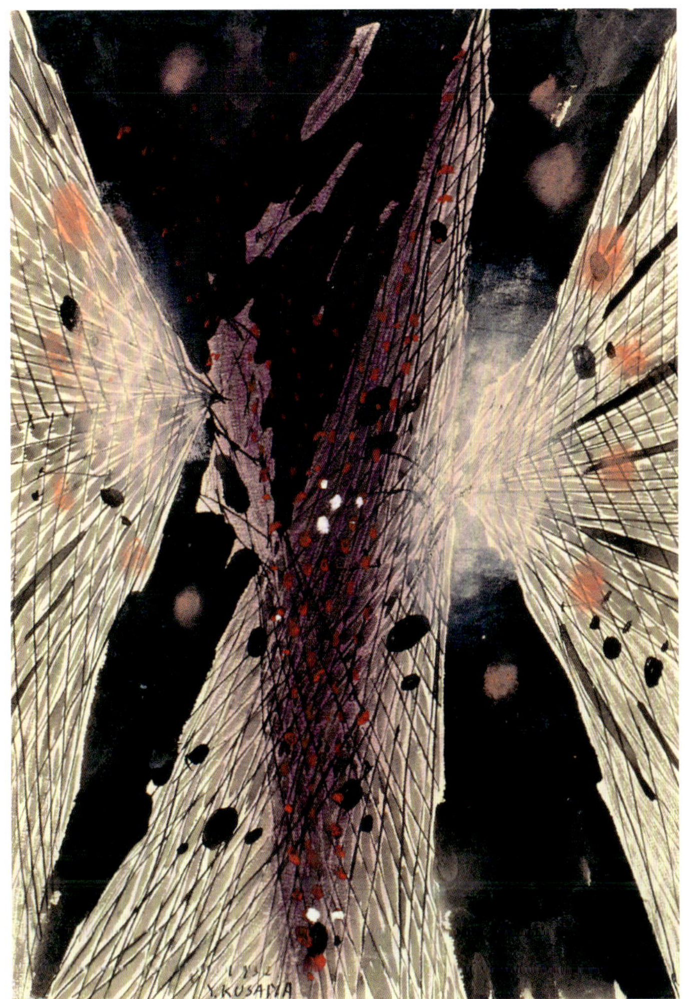

19 | **Flower Bud** 1952

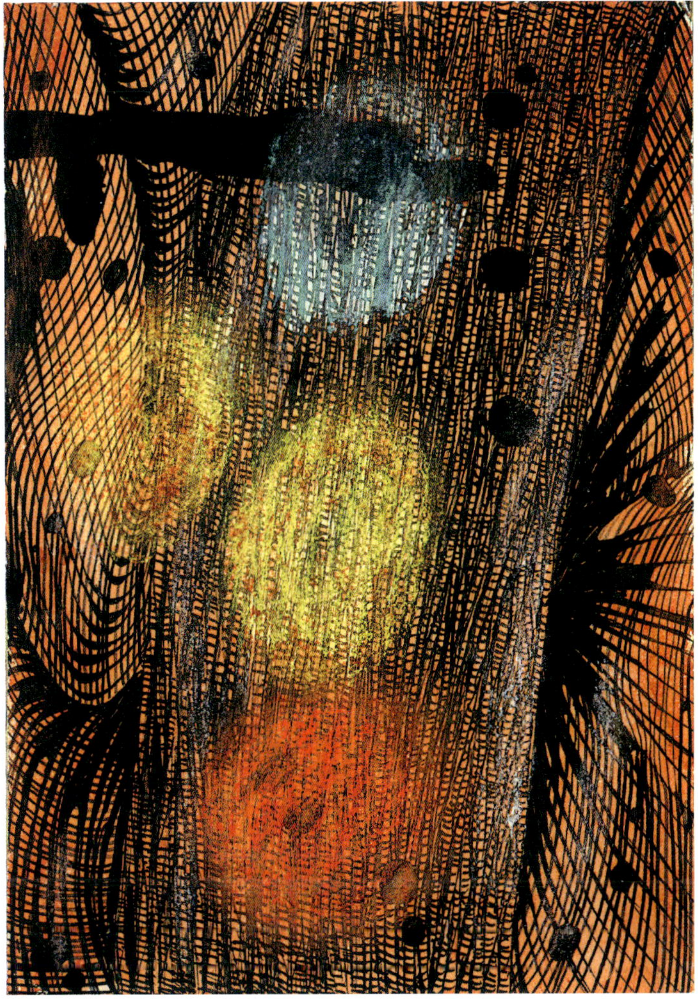

20 | **Phosphoresce in the Daytime** c.1950

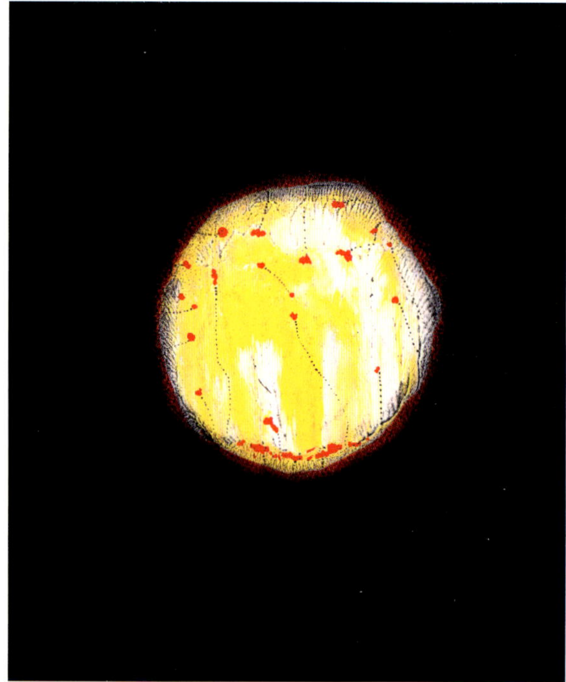

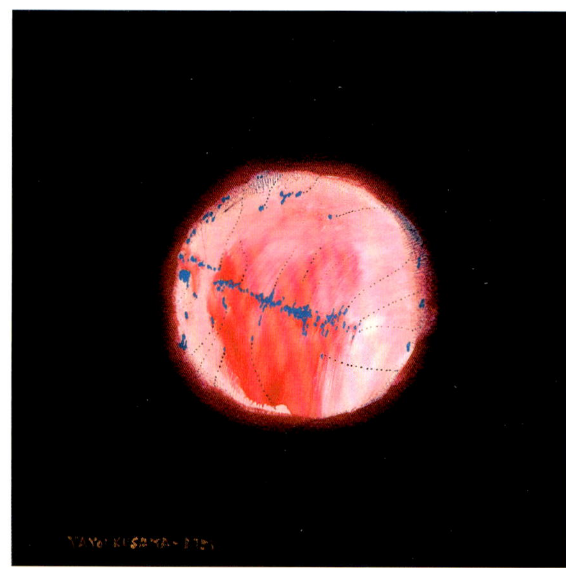

21 | **Island No.7** 1953

22 | **Dots on the Sun** 1953

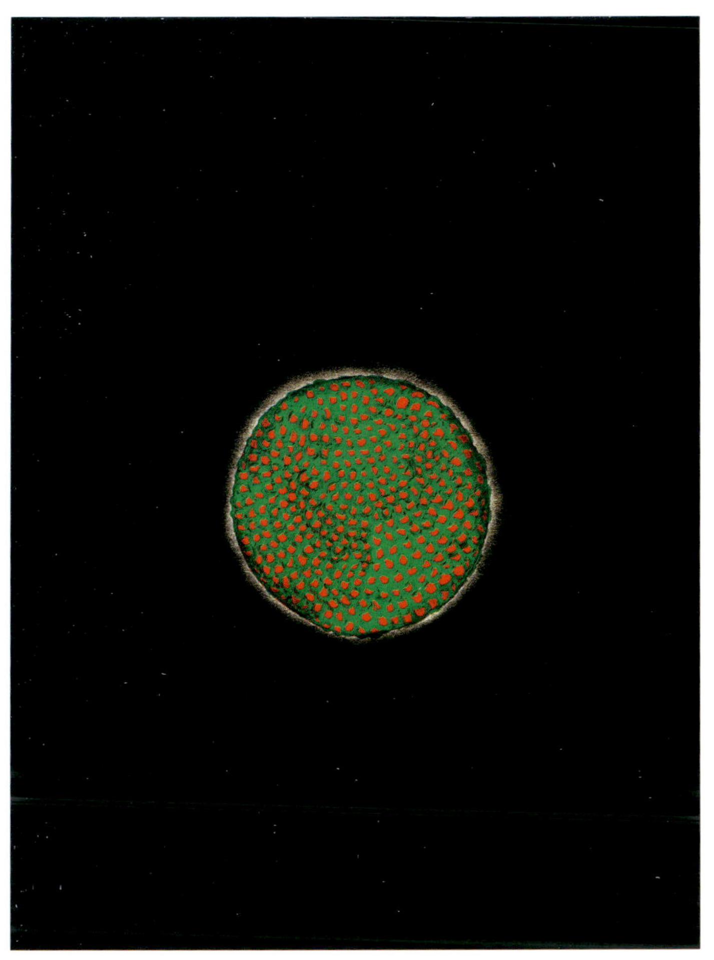

23 | **No.19 H.S.W.** 1956

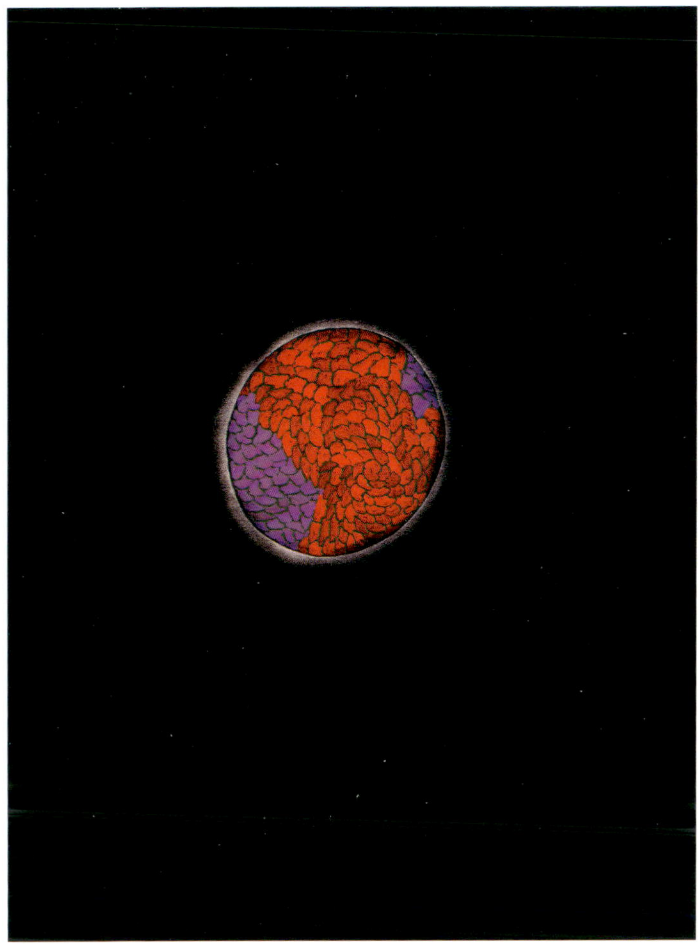

24 | **No.8 H.A.P.** 1956

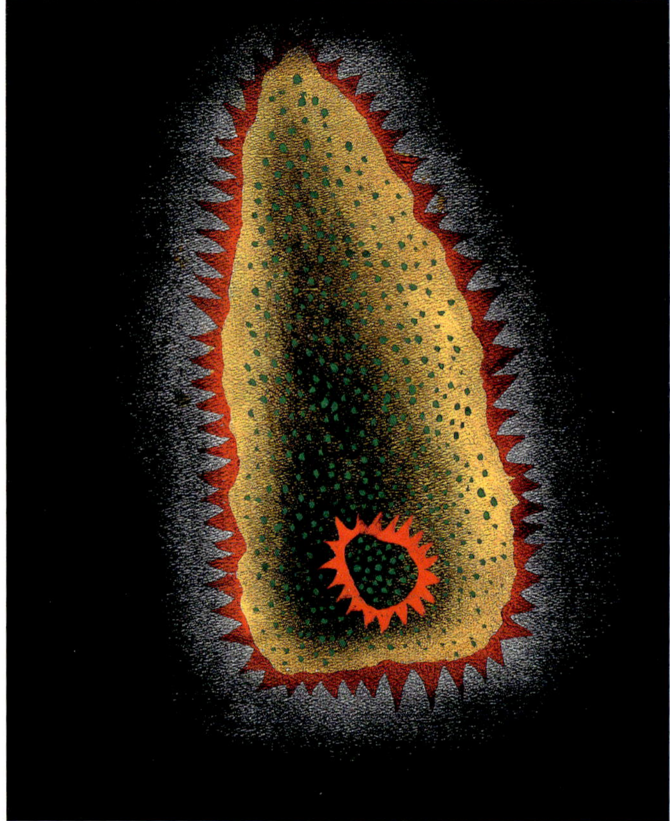

25 | **The Woman** 1953

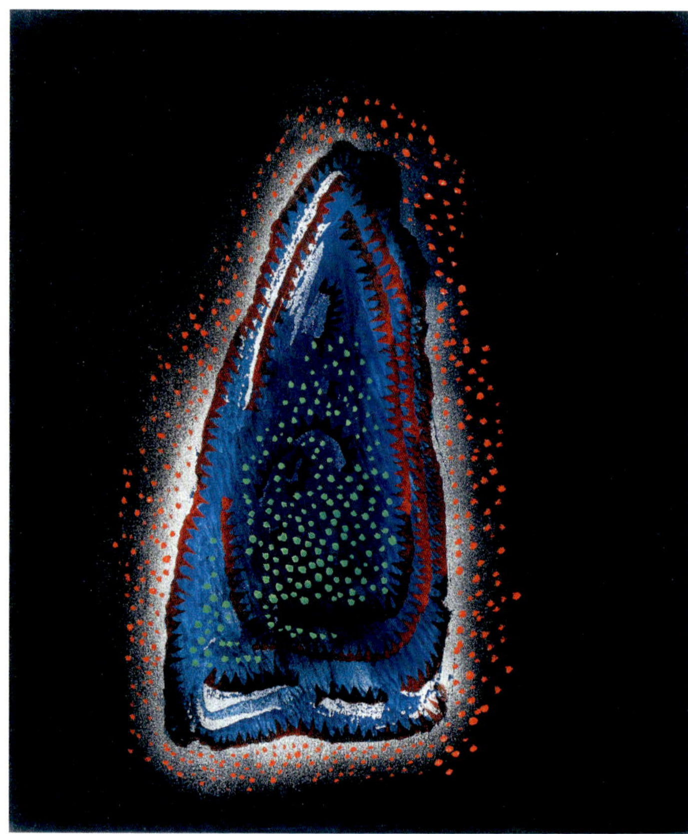

26 | **The Woman (33)** 1953

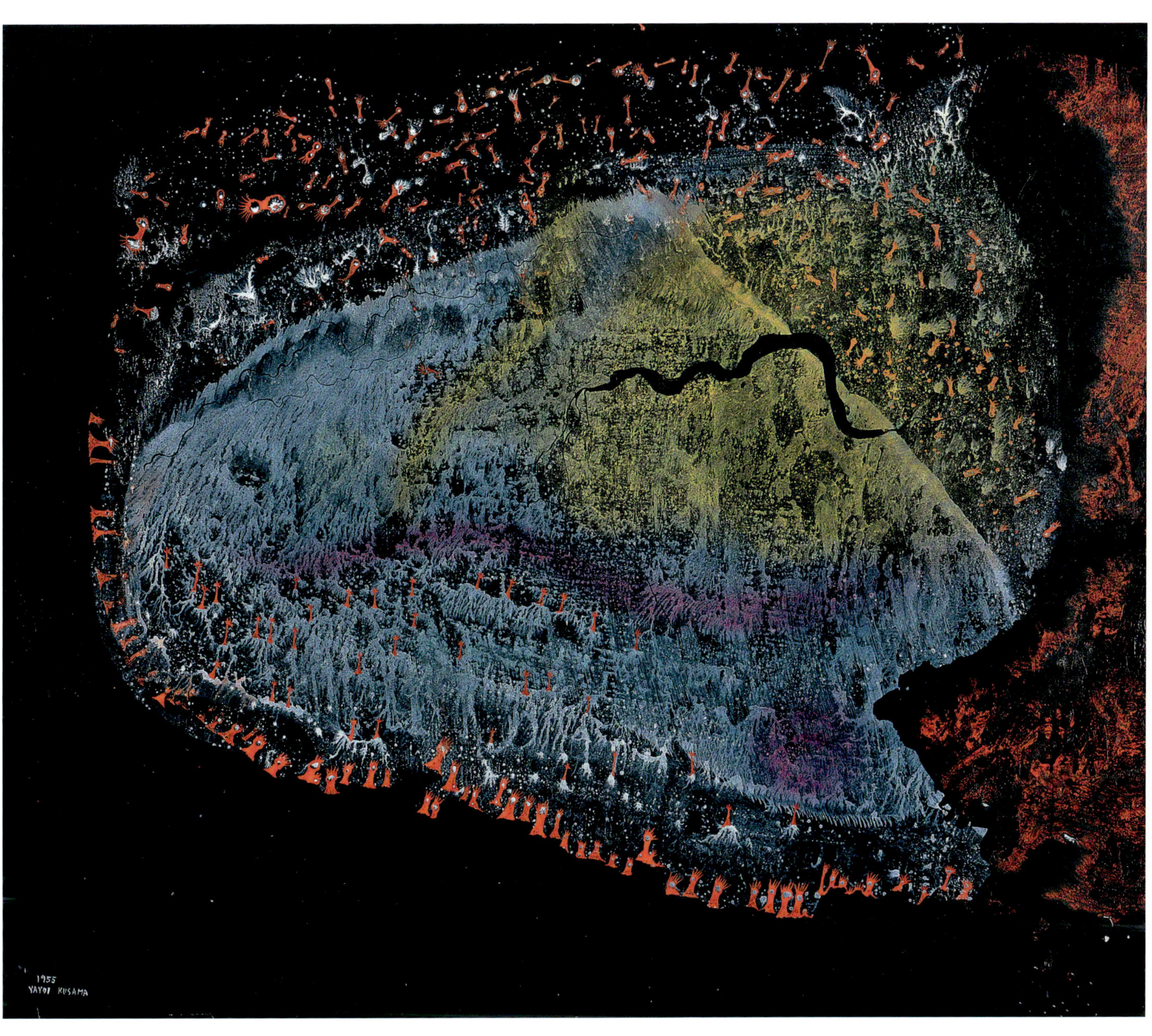

A Gill 1955

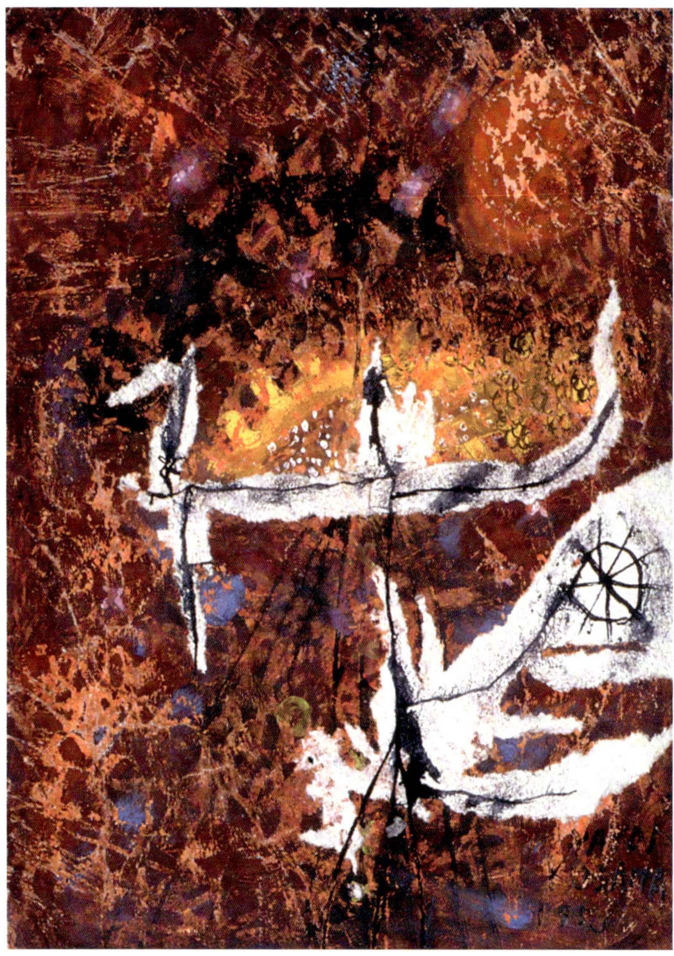

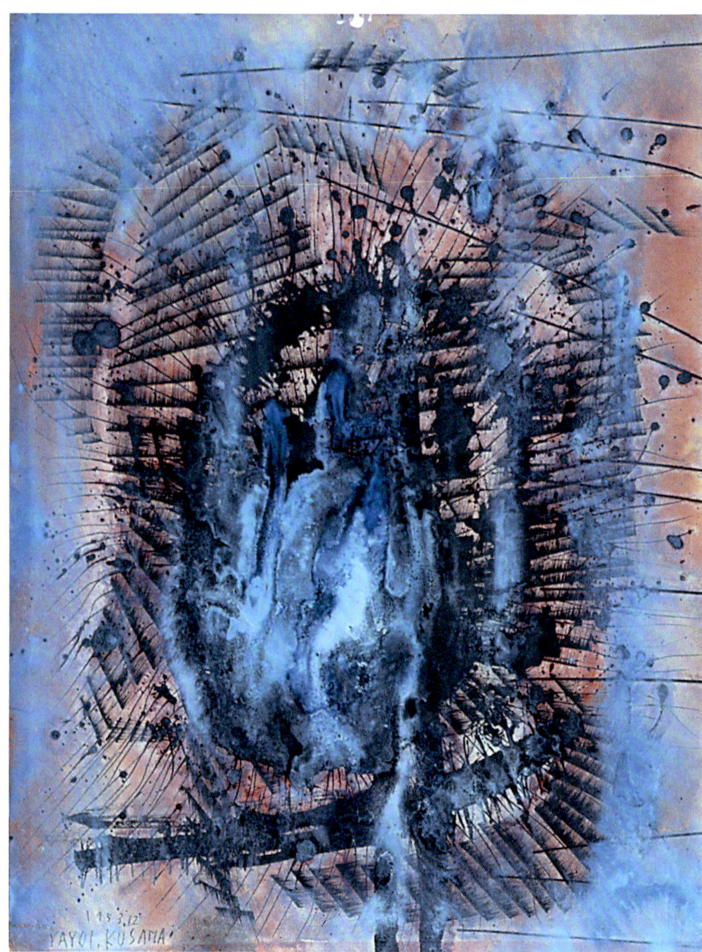

28 | **Flying People** 1953

29 | **Ancient Fire** 1953

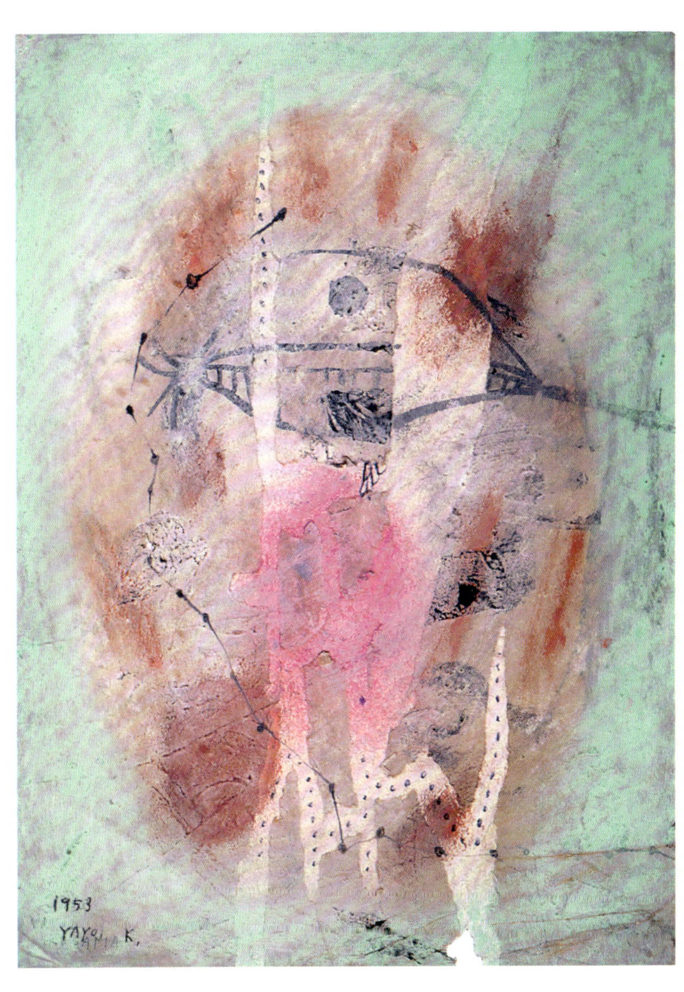

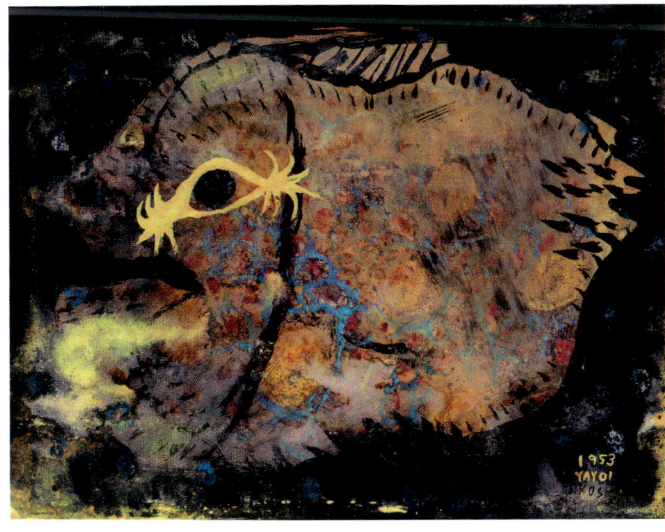

30 | **An Eye** 1953

31 | **Fish** 1953

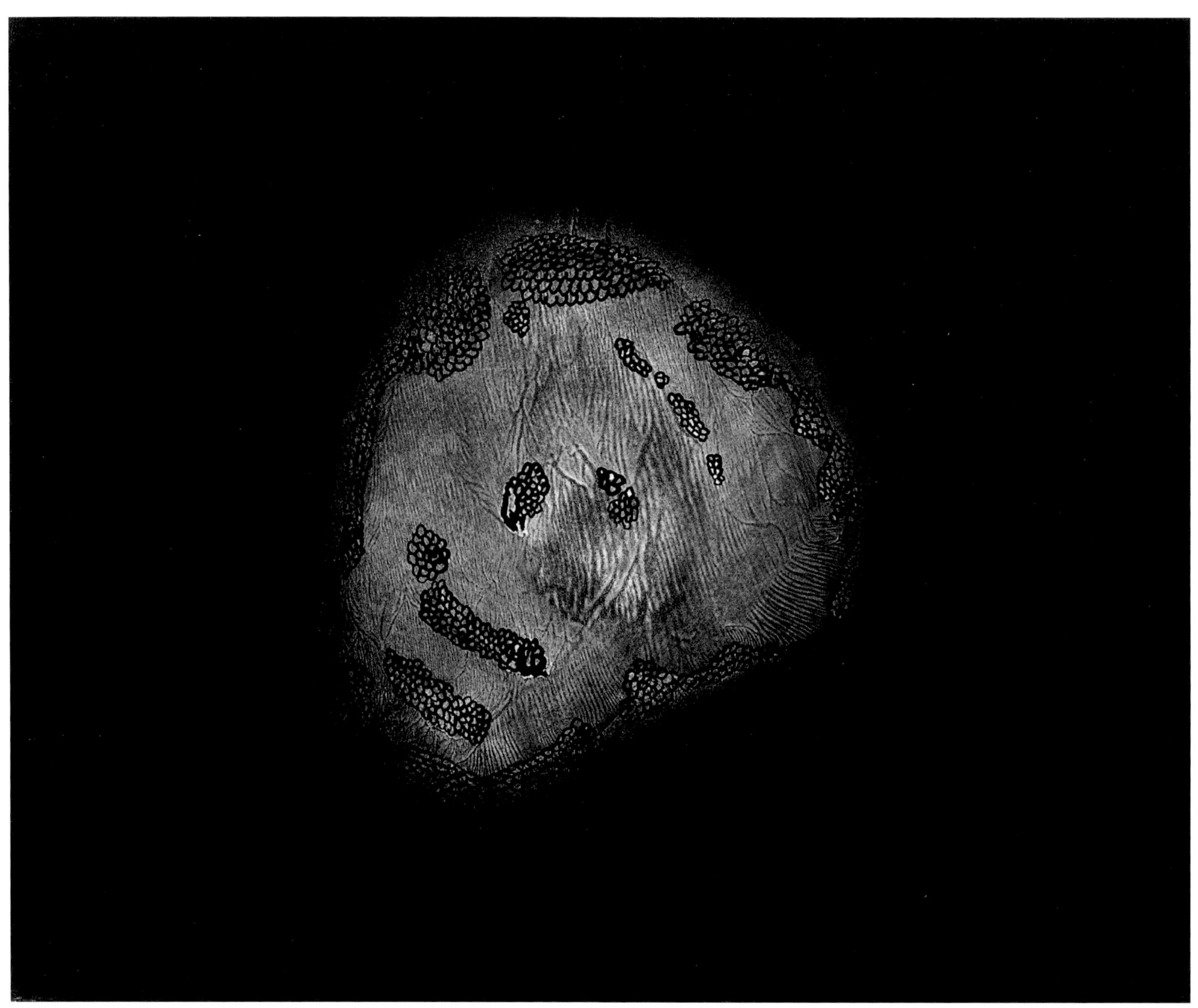

42.43

Inward Vision No.4 1953

33 | **Inward Vision No.1** 1953

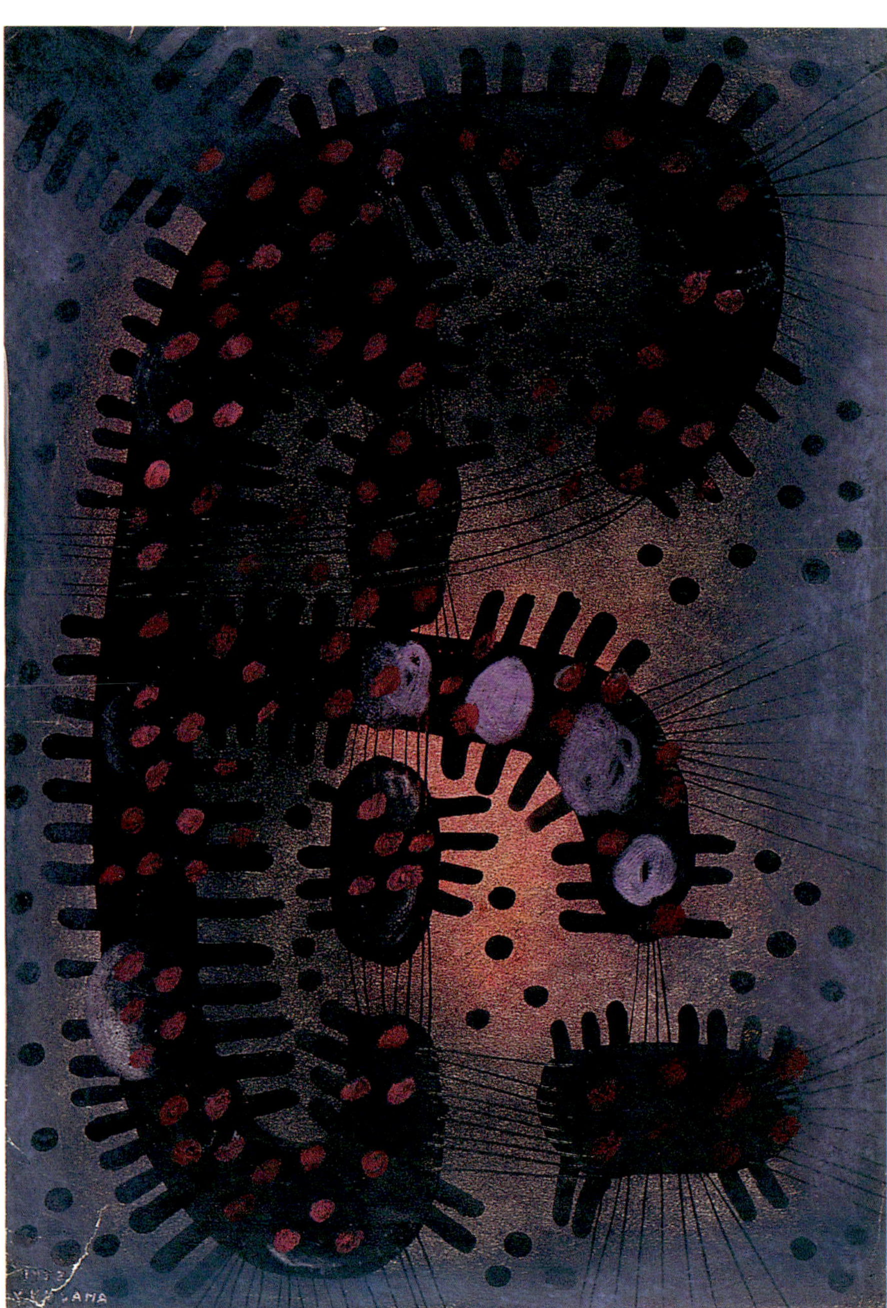

34 | **'Girden' (Festival)** 1953

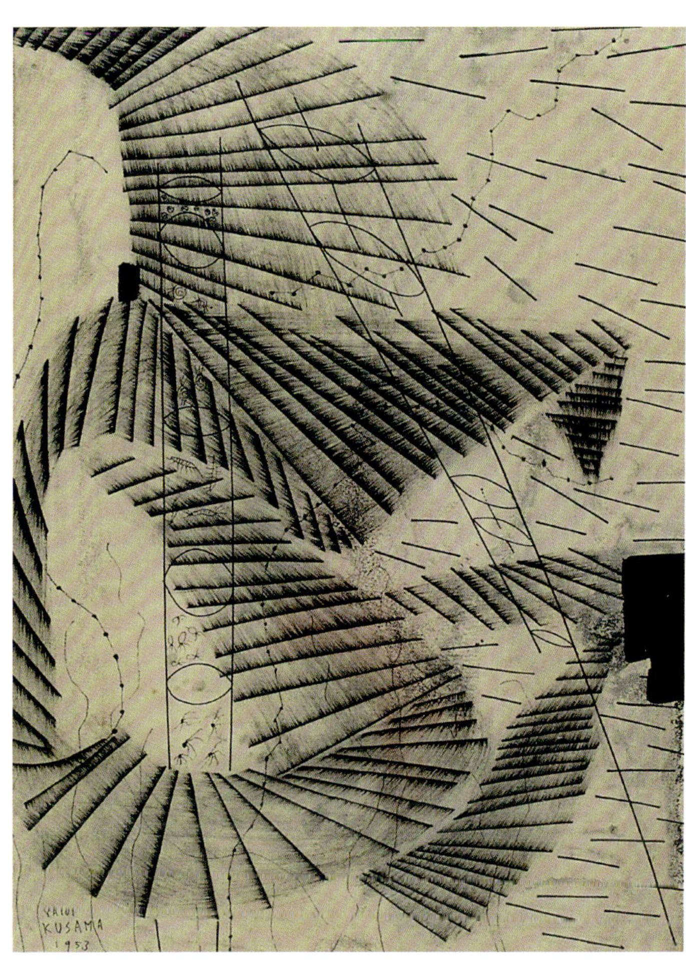

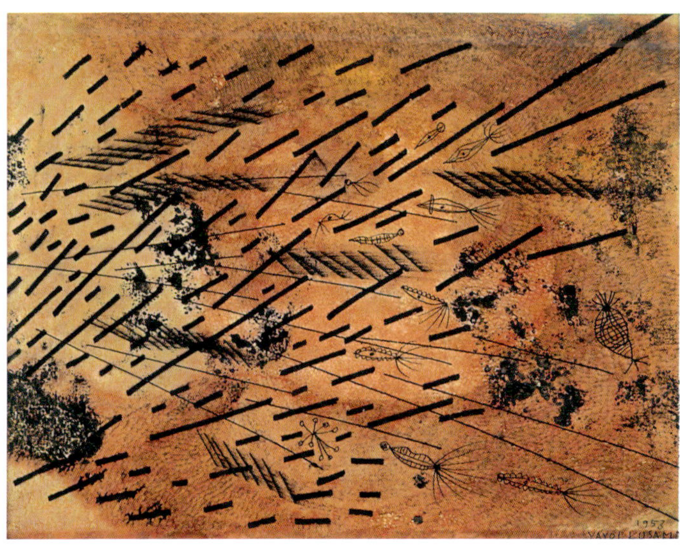

35 | **The Sky** 1953

36 | **Fleeing Eye** 1953

46.47

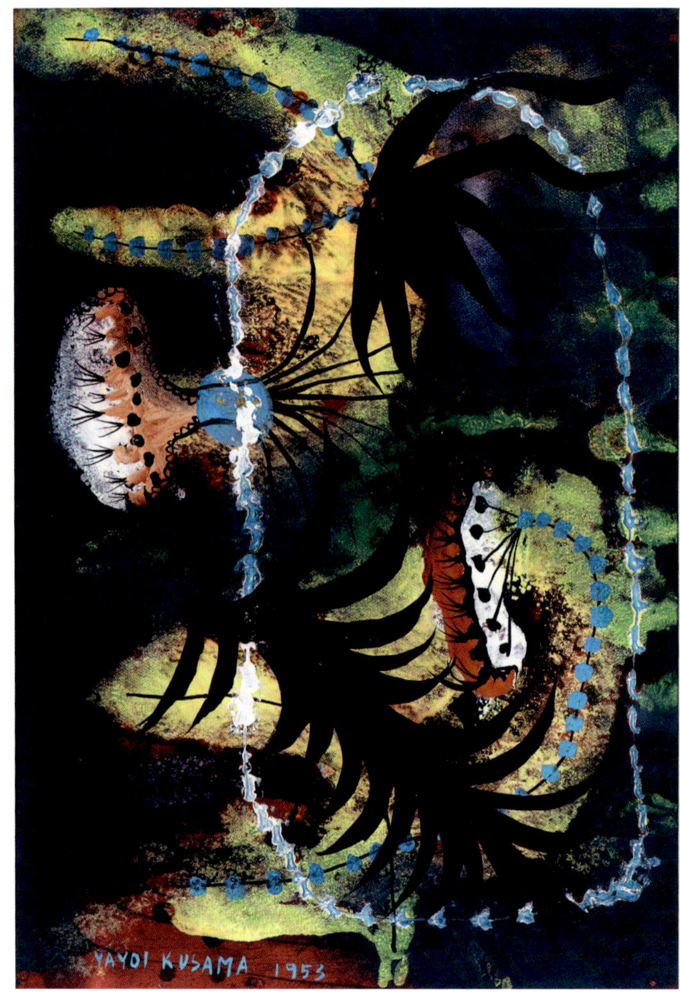

37 | **Fern Kingdom** 1953

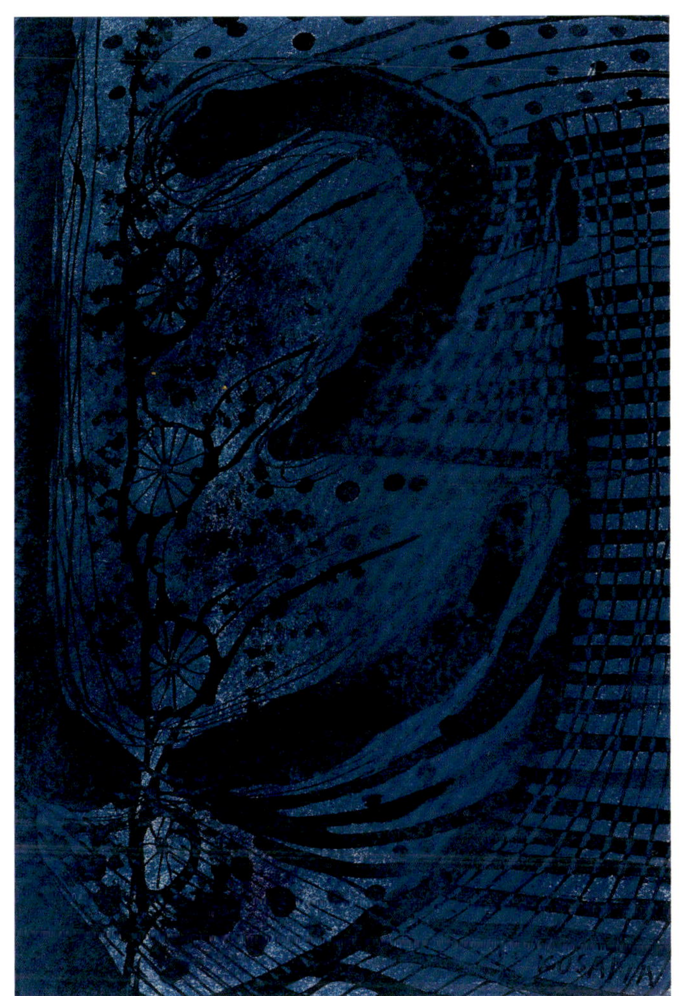

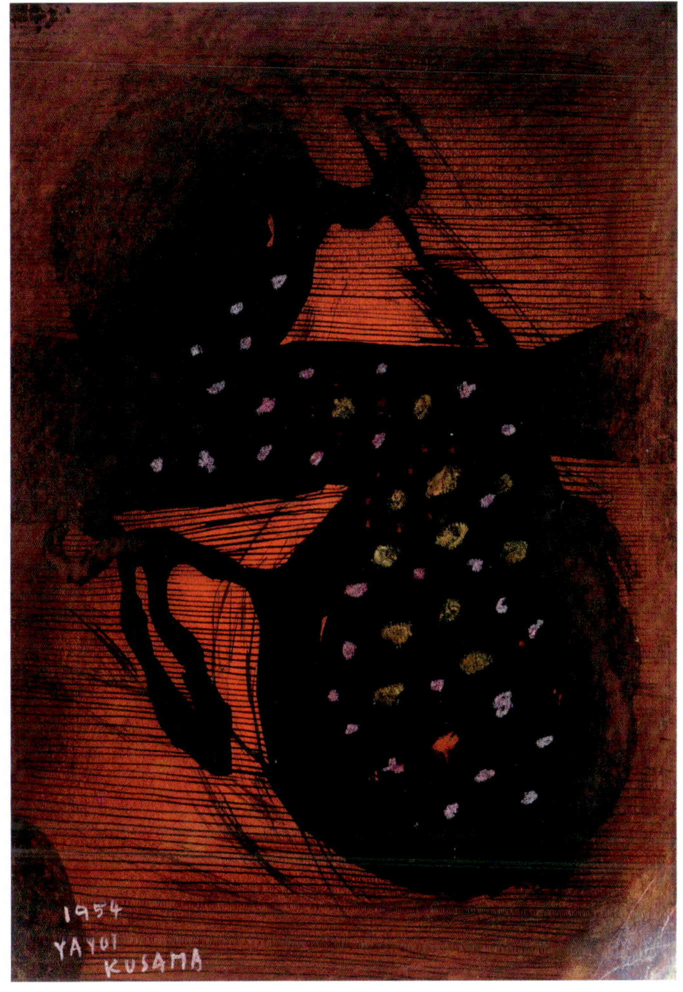

38 | **Untitled** 1950s

39 | **Flower Buds** 1954

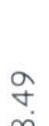

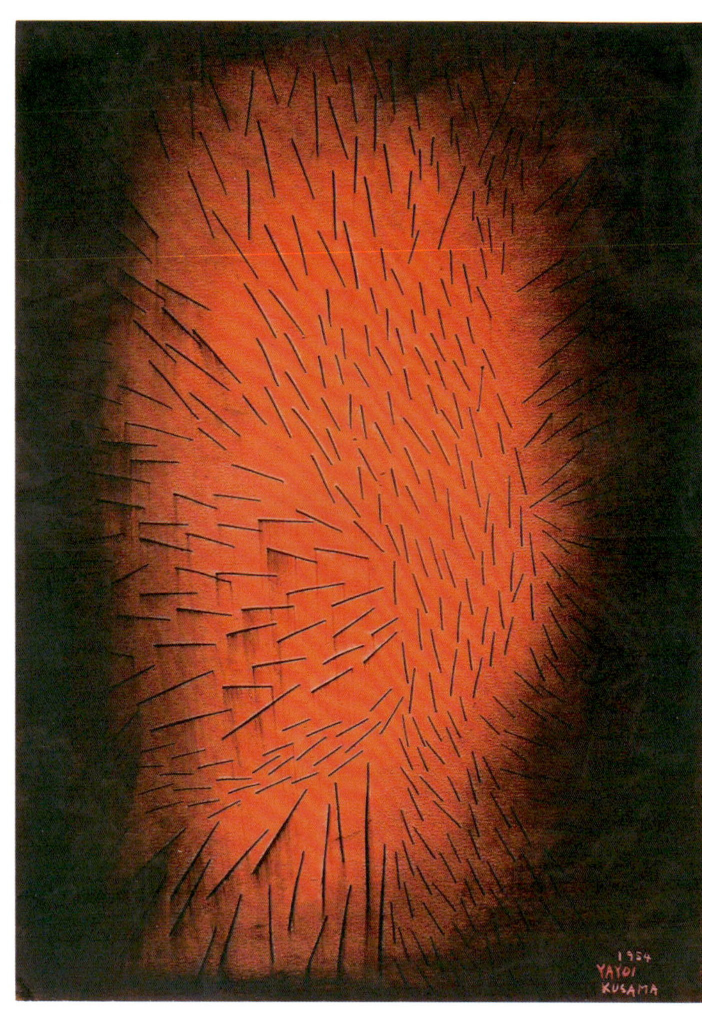
1954
YAYOI
KUSAMA

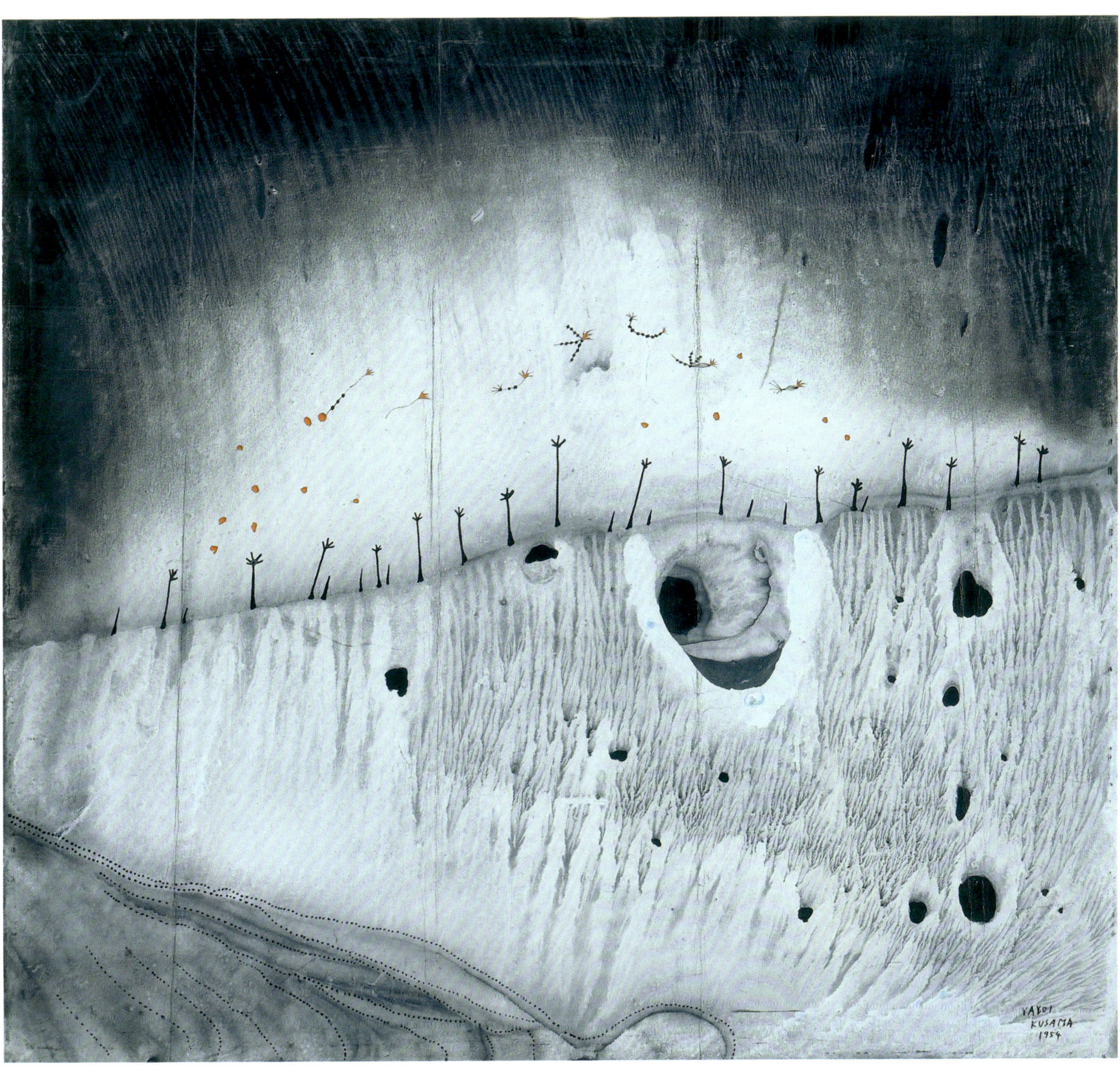

41 | **Untitled** 1954

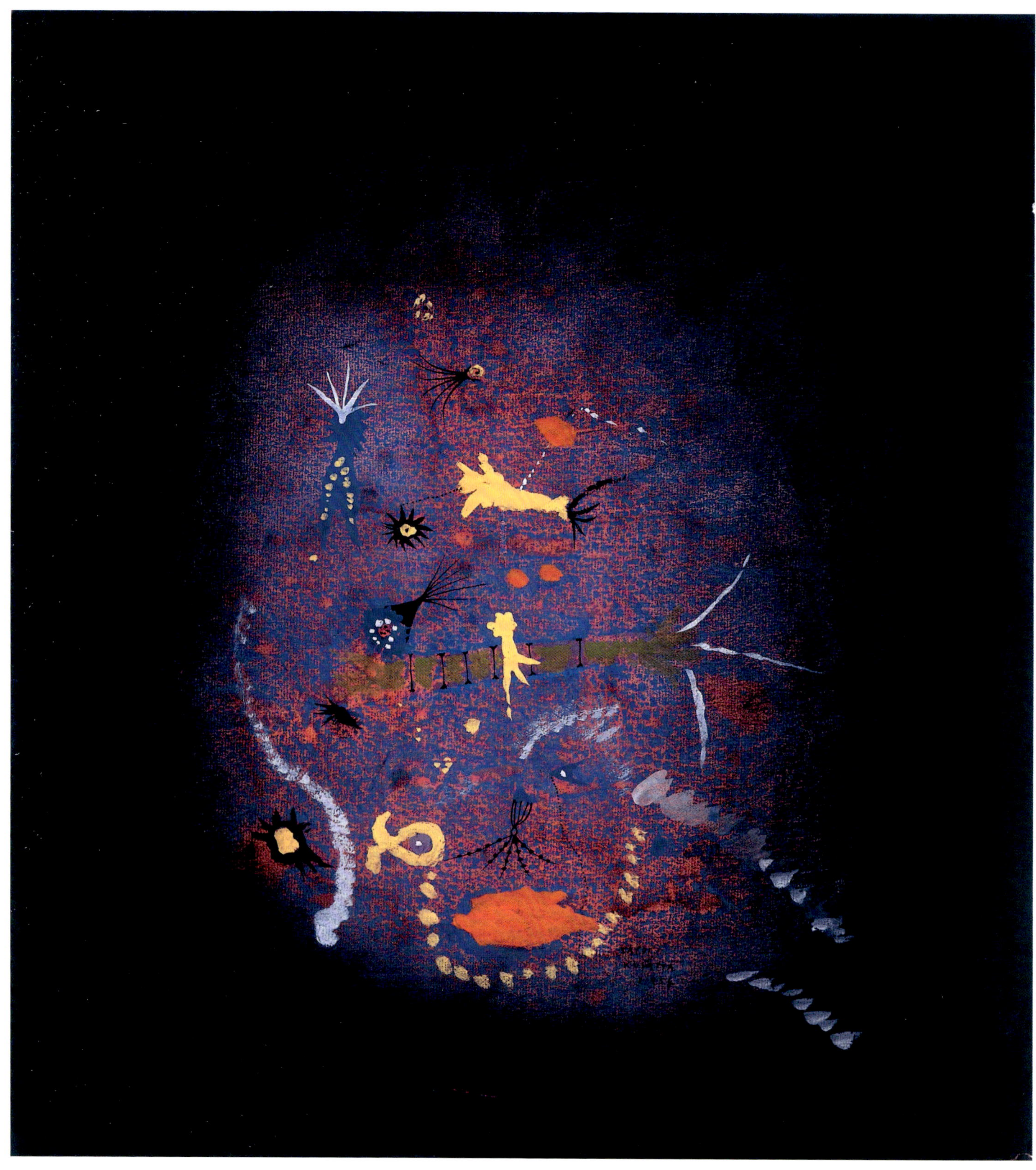

50.51

 Untitled 1954

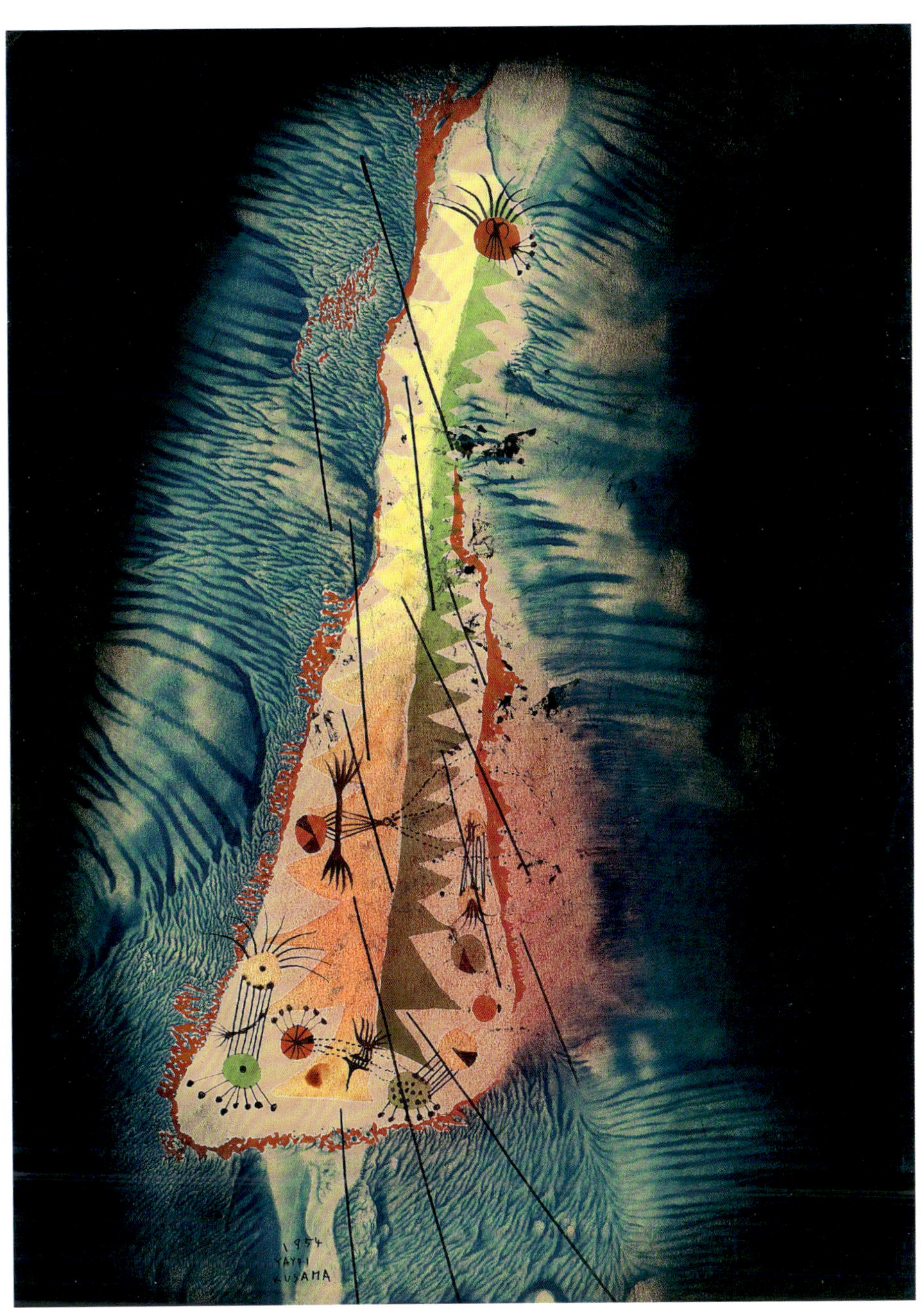

43 | **The Coral Reef in the Sea** 1954

1957–1961

Kusama in her New York studio, c.1960–1

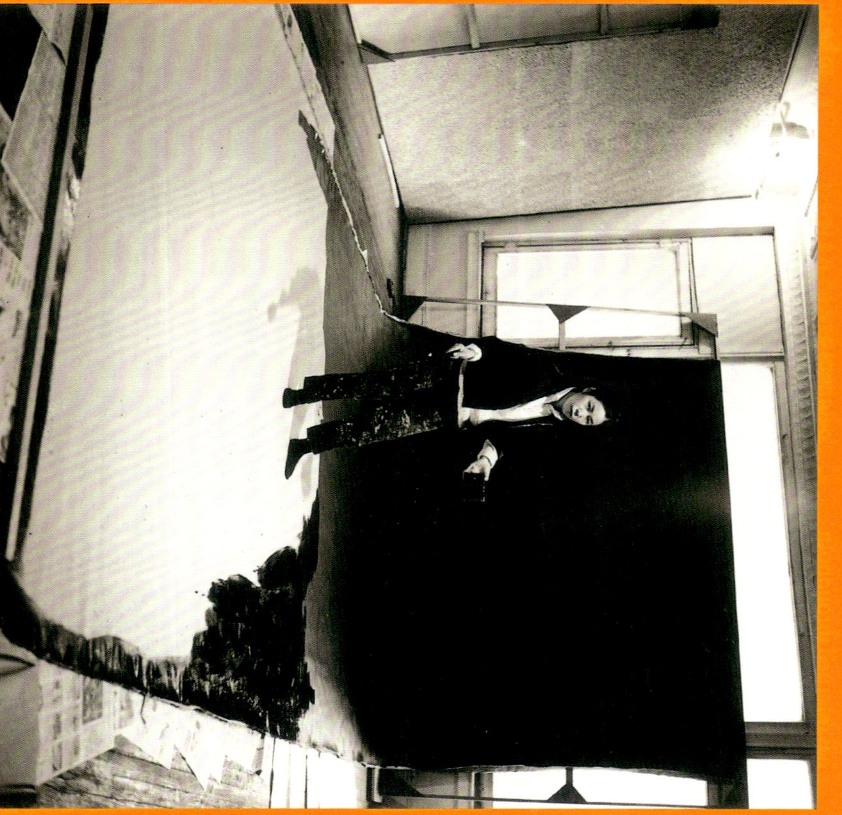

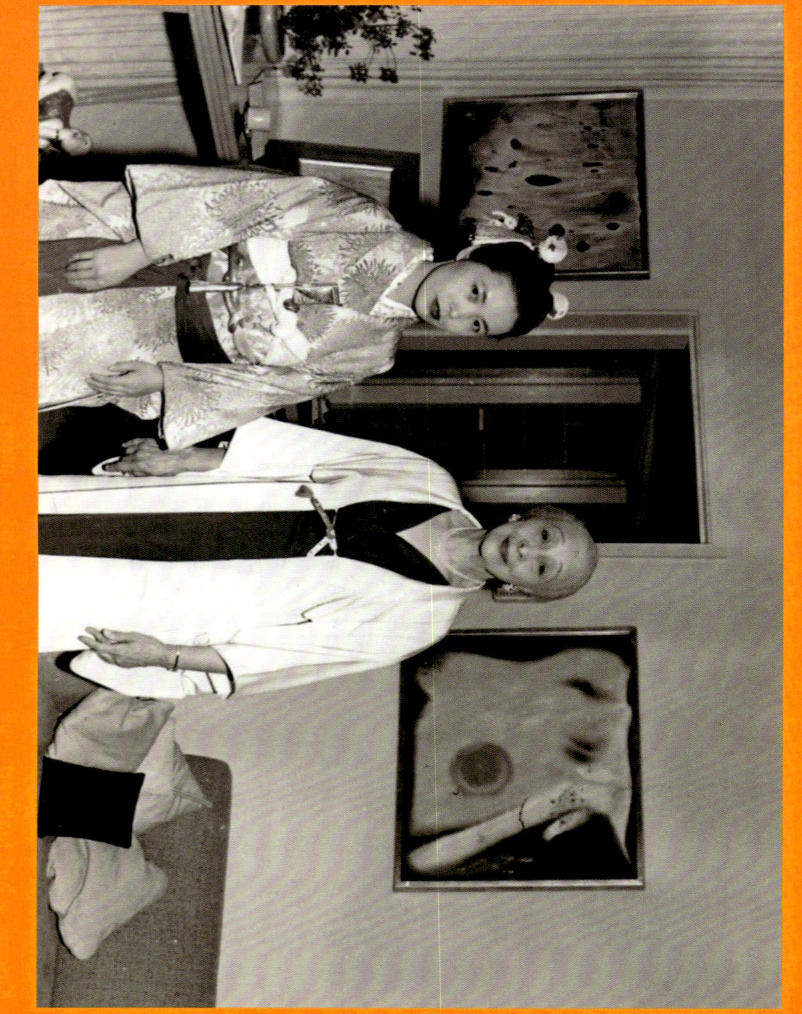

With Zoe Dusanne at Dusanne Gallery, Seattle, 1957

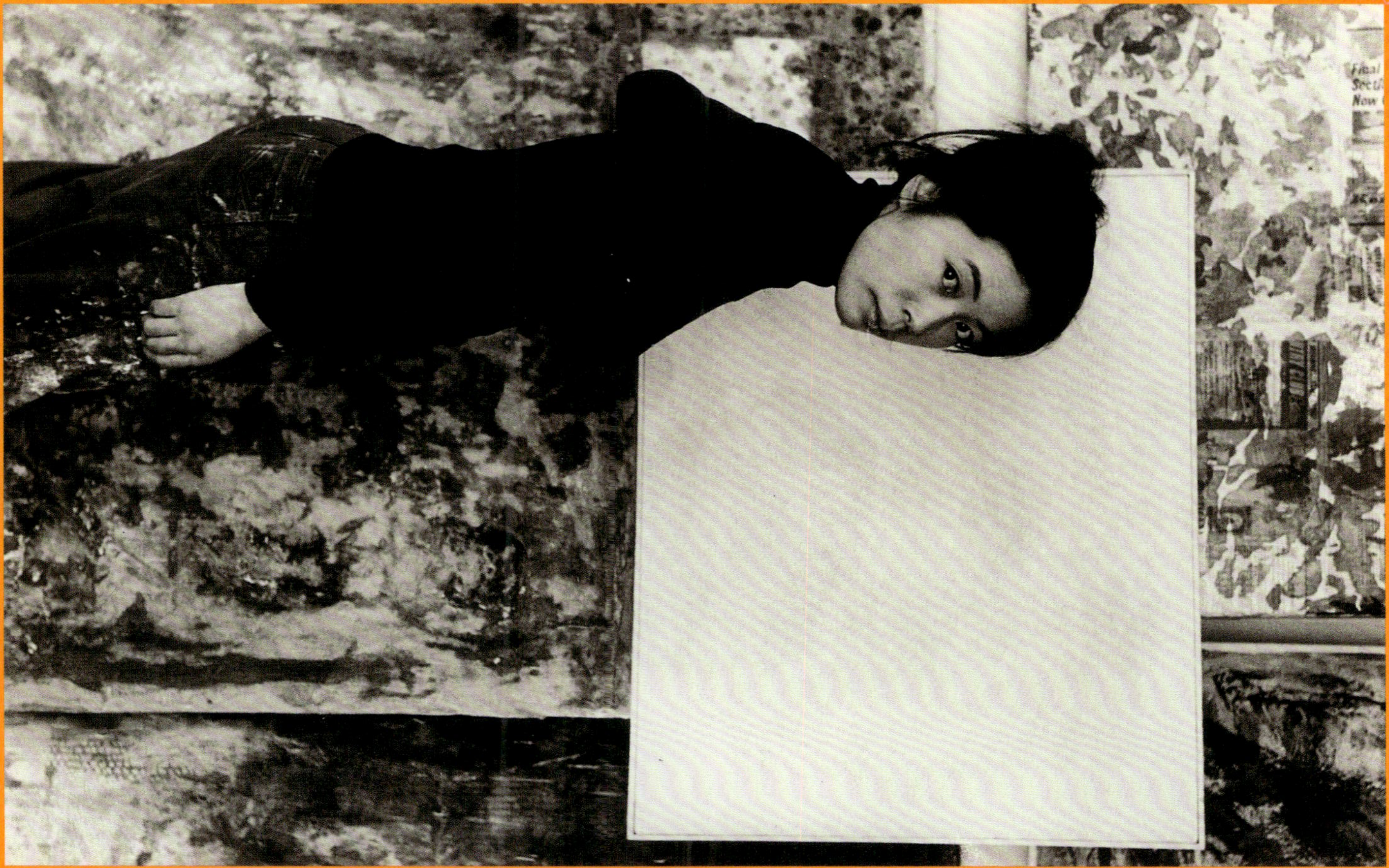

Kusama in her New York studio, c.1958–9

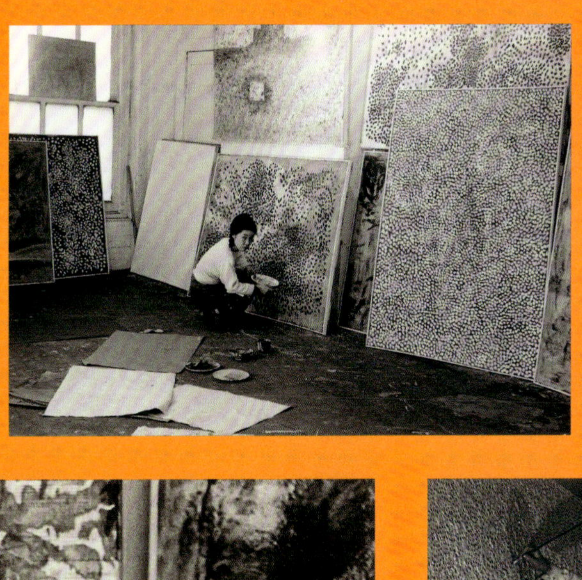

Kusama in her New York studio, 1958–9

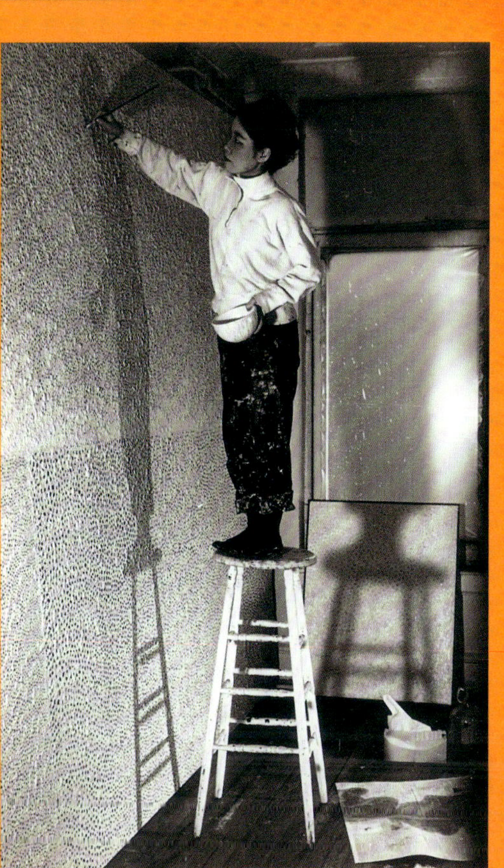

Kusama in her New York Studio, c.1960–1

56.57

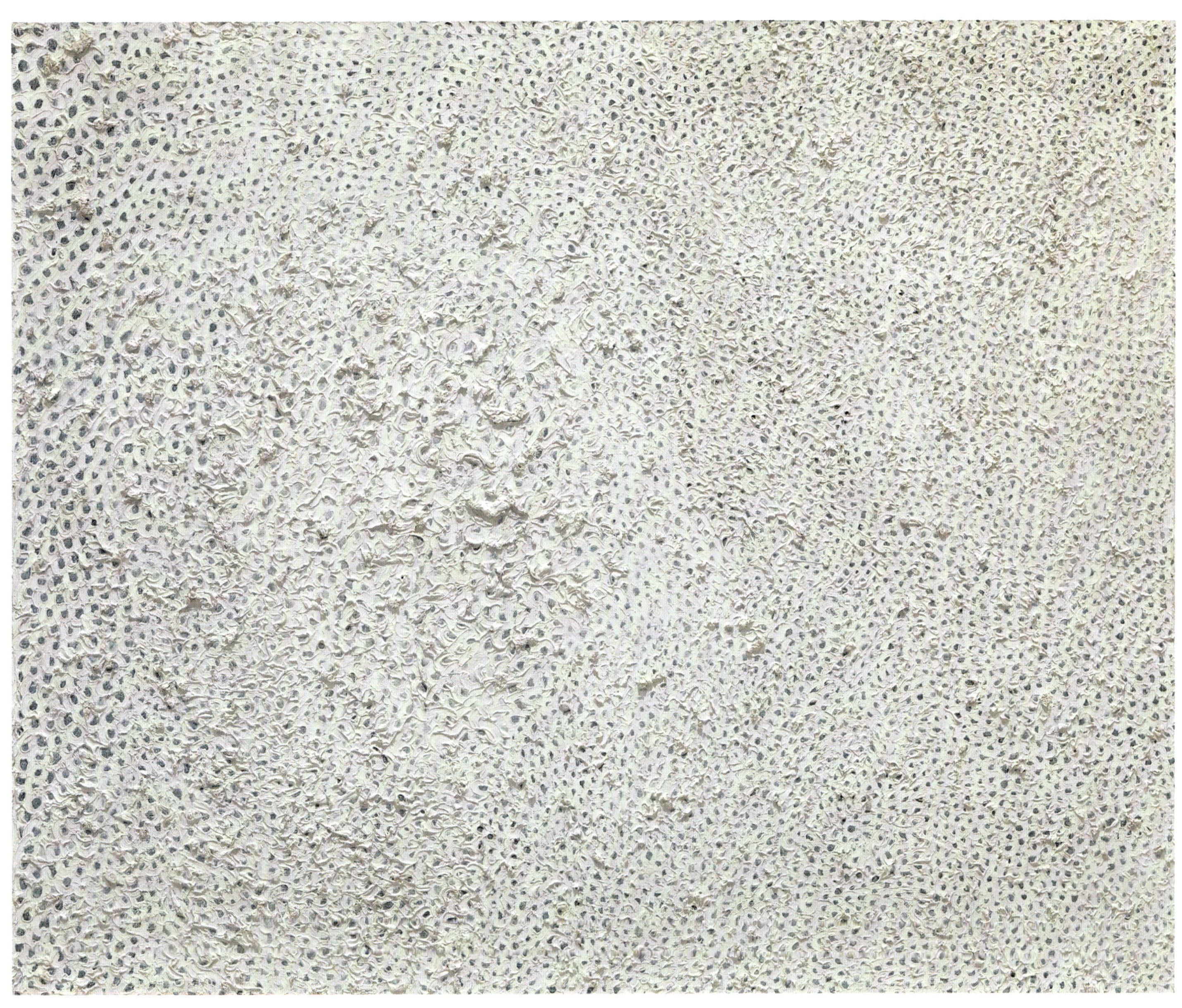

 No.F 1959

 No.B White 1959

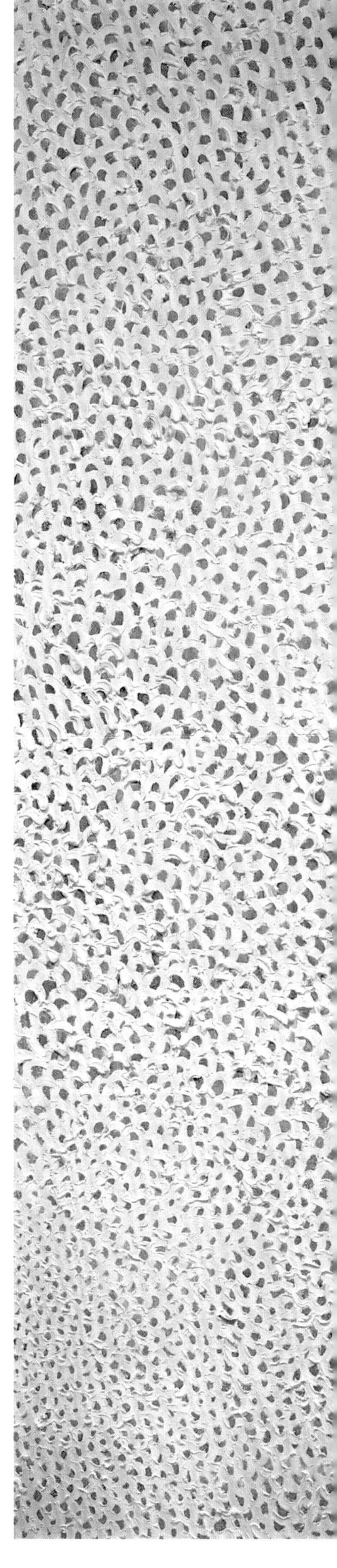

 Pacific Ocean 1960

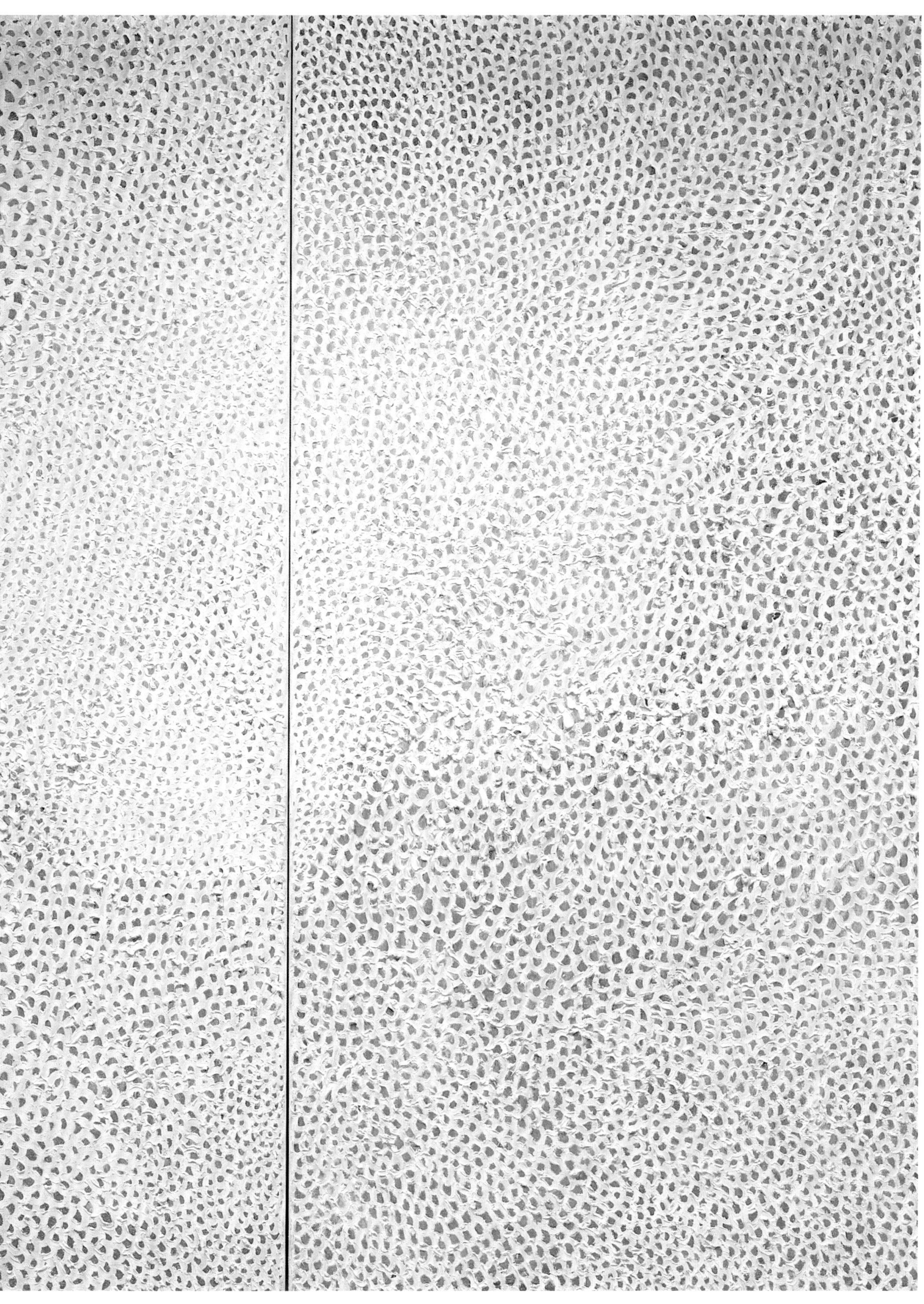

68.69

Accumulation Sculptures and Collages 1961–1965

In September 1961 Kusama moved to a new studio at 53 East 19th Street, on the floor below a studio occupied by Donald Judd; she was to remain there until the summer of 1964. Kusama had met Judd soon after her arrival in New York and counts him as her first friend in the New York art world. At the time Judd was supporting himself as an art critic. He wrote favourably about Kusama's work, praising her painting from the time of her solo exhibition at the Brata Gallery in October 1959, at which time he also became the first collector to buy an Infinity Net painting. By 1961 the two artists had become close and supportive colleagues.

Around the time of her move to the 19th Street studio Kusama began a new body of work, extending her practice into sculpture for the first time. Growing out of the compulsive practice of the Infinity Nets, Kusama began fabricating three-dimensional objects covered with repeated forms. Her first Accumulation sculptures featured everyday objects covered with a proliferation of sewn, stuffed fabric phalli. Kusama's perversely multiplied and proliferating phalli cover the surfaces of a range of furniture, clothing and accessories, objects often associated with the domestic sphere. Her *Compulsion Furniture* works have a surreal quality, suggesting a dreamlike world in which an internal obsession is projected into the physical realm.

Kusama first exhibited her Accumulation sculptures in a group show at the Green Gallery in New York in June 1962. That show included an armchair (*Accumulation No.1*, no.53) and sofa (*Accumulation No.2*, no.52), both of which are covered in white-painted soft-sculpture phalli. The Green Gallery show was significant as it marked one of the first exhibitions of the burgeoning American pop art movement, featuring work by Andy Warhol, Claes Oldenburg, George Segal and James Rosenquist. Kusama is arguably unique amongst artists working in New York in the early 1960s in that her work came to be associated and contextualised with minimal and post-minimal practice as well as pop art.

By this time Kusama was deeply embedded in the heart of the avant-garde scene in New York. She was part of an emerging group of young artists, including Warhol, Oldenburg, Judd and Robert Morris, who were making their names and competing for gallery shows and critical plaudits. Kusama was aware of her 'outsider' status as an Asian woman and this seems to have inspired her to work

1962

Accrochange 1962, Galerie A, Amsterdam, January

**Yayoi Kusama*, Robert Hanamura Gallery, Chicago, 18 March – 1 April

Tentoonstelling Nul (Exhibition Nul), Stedelijk Museum, Amsterdam, 9–25 March

Nieuwe Tendenzen (New Tendencies), State University Gallery, Leiden, 14 March – 2 April

(Group Exhibition), Green Gallery, New York, June

(Group Exhibition), Museum of Modern Art, Penthouse Gallery, New York, November

Anno 62, Galerie't Venster, Rotterdam, 3–23 November

1963

New Work Part 1, Green Gallery, New York, 8 January

Panorama van de nieuwe tendenzen (Panorama of the New Tendency), Gallery Amstel, Amsterdam, 5–25 May

No Show, Gertrude Stein Gallery, New York, 8 October – 2 November

1963–4

**Aggregation: One Thousand Boats Show*, Gertrude Stein Gallery, New York, 17 December 1963 – 11 January 1964

1964

The New Art, Davison Art Centre, Wesleyan University, Connecticut, 1–22 March

**Kusama: Driving Image Show*, R.Castellane Gallery, New York, 21 April – 9 May

Around Travel, PVI Gallery, New York, 30 April

Best of 1964, Southampton Art Gallery, New York, 2 June

Mikro Zero/Nul/Mikro nieuwe realisme, Galerie Delta, Rotterdam, 7–20 August

1965

New Eyes, Chrysler Museum of Art, Provincetown, Massachusetts, 21–30 April

The New Style of Works of International Avant-garde, Galerie de Bezige, Amsterdam, 8 April

Nul 1965, Stedelijk Museum, Amsterdam, 15 April – 8 June

**Yayoi Kusama*, Internationale Galerij Orez, The Hague, 1 May – 3 June

Zero Avanguardia, Galleria del Cavallino, Venice, 4–14 May, touring to Galleria il Punto, Turin, May

Recent Acquisitions, Whitney Museum of American Art, New York, 26 May

Yayoi Kusama and Clifford La Fontaine, R. Castellane Gallery, New York, July

White on White, De Cordova Museum, Lincoln, Massachusetts, 10 October – 21 November

Japanese Artists abroad Europe and America, National Museum of Modern Art, Tokyo, 15 October – 28 November

**Floor Show*, R. Castellane Gallery, New York, 3–27 November

more assiduously and experiment more vigorously, exploring and innovating to demonstrate her creative ingenuity to her peers and the greater art world.

In December 1963 Kusama showed *Aggregation: One Thousand Boats Show* (no.65) for the first time at the Gertrude Stein Gallery in New York. This work features a white-painted fabric phallus-encrusted rowboat complete with oars. The boat that formed the support for this sculpture was scavenged by Kusama and Judd from the street; Judd helped her stuff the fabric phalli. The boat is installed in a room, the walls and ceiling of which are covered with 999 black and white posters depicting the same boat seen from above. Kusama's use of a repeated motif to line the walls of a gallery space predates Andy Warhol's *Cow Wallpaper* by three years. Brian O'Doherty described *Aggregation* as a 'genuine, obscurely poetic event'.[1]

This work was Kusama's first complete room installation, and was to signal the beginning of a wholly new and expansive mode for the artist. Since then she has repeatedly returned to making full-scale environments that immerse the viewer in her obsessively charged vision.

Kusama refers to her phallus-covered works as the *Sex Obsession* series. A parallel sculptural project is her related *Food Obsession* series. The *Food Obsession* works are objects covered with dry macaroni. Just as the phalli can be seen to represent Kusama's fear of sex, the macaroni can be seen to represent her disgust at the overabundance of foodstuffs in the boom-time post-war years of the United States. Many of her macaroni-clad objects were displayed in *Driving Image Show*, a series of room-sized installations she first created at New York's Richard Castellane Gallery in April 1964. For this show Kusama also created a 'Macaroni Carpet', covering the floor with loose dried pasta on which the audience trod as they entered the gallery.

In November 1965 Kusama unveiled her most ambitious gallery presentation to date. *Floor Show* at Castellane Gallery featured a number of large Accumulation works including a phallus-encrusted *Baby Carriage* from c.1964–6 and *My Flower Bed* 1962 (p.191). The latter is a dramatic red-painted construction suspended from the ceiling in which a 'stalk' comprised of dozens of stuffed cotton gloves appears to rise out of a 'ground' made of bedsprings. The exhibition also included *Infinity Mirror Room – Phalli's Field*, a room-sized installation with mirrored walls and ceiling that appeared to reflect endlessly a sea of red on white polka-dotted phallic protrusions covering the floor (see p.186). The following year the artist presented *Kusama's Peep Show* at the same gallery. This work, otherwise known as *Endless Love Show*, consisted of a mirrored hexagonal box into which viewers were invited to look. The mirrored ceiling of the interior was embedded with coloured lights that flashed on and off, appearing to multiply infinitely in the reflections.

In parallel with her experiments in sculpture and installation, in the early 1960s Kusama began making collages in earnest. These two-dimensional works are closely linked to the Infinity Nets and Accumulation sculptures, as they also feature proliferations of identical or similar motifs. Her collages of this period consist of pages covered with ready-made objects: airmail stickers, adhesive labels, toy money, or photographs of details of her own Infinity Net paintings. These works resonate with contemporary explorations of systematic repetition in minimalism and conceptual art.

Many years later, Kusama explained that her approach to making her sculptural and collage accumulations was her philosophy of 'self-obliteration'. She has written:

> Artists do not usually express their own psychological complexes directly, but I use my complexes and fears as subjects. I am terrified by just the thought of something long and ugly like a phallus entering me, and that is why I make so many of them. The thought of continually eating something like macaroni, spat out by machinery, fills me with fear and revulsion, so I make macaroni sculptures. I make them and make them and then keep on making them, until I bury myself in the process. I call this 'obliteration'.[2]

The repetitions of phalli and macaroni in Kusama's work of this period may be understood to represent the artist's attempts to depict and thereby neutralise her neurotic anxiety of the male sex organ and industrially produced foodstuffs. Her compulsion to 'make them and make them and then keep on making them' can be seen as an attempt to lose herself in the act of creation. The obliteration of furniture by fabric phalli and the obliteration of paper by stickers may be understood as a visible manifestation and metaphor of the artist's own attempt to surrender herself to her art.

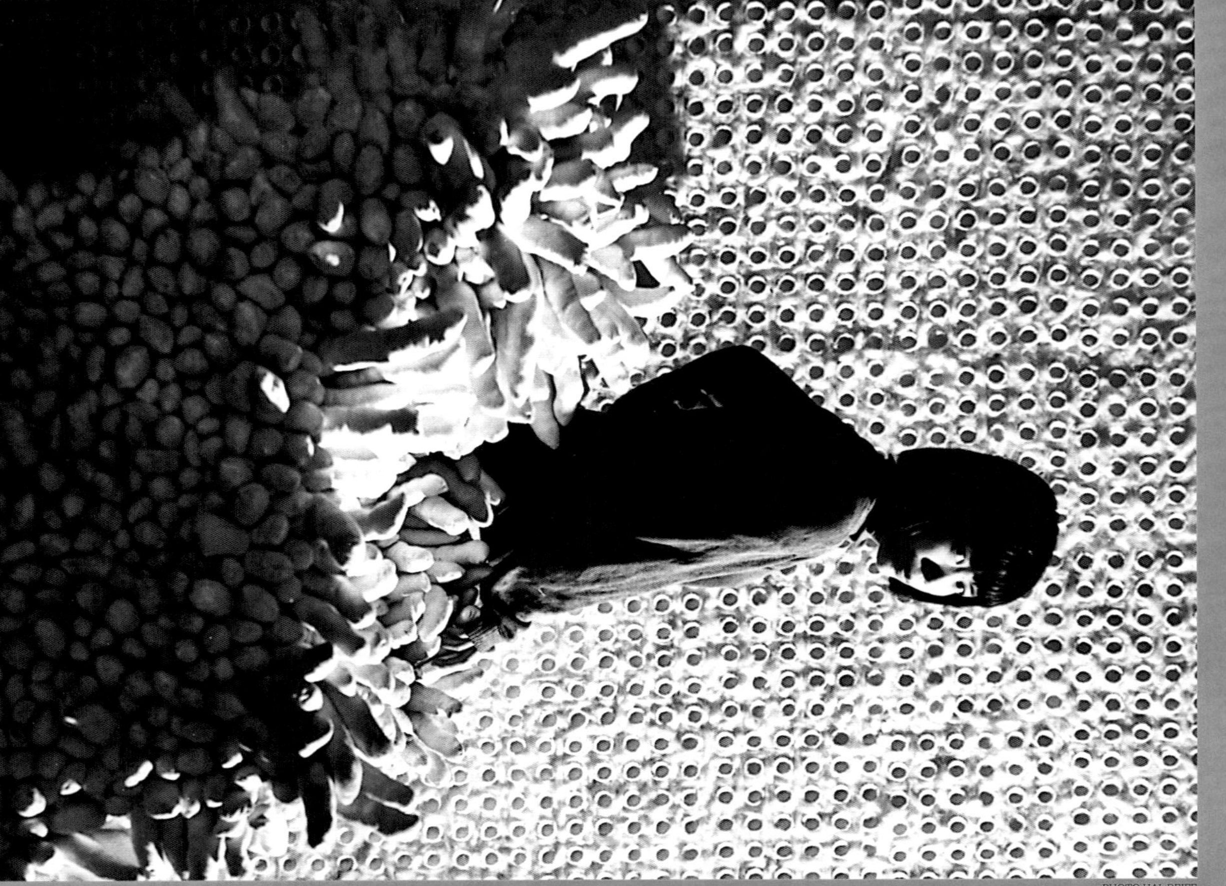

PHOTO HAL REIFF

Kusama with *Accumulation No.1* 1962 and egg-carton relief *No.B,3* 1962, c.1963–4

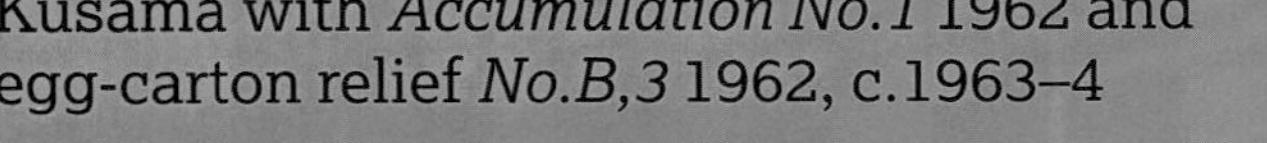

Kusama with sculptures in her New York studio, 1963–4

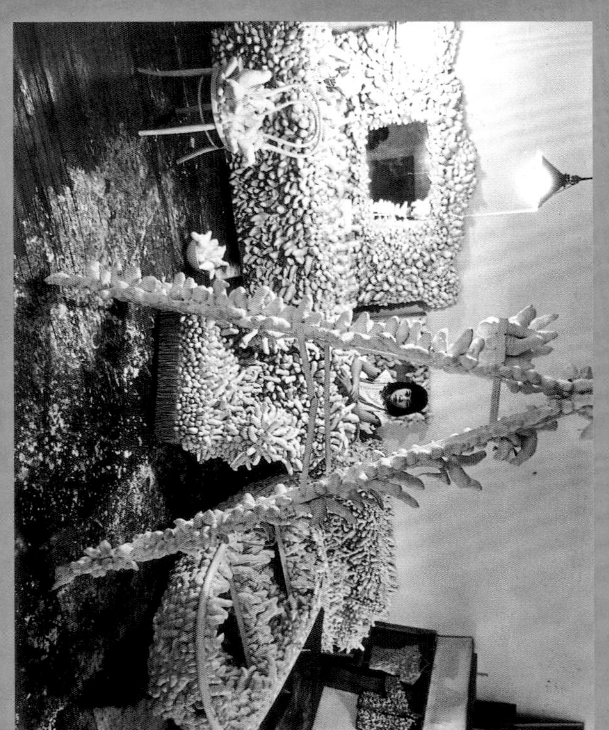

Published materials concerning
Kusama between 1962 and 1965

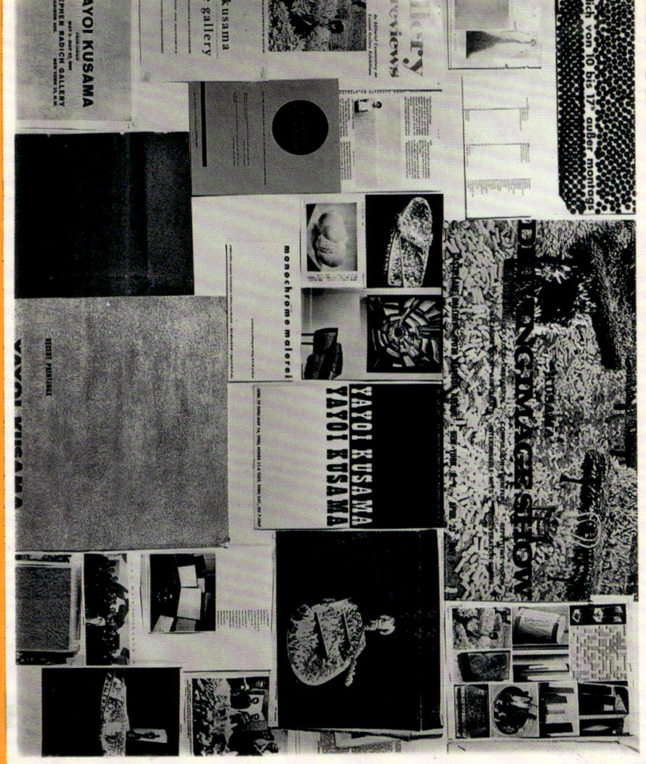

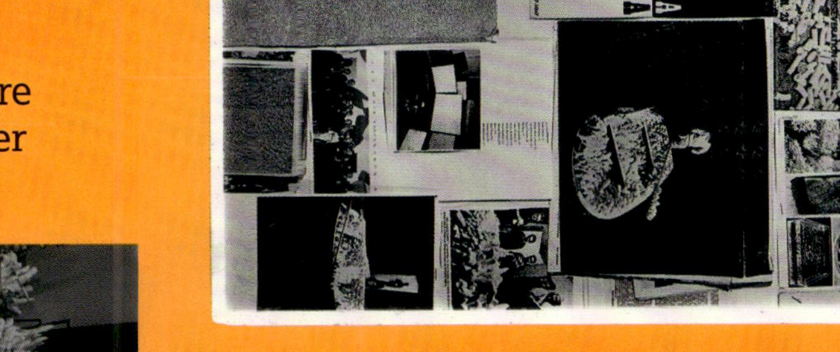

Kusama and her soft sculpture *Accumulation No.2* 1962 in her New York studio, 1964

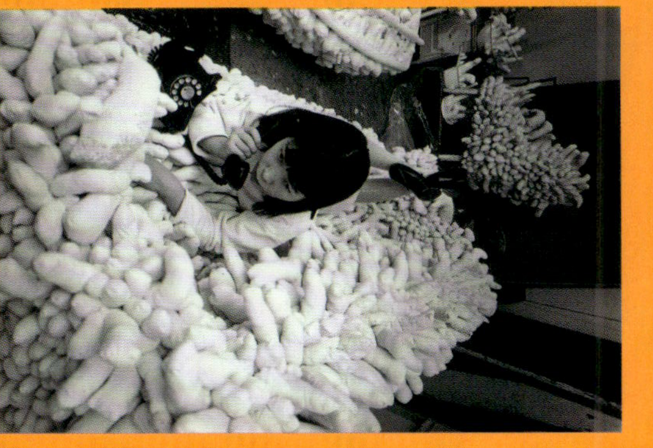

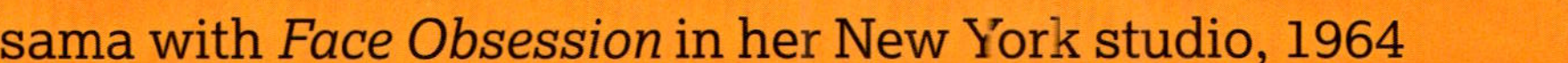

Kusama with *Face Obsession* in her New York studio, 1964

74, 75

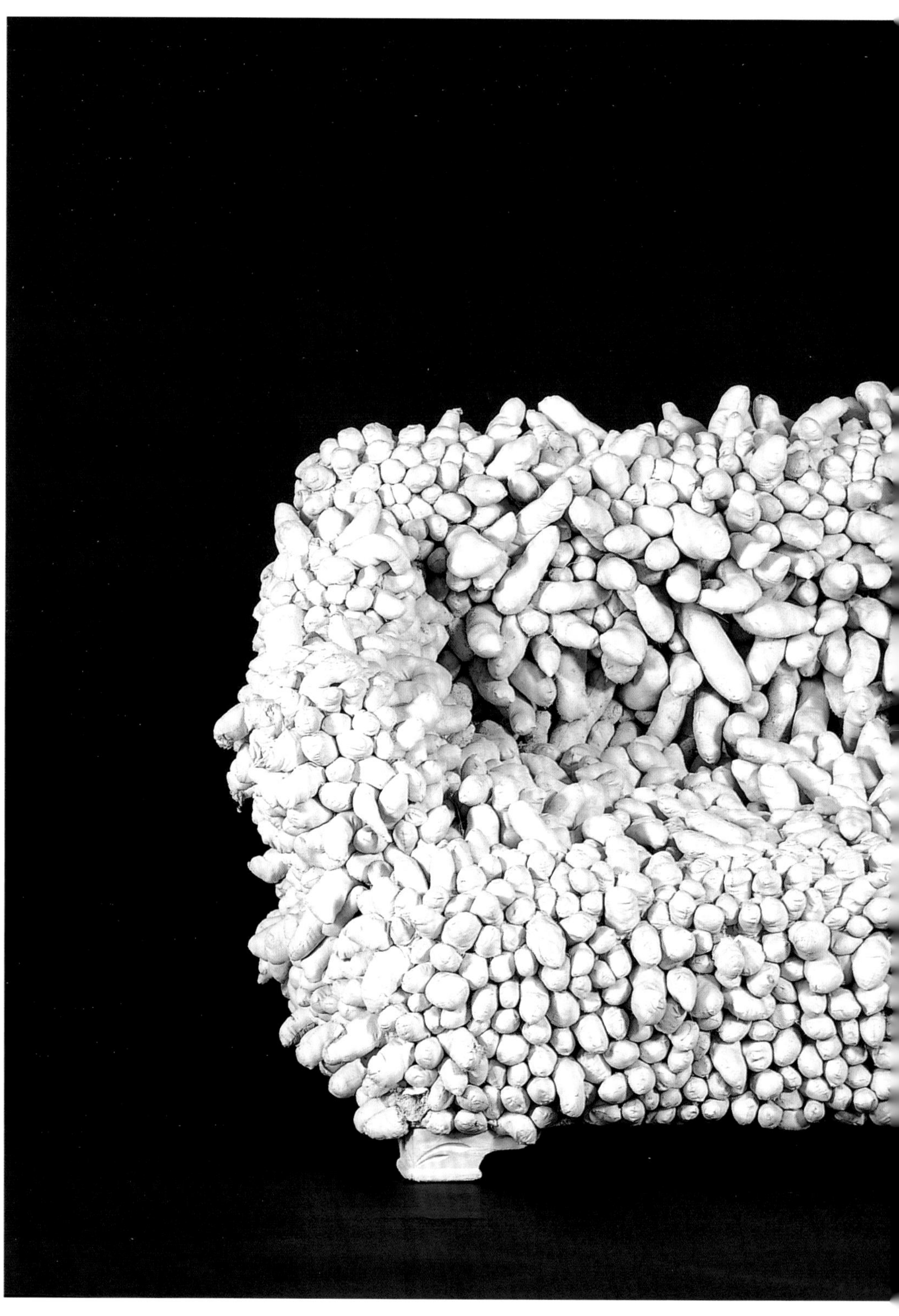

Accumulation No.2 1962

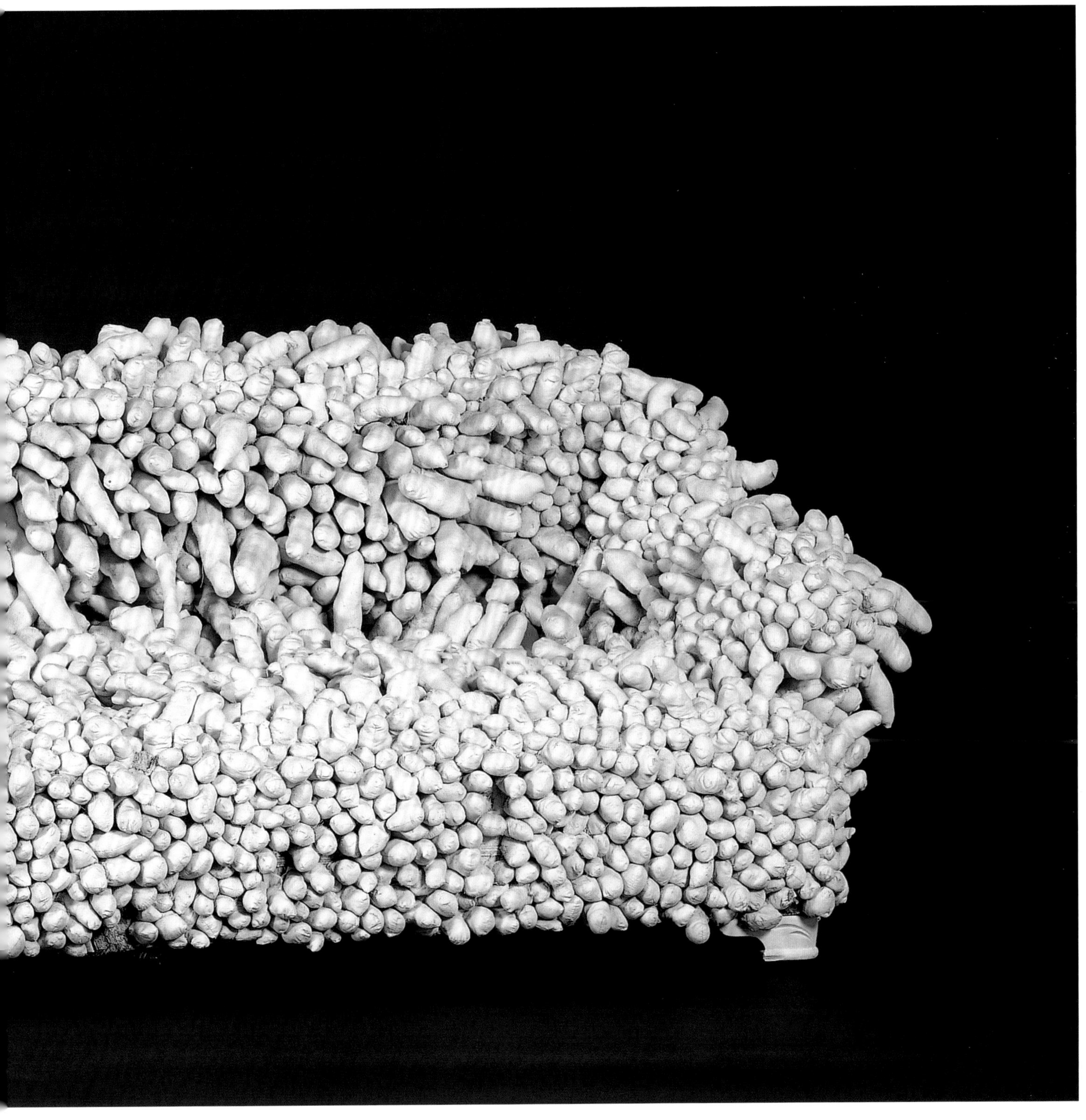

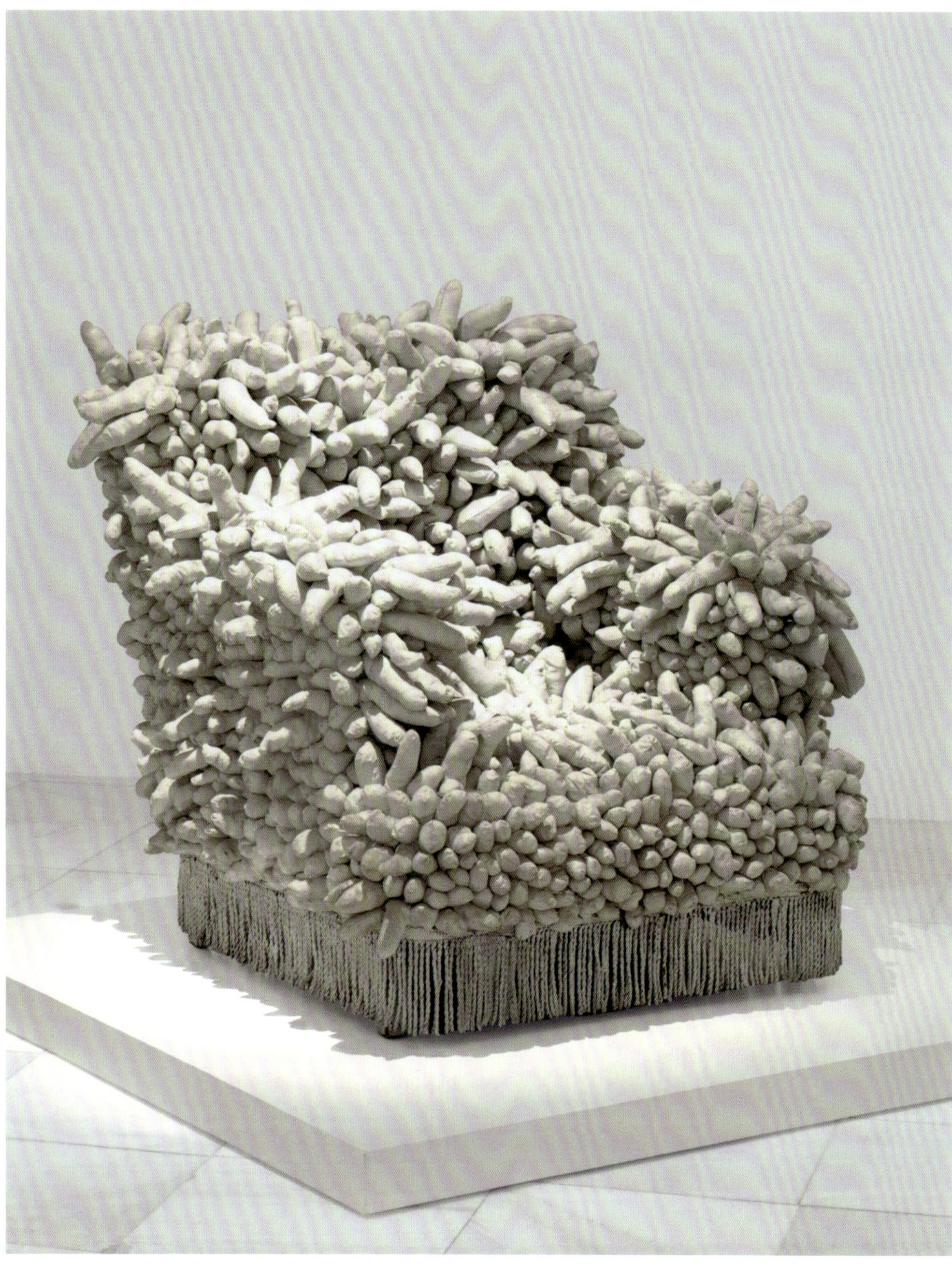

53 | **Accumulation No.1** 1962

54 | **The Man** 1963

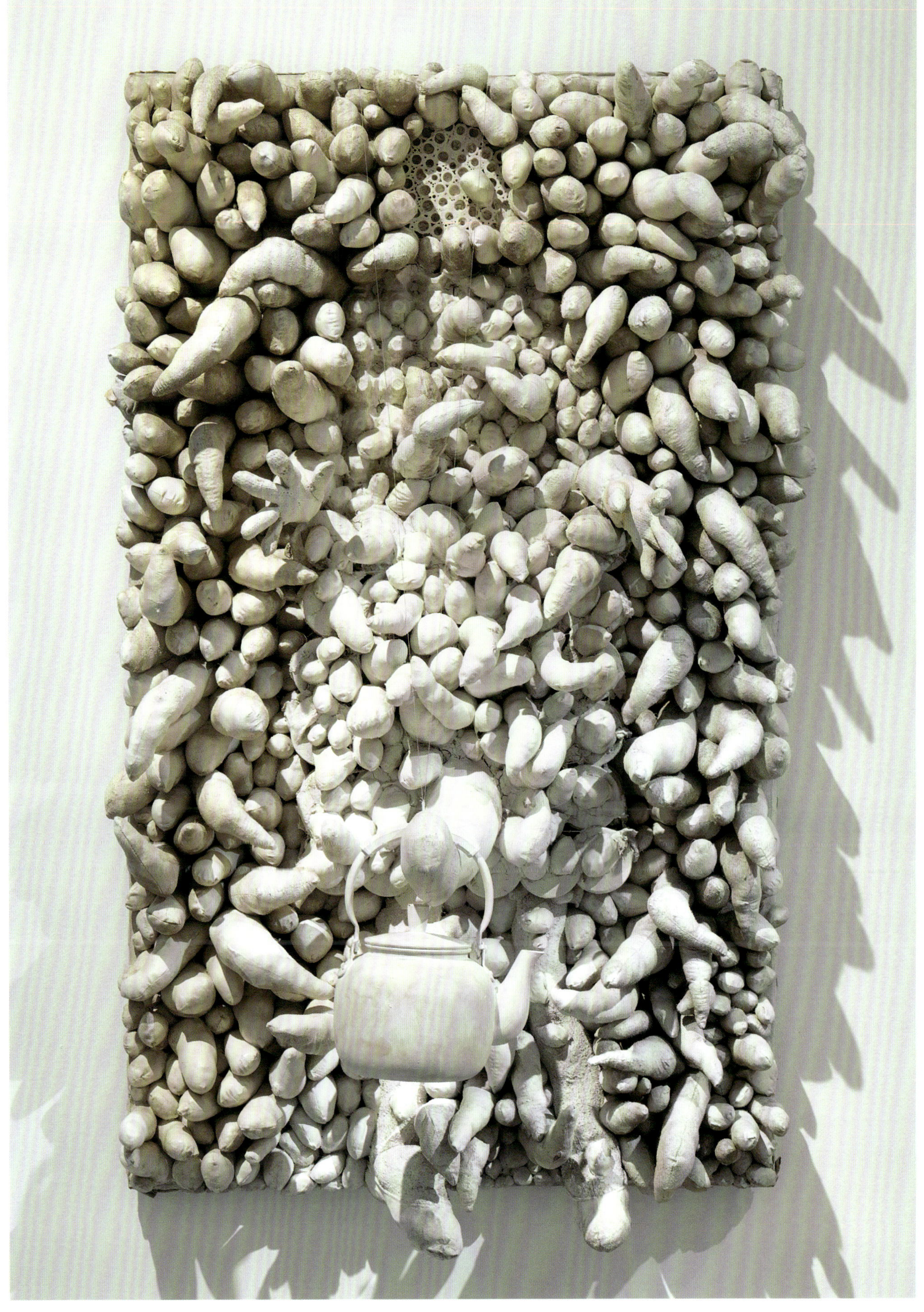

78.79

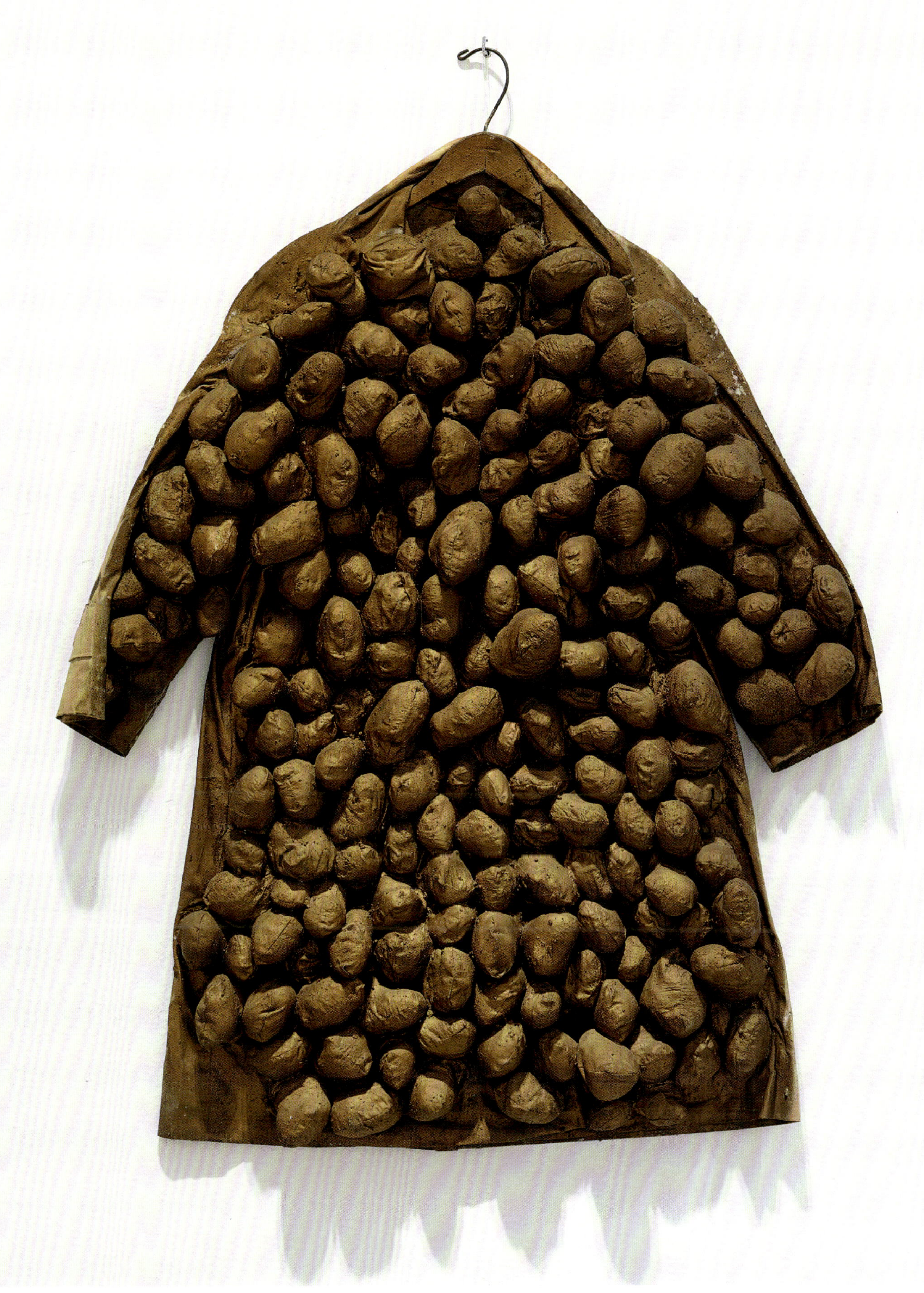

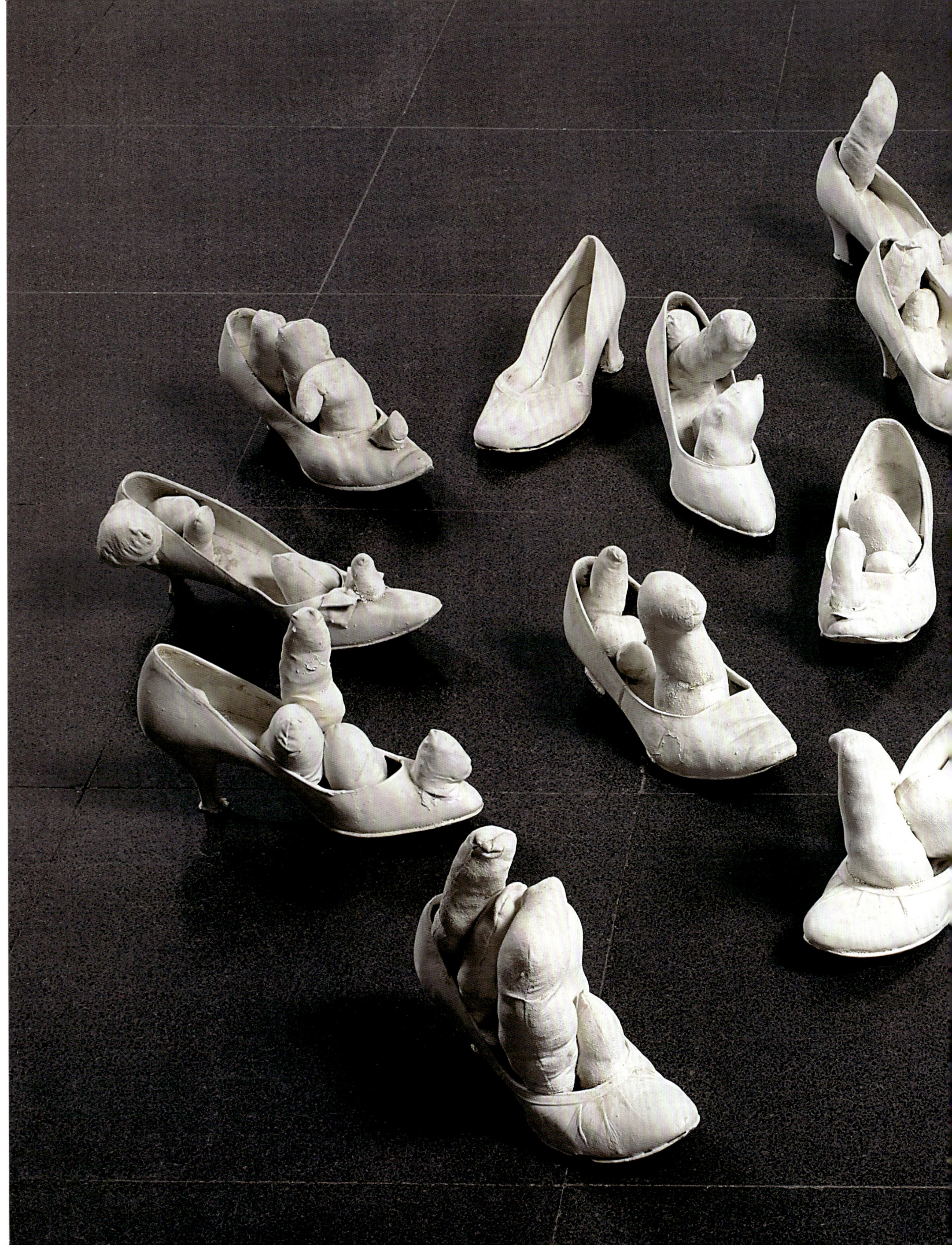

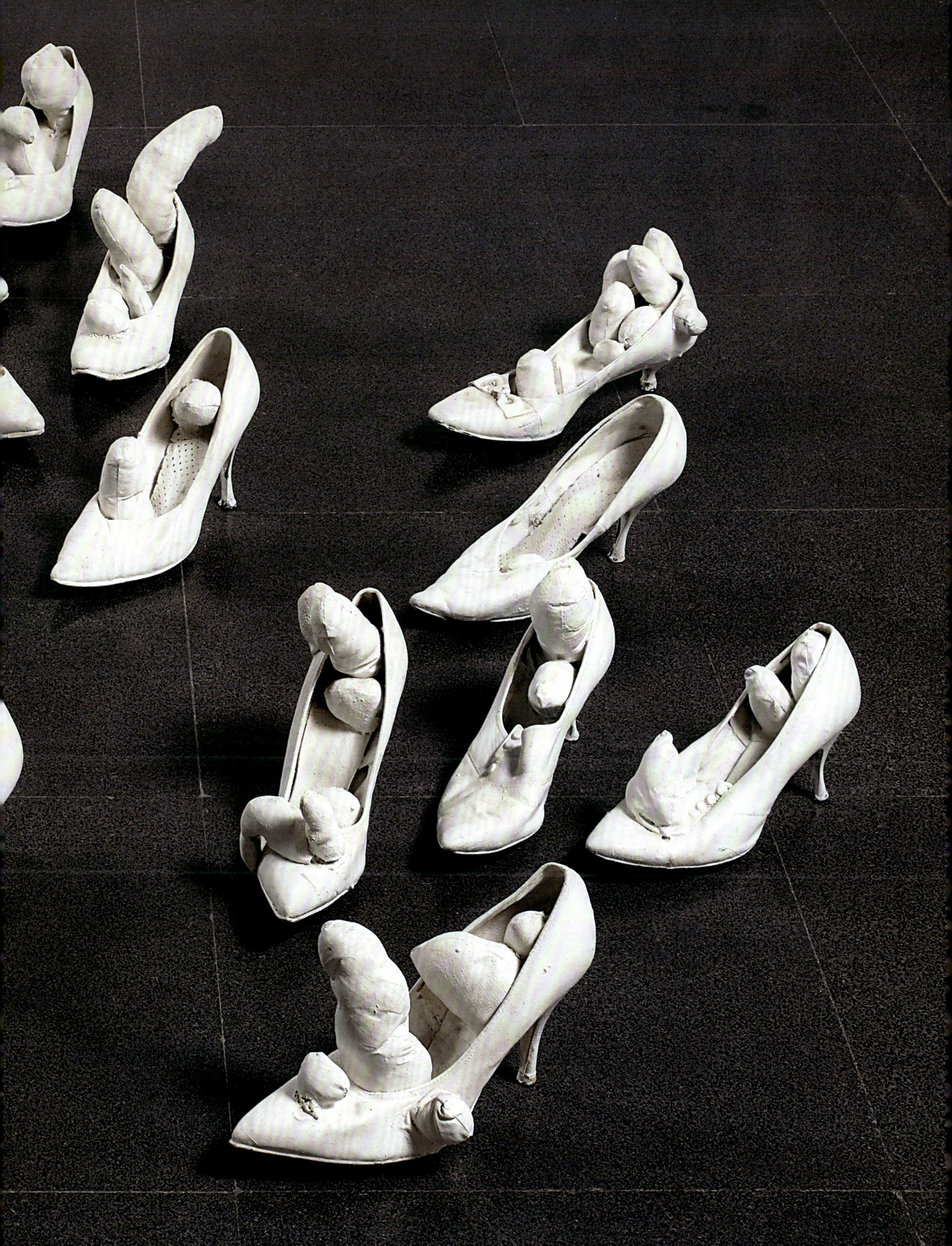

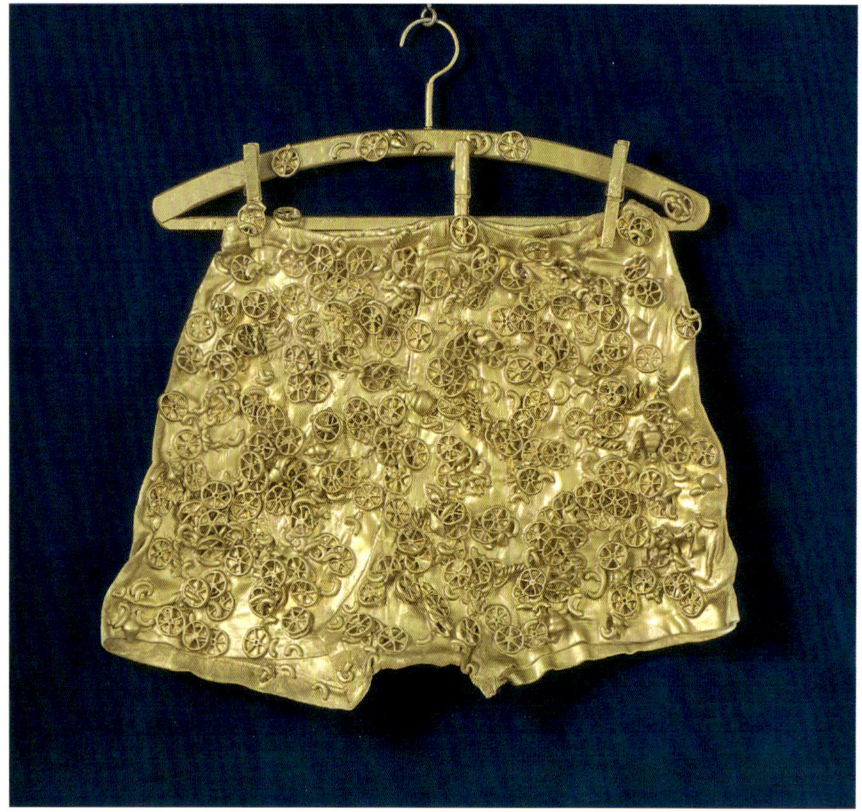

59 | **Macaroni Pants** 1968

60 | **Flower Overcoat** 1964

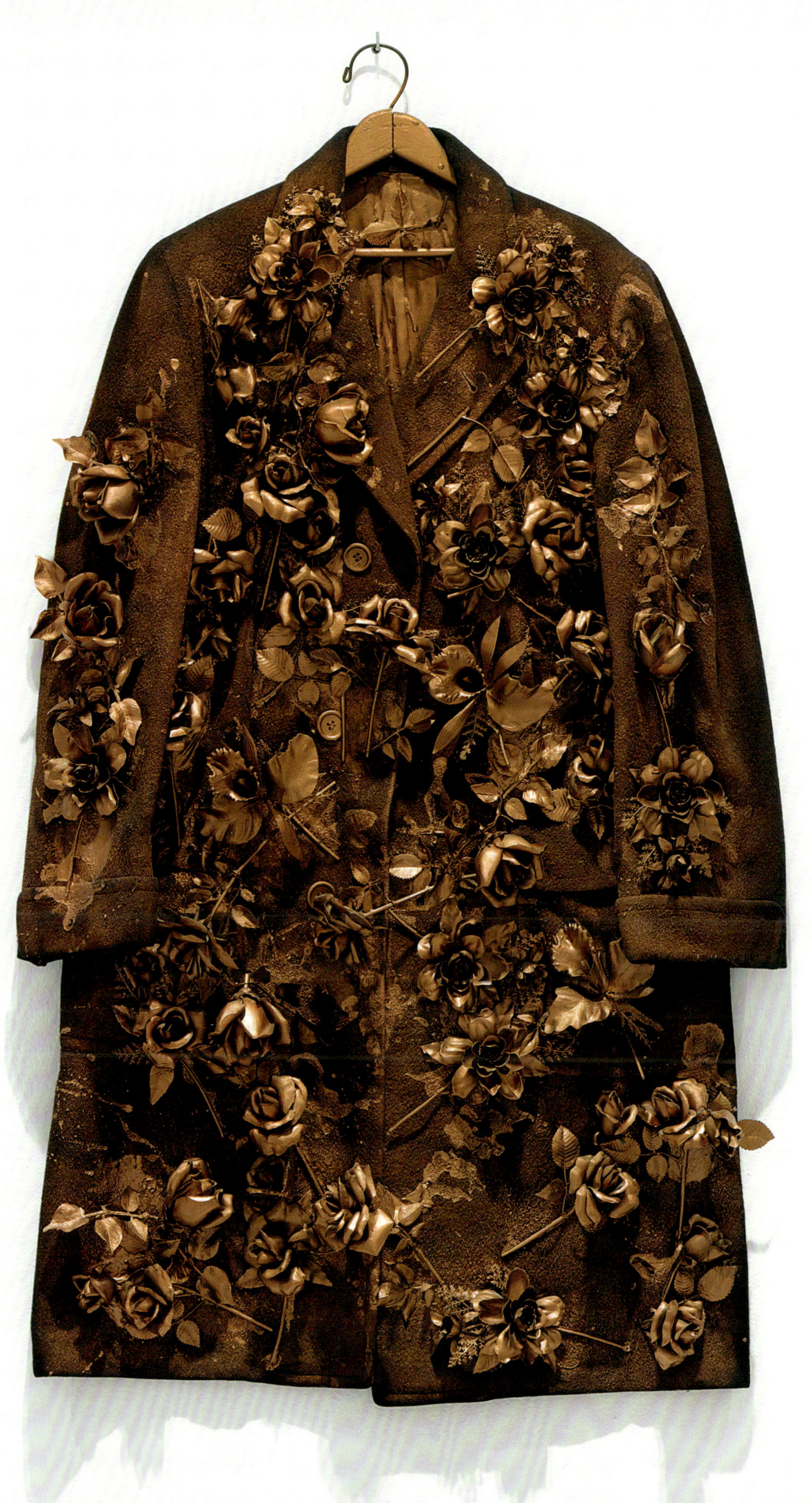

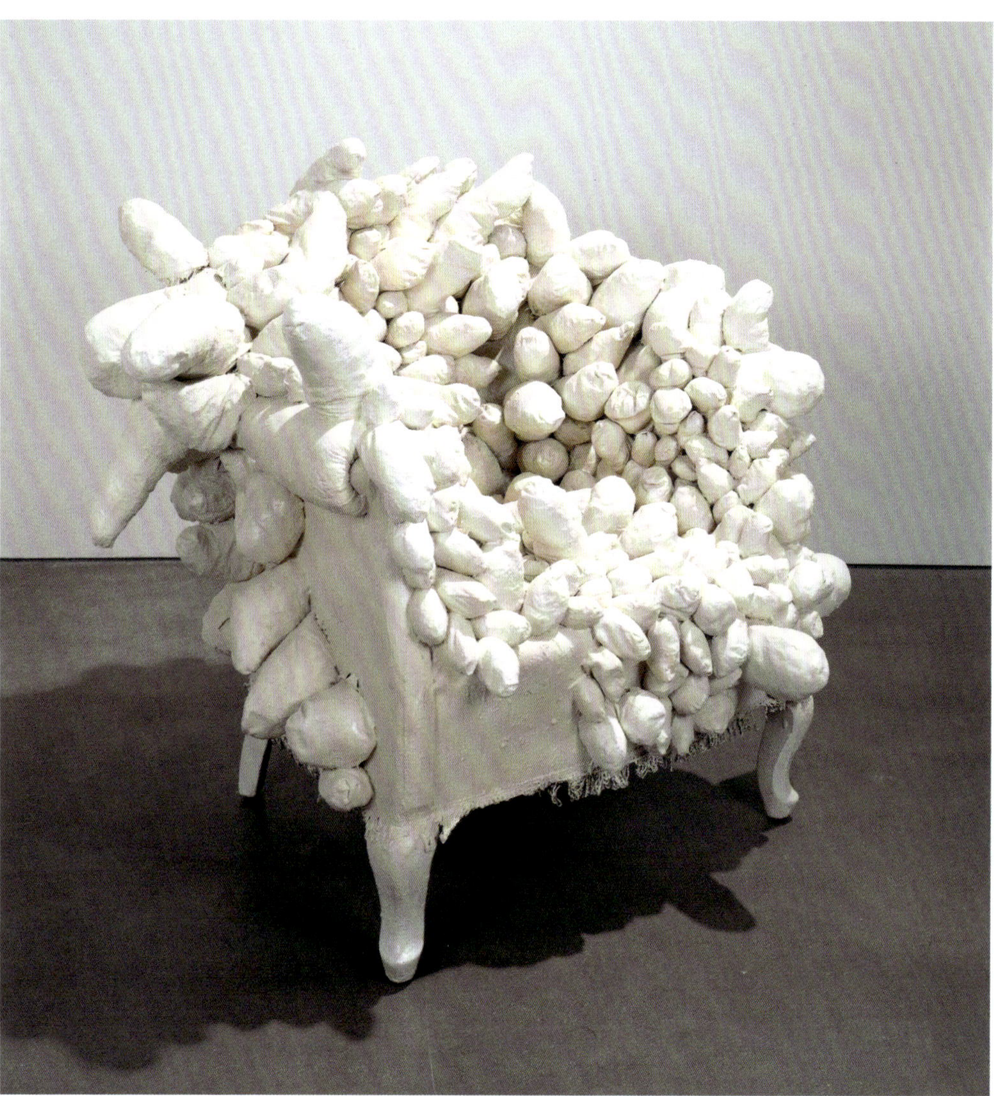

61 | **Accumulation** c.1963

62 | **Arm Chair** 1963

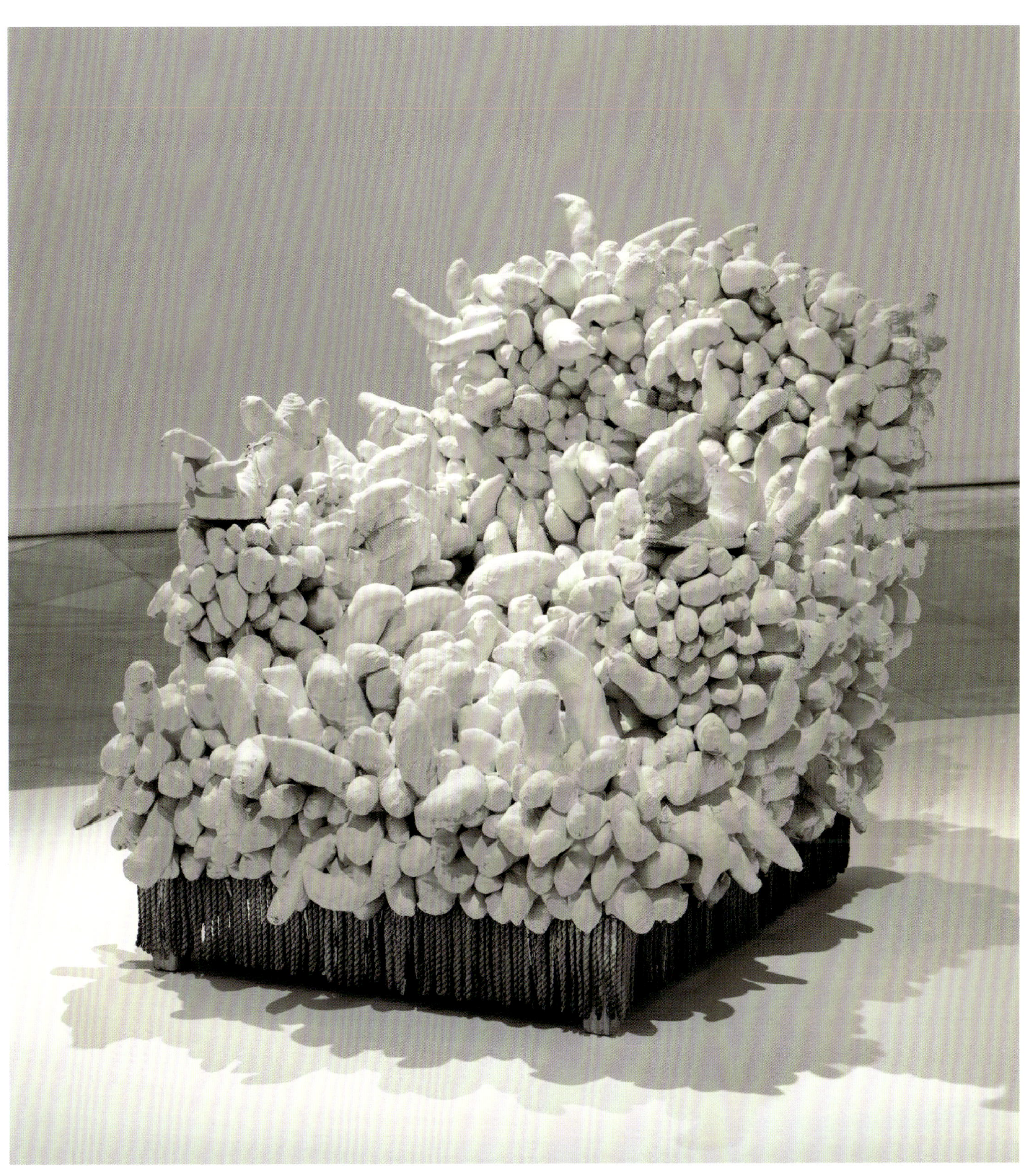

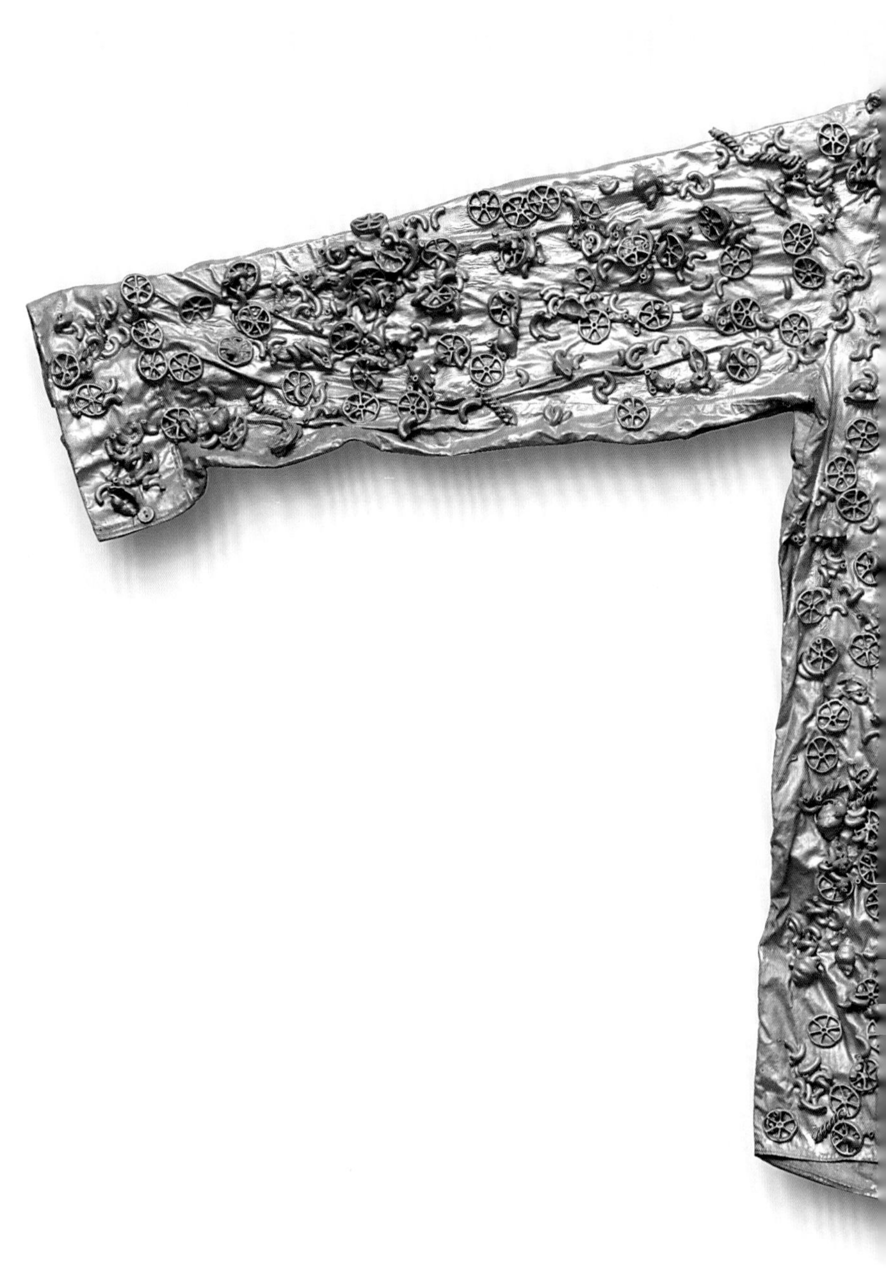

88.89

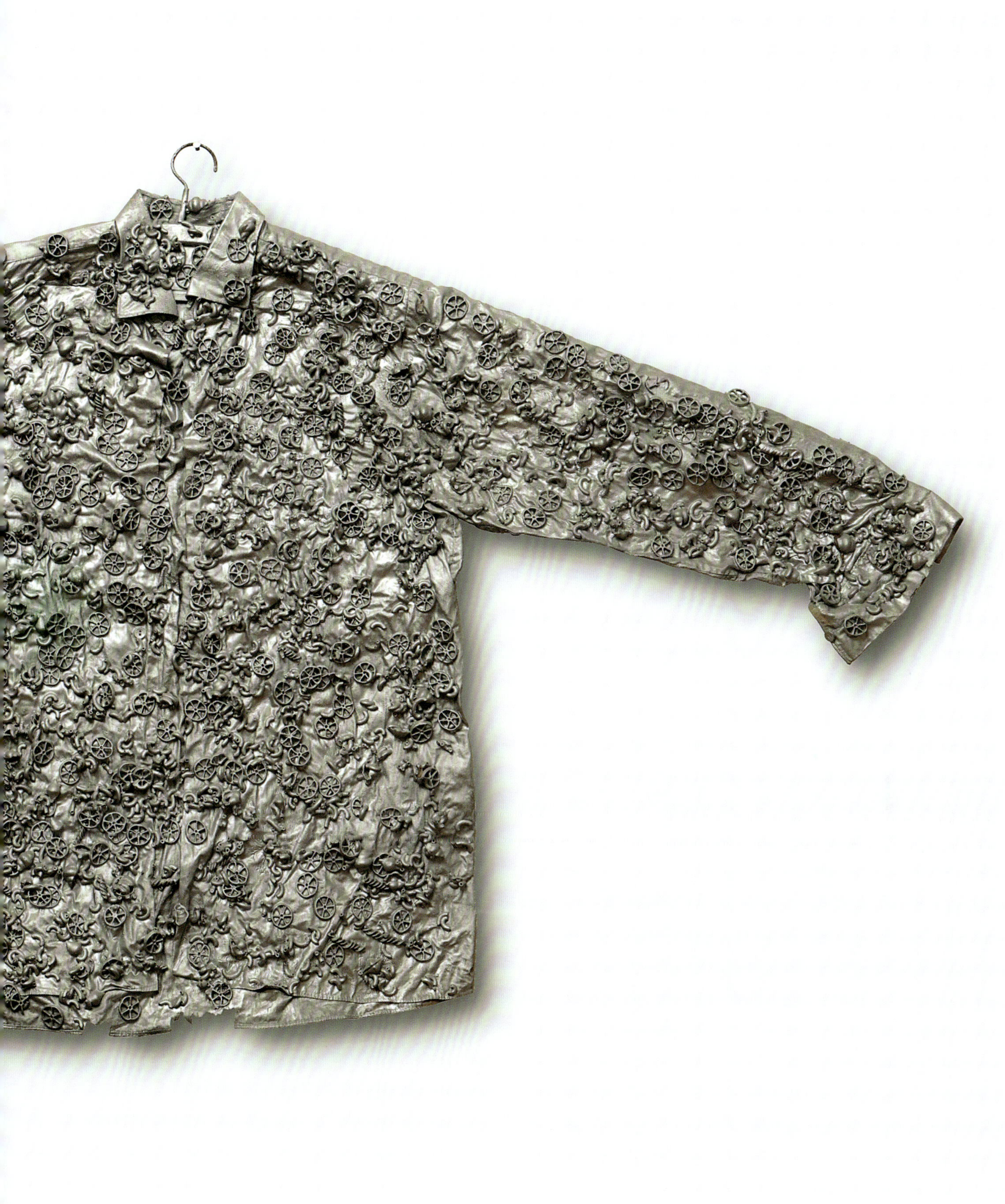

90.91

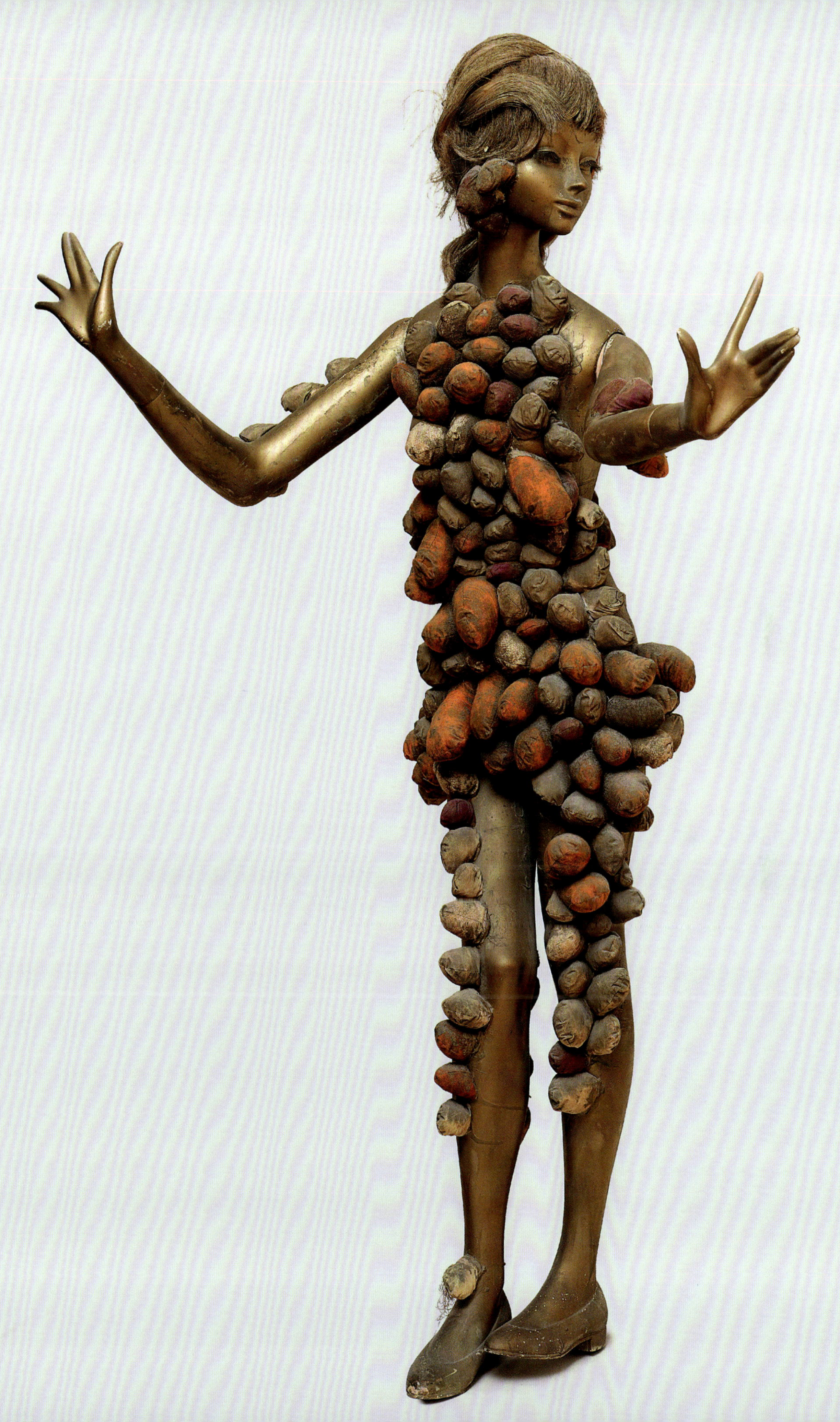

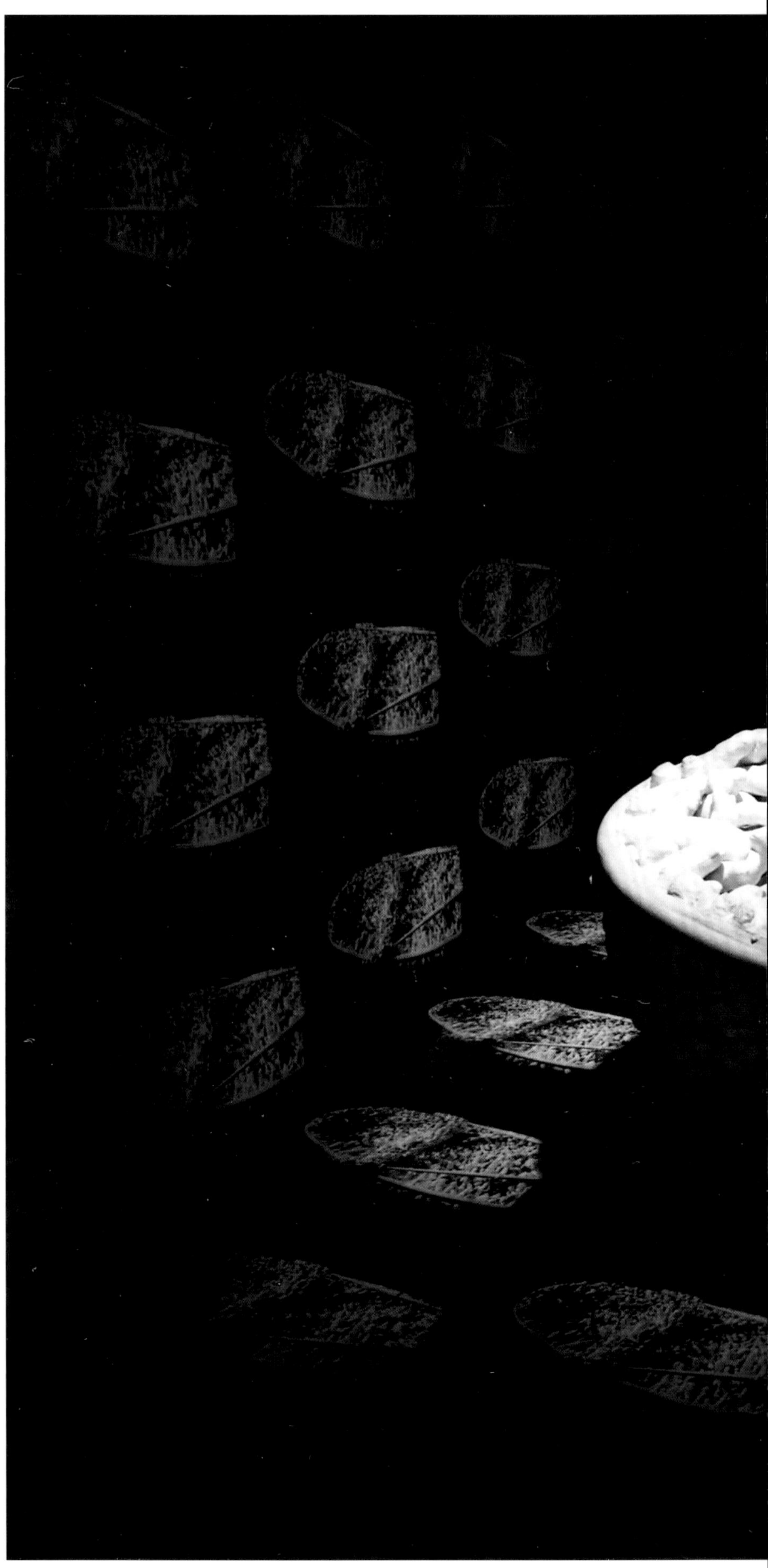

92.93

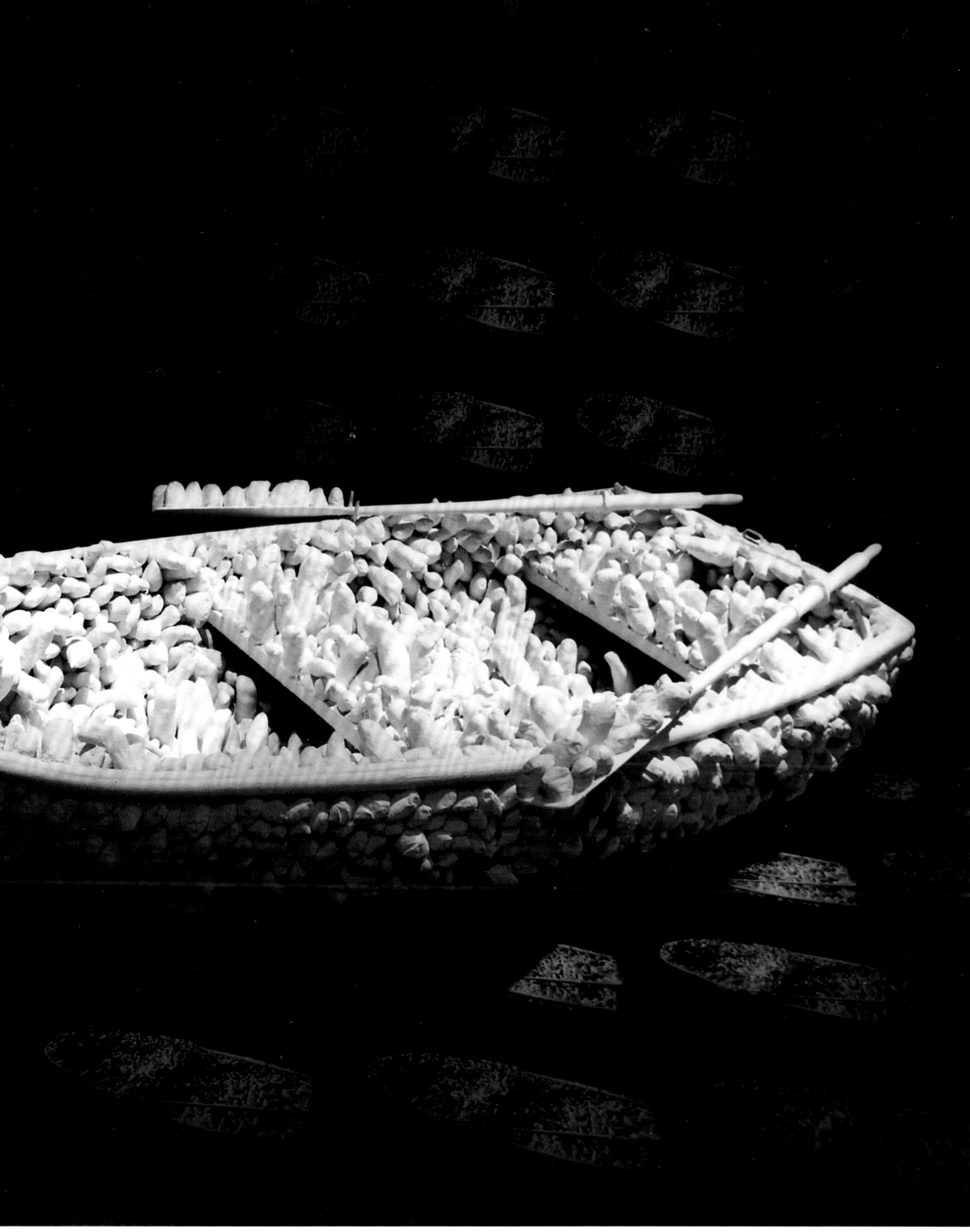

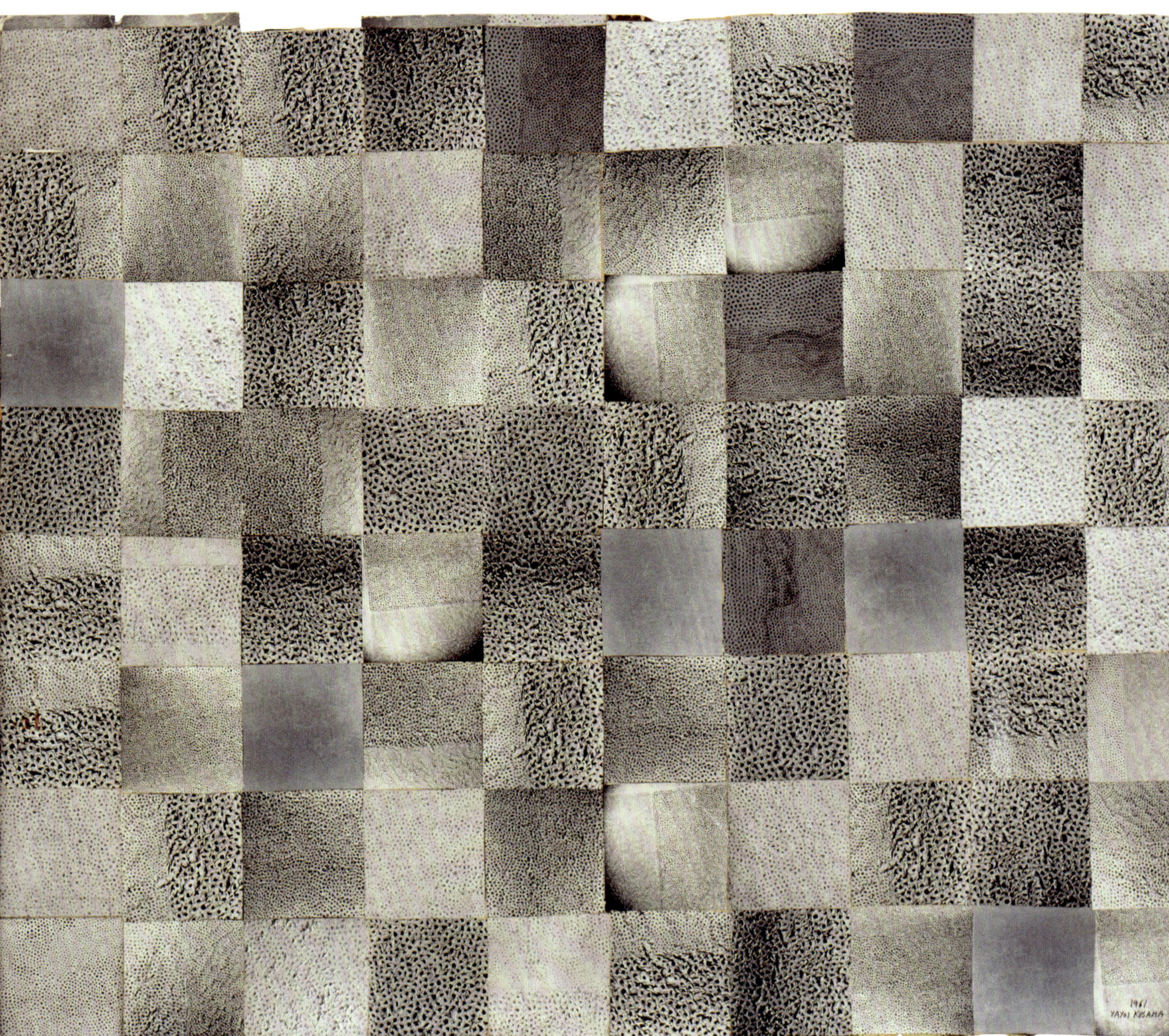

94.95

 | **Accumulation of Nets** 1961

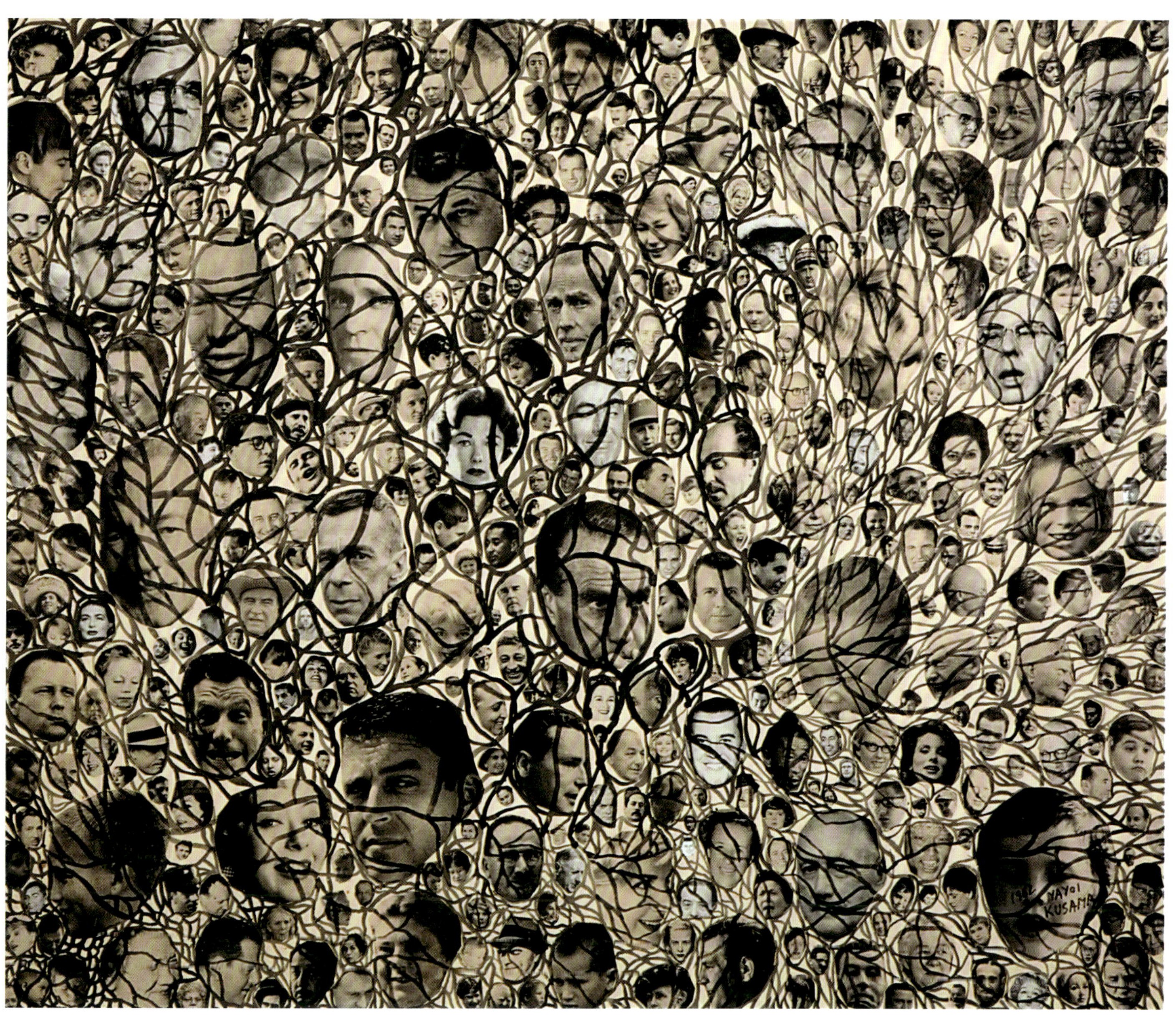

Accumulation of Faces No.2 1962

96.97

68 | **Accumulation No.18a** 1962

ONE ROLLAR
THE UNTIED SKATES OF ARNICA
1004180 C
THIS IS STAGE MONEY NO VALUE
Warry P. Zilch
STENOGRAPHER
DETROIT MICH
Ima Nutt
SECRETARY
WON HOLLAR

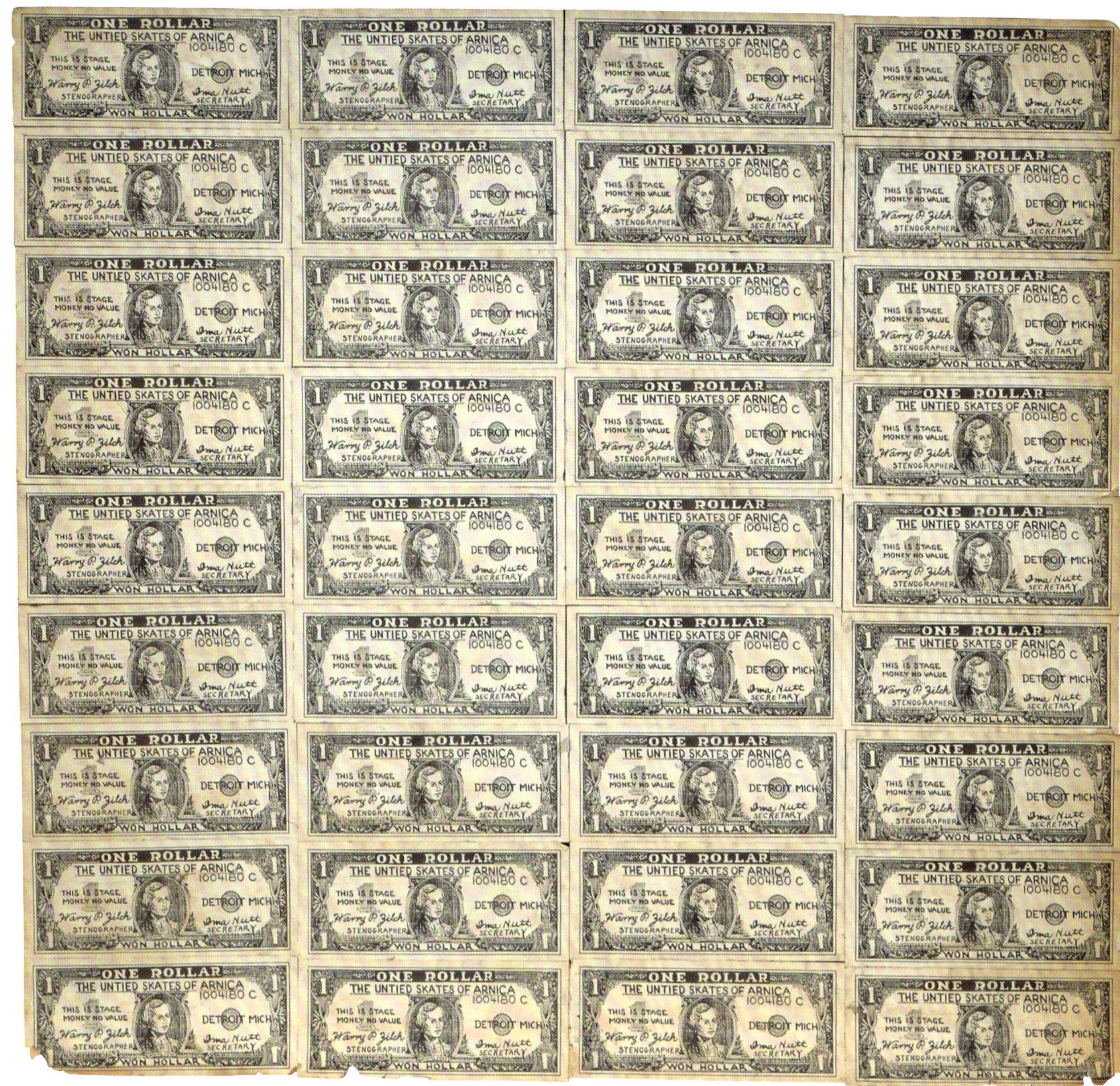

98.99

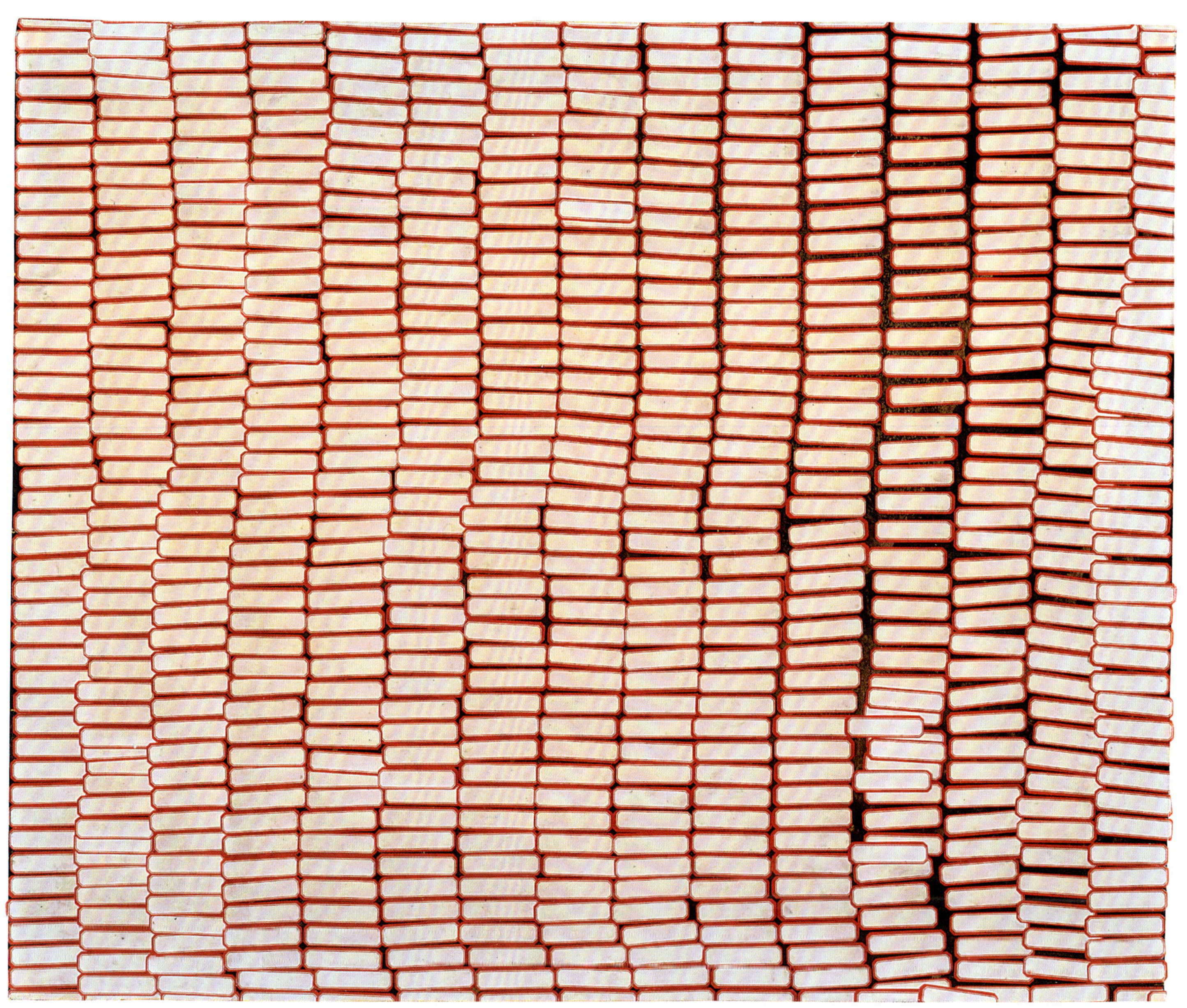

 | **Accumulation of Stamps, 63** 1962

74 | **Self-Obliteration No.1** 1962–7

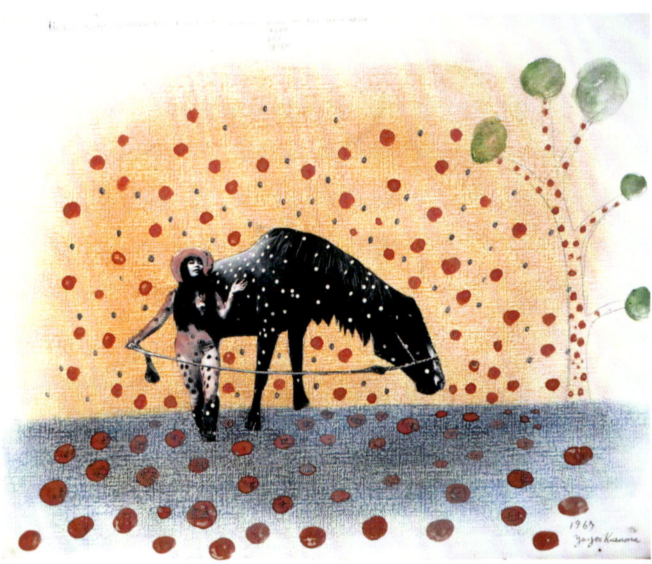

75 | **Self-Obliteration No.2** 1967

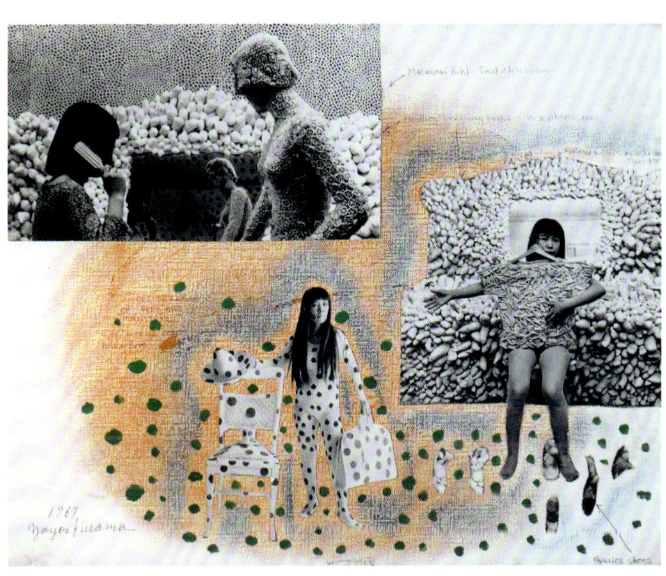

 Self-Obliteration No.3 1967

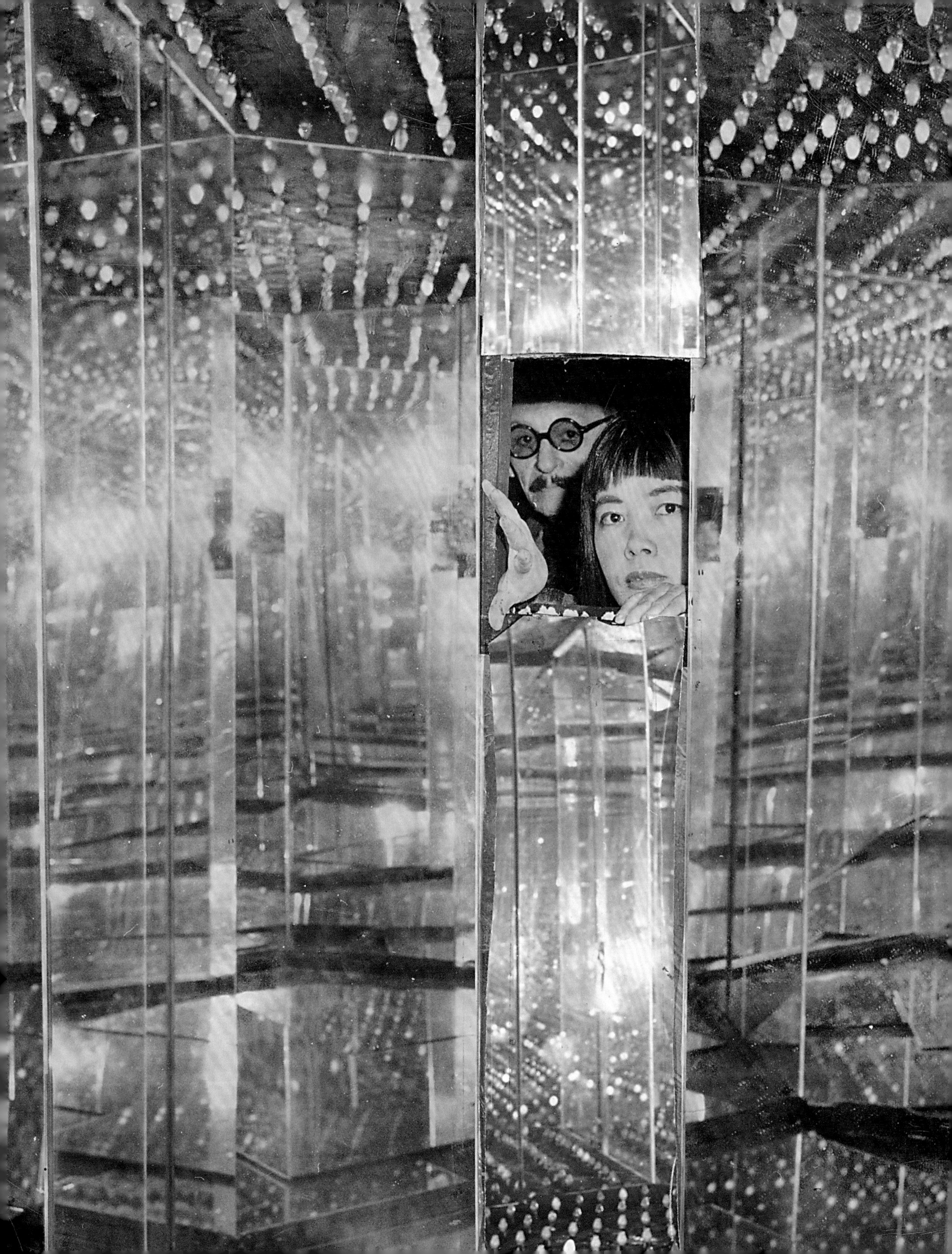

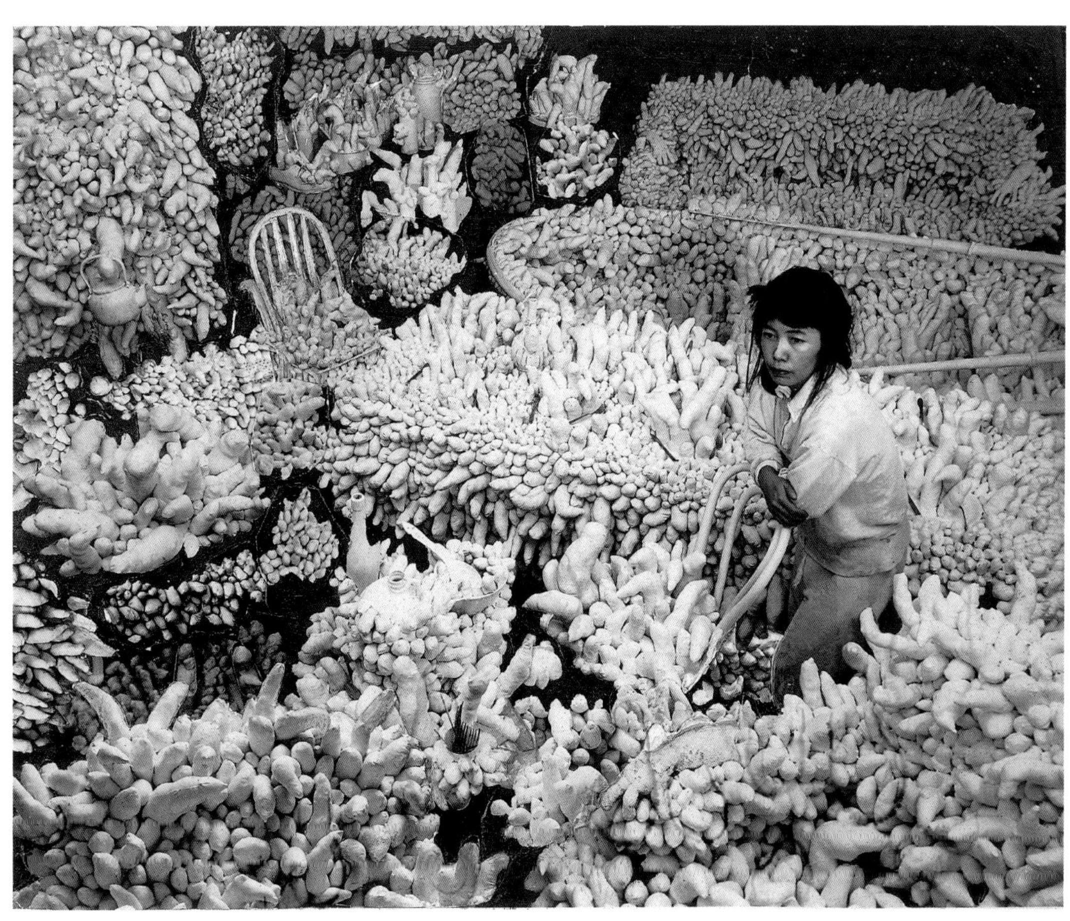

77 | **Love Forever Collage** 1966

78 | **Compulsion Furniture (Accumulation)** c.1964

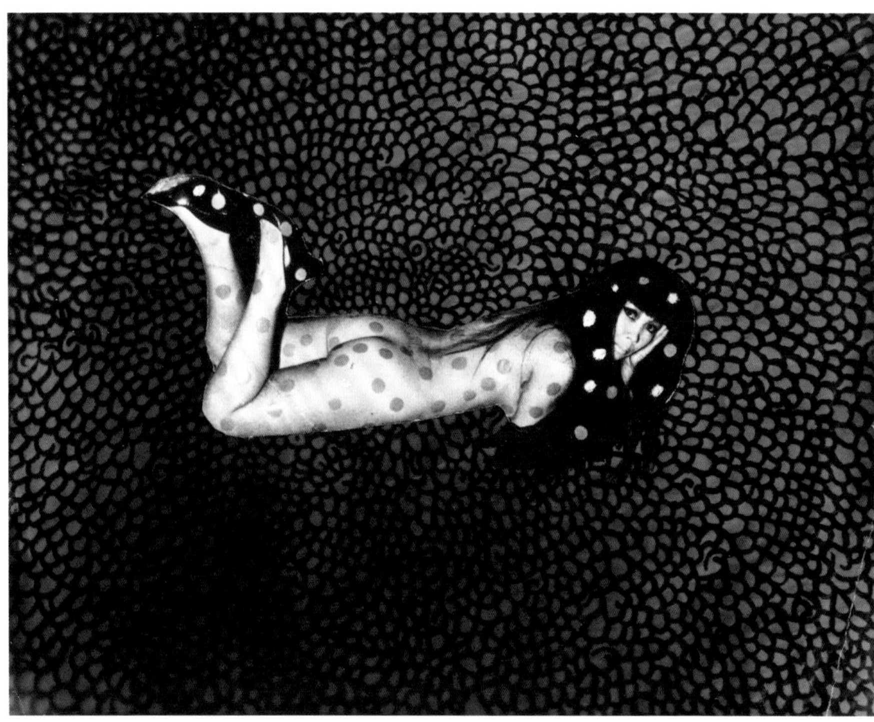

79 | **Self-Obliteration (Net Obsession Series)** c.1966

80 | **Self-Obliteration** (original design for poster) 1968

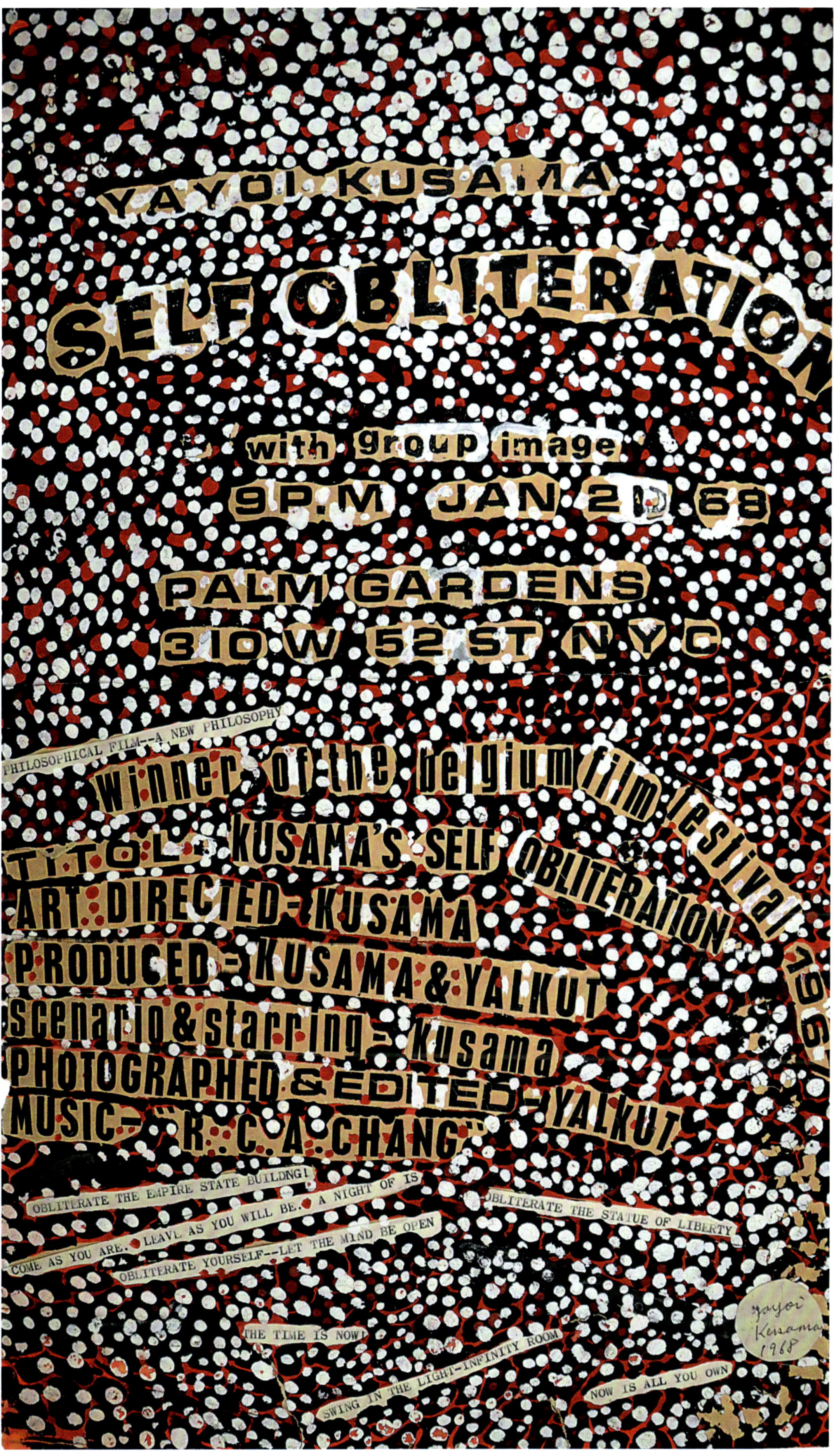

YAYOI KUSAMA
SELF OBLITERATION
with group image
9P.M JAN 21 68
PALM GARDENS
310 W 52 ST NYC
PHILOSOPHICAL FILM--A NEW PHILOSOPHY
winner of the belgium film festival 196
TITOL - KUSAMA'S SELF OBLITERATION
ART DIRECTED - KUSAMA
PRODUCED - KUSAMA & YALKUT
scenario & starring - kusama
PHOTOGRAPHED & EDITED - YALKUT
MUSIC - "R.C.A. CHANG"
OBLITERATE THE EMPIRE STATE BUILDNG!
COME AS YOU ARE. LEAVE AS YOU WILL BE. A NIGHT OF IS
OBLITERATE YOURSELF--LET THE MIND BE OPEN
OBLITERATE THE STATUE OF LIBERTY
THE TIME IS NOW!
SWING IN THE LIGHT-INFINITY ROOM
NOW IS ALL YOU OWN
Yayoi Kusama 1968

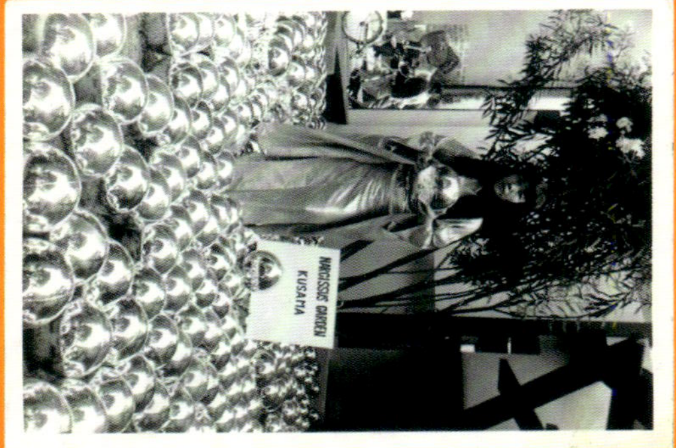

Narcissus Garden 1966, at the 33rd Venice Biennale

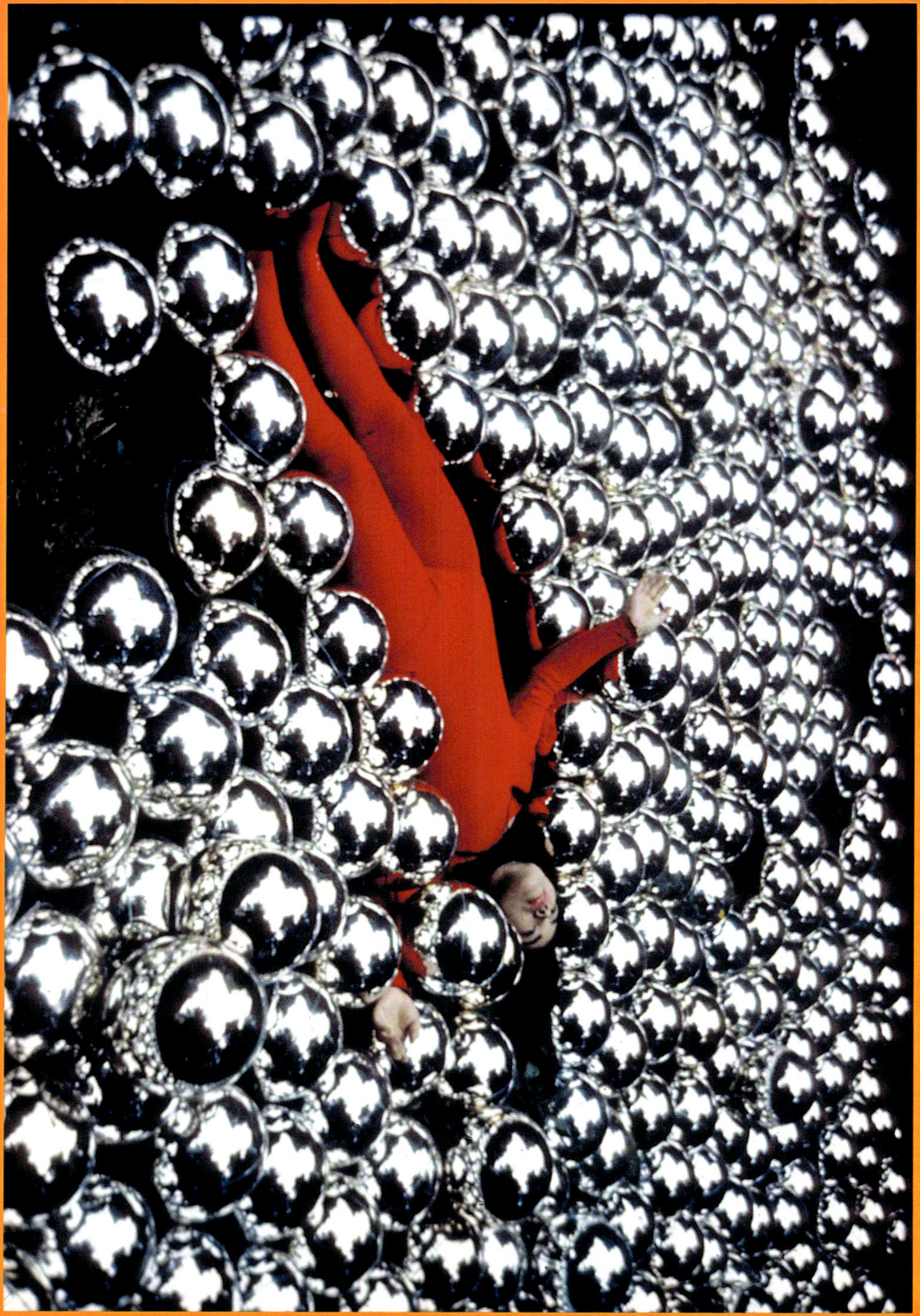

Kusama in *Narcissus Garden* 1966, at the 33rd Venice Biennale

Yayoi Kusama photocollages, 1968

1966

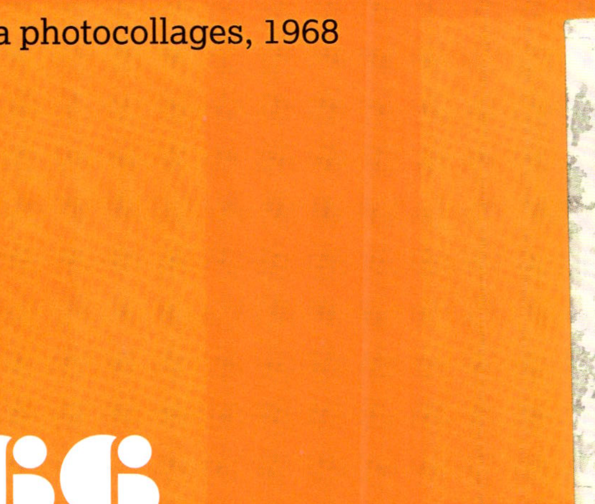

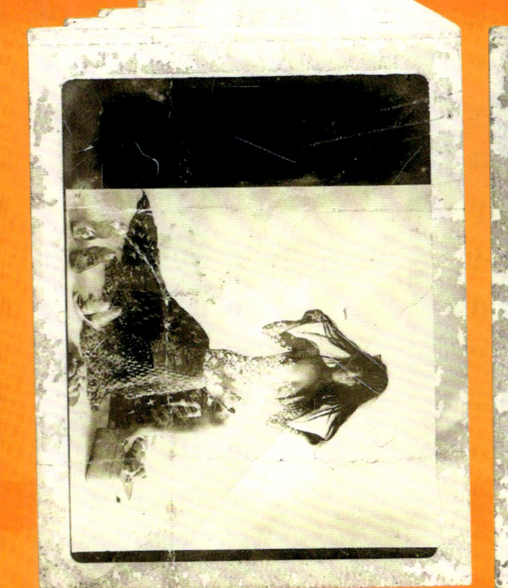

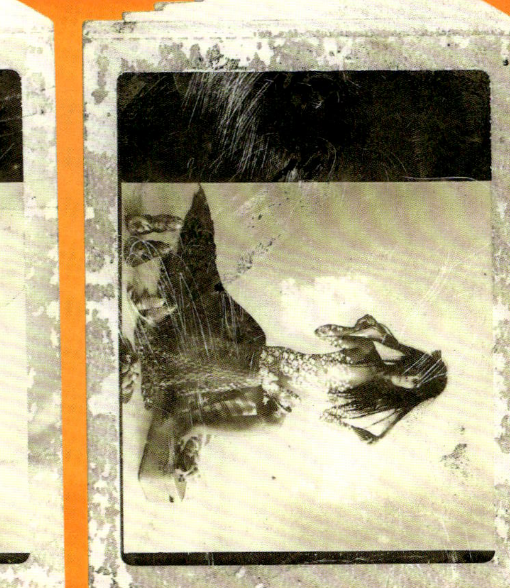

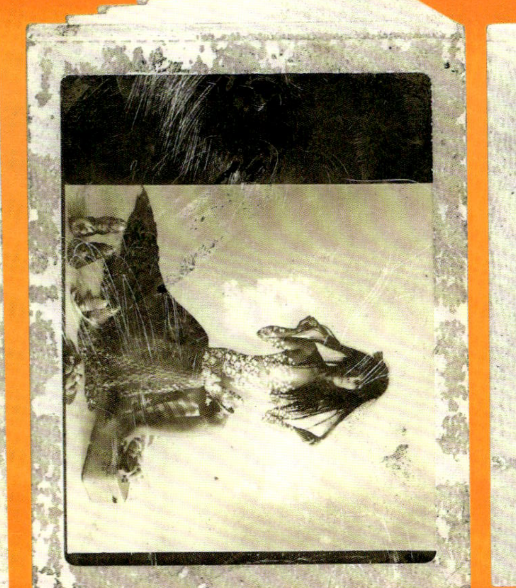

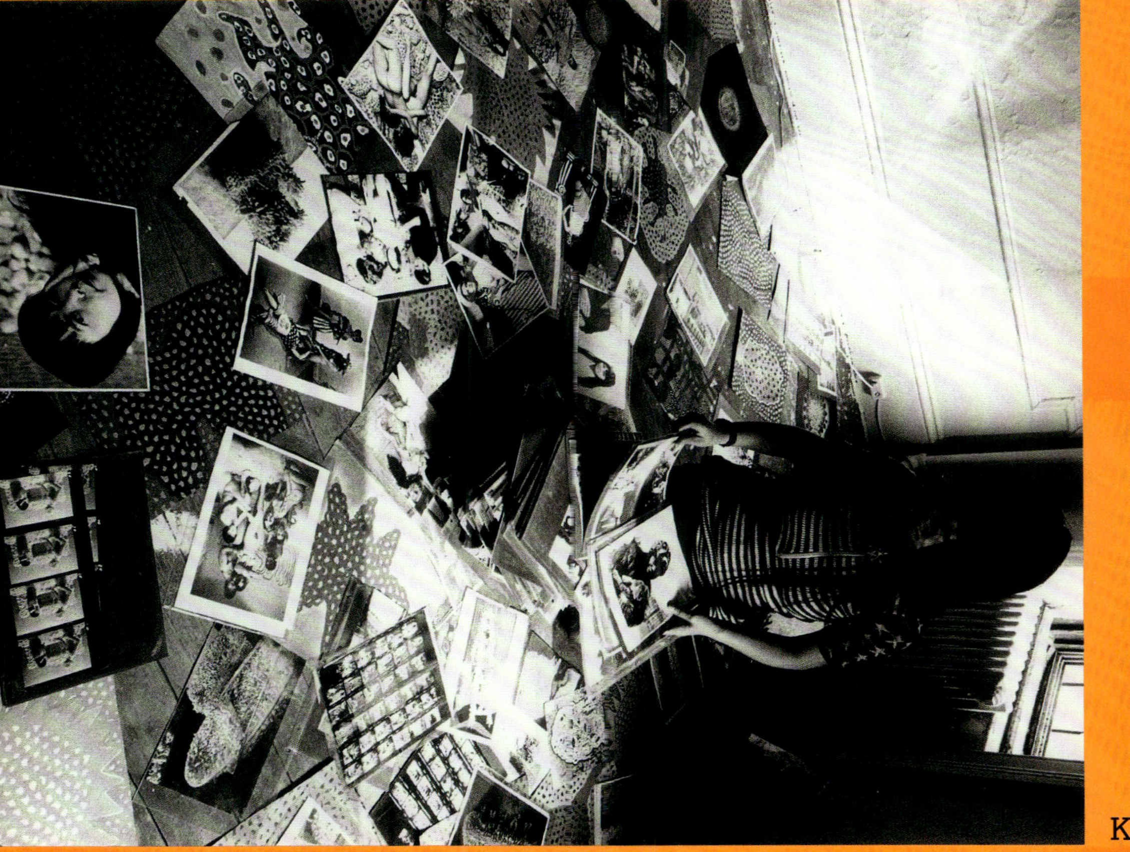

Kusama in her studio in New York, 1970

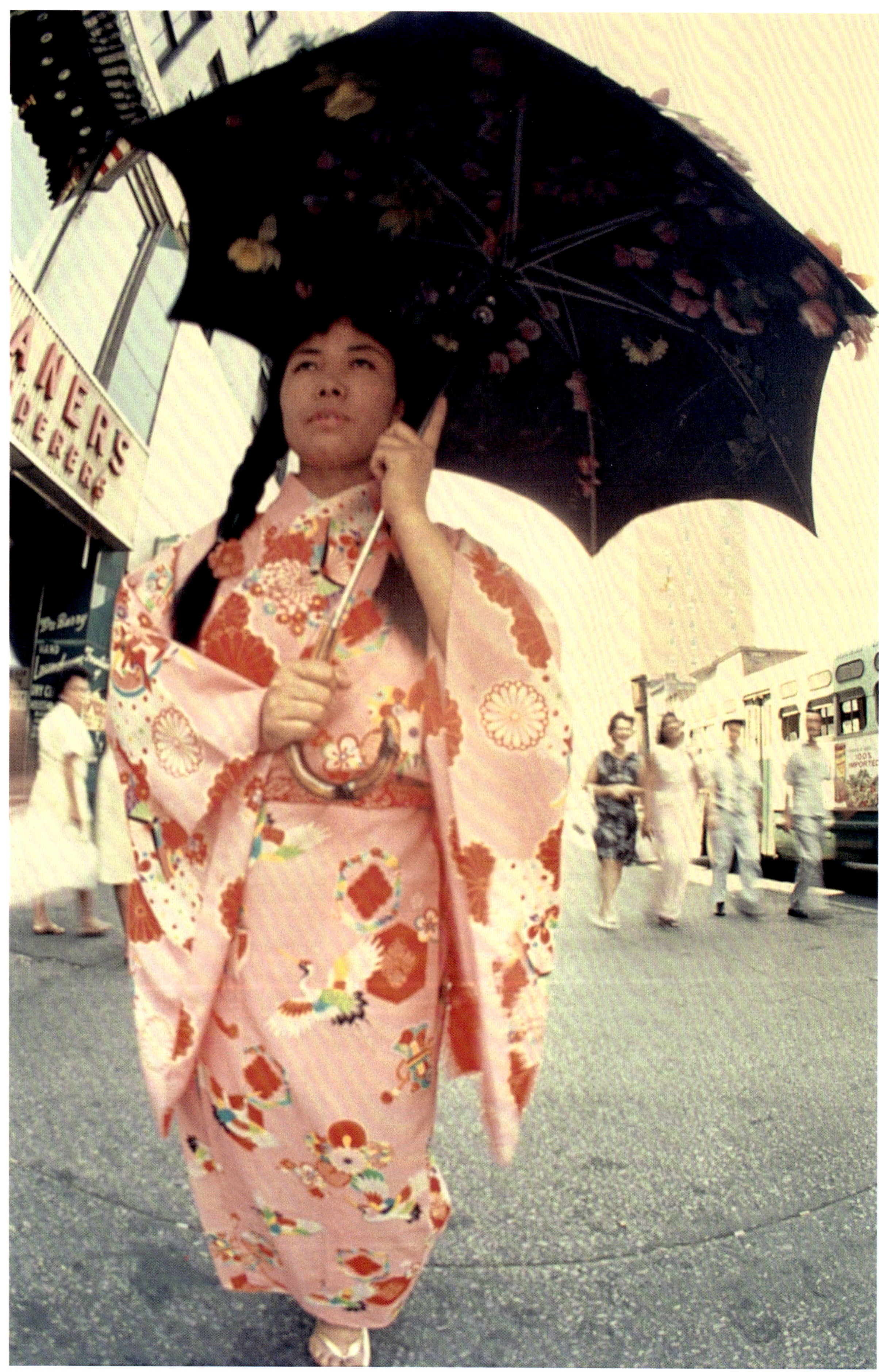
ANERS

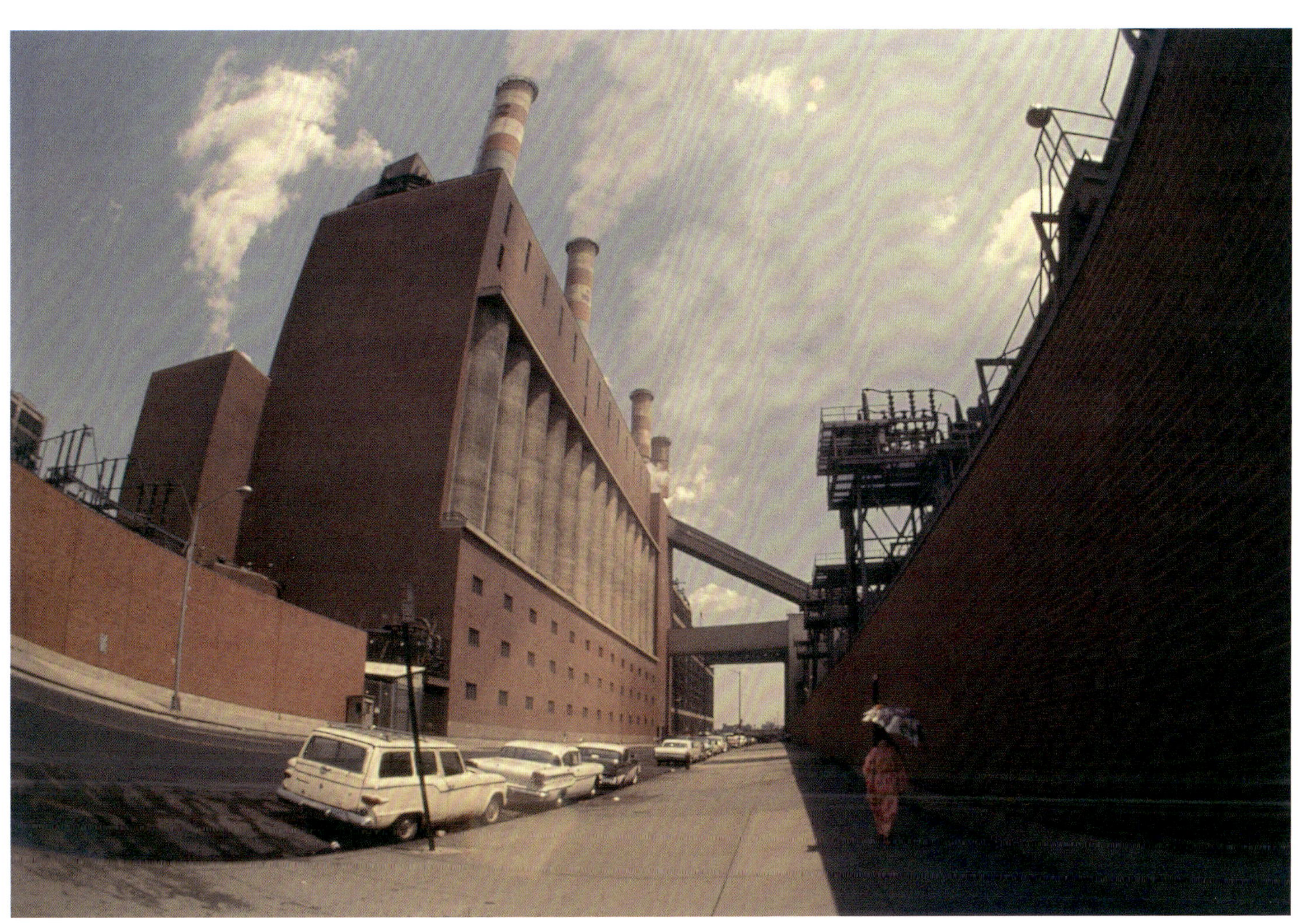

Walking Piece 1966 (details)

Kusama's Self-Obliteration and the Rise of Happenings 1967–1973

By 1967 Kusama had achieved a level of critical and popular exposure in the art world, but she was still struggling to make a living from her work. She had moved studios again in March 1965; initially, she shared a lease on a space at 404 East 14th Street with fellow Japanese émigré On Kawara, but by early 1967 Kusama had taken on the whole studio, with concomitant financial responsibilities. Responding to the socio-political mood of the times, she began looking for new ways to make money and shifted her new-found interest in performance to more popular and inclusive happenings.

America was in the throes of cultural upheaval, with the Civil Rights and Vietnam protest movements changing the political landscape. The rise of hippie culture was challenging social mores with an increasingly open and experimental attitude to sexuality, drug use and mysticism. Kusama wholeheartedly embraced the new cultural mores, seeing in the iconoclastic, revolutionary flower children kindred spirits and potential collaborators and audiences for her work. Her response to the shifting socio-political climate was to position herself as the High Priestess of the increasingly visible hippie scene, channelling its energies of instigation and provocation to her own artistic ends.

Kusama embarked on a period of performative experimentation, staging happenings that, unlike her earlier performances, relied on the participation of groups of young 'scenesters' and curious onlookers. The first of these were audio-visual-light performances in which Kusama painted models in bikinis with colourful fluorescent paints under black lights. On 16, 17 and 18 June 1967 Kusama presented *Self-Obliteration: An Audio-Visual-Light Performance* at the Black Gate Theater in New York. Tickets were $1.50 each; participants were enticed by the promise that 'during the course of the happening Kusama will obliterate her environment, live bikini models and herself… [in] a polka-dot dance party'.[1] Subsequent Body Festivals took place in the city during the following months. In autumn 1967 Kusama took her Body Festivals to Europe for the first time, staging happenings in the Netherlands to coincide with an exhibition at Galerij Orez in the Hague.

She directed *Kusama's Self-Obliteration* (no.82), a film that features footage shot by filmmaker Jud Yalkut during many of her 1967 happenings. The film is an attempt to visualise Kusama's world, featuring images of many

1967

Objecten: Made in USA, Galerie Delta, Rotterdam, 10 February – 17 March

**Love Room*, Internationale Galerij Orez, The Hague, 3 November

1968

Three Blind Mice de Collecties: Visser, Peeters, Becht, Stedelijk van Abbemuseum, Eindhoven, 6 April – 15 May, touring to Sint Pietersabdij, Ghent, 6 April – 19 May

**Yayoi Kusama*, Mickery Gallery, Holland, 9 June – 7 July

**Yayoi Kusama*, Lichter Gallery, Germany, 1 October

1970

Zero Unexecuted, Institute of the History of Arts, University of Amsterdam, 24 April – 13 May

Cage/Painting/Woman, Internationale Galerij Orez, The Hague, October

of her paintings and installations, set to a score by pop-rock band The Group Image. It begins with images of the artist in rural upstate New York, dressed in a spotty ensemble, covering animals, plants, and finally a naked male body with polka dots and leaves. Later scenes depict body-painting happenings and orgy parties staged in the artist's installation environments. The film was popular on the arthouse festival circuit, winning prizes at the Fourth International Experimental Film Competition at Knokke-le-Zoute, Belgium, the Ann Arbor Film Festival, and the Second Maryland Film Festival in 1968. Kusama organised repeated screenings and set up a company to sell prints of the film to the public by mail order.

Kusama followed up the Body Festivals with a series of Anatomic Explosion happenings. The first of these took place on 14 July 1968 in front of a statue of George Washington across the street from the New York Stock Exchange. For the Anatomic Explosions, Kusama employed young performers who would dance in the nude under the artist's direction. Kusama herself remained fully clothed, painting polka dots on her performers and orchestrating the scenarios until they were inevitably broken up by police. The happenings were staged in strategic public locations across New York: over the next four months they took place at venues including the Statue of Liberty, the Alice in Wonderland statue in Central Park and the United Nations Headquarters. The penultimate Anatomic Explosion was staged outside the New York Board of Elections two days before the 1968 American presidential elections; for this performance the nude dancers carried large photographic cut-outs depicting the faces of presidential candidates Richard Nixon, Hubert Humphrey and George Wallace. Following Nixon's election, Kusama staged a nudist protest in lower Manhattan, distributing copies of her 'Open Letter to My Hero Richard M. Nixon'.

These performances were prefaced by press releases circulated by Kusama's studio that ensured the artist's continued exposure in the popular media. Her notoriety was now growing, not only in the United States but in Japan. After a decade in which she had been largely ignored by the press in her home country, Kusama was being discussed by commentators in the Japanese media, many of whom picked up on the more sensational aspects of her practice.

In parallel to the public happenings, Kusama organised ticketed naked performances and orgies in her studio and other venues in the city. Spurred on by her celebrity, she courted more and more publicity. On 25 November 1968 she staged a *Homosexual Wedding* for which she had designed an '"orgy" wedding gown, designed for two instead of one' for the couple. Her intervention at the Museum of Modern Art on 24 August 1969, *Grand Orgy to Awaken the Dead at MoMA (Otherwise Known as the Museum of Modern Art) – Featuring their Usual Display of Nudes*, in which dancers stripped and posed in the fountain of the museum's sculpture courtyard, made the front page of the *Daily News*.

By April 1969 Kusama had also set up a clothing boutique at 404 Sixth Avenue to sell her fashion designs, which were typically covered in polka dots, the most daring featuring strategically placed holes to reveal breasts, buttocks or genitalia. This aspect of her work was commercialised as the Kusama Fashion Institute. This initiative followed the establishment of Kusama Enterprises, a company she set up to market her artistic activities on a commercial basis. Advertisements in the *Village Voice* and other underground media offered 'Beautiful boy and girl models available for skin painting and photo work' in the same venue. By November 1969 Kusama's name had become so synonymous with sex that her name was licensed to a pornographic tabloid, *Kusama's Orgy*.

Kusama's provocative performances brought her fame, but as the cultural and political climate shifted at the end of the decade her notoriety began to wane. She had staged her happenings outside the traditional gallery scene and had thus distanced herself from many of the dealers and collectors who had supported her work in the early 1960s. Media coverage of her work had shifted from critical attention in the art press to exposés in tabloid newspapers and underground periodicals. Over time even the popular press that had celebrated her counter-cultural activities began to turn critically aloof. As early as 1968 one commentator derisively proclaimed 'Kusama is definitely suffering from over-exposure of over-exposure'.[2] Under increasing pressure, Kusama was plagued by recurring bouts of depression and ill health. By the early 1970s, despite still participating regularly in group exhibitions in Europe, she faced an uncertain future in her adopted home.

1967-1973

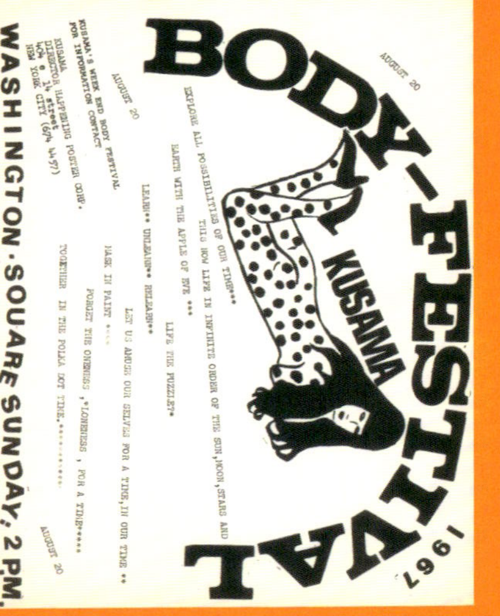

Flyer for *Kusama's Weekend Body-Festival* in Washington Square, New York, 20 August 1967

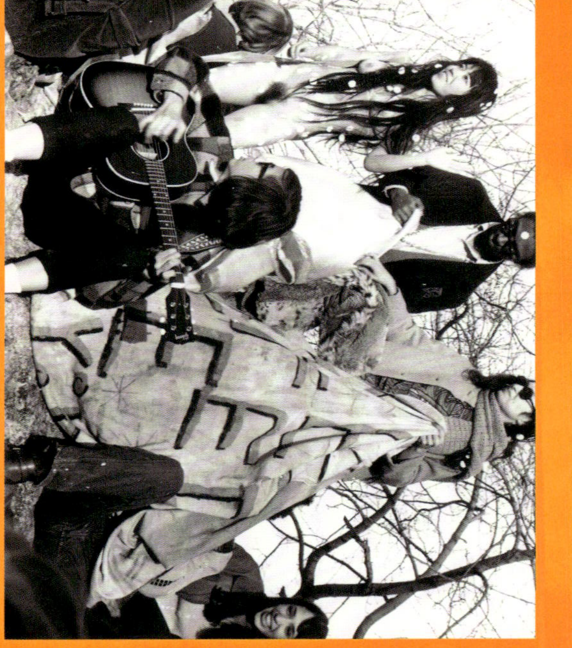

Bust Out happening, Sheep Meadow, Central Park, New York, 6 April 1969

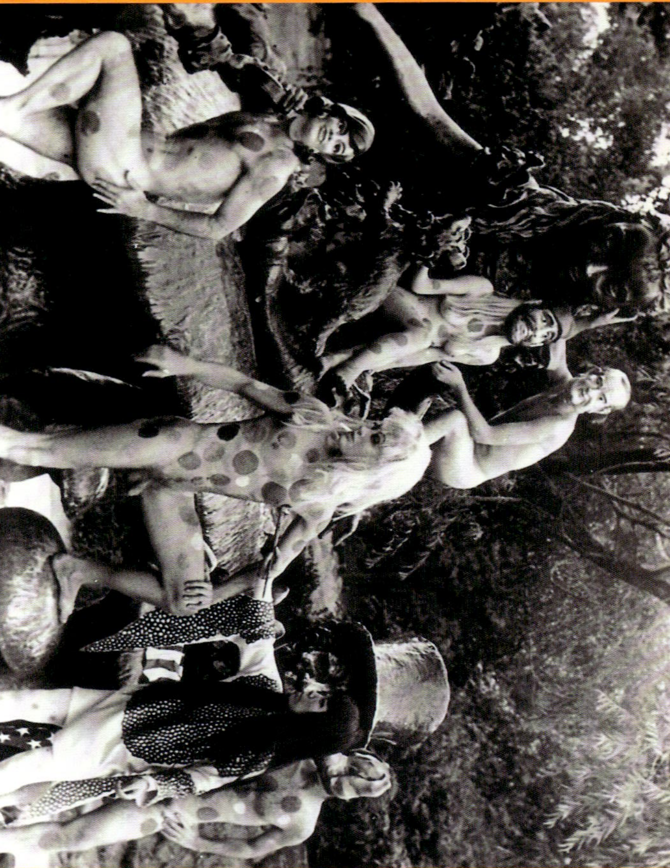

Anatomic Explosion happening in front of Alice in Wonderland sculpture in Central Park, New York, 11 August 1968

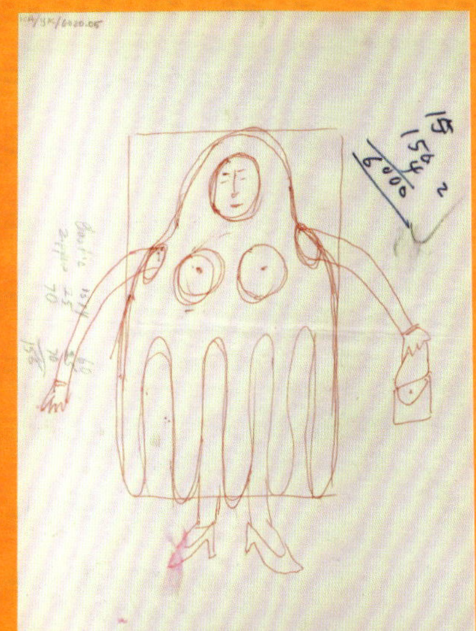

Fashion drawing by Kusama, c.1968

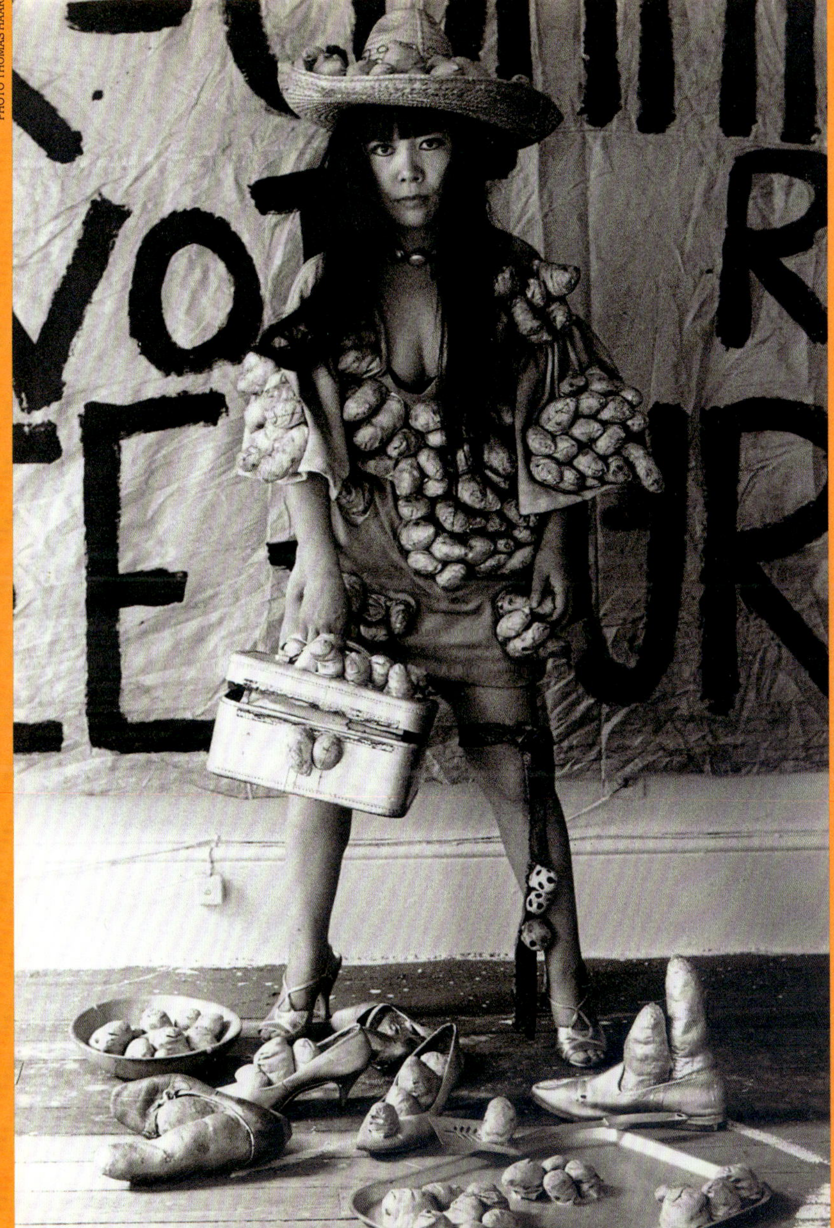

PHOTO THOMAS HAAR

Kusama Fashion, New York, 1970

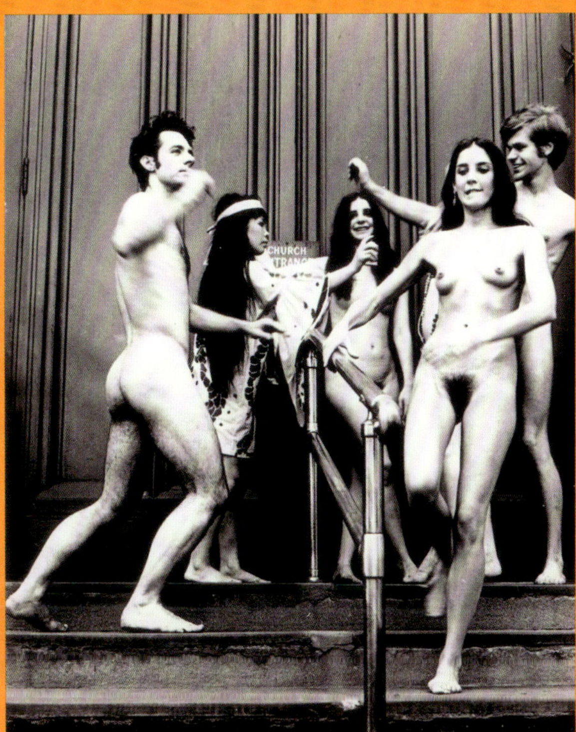

Naked happening in front of church, New York, 1968

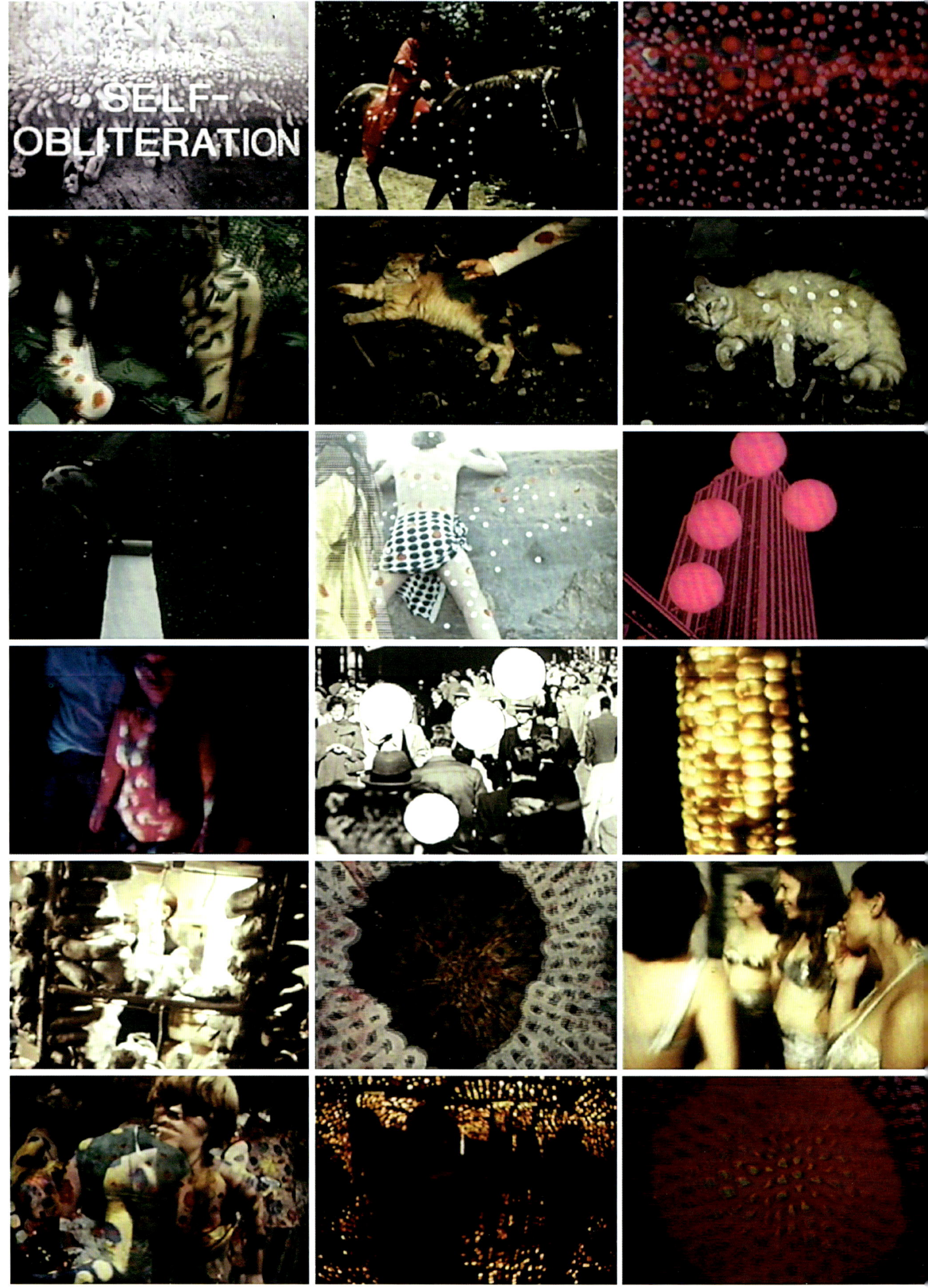
SELF-
OBLITERATION

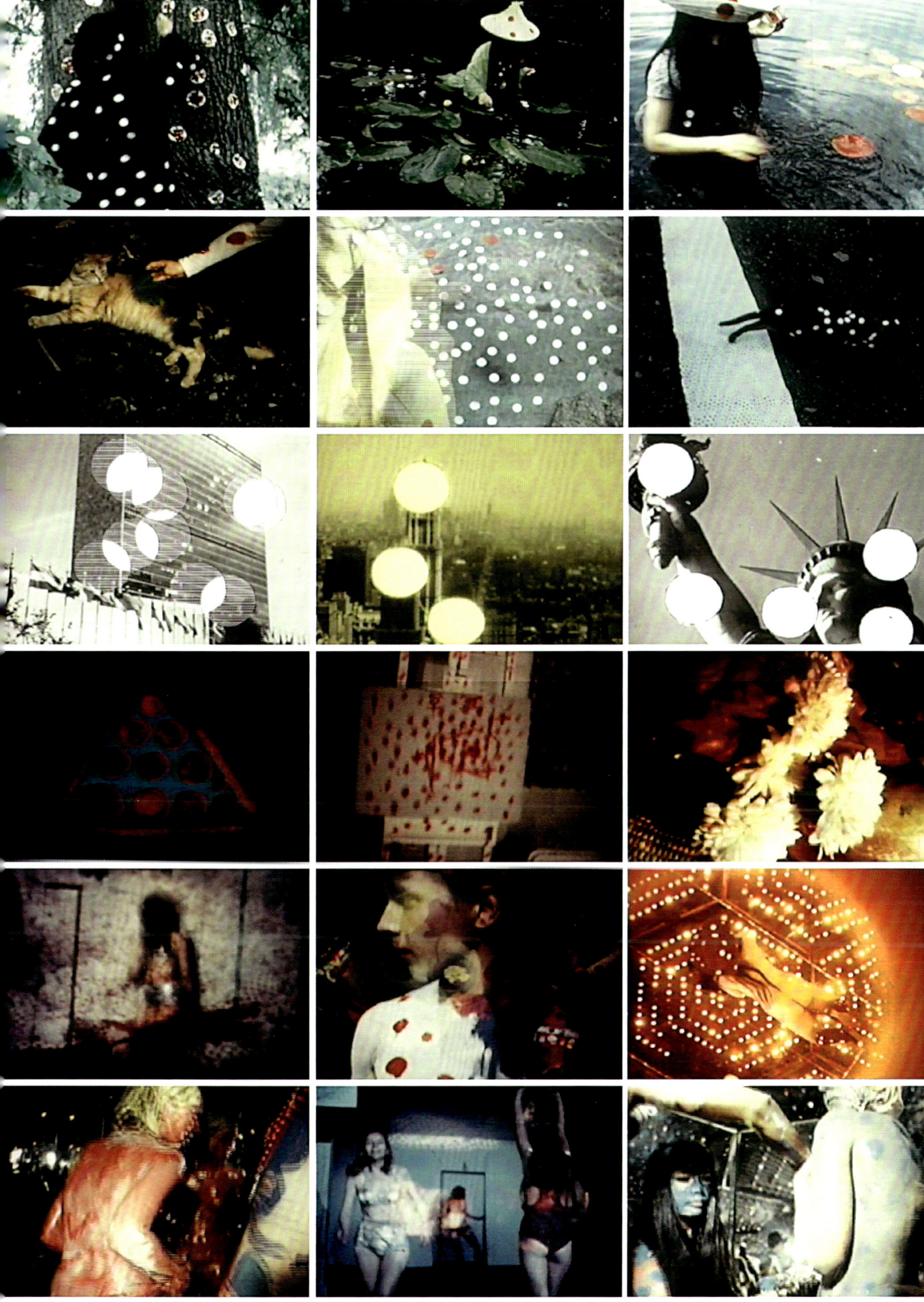

Joseph Cornell collage, untitled, 1967

COLLECTION YAYOI KUSAMA

1973–1983

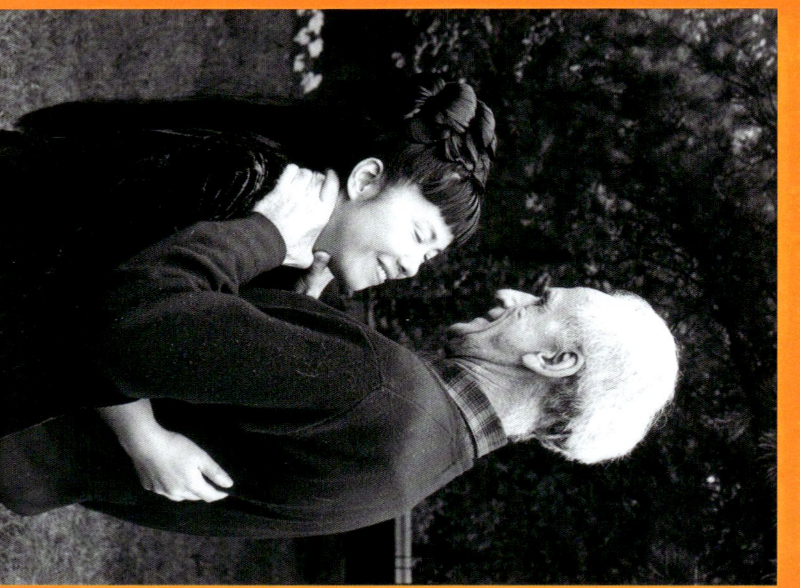

Kusama with Joseph Cornell in New York, 1970

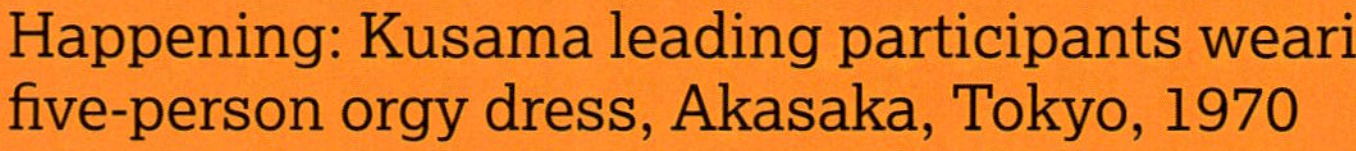

Happening: Kusama leading participants wearing five-person orgy dress, Akasaka, Tokyo, 1970

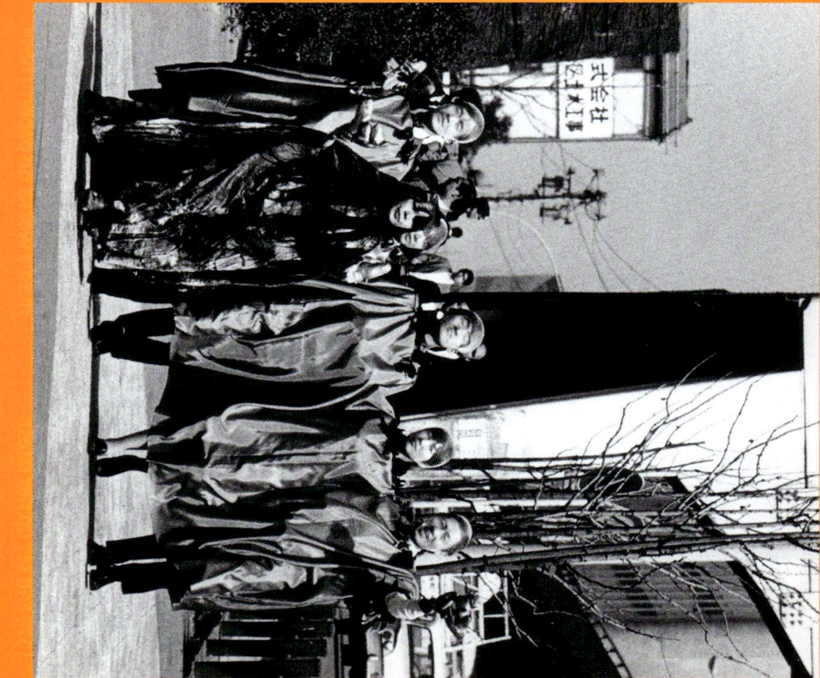

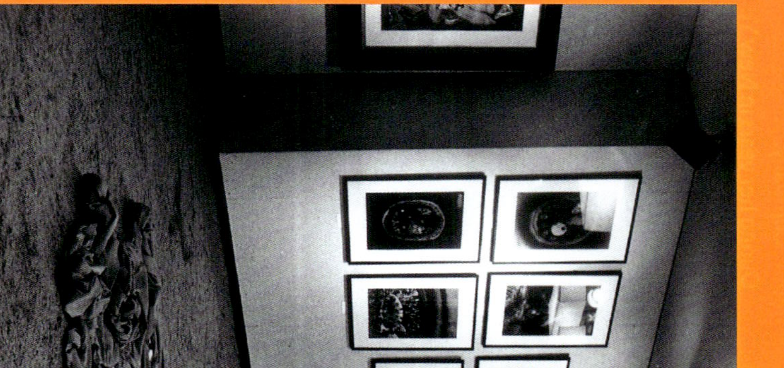

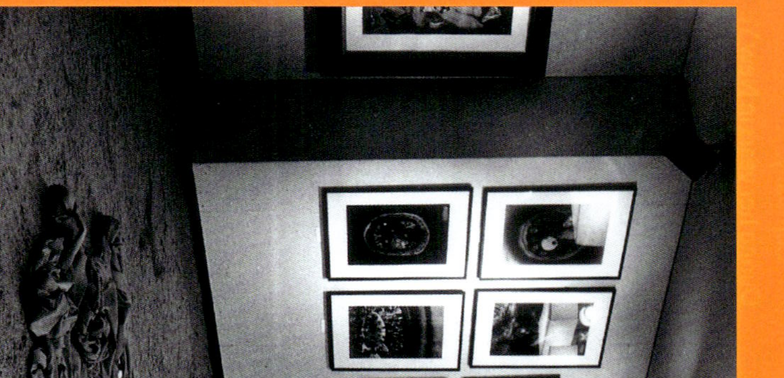

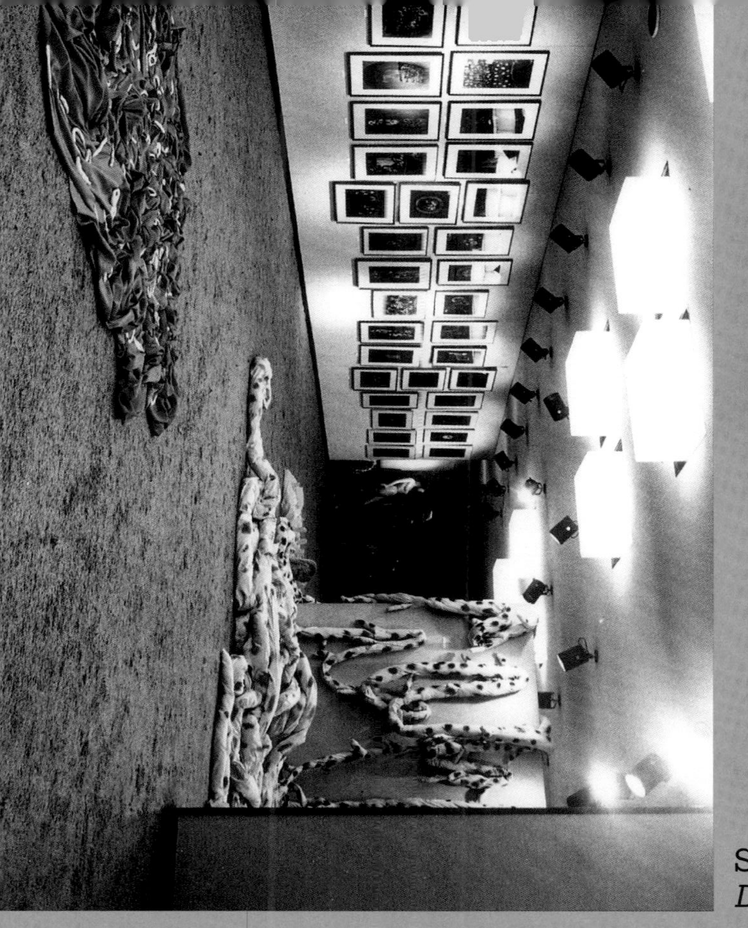

Solo exhibition *Obsessional Art, A Requiem for Death and Life*, Osaka Forms Gallery, Tokyo, 1976

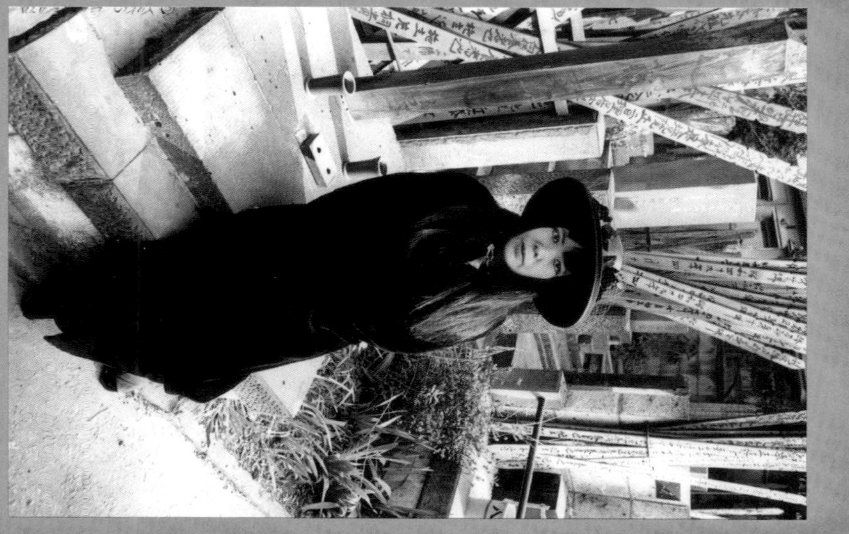

Kusama photographed in a cemetery for a Yomiuri newspaper, c.1976

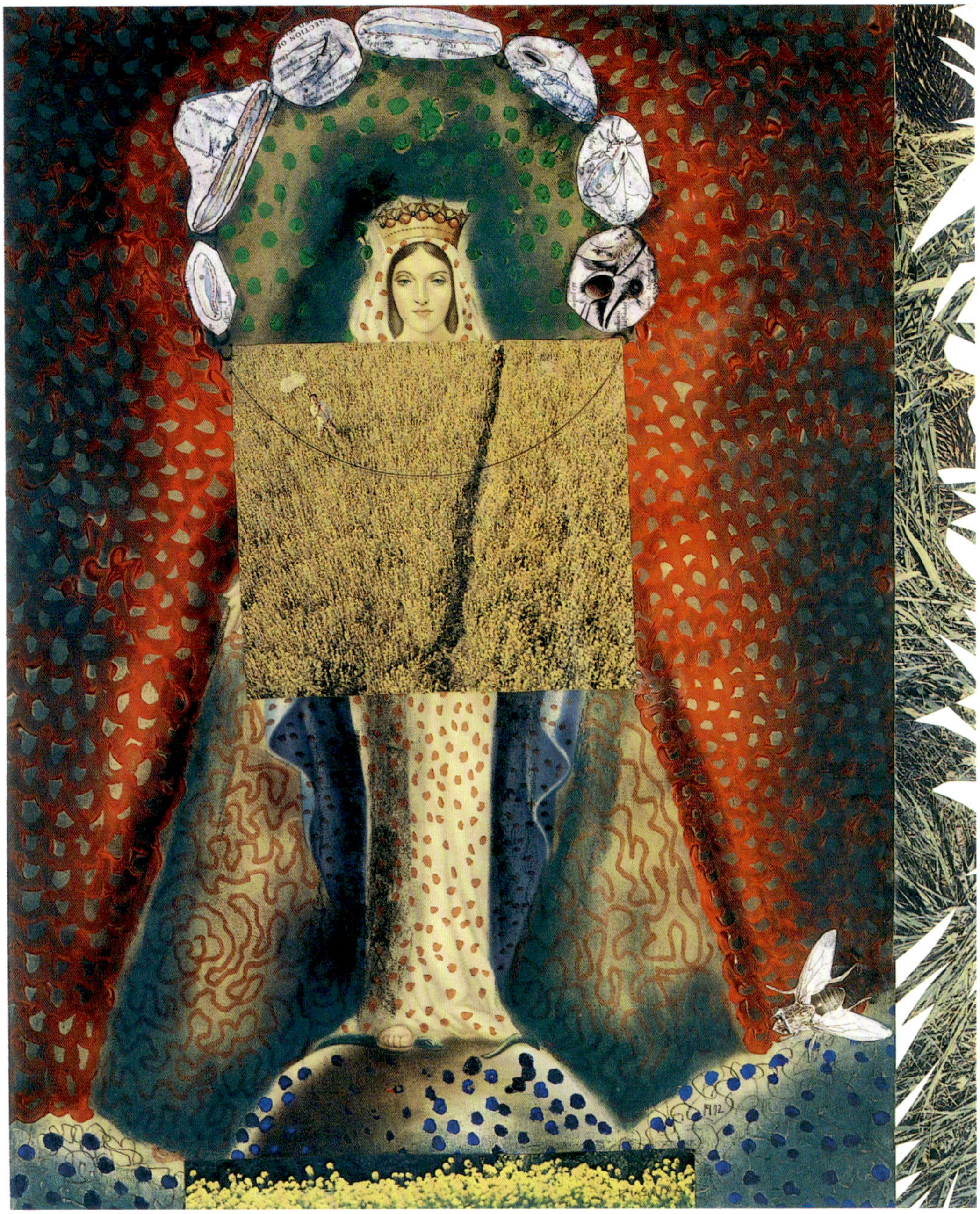

83 | **Man Catching the Insect** 1972

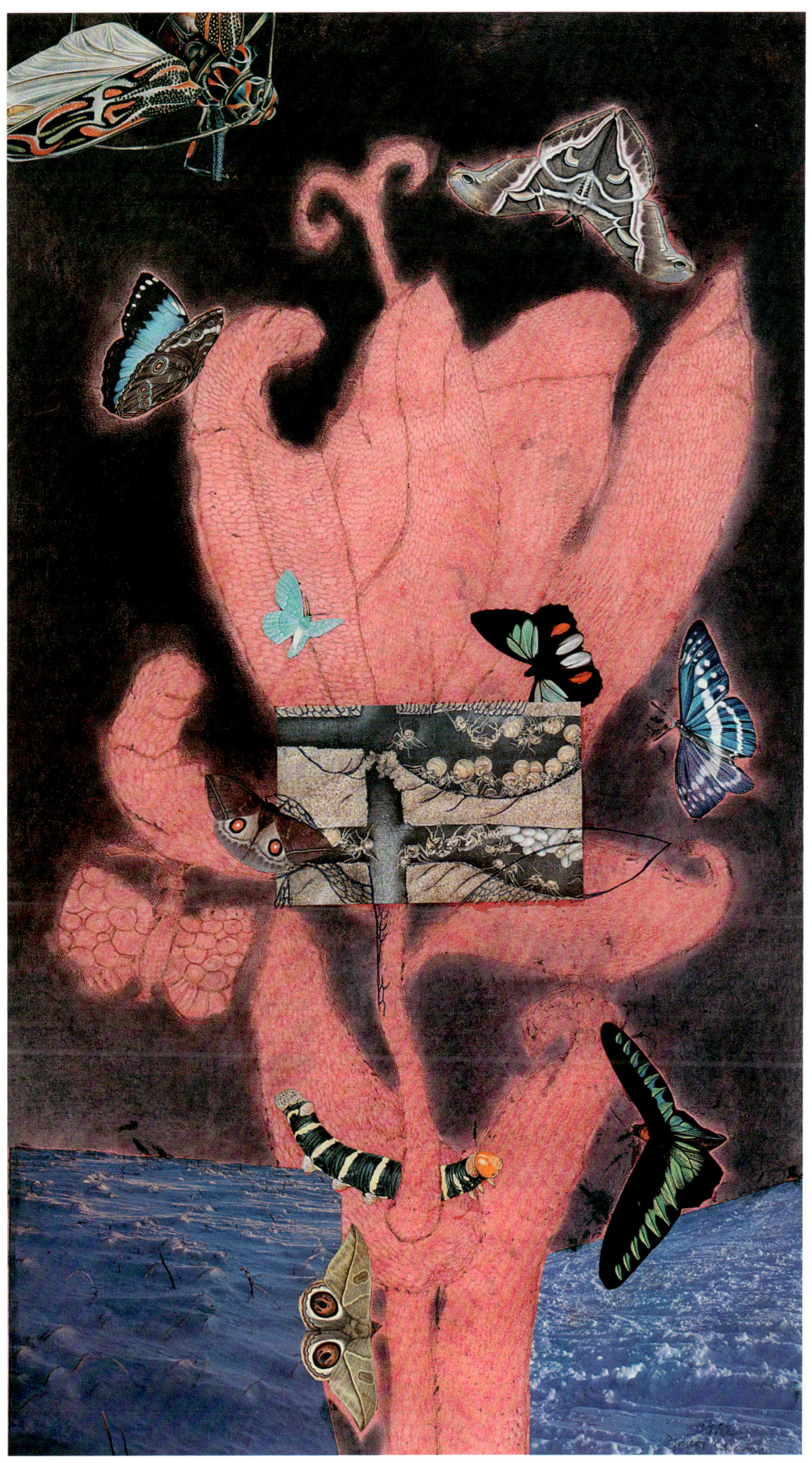

 Self-Portrait 1972

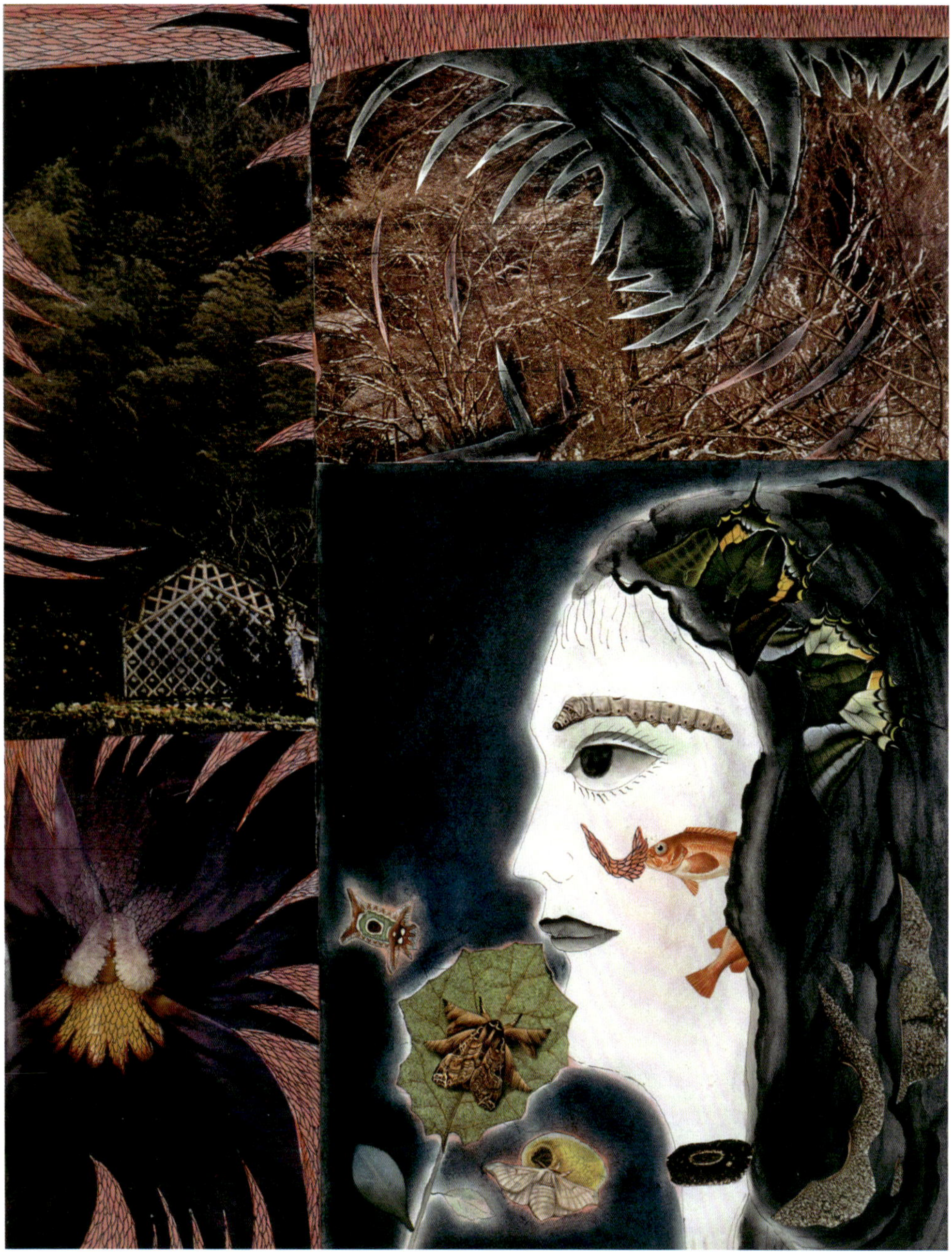

85 | **Flowers and Self-Portrait** 1973

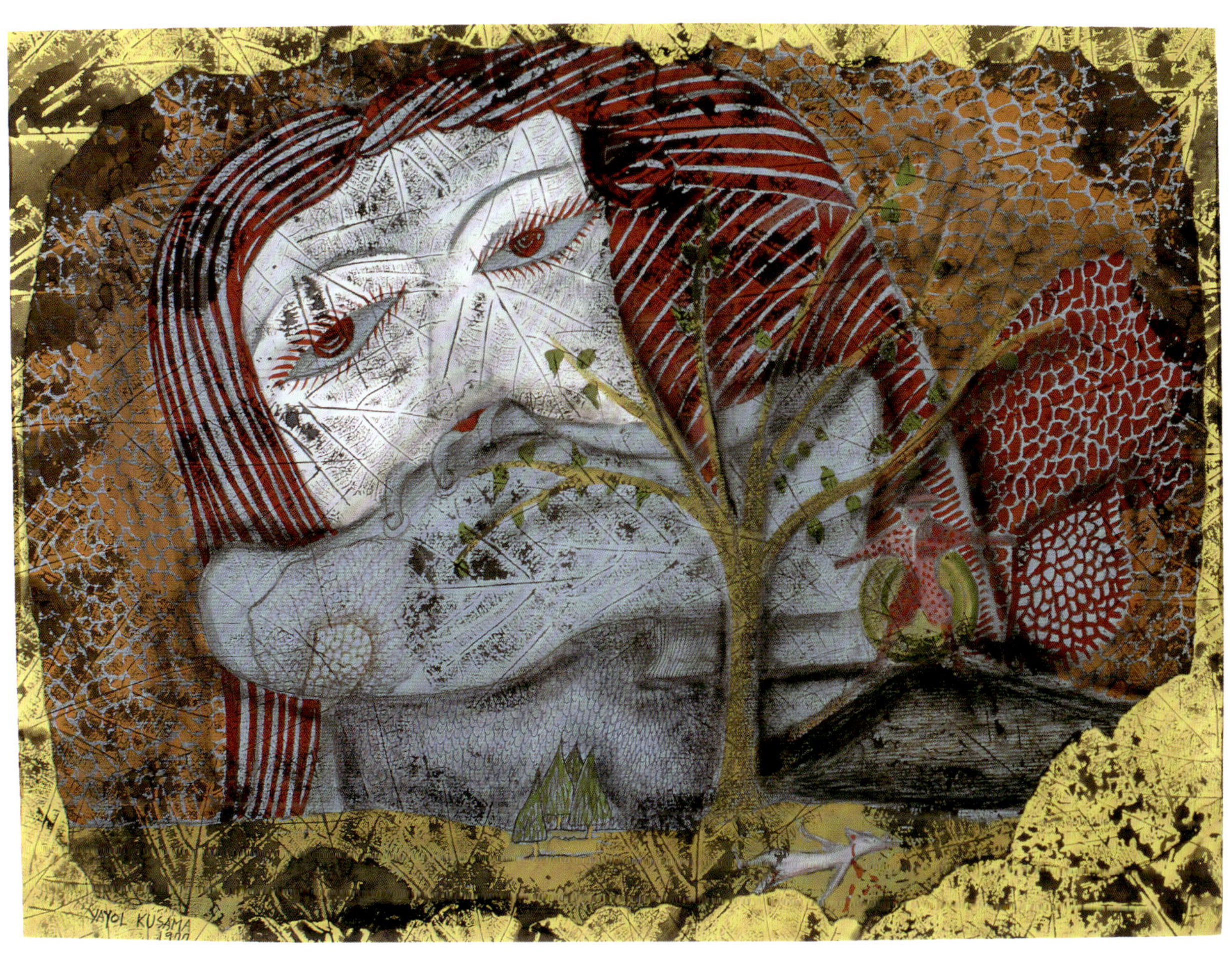

 I Who Committed Suicide 1977

1984

Collectie Becht, Stedelijk Museum, Amsterdam, 16 March – 6 May

Blam! The Explosion of Pop, Minimalism and Performance 1958–1964, Whitney Museum of American Art, New York, 20 September – 2 December

1985

40 Years of Japanese Contemporary Art, Tokyo Metropolitan Art Museum, 12 October – 8 December

Japanese Contemporary Paintings, National Gallery of Modern Art, New Delhi, 18 October

1985–6

Reconstruction: Avant-garde Art in Japan, 1845–1965, Museum of Modern Art, Oxford, 8 December 1985 – 9 February 1986

1986

Japanese Art Today, Mandeville Gallery, University of California, San Diego, 16 May – 22 June

1986–7

Japon des Avant Gardes 1910-1970, Musée national d'art moderne, Centre Georges Pompidou, Paris, 11 December 1986 – 2 March 1987

**Yayoi Kusama*, Musée des Beaux-Arts de Calais, 13 December 1986 – 31 January 1987

1987

**Yayoi Kusama*, Kitakyushu Municipal Museum of Art, Fukuoka, 3–29 March

**Yayoi Kusama*, Musée Municipal de Dole, France, 21 March – 31 May

Medusa's Magic: European Mannerism, Kunstlerhaus, Vienna, April

Collection Agnes et Frits Becht, Centre régional d'art contemporain Midi-Pyrenees, Lagere, France, 23 September – 8 November

1988

Large Works from the Permanent Collection, Neuberger Museum, State University of New York, Purchase, April

**Yayoi Kusama: Soul Burning Flashes*, Hakone Open-Air Museum, Kanagawa, 1 July – 7 September

1989

Art Kite, Miyagi Museum of Art, touring to 8 venues in Japan, 13 venues in Europe, 3 venues in South America, 11 June – 10 July

Art Exciting '89, Museum of Modern Art, Saitama, 17 June – 23 July, touring to Queensland Art Gallery, 20 September – 12 November

20ste Biennale Middelheim-Japanese: Europalia 89, Openluchtmuseum voor Beeldhouwkunst Middelheim, Antwerp, 18 June – 29 October

The 'Junk' Aesthetic: Assemblage of the 1950s and Early 1960s, Whitney Museum of American Art at Equitable Centre, New York, 30 June

1989–90

**Yayoi Kusama: Retrospective*, Centre for International Contemporary Arts, New York, 27 September 1989 – 31 January 1990

**Soul Burning Flash*, Museum of Modern Art, Oxford, 5 November 1989 – 7 January 1990

**Yayoi Kusama: Soul Burning Flashes*, Bunkamura Gallery, Tokyo, 26 December 1989 – 7 January 1990

1990

Pharmakon '90, Nippon Convention Centre (Makuhari Messe), Chiba, 28 July – 20 August

1990–1

AERONART (a hot-air balloon exhibition designed by various artists), Grand Palais, Paris, 1 November, touring to CNIT, Paris, 10–30 June 1991; Loire Castles, 28–9 September 1991; Kronenbourg Gallery, Paris, 12–22 November 1991

1991

**Yayoi Kusama-Collage 1952–83*, Nabis Gallery, Tokyo, 8–19 January

1992

**Bursting Galaxies*, Sogetsu Art Museum, Tokyo, 21 September – 31 October and touring to Niigata City Art Museum, 7 November – 13 December

1993

**HAM Collection Yayoi Kusama 1952–1993*, Gallery HAM, Nagoya, 6 February – 6 March

**Yayoi Kusama*, Galleria Valentina Moncada, Rome, 1 June – 30 September

**Yayoi Kusama*, Galleria d'Arte del Naviglio, Venice, 10 June – 30 September

**Yayoi Kusama*, 45th Venice Biennale, Japanese Pavilion, 30 June – 10 September

Abject Art: Repulsion and Desire in Contemporary Art, Whitney Museum of American Art, New York, 23 June – 29 August

1994

Japanese Art after 1945: Scream Against the Sky, Yokohama Art Museum, 5 February – 30 March, touring to Solomon R. Guggenheim Museum, New York, 14 September – 8 January 1995; San Francisco Museum of Modern Art, 14 September – 31 May 1995

**Yayoi Kusama*, Komagane Kogen Art Museum, Nagano, 16 March – 20 April

**Yayoi Kusama*, Nagano Prefectural Shinano Art Museum, 22 April – 22 May

**Yayoi Kusama*, Galleria Cardazzo, Venice, 1 June

Out of Bounds, Benesse House Naoshima Contemporary Art Museum, Okayama, 15 September – 27 November

Infinity of Space and Light in the 1950s and 1960s: Yayoi Kusama from the Collection of Richard Castellane, Esquire, Picker Art Gallery, Colgate University, Hamilton, New York, 16 November

1995

ARS 95, Museum of Contemporary Art/Finnish National Gallery, Helsinki, 11 February – 28 May

Division of Labor: 'Women's Work' in Contemporary Art, Bronx Museum of the Arts, New York, 17 February – 11 June, touring to Museum of Contemporary Art, Los Angeles 24 September – 7 January 1996

**'Yayoi Kusama: I Who Committed Suicide'*, Ota Fine Arts, Tokyo, 1 July – 5 August

NO!art, Neue Gesellschaft für Bildende Kunst, Berlin, 22 October – 26 November

1995–7

Japan Today, Louisiana Museum of Modern Art, Humlebæk, Denmark, 23 June – 1 October, touring to Kunstnernes Hus, Oslo, January – May 1996; Wäinö Aaltosen Museo, Turku, Finland, June – September 1996; Liljevalchs Konsthall, Stockholm, October – December 1996; MAK-Austrian Museum of Applied Arts, Wien, 26 February – 1 June 1997

1996

Drawing International, Galerie A/Harry Ruhe, Amsterdam, 24 February – 30 March

**Yayoi Kusama: The 1950s and 1960s*, Paula Cooper Gallery, New York, 3 May – 21 June

Now Here, Louisiana Museum of Modern Art, Humlebæk, Denmark, 15 May – 8 September

L'informe: Mode d'emploi, Musée national d'art moderne, Centre Georges Pompidou, Paris, 22 May

**Yayoi Kusama Recent Works*, Robert Miller Gallery, New York, 17 September – 19 October

Unveiling ceremony of open-air sculpture Three Hats, Fukuoka Health Promotion Foundation, 5 October

New Installations, Mattress Factory, Pittsburgh, 20 October – 29 June

1996–7

**Repetition*, Art Gallery Artium, Fukuoka, 13 December 1996 – 19 January 1997

1997

**Yayoi Kusama*, Baumgartner Galleries Inc, Washington DC, 17 January – 28 February

The Maximal Sixties, The Museum of Modern Art, New York, 18 January – 29 April

Art Fashion, Solomon R. Guggenheim Museum, New York, 12 March – 8 June

Exhibition by Three Women Artists from Shinshu, Suzaka Prints Museum, Nagano, 16 April – 1 June

**Yayoi Kusama*, Arts Club of Chicago, 11 June – 31 July

**Yayoi Kusama*, Margo Leavin Gallery, Los Angeles, 1 September – 1 October

1997–8

Yayoi Kusama: A Snake; Andy Warhol: Silver Clouds, D'Amerio Terras, New York, 11 November 1997 – 31 January 1998

1998

**Yayoi Kusama Prints*, Toki no Wasuremono, Tokyo, 16 January – 31 January

Out of Actions: Between Performance and the Object, 1949–1979, Museum of Contemporary Art, Los Angeles, 8 February – 10 May

1998 Taipei Biennial: Site of Desire, Taipei Fine Arts Museum, 13–16 June

**Yayoi Kusama: Works from the 1950s*, Peter Blum Gallery, New York, 20 June – 1 September

XXI Bienal de Sao Paulo, 4 October – 13 December

1998–9

**Yayoi Kusama*, Victoria Miro Gallery, London, 18 November 1998 – 8 January 1999

**Yayoi Kusama*, Piece Unique, Paris, 17 December 1998

**Love Forever: Yayoi Kusama 1958–1968*, Los Angeles County Museum of Art, 8 March – 8 June, touring to The Museum of Modern Art, New York, 9 July – 22 September 1998; Walker Art Centre, Minneapolis, 13 December 1998 – 7 March 1999; Museum of Contemporary Art, Tokyo, 29 April – 4 July 1999

Inner Eye: Contemporary Art from the Marc and Livia Straus Collection, Samuel P. Harn Museum of Art, University of Florida, Gainesville, 22 March 1998 – 3 January 1999, touring to Knoxville Museum of Art, Tennessee, Spring 1999; Georgia Museum of Art, University of Georgia, Athens, Summer 1999; Chrysler Museum of Art, Norfolk, Virginia, Autumn 1999

Mirror Images: Women, Surrealism and Self-Representation, MIT List Visual Arts Centre, Massachusetts, 9 April – 18 June 1998, touring to Miami Art Museum, 28 September – 29 November 1998; San Francisco Museum of Modern Art, 8 January – 20 April 1999

1999

Contemporary Classicism, Neuberger Museum of Art, 20 February – 6 June

Love Forever: Yayoi Kusama 1958–1968/In Full Bloom: Yayoi Kusama, Years in Japan, Museum of Contemporary Art, Tokyo, 29 April – 4 July

**Message from Yayoi Kusama*, Matsumoto Municipal Museum, Nagano, 18 September – 17 October

1999–2000

**Yayoi Kusama*, Victoria Miro Gallery, London, 18 November 1999 – 8 January 2000

Experiments in Sculpture and Painting 1980s & 1990s

For Kusama, the 1980s and 1990s were a period of continued and constant activity. Now firmly committed to remaining in Japan, she used the hospital as a base, initially setting up a studio within the medical faculty. As she adjusted to more confined living arrangements, her approach to art making changed. She returned to sculpture, making objects by hand. The scale of the individual objects she created was small, but she combined these to create large multi-part installations. *The Clouds* 1984 (no.87) consists of one hundred unique sewn stuffed cushions. These bulbous, biomorphic objects are arranged on the floor, creating a constellation of singular yet interrelated forms.

As if in response to her own more contained environment, Kusama began making box constructions, filling these dioramas with her signature motifs. In these works the phalli of her Accumulation sculptures are extended and elongated into snake-like forms that appear to writhe in dense layers, or extrude like overgrown foliage. Ovoid forms proliferate like barnacles at the edges of some of her constructions. These sculptural installations vary in colouration: some works are monochrome whereas others are vibrantly coloured and densely covered in polka dots.

In parallel with her sculptural output Kusama was painting again with a renewed vigour and on a scale unmatched since the high mark of her production of Infinity Nets in the early 1960s. Kusama had turned to acrylic as a medium, and was filling her canvases with all-over compositions in a rich palette of bright colours. Although she also made smaller paintings, in the late 1980s and early 1990s she began experimenting with multi-panel paintings that suggest an endless expansion of the visual field. The largest of these extends to sixteen canvases; more typically she worked with diptychs and triptychs. Kusama's paintings of this period suggest microscopic or macroscopic worlds, with repeated abstract patterning recalling biological or astronomical imagery. In about 1988 a new motif emerged in her paintings: a sperm-like form that harks back to some of her earliest works on paper. Bhupendra Karia has described this pattern: 'It [is] as if her polka-dots [are] sprouting, or eggs [are] hatching into tadpoles.'[1] As this description suggests, Kusama's paintings, like her sculptures, continue to evoke fecundity and growth.

Kusama showed these new works in numerous solo and group exhibitions during this period, including a series of monographic presentations at Tokyo's Fuji Television Gallery, which now acted as her primary dealer. Although she was regularly exhibiting in Japan and to a lesser extent in Europe, her exposure in the United States was relatively modest until the Center for International Contemporary Arts in New York staged the first major international retrospective of her work in 1989. This exhibition sought to reintroduce Kusama's practice to an American audience. As part of an extended research project leading up to the exhibition, the CICA catalogued extensive parts of Kusama's vast personal archive, paving the way for subsequent academic explorations of her career.

In 1993, twenty-seven years after she staged *Narcissus Garden* in the Giardini, Kusama returned to the Venice Biennale, this time representing her country in the Japanese Pavilion. This exhibition marked the extent to which Kusama had been embraced by the Japanese artistic establishment. Far from the scandalous provocateur the media had cast her as in the late 1960s, Kusama was now a respected and revered grande dame of the avant-garde. Her exhibition in Venice featured large sculptural statements, including two versions of her signature phallic rowboat: one a bright pink monochrome, the other featuring a multi-coloured array of polka-dotted fabric.

The Venice exhibition only served to increase international interest in Kusama's work. By the end of the decade her oeuvre became the subject of comprehensive historical re-evaluation in a major trans-continental curatorial project. In 1998 and 1999 two related exhibitions focused on the artist's practice in the United States and Japan respectively. *Love Forever: Yayoi Kusama, 1958–1968* opened at the Los Angeles County Museum of Art in March 1998, and subsequently toured to the Museum of Modern Art, New York; the Walker Art Center, Minneapolis; and the Museum of Contemporary Art, Tokyo. At the final venue in April 1999 this show coincided with the complementary exhibition *In Full Bloom: Yayoi Kusama, Years in Japan*. These major retrospectives signalled a renewed critical and intellectual engagement with Kusama's work, and emphasised the extent to which her work had finally achieved the level of international recognition and success she had courted for so many years.

1980s & 1990s

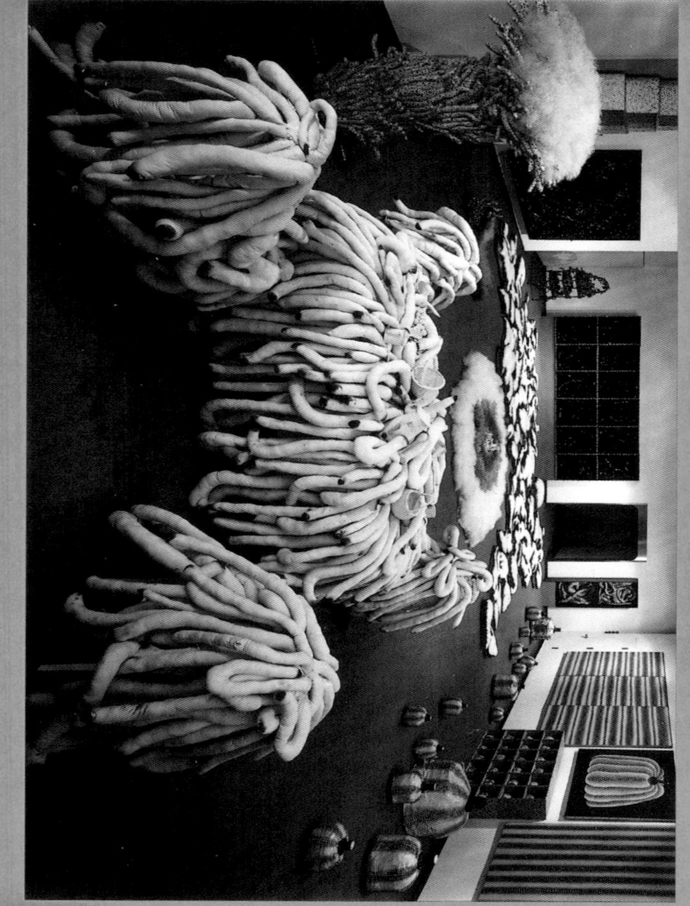

Solo exhibition at Fuji Television Gallery, Tokyo, 1984

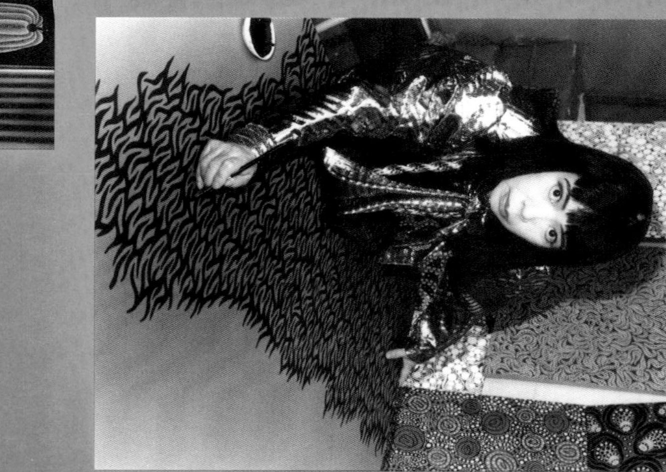

Kusama in her studio in Tokyo, 1989

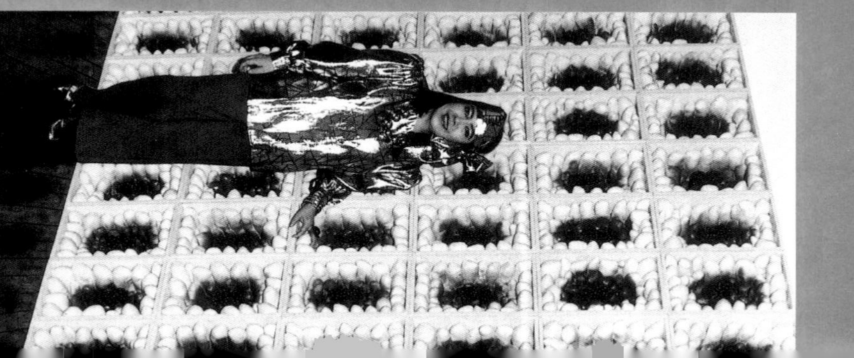

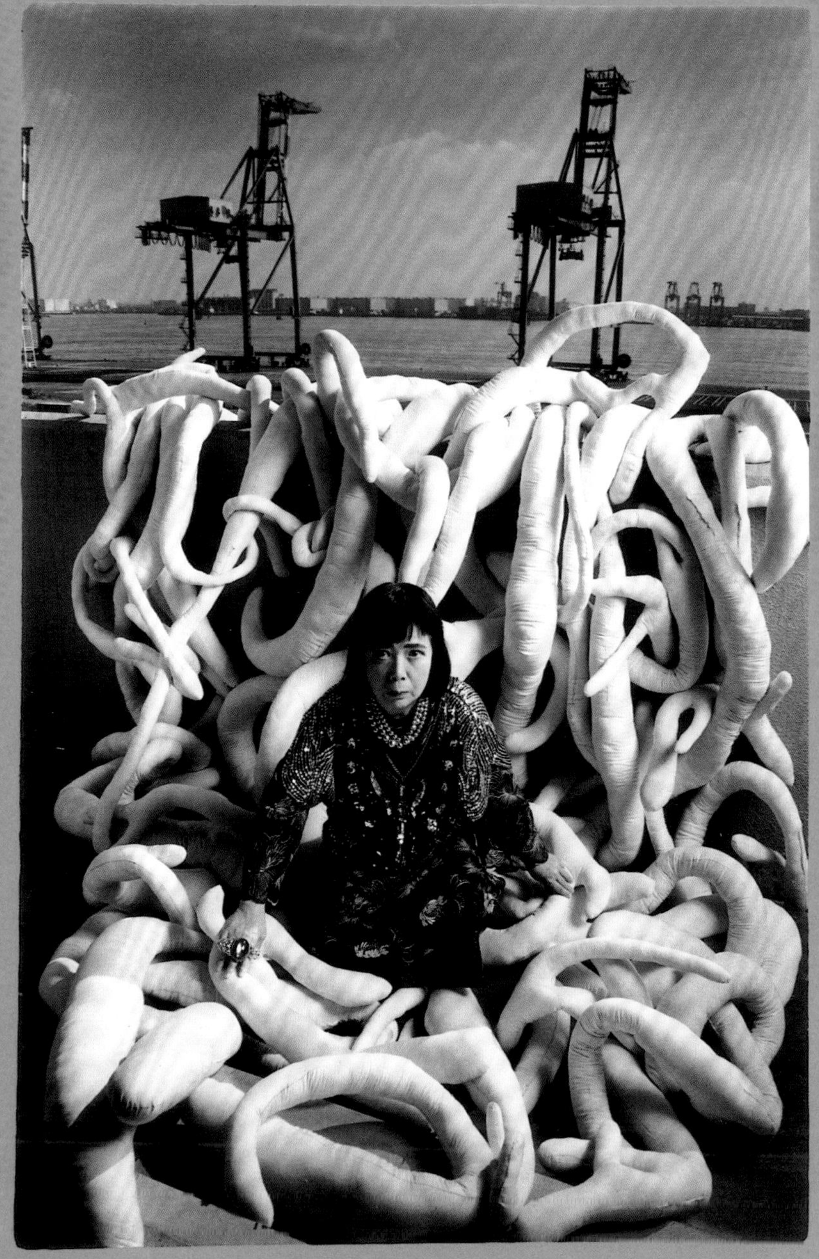

Portrait of Kusama in Tokyo, 1993

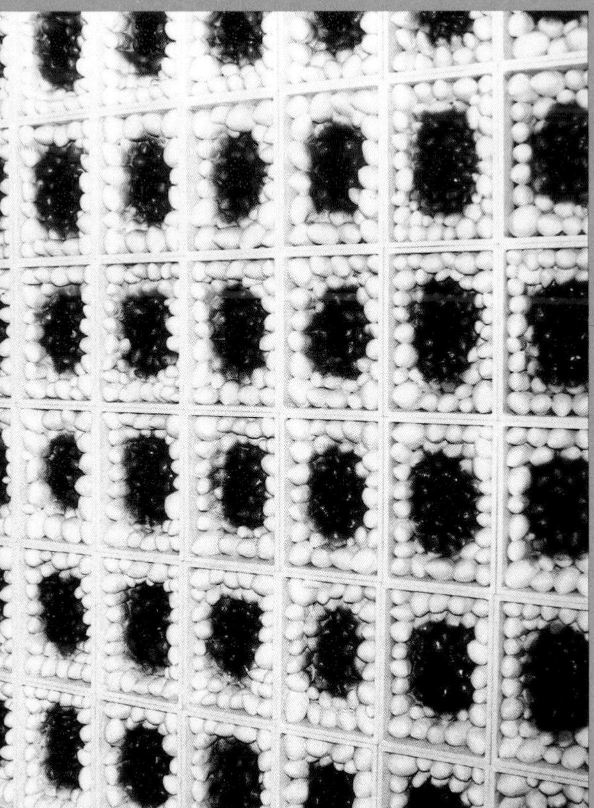

Solo exhibition at Fuji Television Gallery, Tokyo, 1991

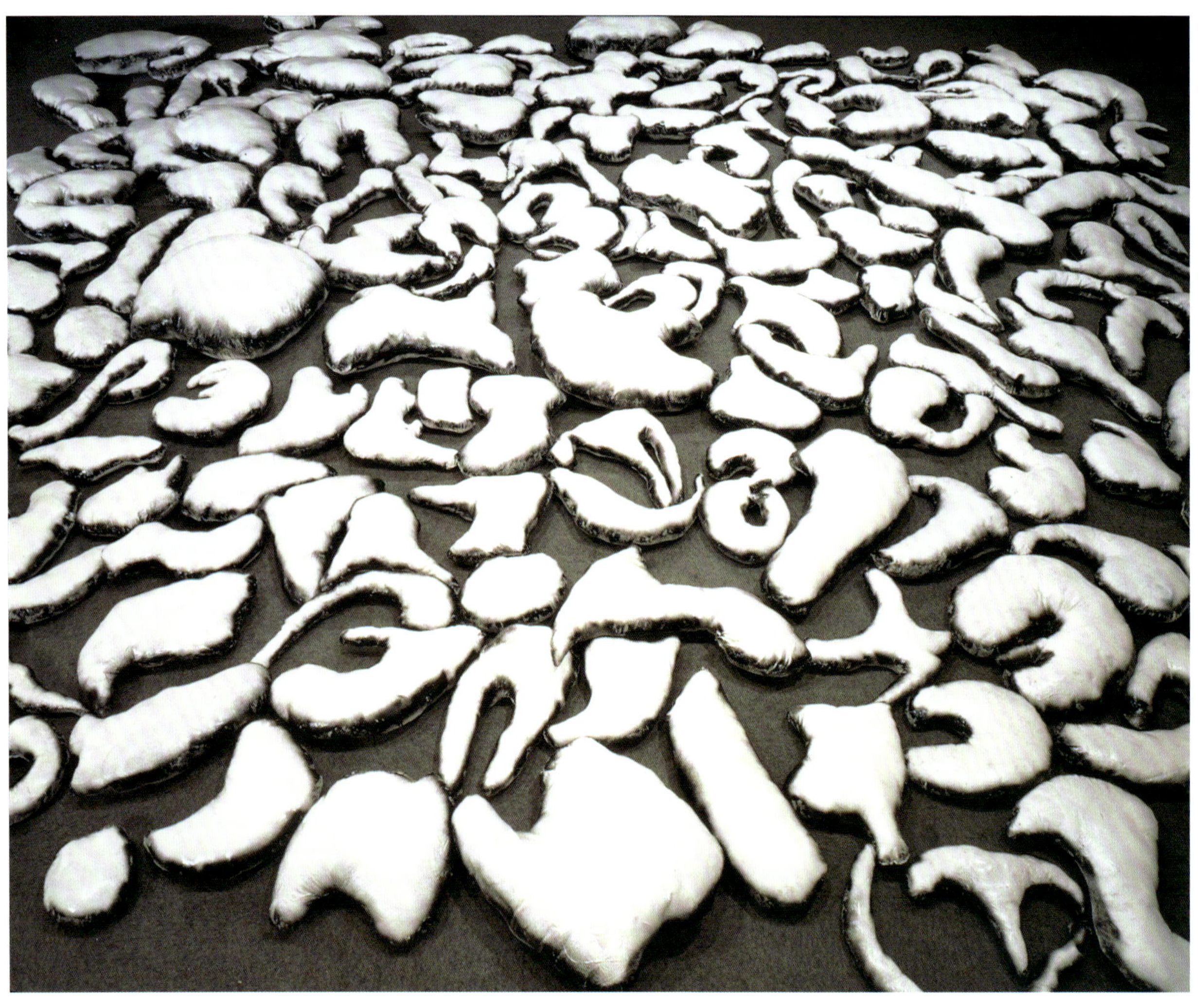

87 | **The Clouds** 1984

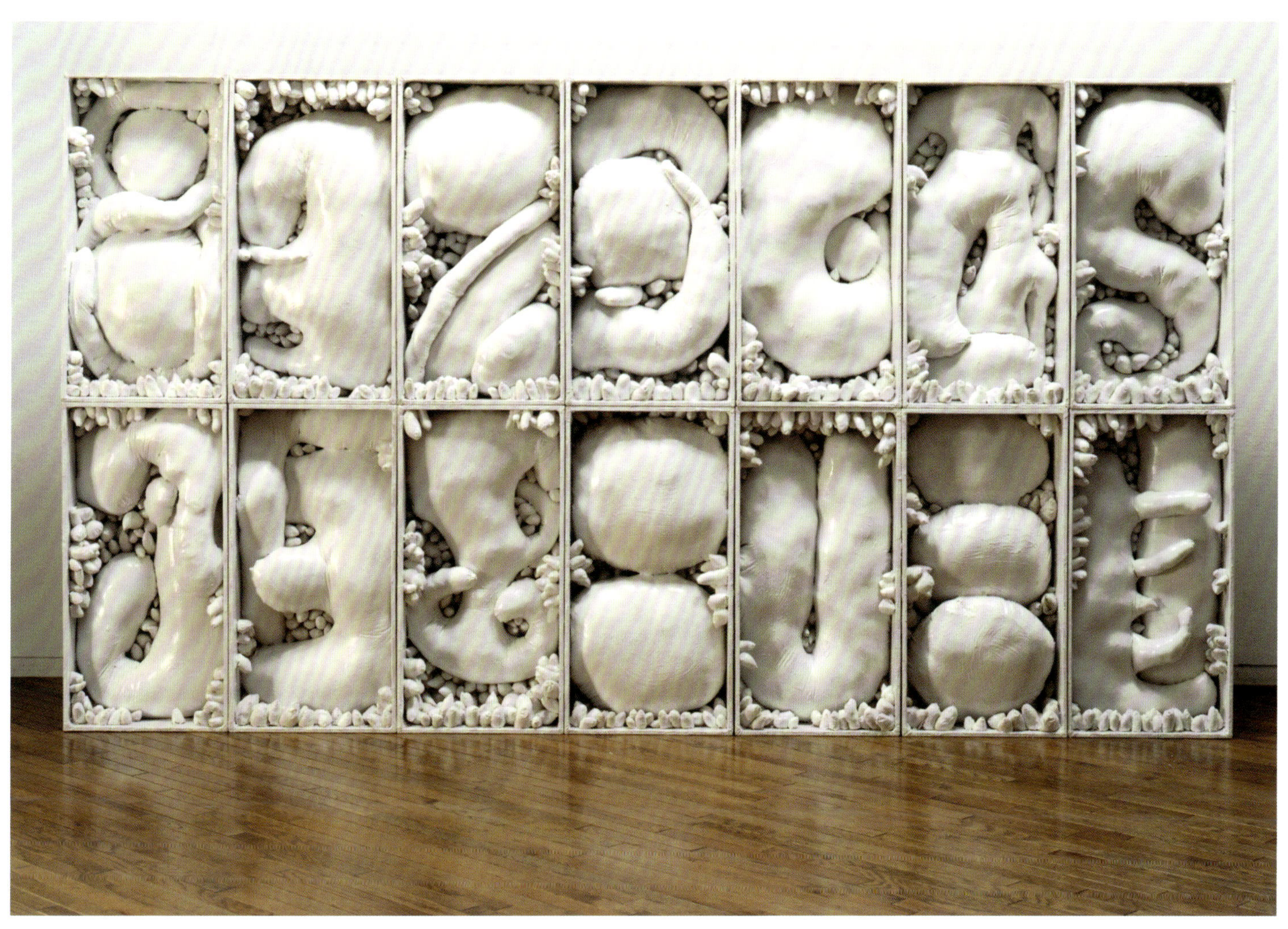

 Leftover Snow in the Dream 1982

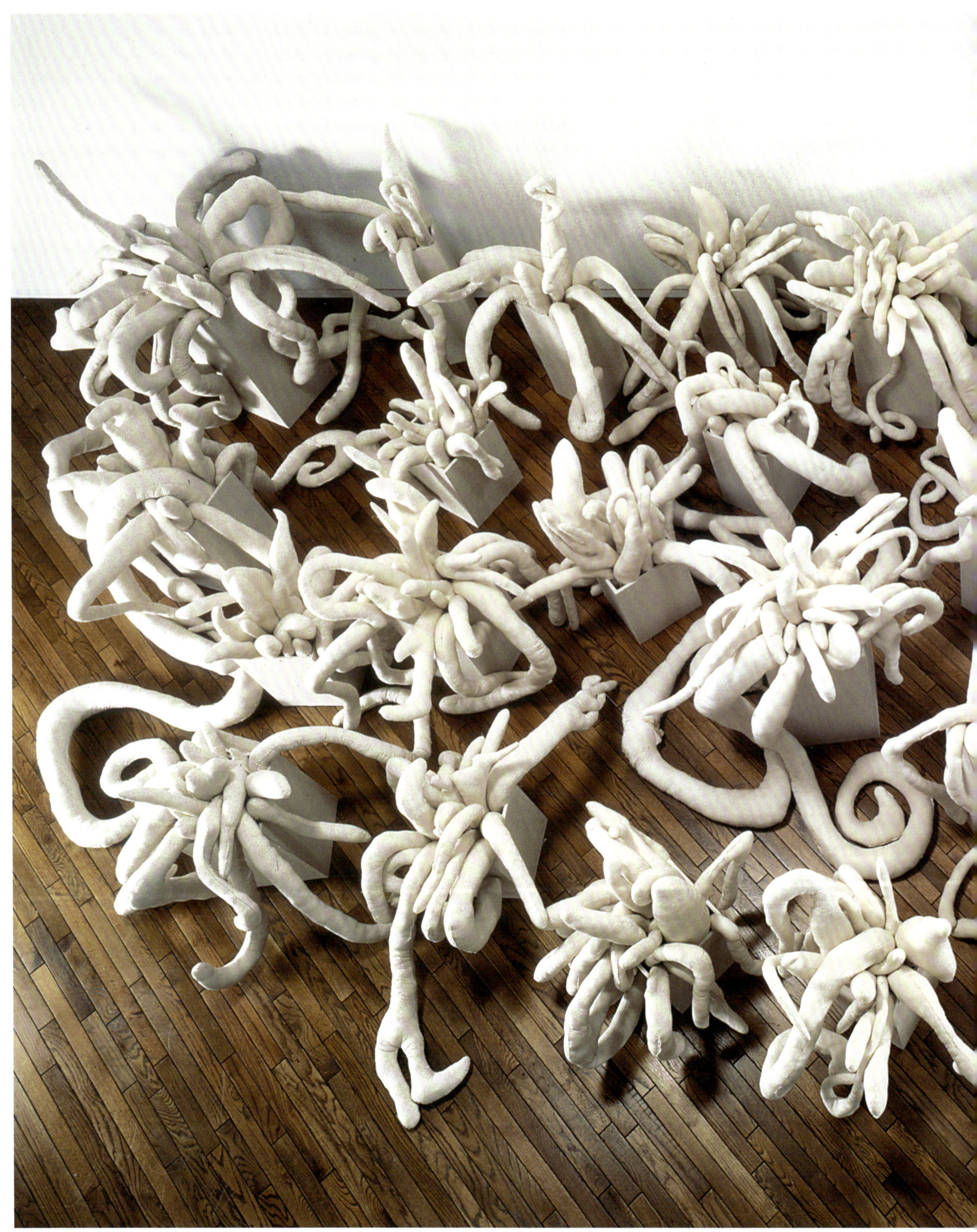

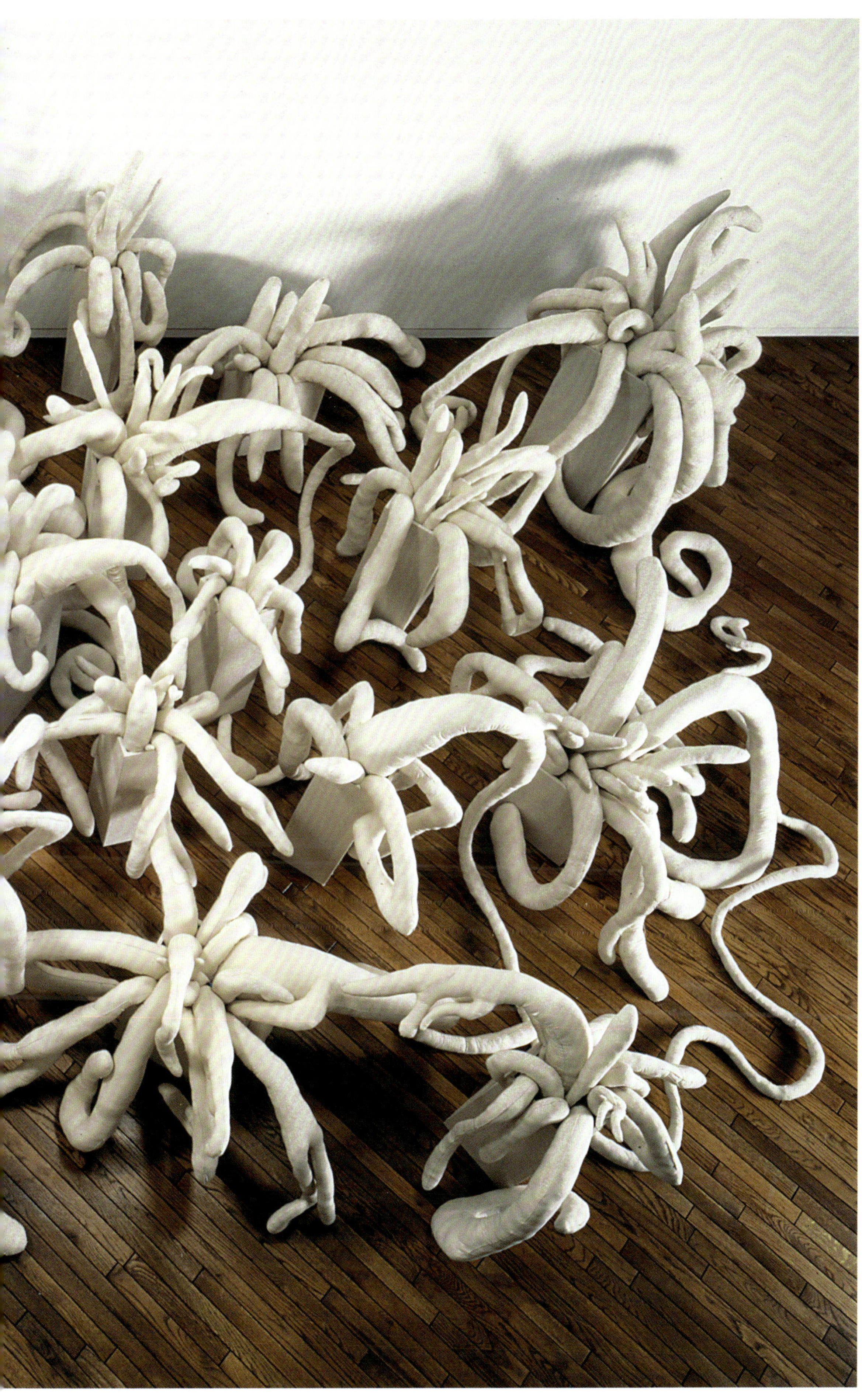

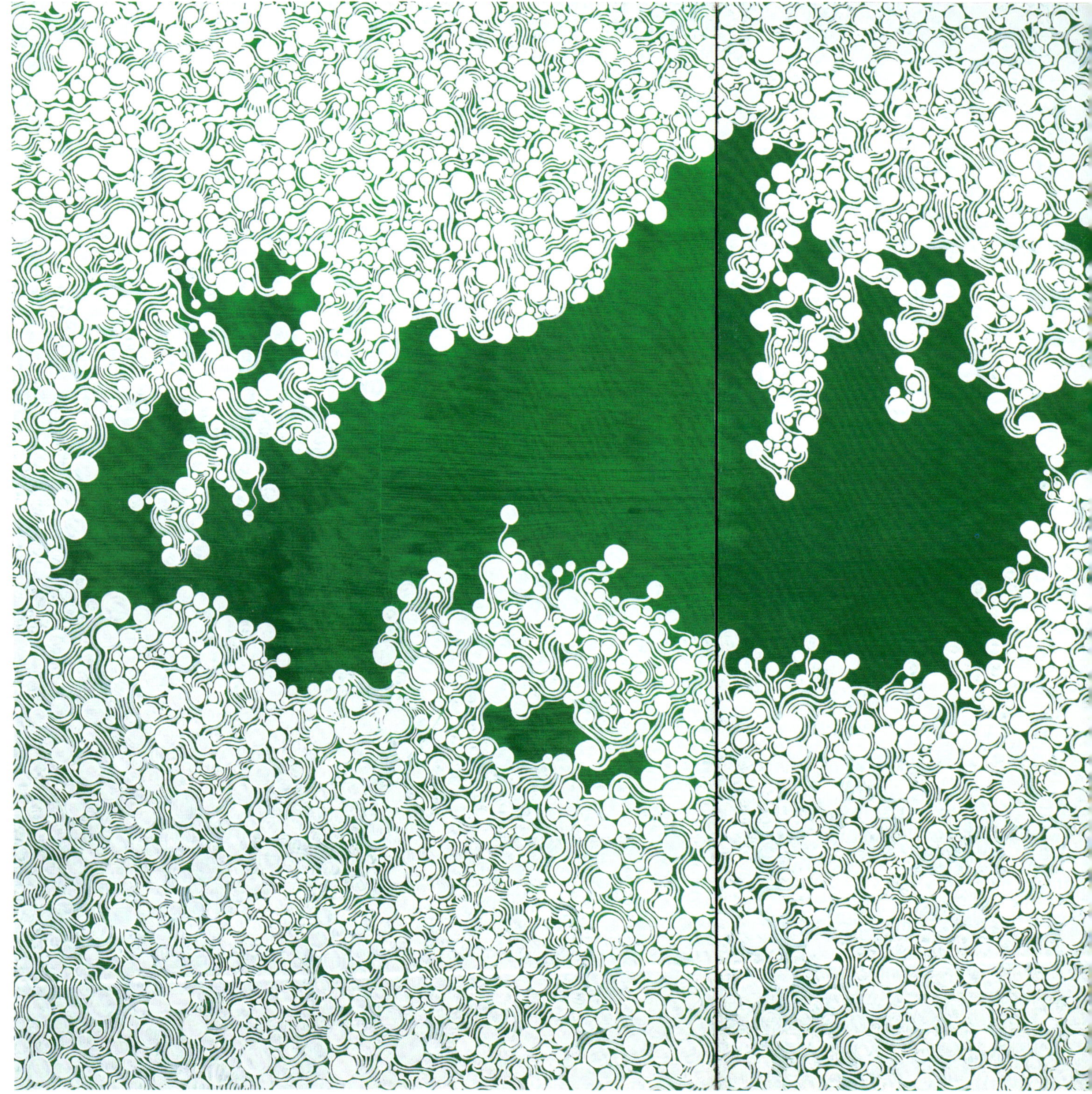

138.139

 Sprouting (The Transmigration of the Soul) 1987

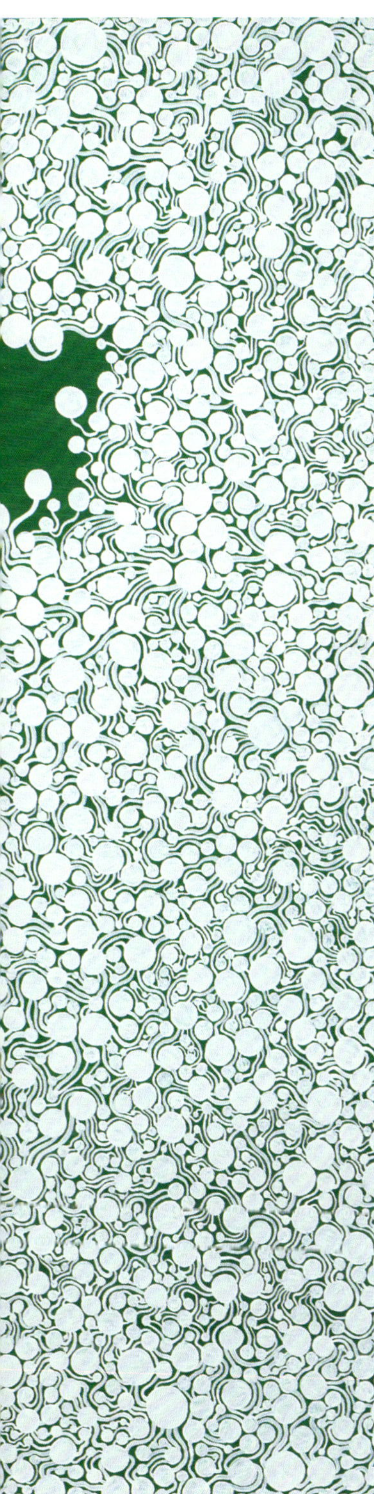

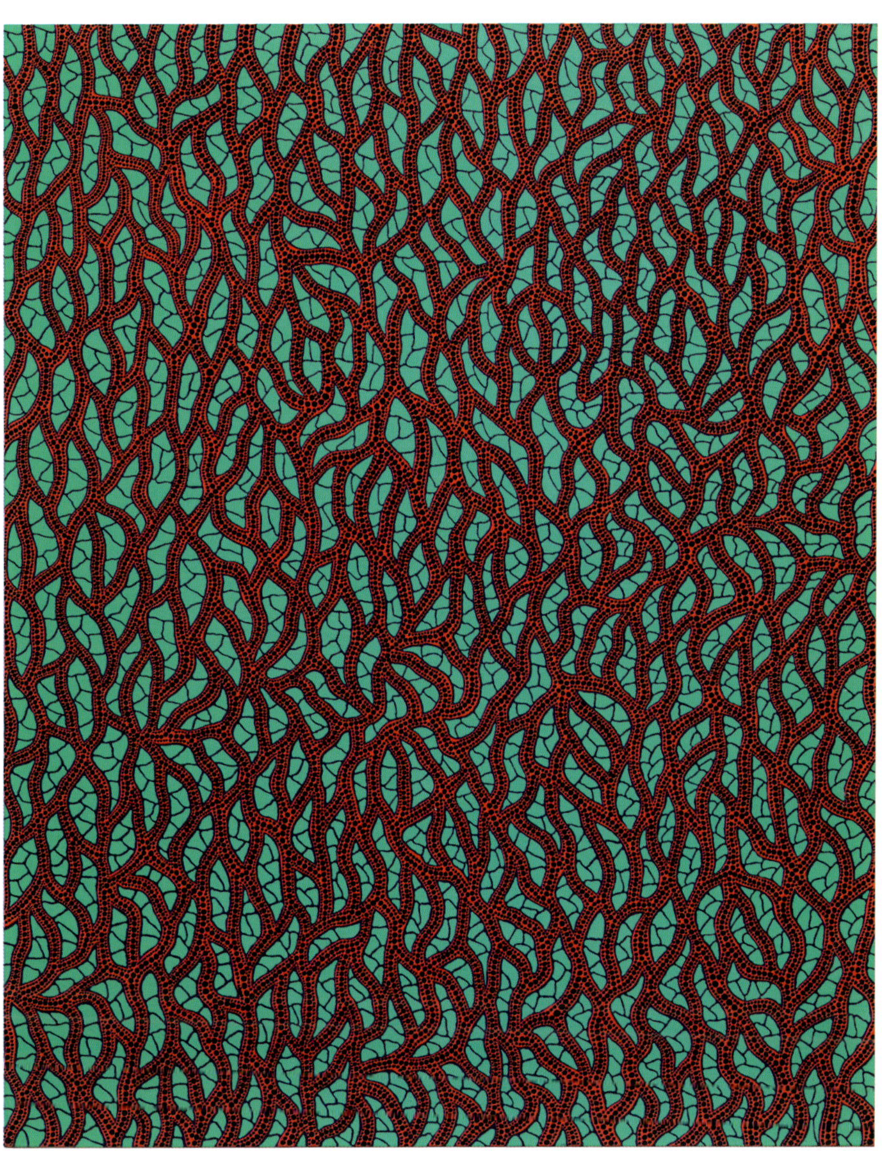

91 | **Gentle are the Stairs to Heaven** 1990

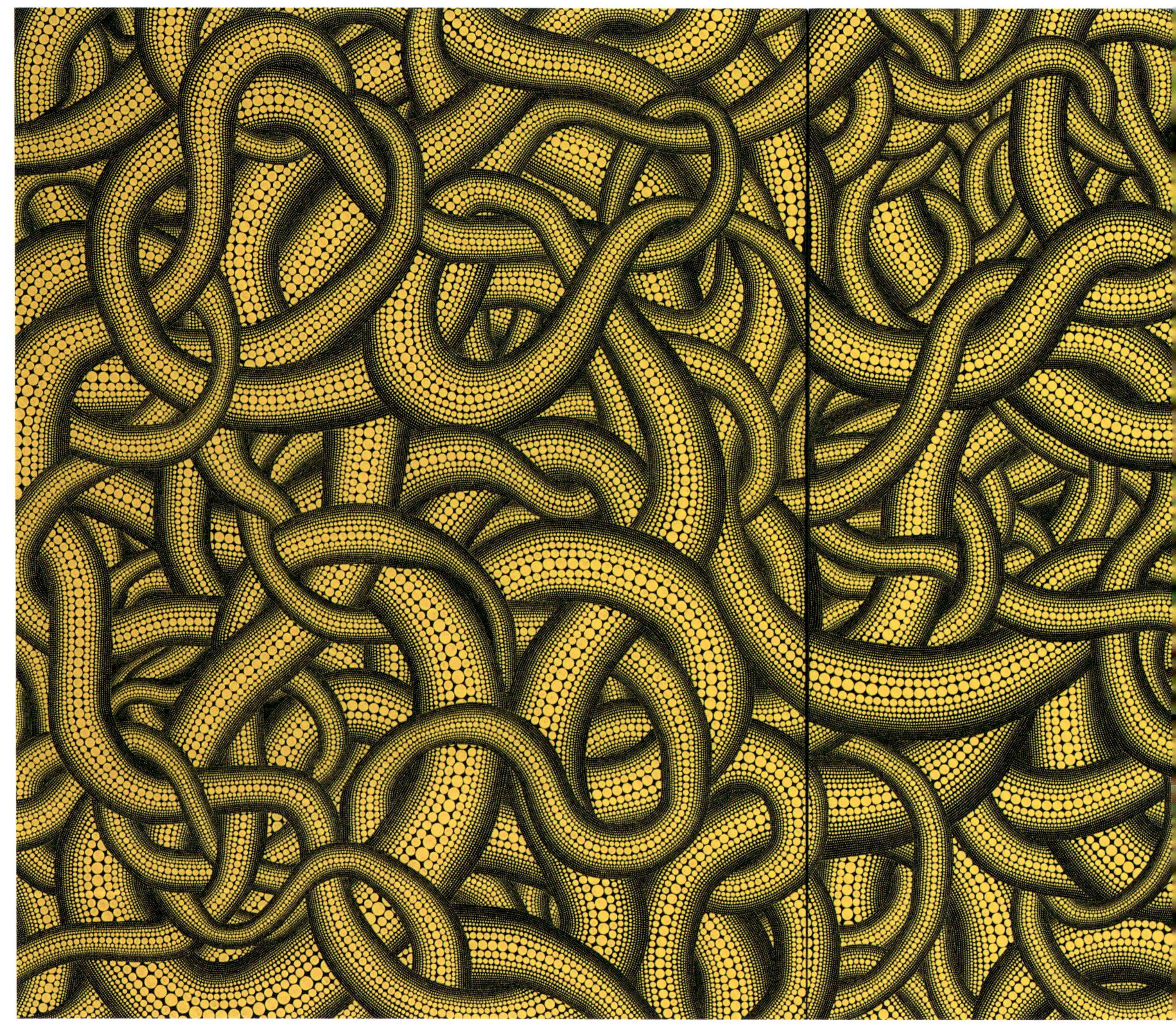

140.141

 Yellow Trees 1992

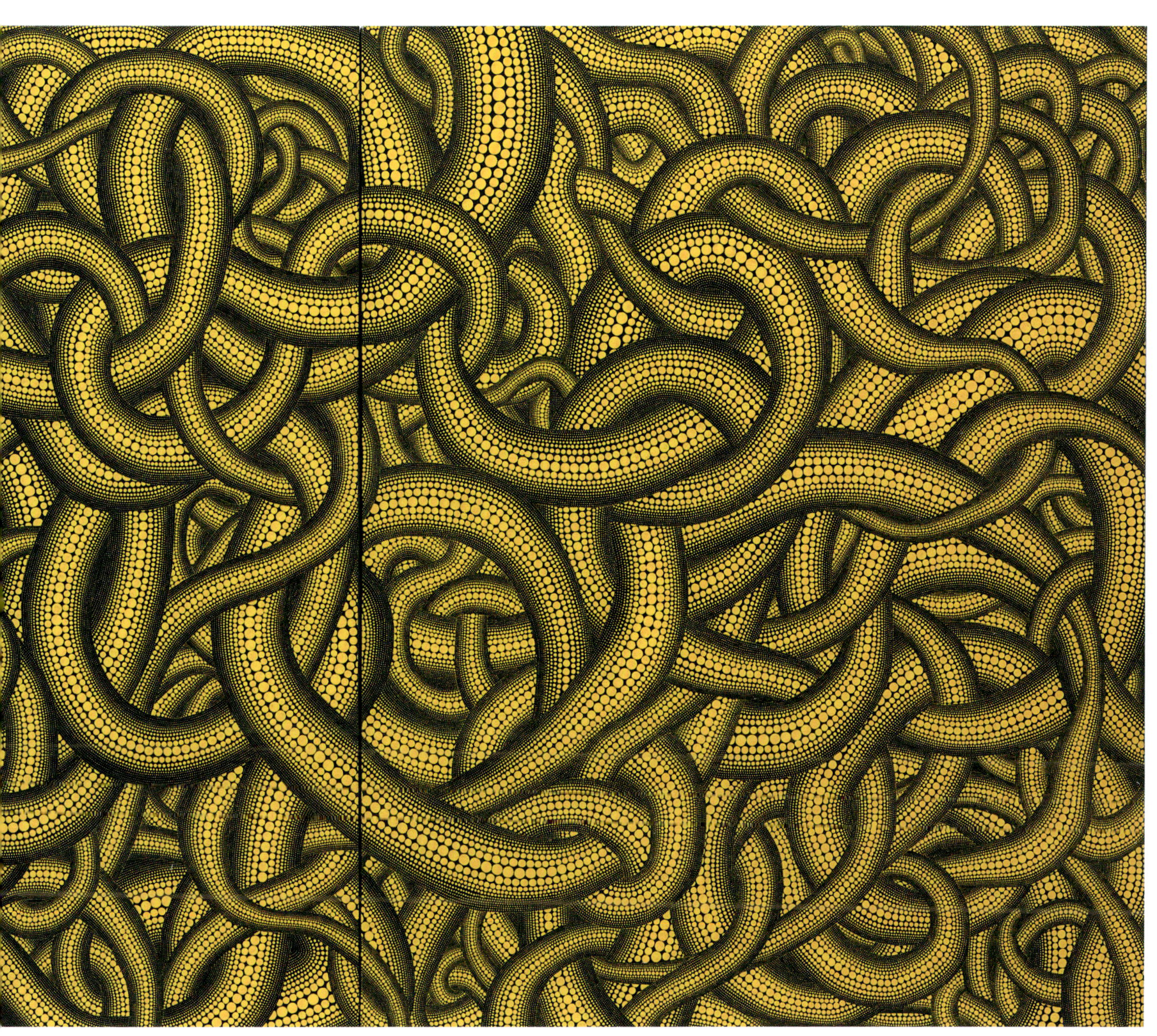

142.143

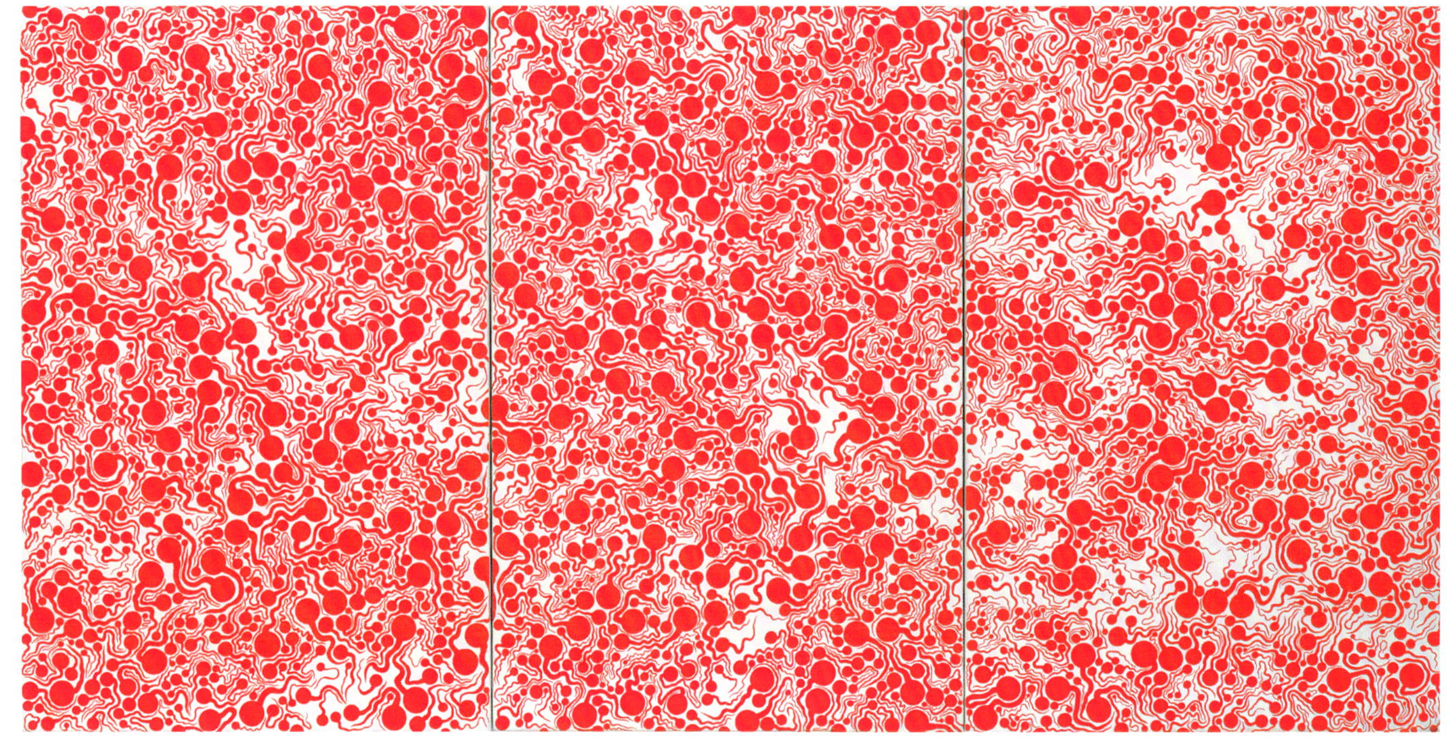

 Flame 1992

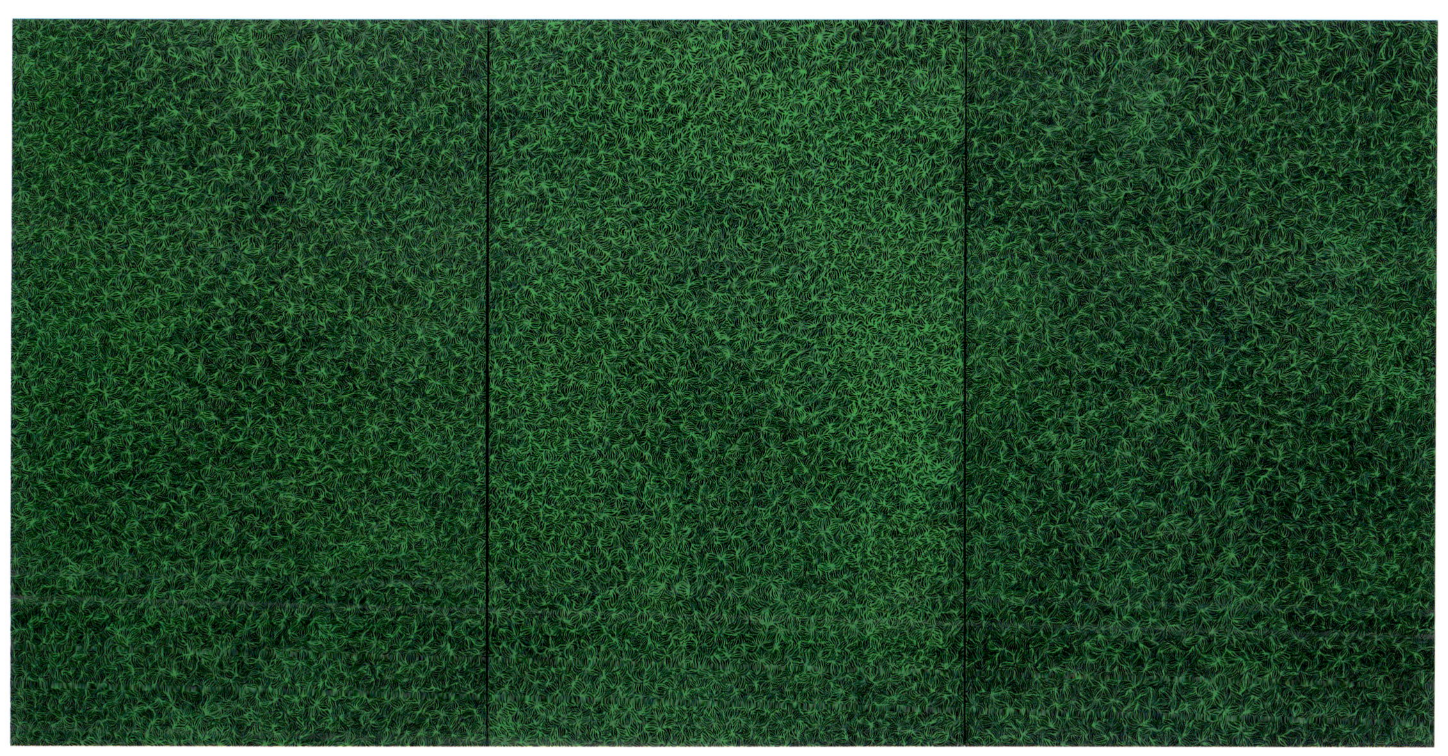

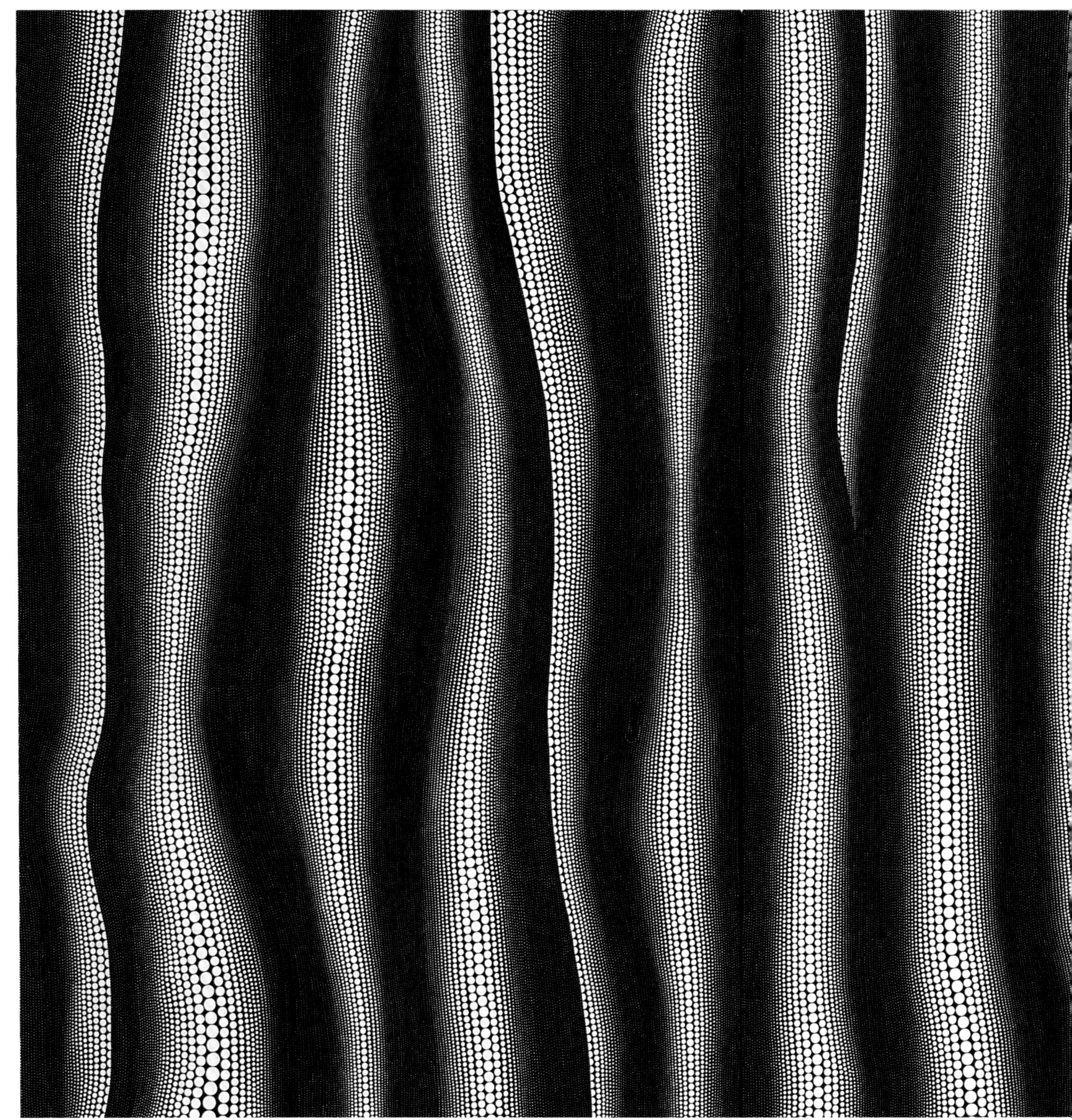

144.145

 Revived Soul 1995

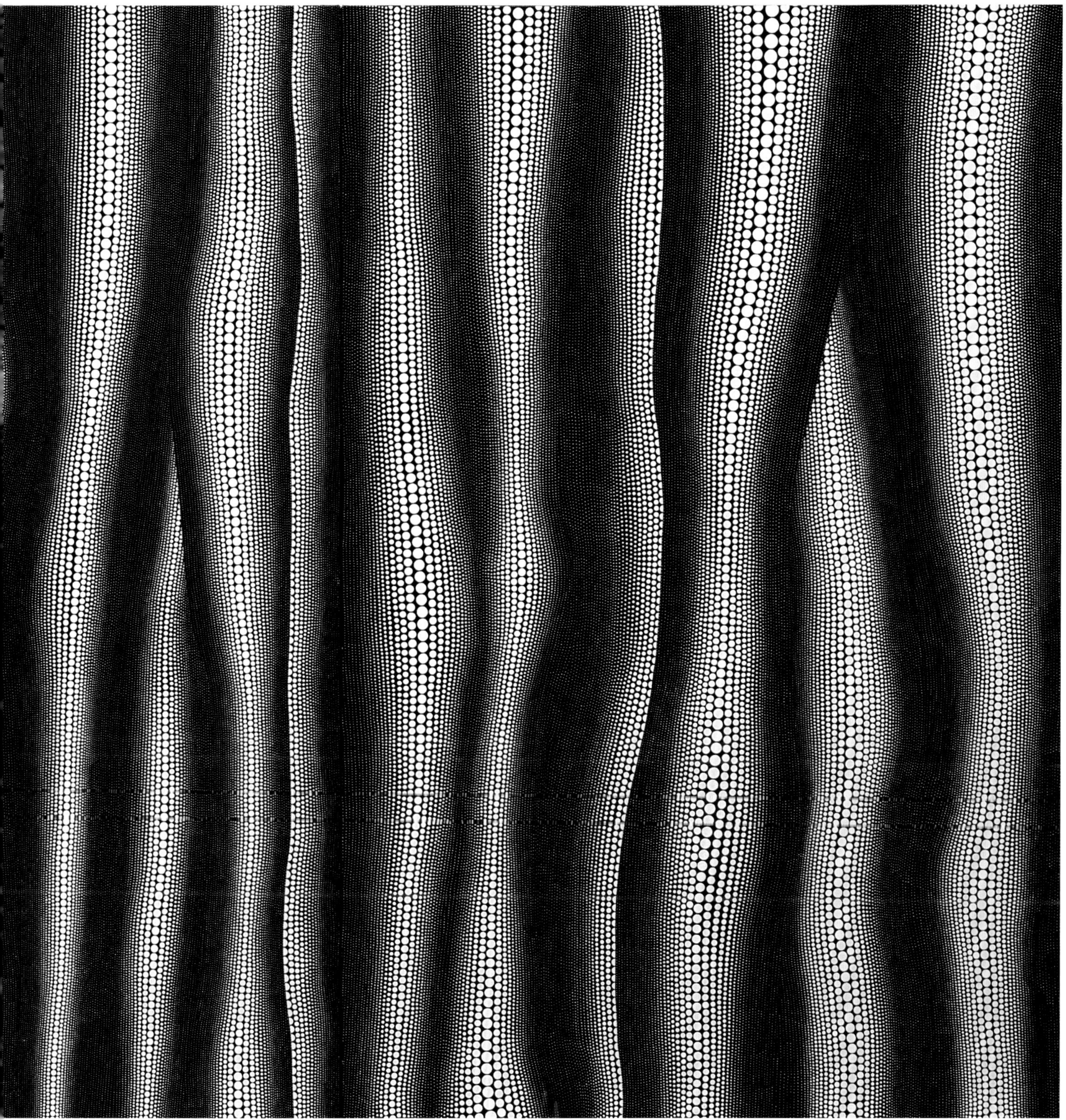

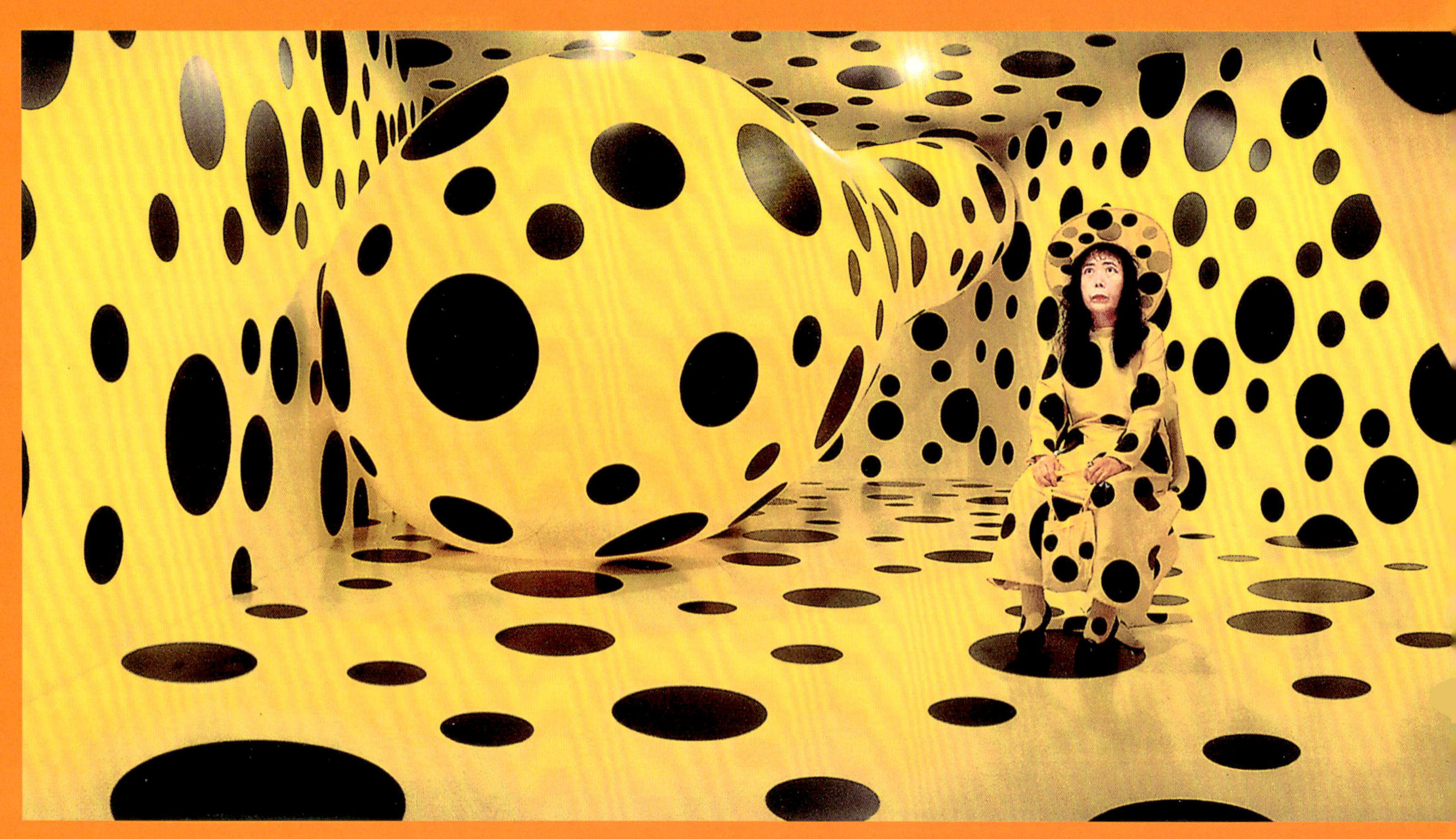

Dots Obsession 1996, at The Mattress Factory, Pittsburgh, 1996

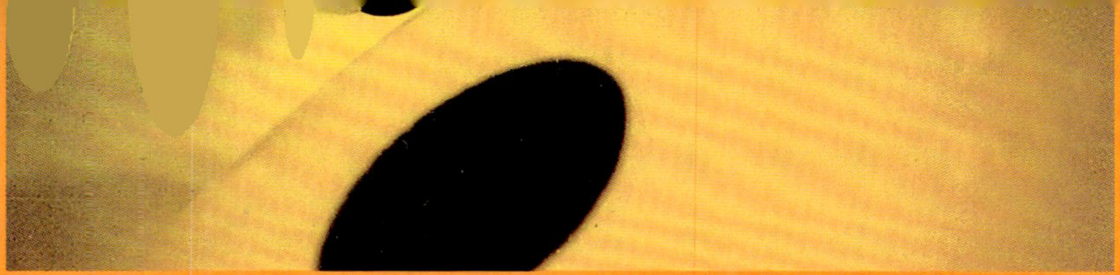

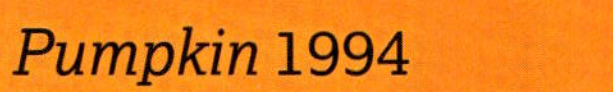

2000–2008

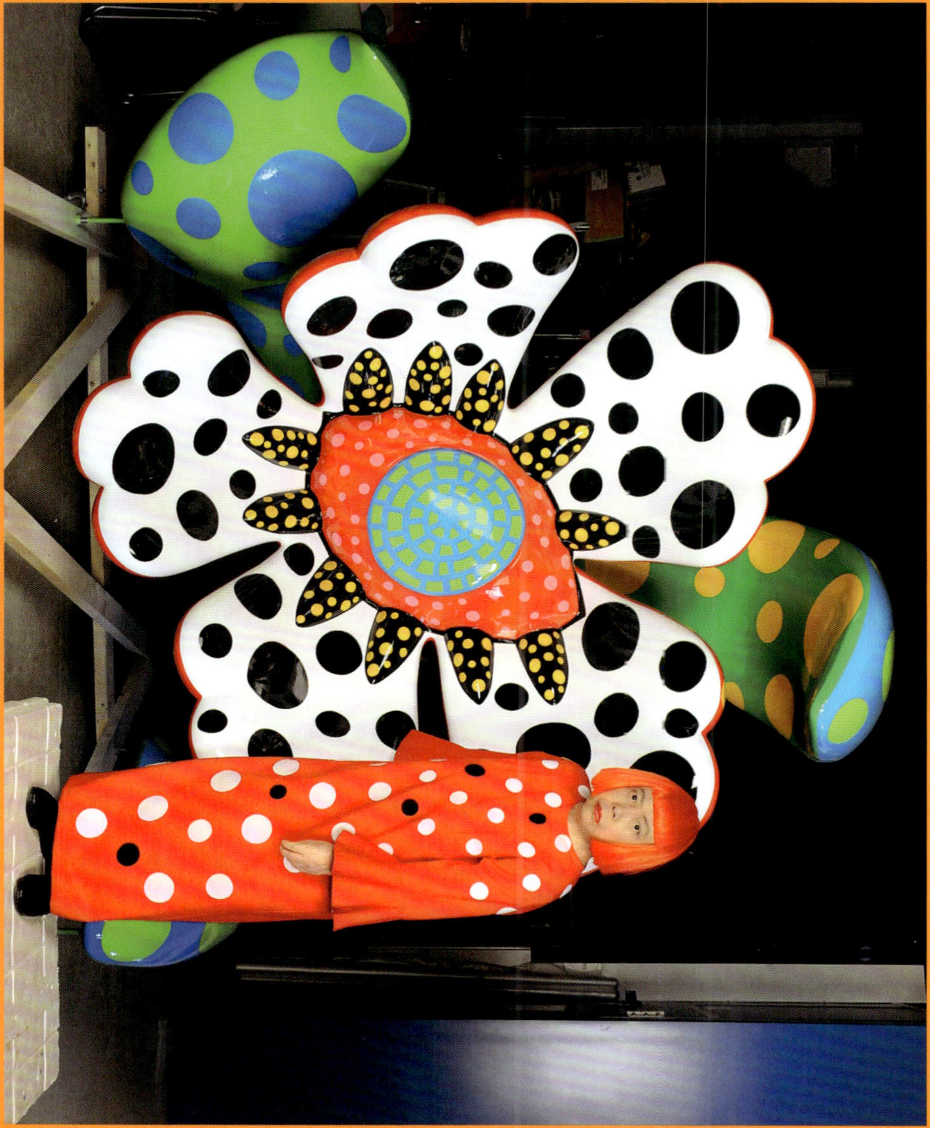

Pumpkin 1994

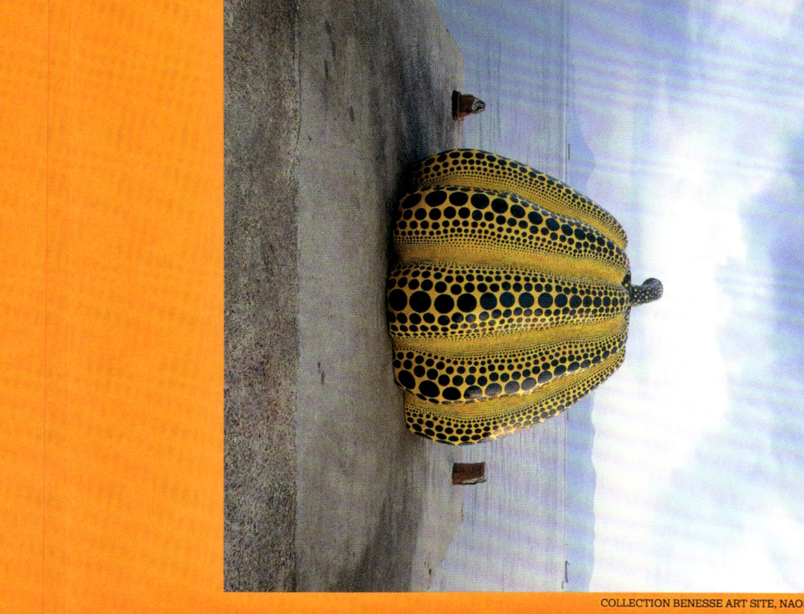

COLLECTION BENESSE ART SITE, NAOSHIMA

Kusama with *Flowers that Bloom at Midnight* 2009

150.151

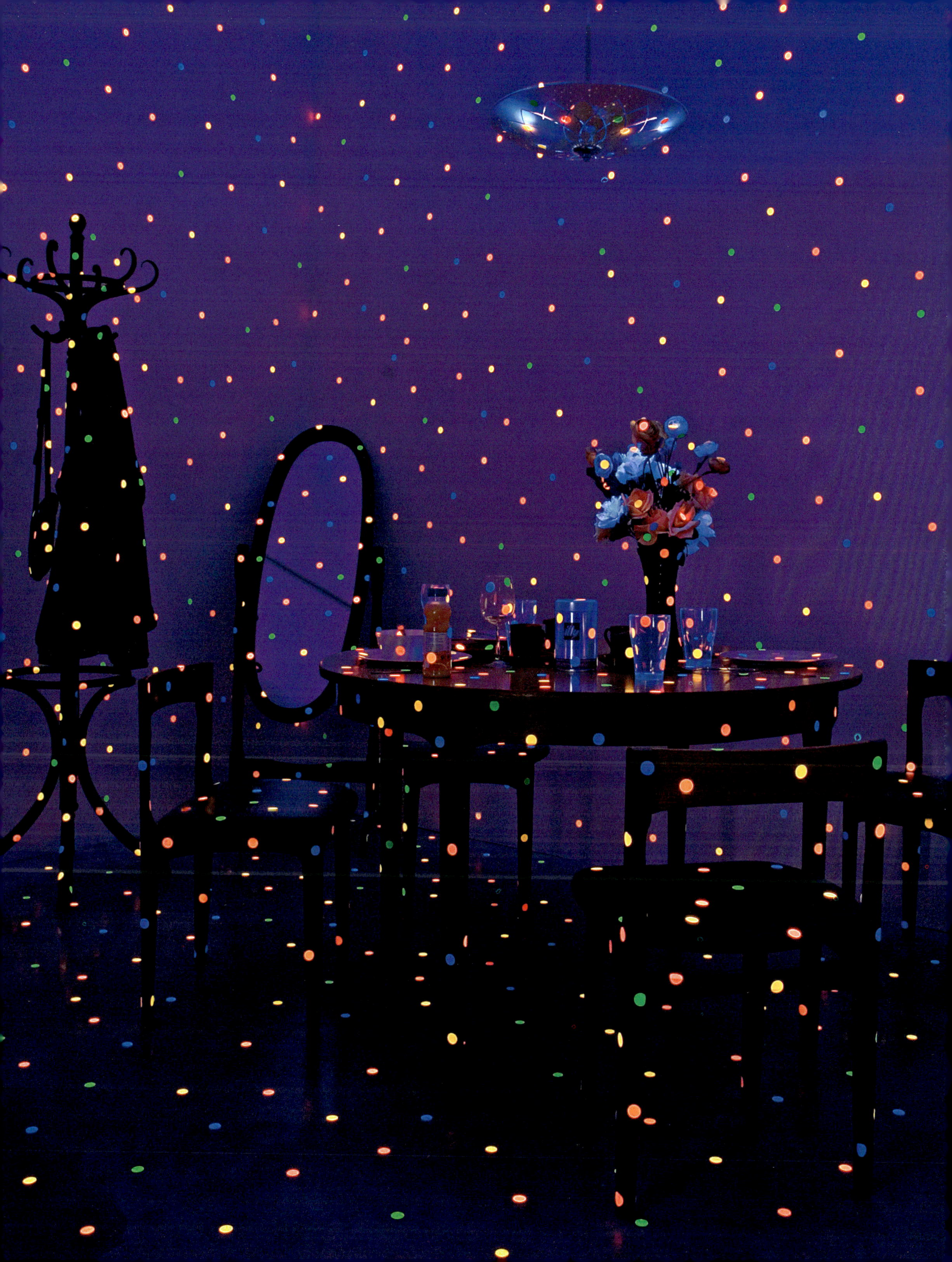

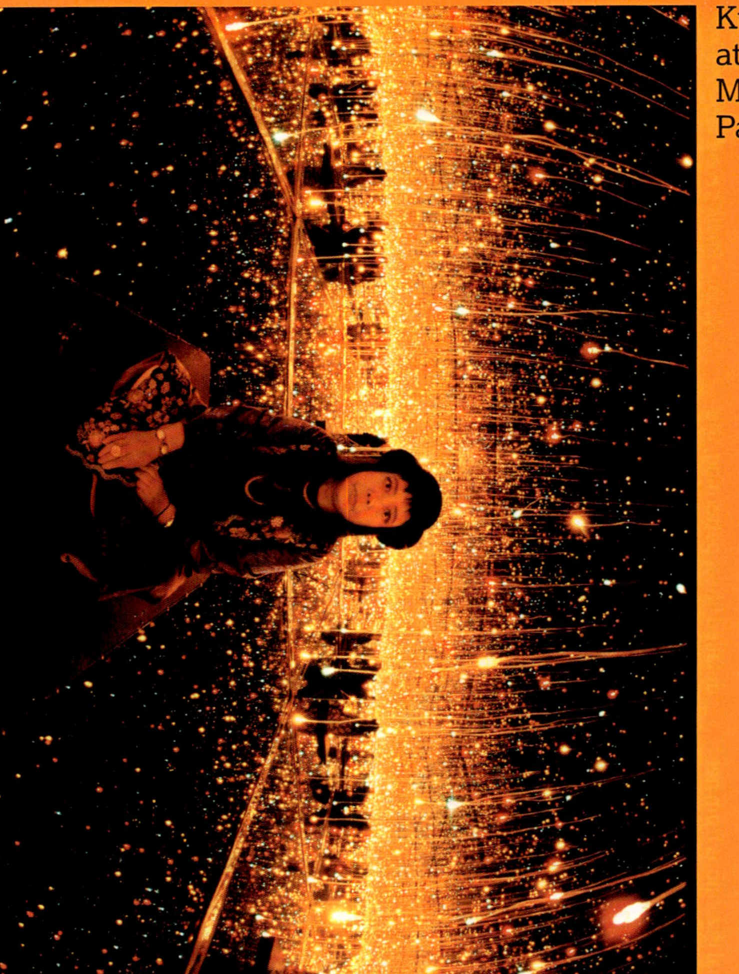

Kusama with *Fireflies on the Water* at her solo exhibition Yayoi Kusama, Maison de la culture du Japon, Paris, 2001

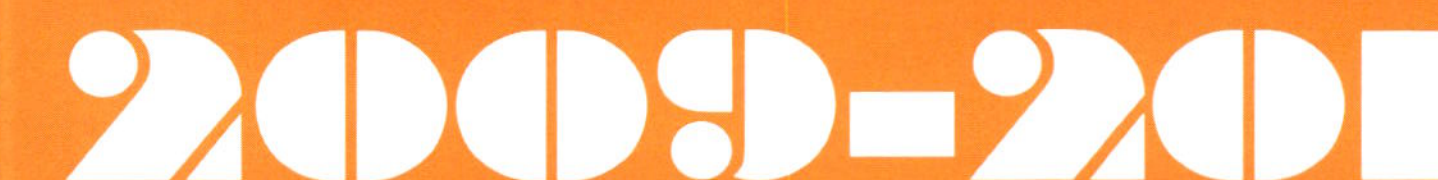

2009-2012

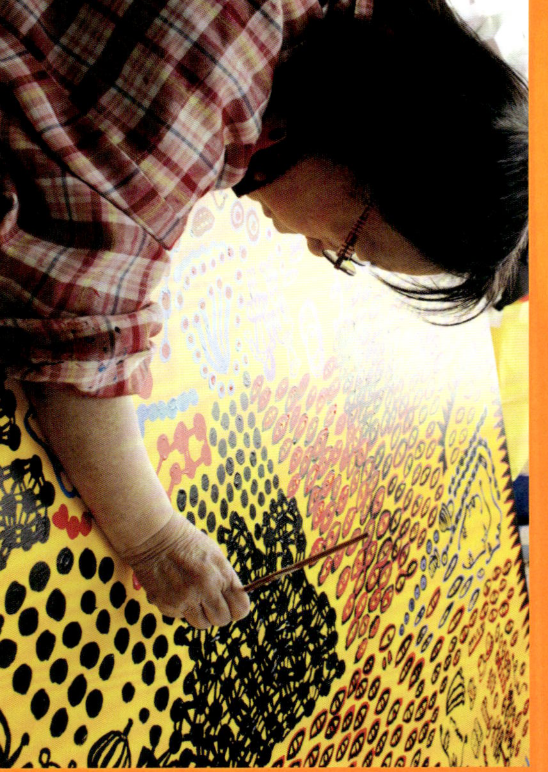

Kusama in her studio, January 2010

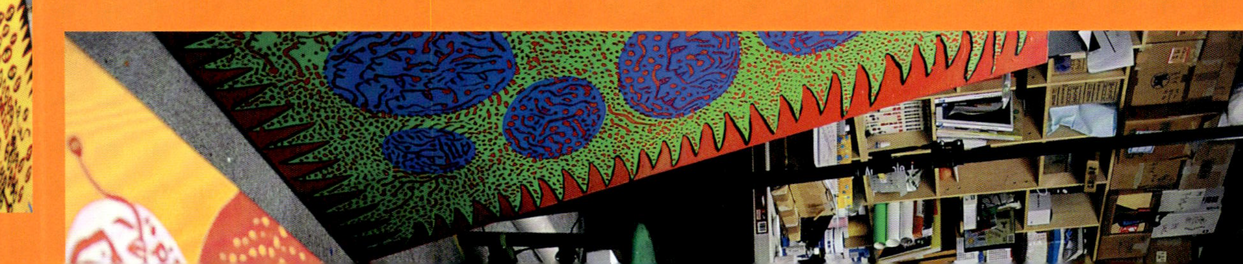

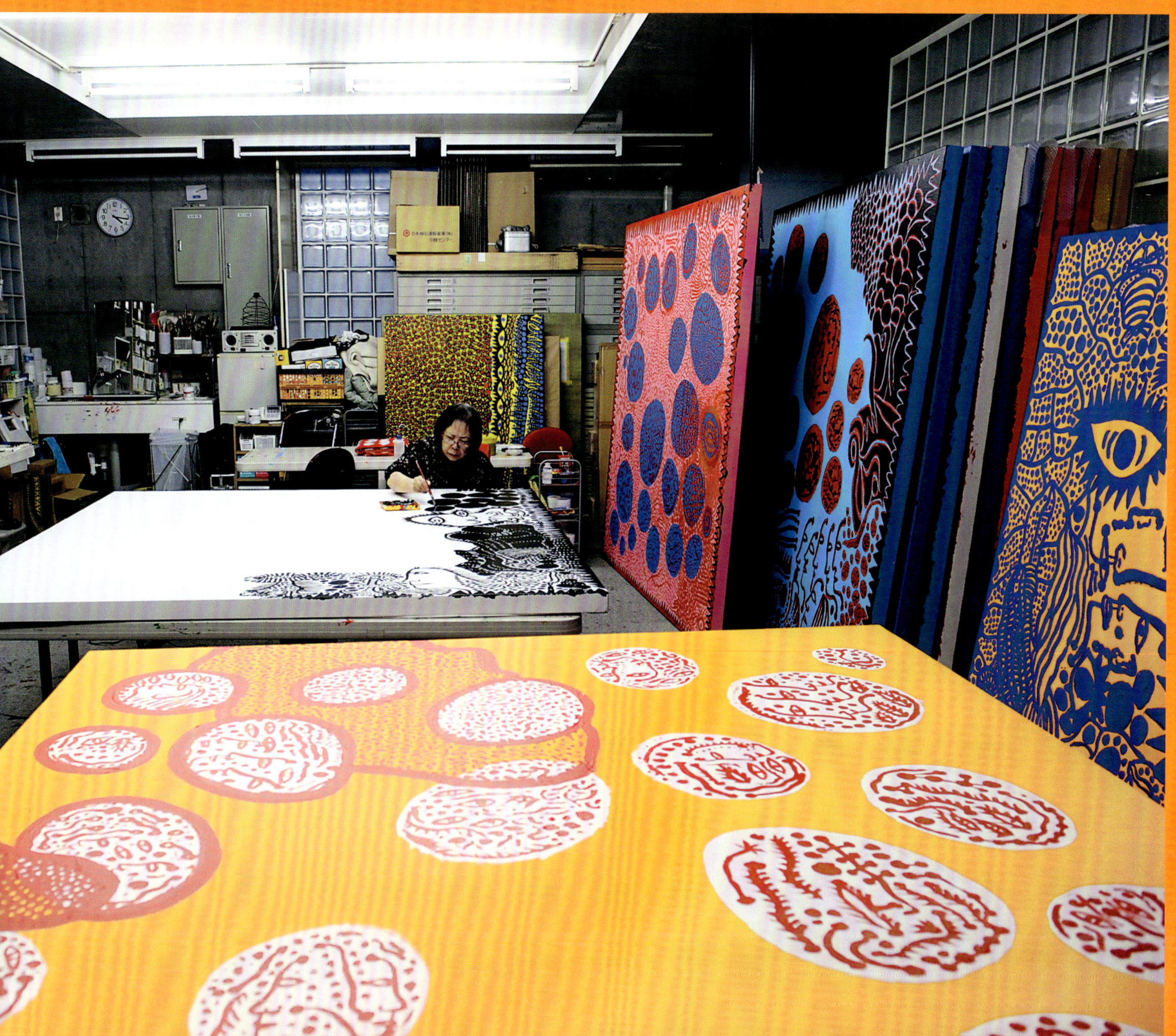

Kusama in her studio, December 2010

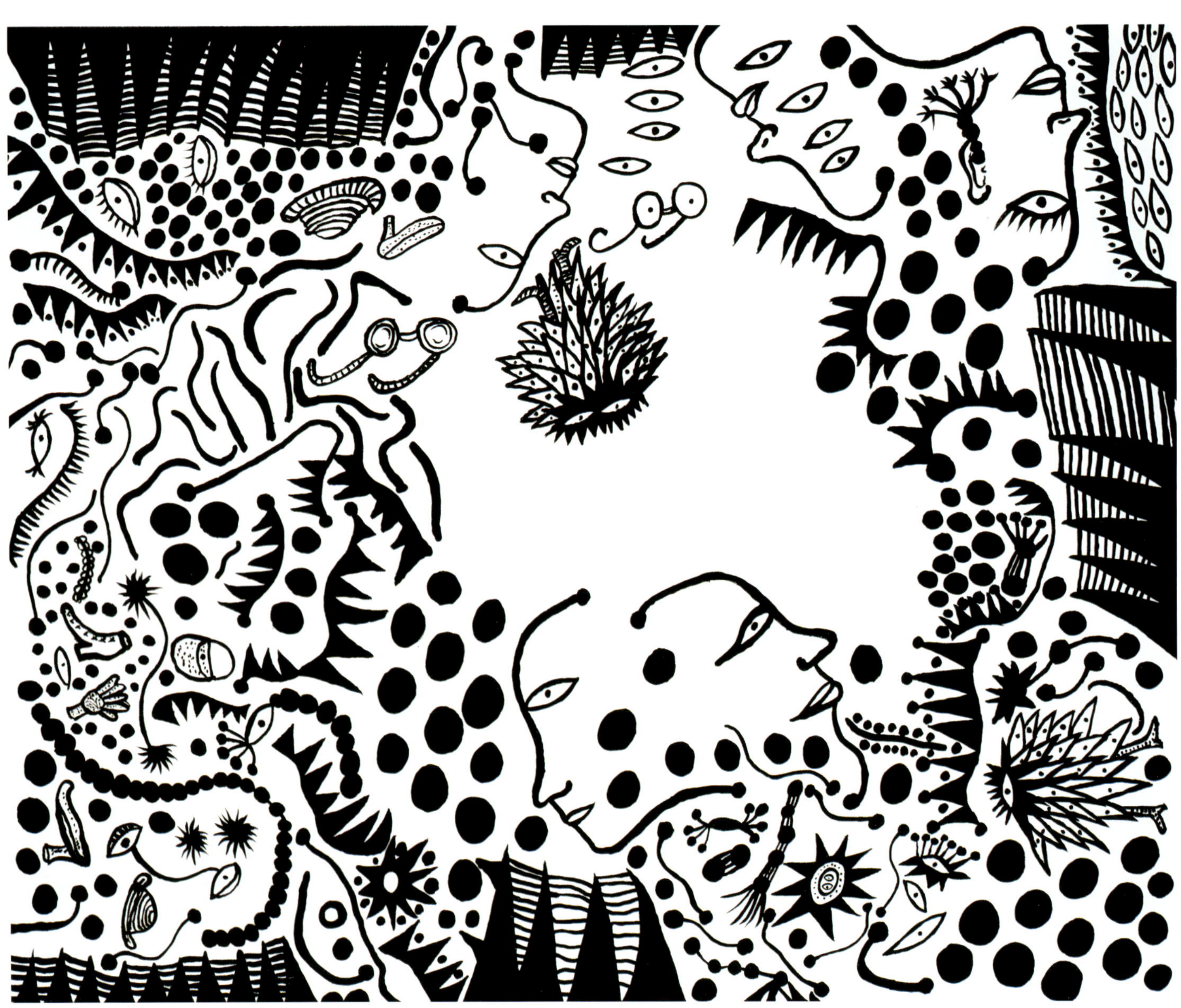

97 | **All About my Love, and I Long to Eat a Dream of the Night** 2009

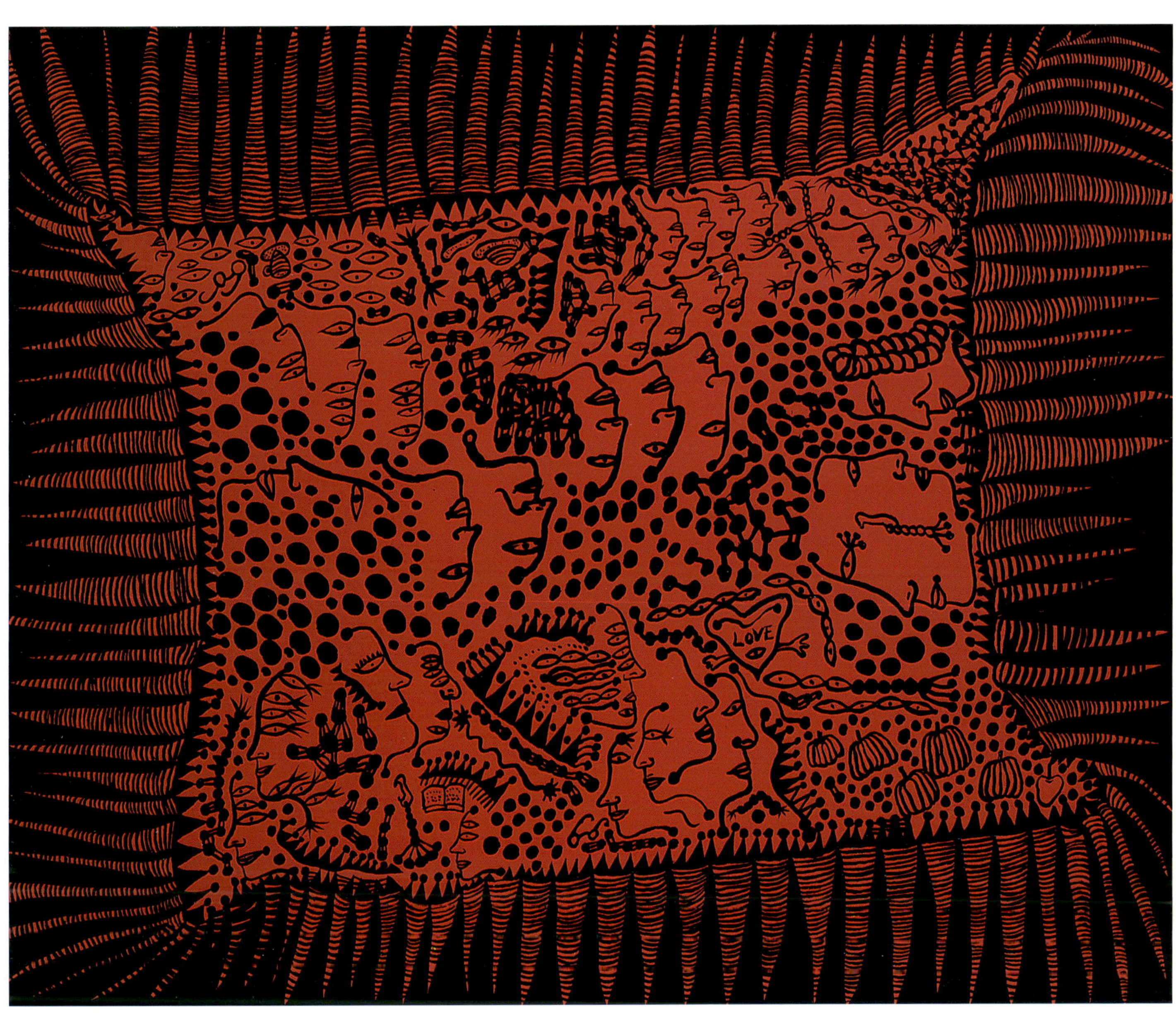

Look at the Gathering of Women in Search of Love 2009

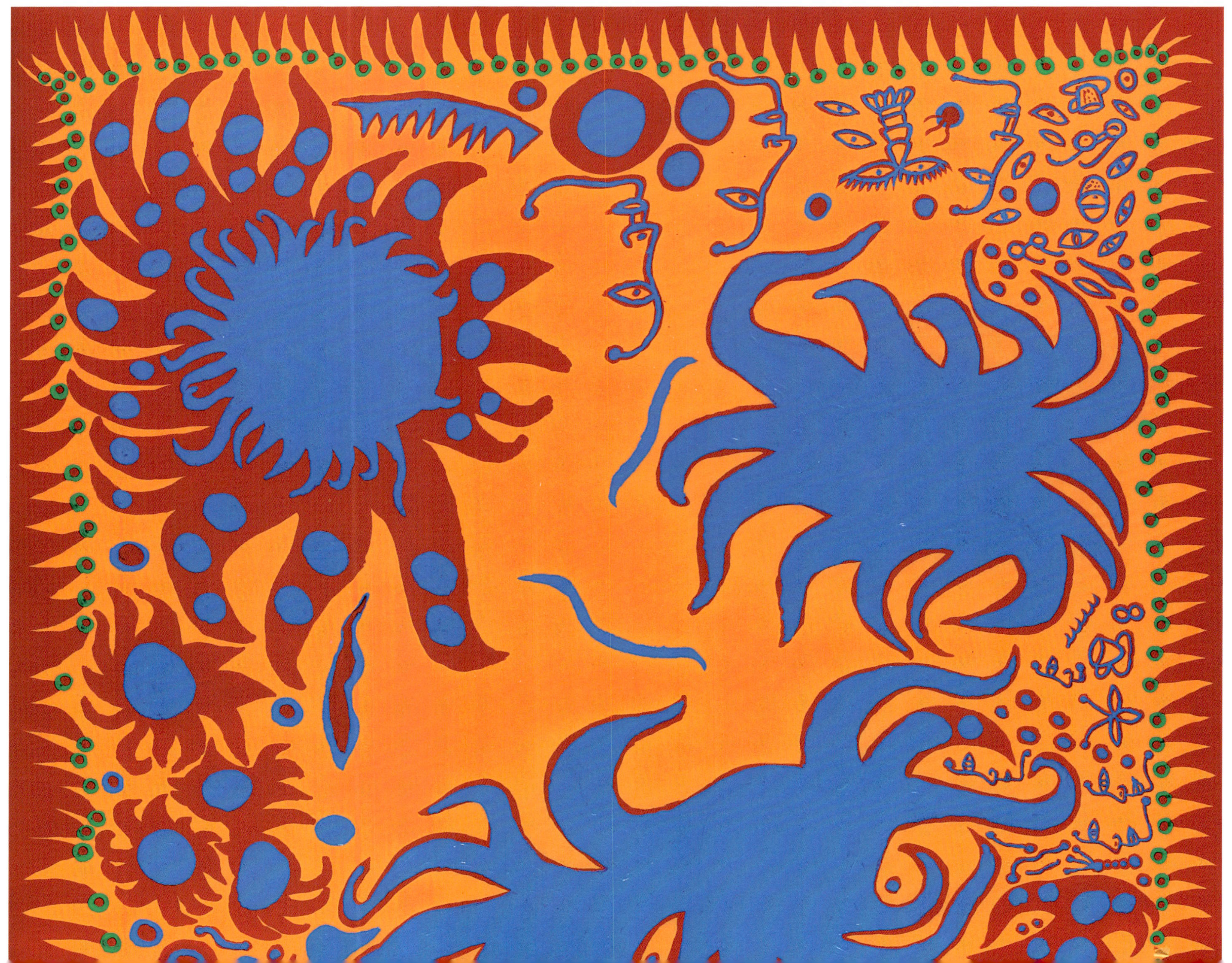

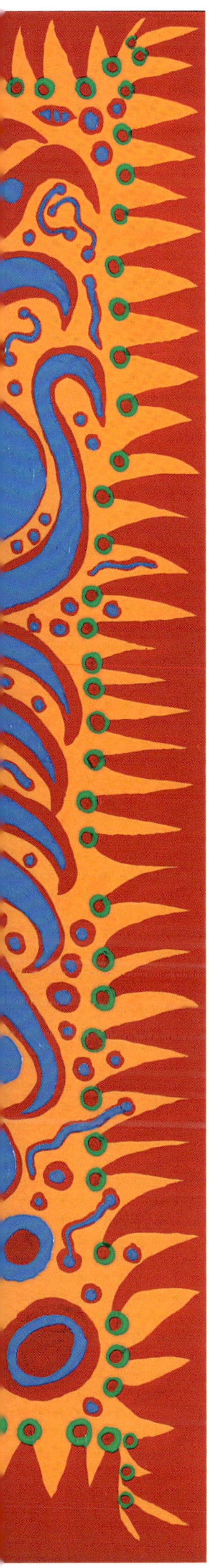

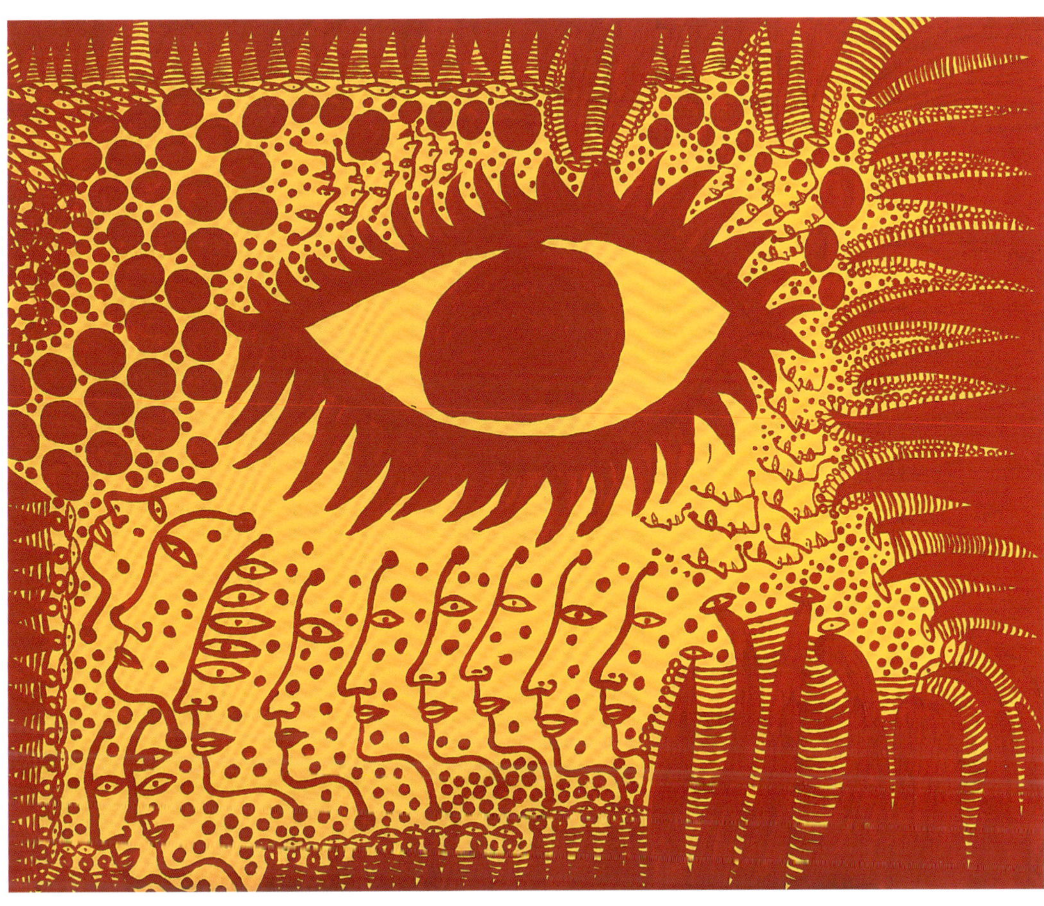

99 | **Joy I Feel when Love has Blossomed** 2009

100 | **I Want to Live Honestly, Like the Eye in the Picture** 2009

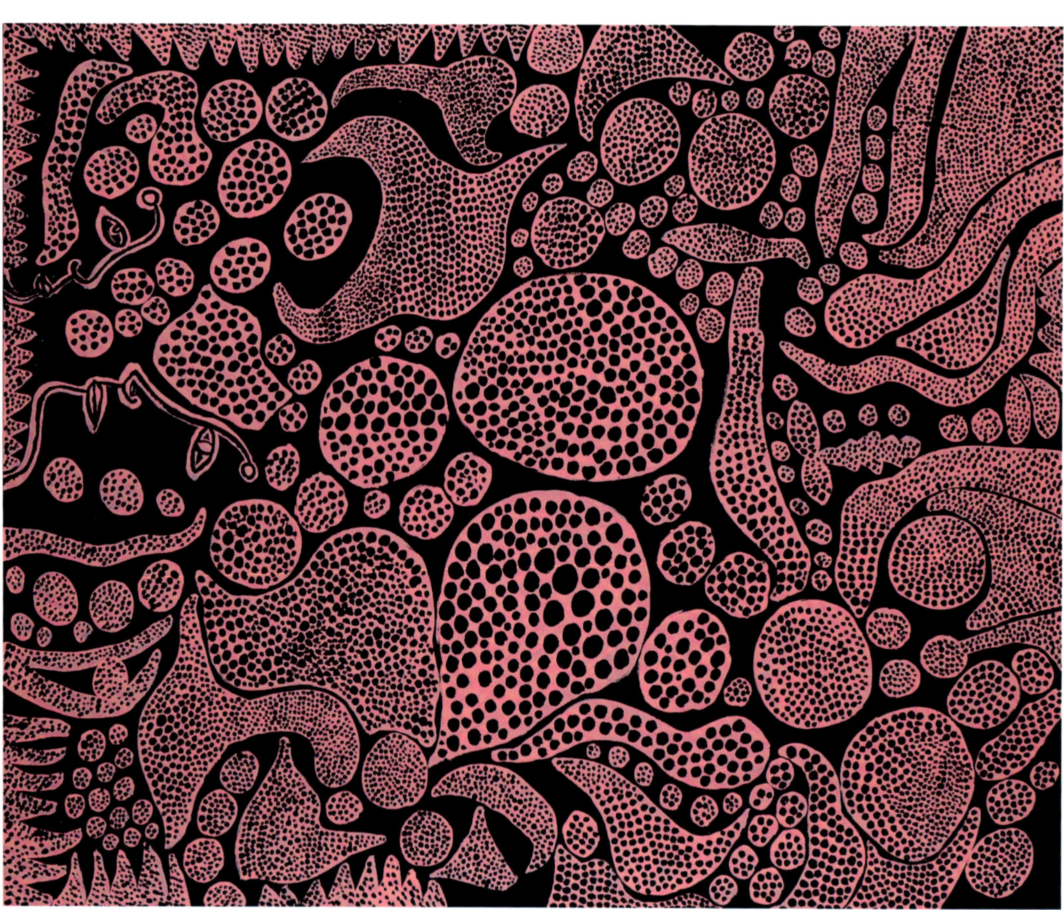

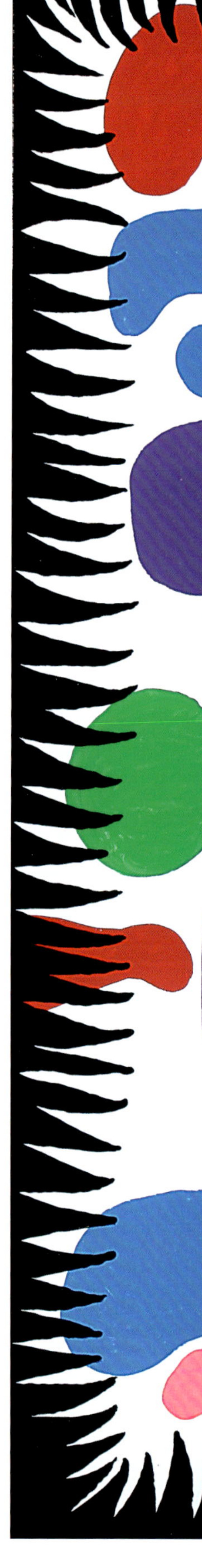

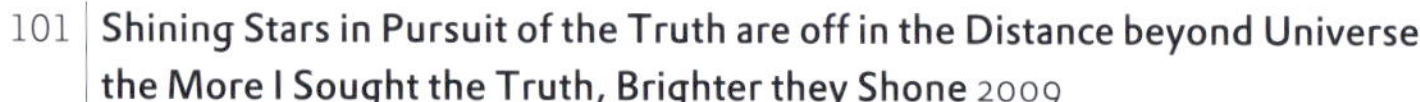

101 | **Shining Stars in Pursuit of the Truth are off in the Distance beyond Universe, the More I Sought the Truth, Brighter they Shone** 2009

102 | **Once the Abominable War is Over, Happiness Fills our Hearts** 2010

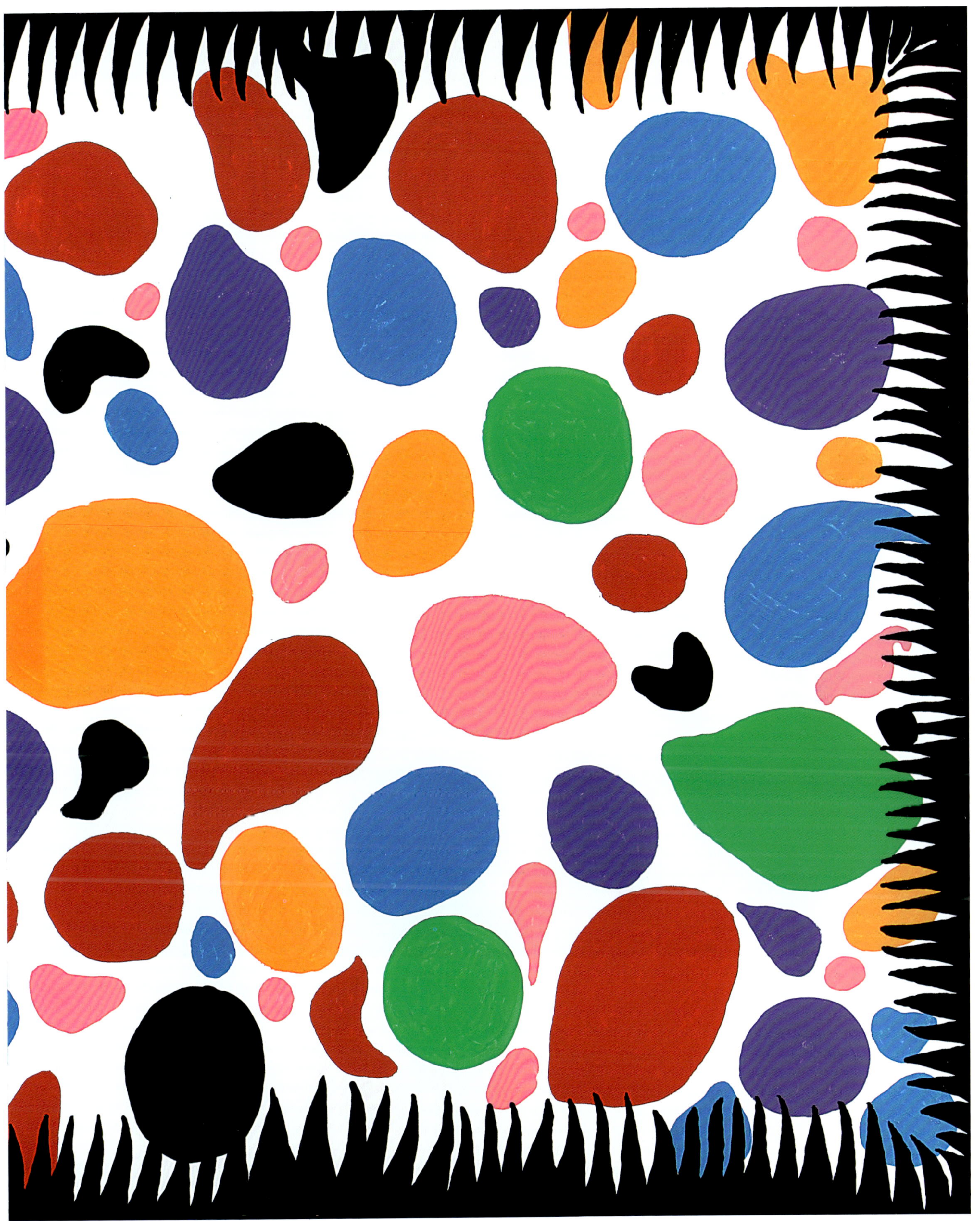

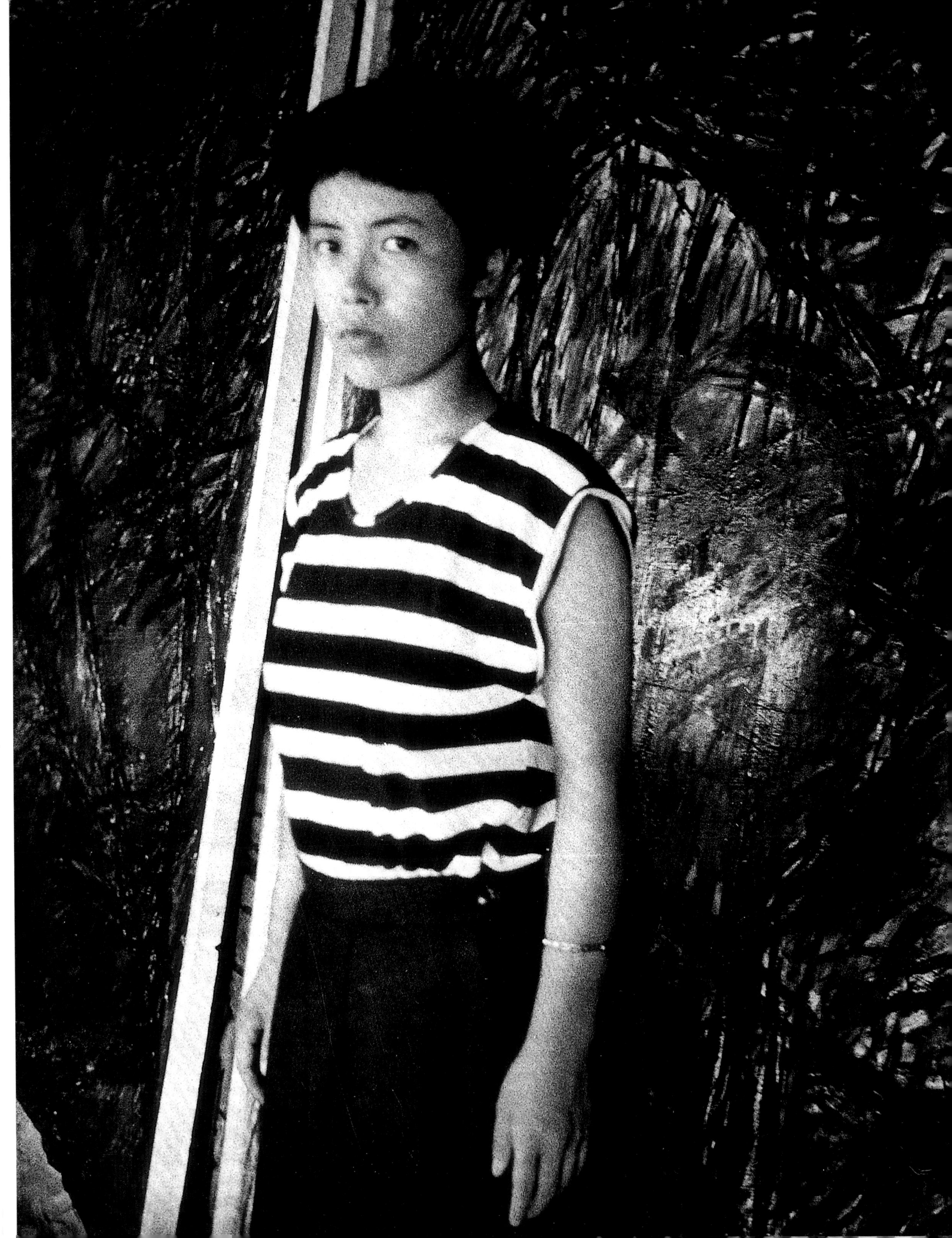

Kusama in her studio at her parents' home in Matsumoto, c.1950

Sometime between January and July of 1956, anticipating her departure for Seattle in 1957, Yayoi Kusama burnt most of her early works on the banks of the Susuki River that runs behind her family home, pledging to 'create better works when I got to New York'.[1] She remembers today that they were mostly *Nihonga* (a modern Japanese style of painting in water-soluble mineral pigment bound by deer-glue), the medium she had been acquainted with since January 1942, when her school replaced Matsumoto Noboru, an art teacher specialising in *yōga* (Western-style painting), with *Nihonga* painter Hibino Kakei (né Teruo).[2] Just a month after Japan's attack on Pearl Harbor of 7 December 1941, this personnel change reflected the state policy of deploying culture to create fanatic nationalism during its aggressive colonial campaign called the Greater East Asia Co-Prosperity Sphere. Born in 1929 in Matsumoto, a mountainous province in Nagano Prefecture, to an affluent family that owned a plant nursery, Kusama, then thirteen and aspiring to become an artist, had no other choice but to take private lessons from Hibino.

Burning her *Nihonga* works at the threshold of Kusama's career might have meant expunging dark memories of the war. She did save some works, however – a diverse array of things that included a wartime sketchbook, some *Nihonga*, and *kōsai* (a defiant genre in *Nihonga* that became prominent immediately after the war). Often marked as '*hibaihin*' or 'not for sale', they were kept by Kusama until 2004, when concerned curators finally convinced her to move them to fireproof storage at her hometown's Matsumoto City Museum of Art. She wanted to keep them close because they were the items most incised with memories of her growing up and maturing as an artist. In other words, they allowed her to remain in touch with her past.

These unsettled works can be seen as the material testimonies of Kusama's response to Japan's tumultuous entry into the war and the post-war period. This essay will focus mainly on the works she exempted from destruction. In particular, four items – a wartime sketchbook from 1945 (p.170), *Lingering Dream* 1949 (no.1), *On the Table* 1950 (no.4), and a mature work from this period, *A Gill* 1955 (no.27), that she included in her first American solo exhibition in Seattle – will be examined in relation to their socio-historical milieu, carefully reconstituted from various archival sources including chronicles, newspaper articles, newsreels and interviews, which will illuminate the genesis of her practice.

Midori Yamamura

Rising from Totalitarianism: Yayoi Kusama 1945–1955

A Sketchbook from 1945

The earliest work preserved in Kusama's Tokyo studio is a sketchbook that bears the English word 'NOTEBOOK' embossed with fancy gold letters on a plain black cover. The date in red letters on the first page reads 'Shōwa 20-nen 6-gatu' (June 1945), two months prior to the end of the Second World War. Kusama remembers how US bombers, finally reaching Japan's mainland in November 1944, 'flew in broad daylight' and 'I could barely feel my life'.[3] The living conditions were terrible, with magazine and newspaper articles listing 'edible' things that included insects and ground straw.[4] Alarmed and hungry, still, she was able to fill the seventy-six pages of her sketchbook with meticulously depicted peonies that bear no trace of haste or confusion.

In an oblique way, the plain-covered sketchbook encapsulates a wartime moment. This type of notebook with an English word on its cover was manufactured before the government's ban on English as a language of the enemy in January 1943, and was most likely kept out of commercial circulation.[5] In 1945, with only three years of professional training, Kusama was ineligible to receive government-rationed art supplies.[6] Yet, pressed by an urgent need to create art, she most likely acquired the notebook from some underground source. Since paper money had no value by that time, she must have traded clothes or foodstuffs – the necessities of life.[7]

Under the military regime, students were reduced to cogs in the machine of a militarised society. In the early days of Japan's entry into the war, Kusama was mobilised to work in the fields, planting crops.[8] After the revision of the Student Mobilisation Act in July 1944, she was sent to work at Kureha Bōseki (Kureha Textile), a factory that produced fabrics for military uniforms and parachutes.[9] Under this new labour law, students fifteen and older (Kusama was fifteen in 1944) toiled until midnight. In 1944 the average weight of a fifteen-year-old was 42.8 kilograms, down from 45.4 kilograms in 1942, and the situation worsened in the final year of the war.[10] The winter of 1944/5 was exceptionally cold. Malnutrition, the smoke from damp wood used for heating, and poor ventilation in factories affected the respiratory system of many workers.[11] Lacking nutritious food and breathing the polluted factory air made Kusama sick with pneumonia. The wartime sketchbook was among the works that she produced while recuperating at home.[12]

Kusama's wartime sketchbook is filled with various details of peonies. In Japan the peony is regarded as the most beautiful of all flowers. However, up until page twenty-two she kept drawing damaged fragments, including withered and deformed flowers with insect-eaten leaves, and darkened and shrivelled pistils. For example, the drawing on the right-hand page illustrated above bears a cluster of worm-eaten leaves. A broken tendril supported by thin unyielding skin conveys the plant's faint resistance against a greater natural force, as though reflecting Kusama's own will.

'I was born the year the stock market crashed': she clearly understood the historical circumstance surrounding her early years.[13] While Kusama was growing up, the global economic depression beset her remote province. Before the depression, Nagano was famous for its silk industry. Raw silk, during the First World War, ranked as Japan's foremost export item.[14] The sudden demise of the export silk market after the war hit local farmers hard. In 1930 Nagano's biggest local bank, Shinano Ginkō (Shinano

Top and middle:
Study of a Peony from a sketchbook, June 1945
15.1 × 21.5
Pencil on paper with a red seal with the artist's surname
Bottom:
Harvest 1945
Pigment on silk
58.5 × 72.5

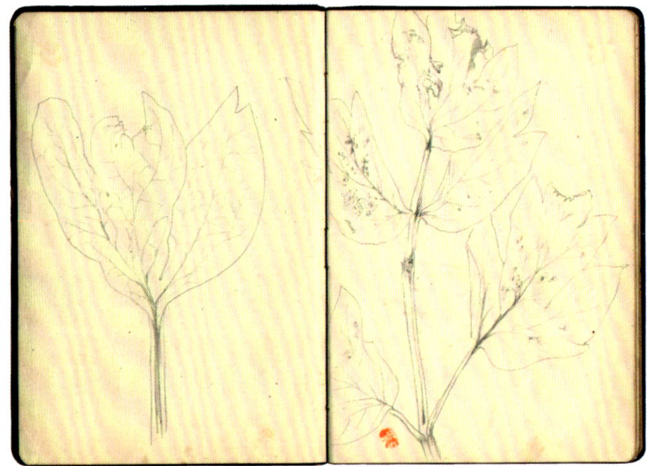

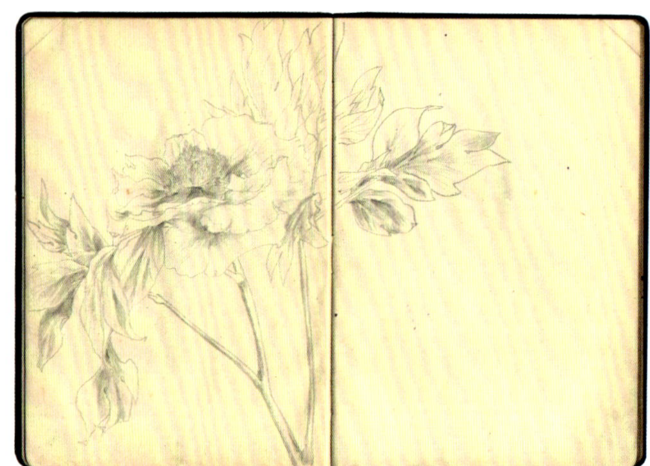

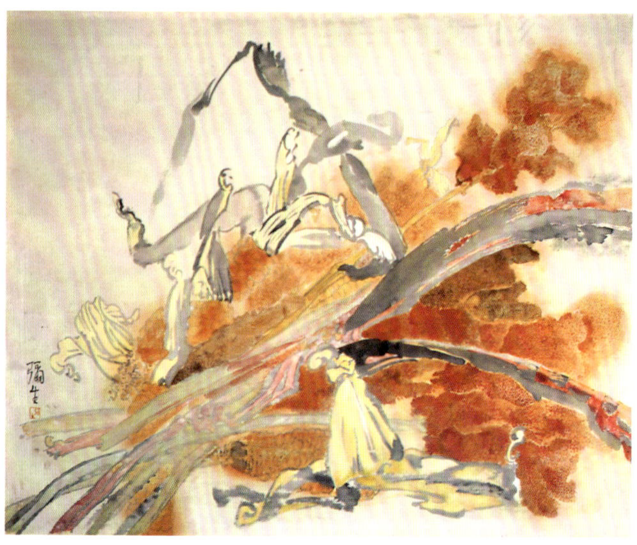

Bank), went bankrupt.[15] These events negatively affected the Kusamas' family business, forcing them to sell parts of their land.[16] Nationwide, the economic calamity led to a chain of political and social unrest. After the Manchurian Incident in 1931, the Japanese finance minister approved major deficit spending in the continent to stimulate the stagnant economy, signalling the onset of the Greater East Asia Co-Prosperity Sphere. Soon after, the government resolved the grave state of unemployment at home by relocating 50,000 Japanese to Manchuria. With its silk industry decimated, Nagano ranked as the nation's top labour exporter, totalling 30,900 people.[17] At the same time, the state authorities tightened the control of information and solidified its hold over cultural representation.

In 1939, under the auspices of the Army Information Section, the Army Art Association was established.[18] In July 1941, anticipating war with the United States, the government consolidated various art magazines into *Shin Bijutsu* (*New Art*), which in October 1943 was divided into *Bijutsu* (*Art*) and *Seisaku* (*Art-Making*). These magazines featured mainly *Nihonga* and the classical arts of Japan's allies, Germany and Italy. The history of *Nihonga* as 'modern Japanese-style painting' dates back to a decade after the Meiji Restoration in 1868.[19] Since its inception, *Nihonga* was deeply intertwined with Japan's self-conscious projection as a modern nation-state modelled after the nineteenth-century European concept of 'culture-based, language-based ethnic collectives'.[20] During Japan's colonial expansion, the role of culture to spur patriotism at home and impart coherent identity in its colonies gained renewed importance. As part of this grand campaign, Hibino Kakei was hired to teach *Nihonga* at Kusama's school, which became a significant influence on her artistry.

Her peony drawings, which often bear notations of the colours and qualities of the plants, are the earliest stage in Kusama's making *Nihonga* works.[21] Notwithstanding its vehement nationalism, what attracted Kusama to this would-be chauvinistic practice was its main principle, *jiko hattatsu*. The Japanese word *jiko* means 'self', and *hattatsu*, 'development'. According to the art historian Kawakita Michiaki, what *Nihonga* truly encouraged at its inception during the Meiji Period (1868–1912) was the creation of a distinctively individual expression by drawing on various Eastern and Western cultures to make Japanese art internationally competitive.[22] For Kusama, the concept of self-development had a twofold significance: first, it presented a mandate to invent her own original form of expression; and second, it necessitated cultivating a unique personality through engaging in art.

Kusama's cultivation of *Nihonga* gained greater importance when propaganda in various material forms permeated the national mindset, whereby the state glossed over daily realities. During the war, all journalistic articles underwent pre-publication censorship under the policy of *genron tōsei* (speech control). Newsreels were made up of bloodless fake battles that always ended in victory for the imperial army.[23] By 1941, 6.6 million radio receivers brought jingoistic news and entertainment to more than 45 per cent of all households.[24] In time, individuals were deprived of all freedom and woven into a system. Given the government's slogan, 'Luxury is the enemy', art that did not assist in the national war effort – that is, if it did not graphically depict battle scenes or broadcast the state propaganda – was deemed superfluous, thus anti-patriotic. Still, Kusama captured breathtakingly beautiful peony blossoms in her sketchbook (p.170). For her, embracing pure beauty during this tumultuous time was, in a sense, a political act of resistance to the irresistible powers of the military government.

Kusama later recounted: 'Imperialism and militarism melded together deprived individuals of their ability to develop free thinking.'[25] And she remembered trying to confirm the actual existence of things by counting endless pebbles on the riverbank behind her family house.[26] Similarly, she engaged in rendering a microcosmic view of plant life – from growth to decay to regeneration in the full life cycle of a peony. Kusama's painstaking efforts to develop craftsmanship, polish her skills and cultivate her aesthetic insights became a means of proving her own existence and becoming her own person. She remembers today that her 'worldview was entirely formulated by engaging myself in painting'.[27]

Due to the lack of resources, it is highly unlikely that Kusama completed any *Nihonga* during the war. After the war, however, she wasted no time in building a career as a professional artist. Already in November 1945, three months after the war's end, she submitted a work entitled *Harvest* (p.170) to the *Zen-Shinshū Regional Art Exhibition*, and was accepted; this is another work she still cherishes. It was during these 'dark, dead-end' days of the war that, disgusted by the rampant chauvinism, Kusama also began to think of going overseas, so that she could 'communicate with a wider audience, especially people abroad, through my art'.[28]

Lingering Dream

Lingering Dream from 1949 (no.1) is among a few *Nihonga* works that Kusama chose not to destroy. Previously regarded as her earliest and 'closest approach to Surrealis[m]',[29] this work manifests more of her conscious decisions and sure hand than her involvement with the unconscious. In stark contrast to *Harvest*, this painting is intended objectively to convey Kusama's inner feelings with coded structures of colour, line and subject matter, reflecting her peculiar interest in Symbolism during this time. The work's principal subject, the sunflower, already evokes the symbolism of Vincent van Gogh's own sunflower paintings. In the immediate post-war years influential art critics such as Uemura Takachiyo, writing in popular Japanese art magazines like *Mizue* and *Atelier*, enthusiastically encouraged artists to create 'alphabets for a plastic language' with colours and forms that would correspond to certain human senses, like the 'constants of visual art'.[30]

In *Lingering Dream* Kusama deftly employs the dark crimson tone laid in the foreground to suppress the entangled withered sunflowers, which conjure up the grim realities of the war. The unified tone in the foreground establishes a visual shield, guiding the viewers' attention to a faint light over the horizon, alluding to an uncharted world beyond.[31] Two opposing colours are juxtaposed in the form of three emerald butterflies against crimson foliage, scientifically engendering, according to European colour theory, a glowing effect that conveyed her buoyant feelings.

In this painting Kusama also modernised the traditional Japanese spatial conception of *yohaku* (blank space), which she employed in her earlier work *Harvest*. In the Japanese painterly tradition, *yohaku* is of paramount importance as an expressive element that speaks of the artist's spiritual attainment: traditional Japanese painters would be evaluated on their achievement of an exquisite balance between the subject and the blank space. *Yohaku* is a charged space where the artist's energy cannot be seen, but only felt. In *Lingering Dream* Kusama replaced the blank space with a descriptive blue sky, which does not belong to the tradition of Japanese painting. Still, she kept the charged space by rendering minutely detailed foliage.

The current *Lingering Dream* evolved from an early state, a photograph of which reveals far more detail in the work's upper-left side cluster of leaves (see below). During the immediate post-war years, Kusama is said to have admired the works of the *Nihonga* artists Hayami Gyoshū (1894–1935) and Murakami Kagaku (1888–1939).[32] Both were known for their fierce originality and salient modern sensibility. Her minute observation of the leaf veins in *Lingering Dream* bears an affinity to Hayami's exhaustive examination of reality, which can be seen in the leaves of his *Sunflowers* (p.173).

Kawakita Michiaki explains that early in his career Hayami attempted to manifest 'mystical feelings informed by religious ideas' in his paintings. However, being a product of modernity, Hayami felt that just illustrating religious subjects was too vague a pursuit. Only when he engaged in tireless scrutiny of an object could he open up an 'earnest spiritual world' in his work.[33] His yearning to attain the spiritual through his tireless scrutiny of the real can best be understood in the context of Zen Buddhism, which had a major impact on traditional Japanese painting.

In Zen, the duality of body and mind – as constructed in Western culture – does not exist. The goal for Zen practitioners is to cultivate a path to *satori* (enlightenment) through engaging in *dō* (the way), which consists of ascetic daily practices characterised by the idea of *munen musō* (no thought, no image). In Zen-based aesthetic, 'skill' is not simply technique or artistry but is equivalent to a spiritual phenomenon deployed to achieve enlightenment; thus the skill for making art can be acquired only through positioning one's self in this state of *dō*.[34] To make his art, Hayami usually rented a room in a Zen temple and lived like a monk during the period when he was painting. He would begin his day at four o'clock by cleaning his studio, attending the sitting (meditation session) and eating plain temple vegetarian food. After breakfast he would concentrate on painting until sunset.[35] In her one year in art school, Kusama would also meditate before she began working on her paintings, as a process of achieving *munen musō*.[36]

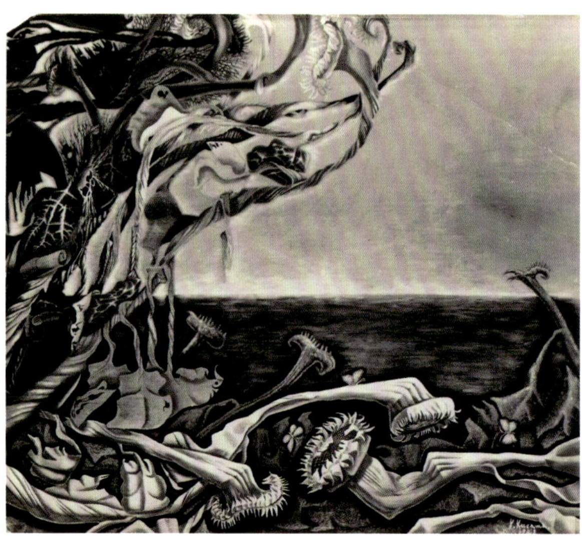

In *Lingering Dream* Kusama practised extraordinary concentration. This is obvious in her intricate depiction of sunflower veins using *Nihonga* pigments. These pigments, ground from natural stones, tend to be heavy and hard to manipulate; they are not a medium suitable for rendering fine details. The detailed foliage in *Lingering Dream* thus suggests a self-imposed challenge to attain great physical and psychic patience through self-discipline, in order to achieve spiritual enlightenment. What can be called her 'ascetic realism' allowed Kusama to establish a charged space where her creative energy can be felt.

Lingering Dream was painted after Kusama's year studying in Kyoto, where she attended a preparatory school for Kyoto Shiritsu Bijutsu Senmon Gakkō (Kyoto City University of Arts).[37] When she arrived in Kyoto in 1948 (most likely in March), *Nihonga* was undergoing a serious crisis, as it had been inextricably compromised by its association with wartime nationalism and conservatism. Striving to revitalise it, young painters in Tokyo and Kyoto courageously left the *Nitten* (the semi-governmental salon) and formed a new organisation, Sōzō Bijutsu (Creative Arts), in January 1948.[38] Kusama's *Lingering Dream* eventually found its way into the second Sōzō Bijutsu exhibition held between September and November 1949. In May 1948, Panreal, another radical *Nihonga* group based in Kyoto, organised their first exhibition at the local Maruzen Gallery, proclaiming that art should profoundly relate to 'the creation and development of social reality'.[39]

On the Table

After one submission to Sōzō Bijutsu, Kusama decided not to associate herself with any 'group or party', and went on her solitary path.[40] On 18 and 19 March 1952 she held her first solo exhibition at The First Community Centre in Matsumoto. The show's invitation card listed a unique genre called *kōsai*.[41] The Chinese character *kō* means *nikawa* in Japanese, signifying the animal-glue used as a binder for *Nihonga*, while *sai* means 'to paint'. Together, *kōsai* is literally 'animal-glue painting'. In post-war Japan, *kōsai* also denoted artists' political response to *Nihonga*'s conservatism. This was articulated in the 'Panreal Manifesto' that said artists must expand and substantiate the possibilities in *kōsai geijutsu* (art using a binder for *Nihonga*). The 'Panreal Manifesto' encouraged 'exhaustive exploration of reality in art, in its *motif* and *matière* (facture)', beyond conventional limits.[42] Among Kusama's extant works, *On the Table* (no.4) from 1950 fits this agenda.

If the Hanoverian Dadaist Kurt Schwitters defied traditional high art in his collages by incorporating urban refuse that reflected post-First World War reality, some *Nihonga* practitioners upheld *kōsai* partly as their response to the severe lack of resources after the Second World War. For instance, Panreal artists sometimes substituted ceramic clay for certain pigments used in *Nihonga*, such as *ōdo* (yellow ochre) or *gofun* (white).[43] Similarly, in her recollection of the early 1950s, Kusama characterised *nikawa* as the least expensive material in *Nihonga*, although it did become 'expensive for me', and she 'bought inexpensive house paints, mixed them with sand'.[44]

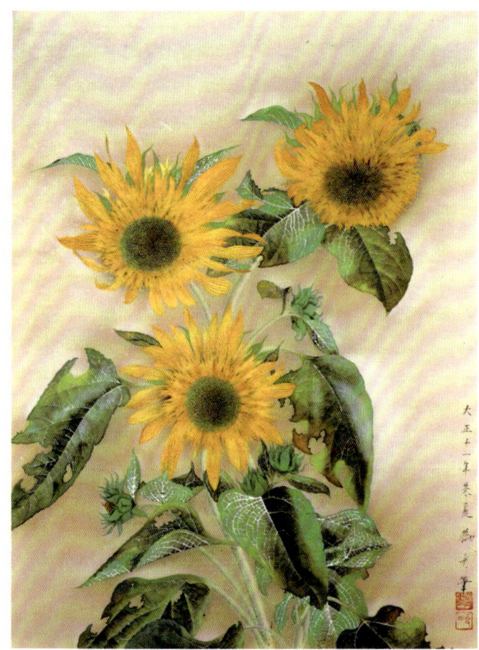

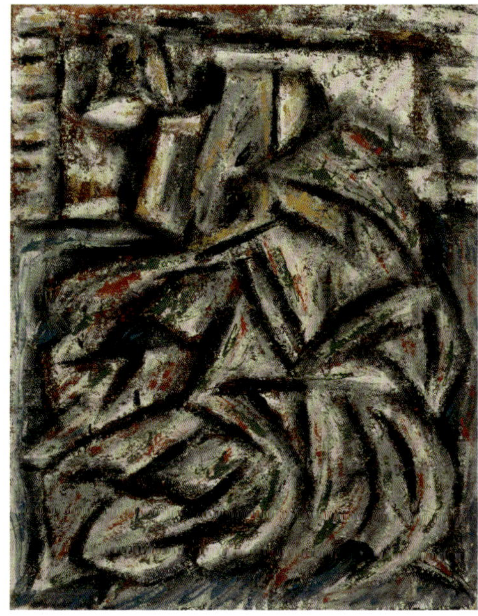

Opposite: Detail of postcard for *Second Sōzō Bijutsu (Creative Arts) Exhibition* 1949, with black and white reproduction of *Lingering Dream* 1949
Top: Hayami Gyōshū
Sunflowers 1922
Pigment on silk
64.5 × 49.7
Reiyu-kai – Myoichi Memorial Museum
Above: *On the Table* 1950
Oil, etc. on seed sack
80.4 × 65.5

A careful scrutiny of *On the Table* reveals Kusama's unique post-war reality. The work was painted on a seed sack she scavenged from her family's plant nursery and stretched over a plywood panel, another *objet trouvé* from the family's house reconstruction. By mixing sand from the riverbank behind her home with *nikawa*, she skilfully built a surface with rough, convex, grey achromatic impastos, mimicking the facture of oil painting. Over this heavily built surface, she applied white (most likely house paint) and colours (most likely oils). All taken together, the work's coarse surface and assemblage of found objects totally debased *Nihonga*'s purported elegance. *On the Table* clearly embodied Kusama's revolt against the conservative hereditary artistic system.

The subject matter of *On the Table*, a cubist-inspired fragmented flower bouquet, points to her active effort to further innovate *Nihonga*. The bold abstraction interfered with the intense concentration she initially poured into the work's details, however. By her second solo show held again at The First Community Centre between 31 October and 2 November 1952, Kusama had found watercolour a more suitable material and discontinued using *Nihonga* media.[45] Unlike *kōsai* that mandates an elaborate preparatory process, and oil, which requires a protracted period of time to dry and must be done in stages, watercolour lends itself more readily to spontaneity. One newspaper article reported that Kusama obsessively produced an average of fifty to seventy watercolours a day, and even over one hundred on some days.[46] In little over six months, the artist produced 270 works she deemed presentable in her second exhibition.[47] Among them, 106 were recorded in five photographs that documented the exhibition. They were bold line drawings that often bore repetitive 'dots' and some elements of 'nets', which would later become her signature pictorial components.

Most importantly, the second solo exhibition sparked Kusama's lifelong interest in psychology. Nishimaru Shihō, a psychology professor at the local Shinshū University, happened to visit the exhibition. He specialised in analysing the brains of geniuses and in detailing artists' pathographies as a way of studying their works.[48] On first seeing her work, Nishimaru determined that Kusama suffered from cenesthopathy; that is, though there was physically nothing wrong with her, she nonetheless experienced strange bodily sensations. In interviews, Kusama often mentions suffering from heart palpitations.[49] This condition was an outcome of taxing herself beyond her limits when she painted, which quickened her heart rate and, in turn, gave rise to these sensations. Immediately after their encounter, Kusama became the focus of Nishimaru's research. A month later, on 13 December 1952, he presented a scientific analysis on her art at the annual conference of the Kantō Psychiatric and Neurotic Association, held at the University of Tokyo.[50]

Kusama's interest in psychology at the time also suggests her attentiveness to surrealism, which is apparent in her close relationship with the Japanese surrealist poet and critic, Takiguchi Shūzō. The Spanish surrealist Joan Miró's various signs allegedly drawn from his unconscious also evoke Kusama's bold, line-based watercolours from this time. After the war, Miró's work first appeared in the August 1949 issue of *Atelier* magazine accompanied by Takiguchi's introduction. Takiguchi also contributed the preface for Kusama's second solo exhibition brochure. Immediately after, Kusama went to Tokyo and for the first time met Takiguchi in person.[51] The meeting propelled her to experiment with decalcomania, with early examples using this technique as part of her painting dating from 1954 (see no.41).[52] Takiguchi, who befriended André Breton, Salvador Dalí, Miró and Marcel Duchamp, avidly collected art books. Through him, Kusama became familiar with various surrealist concerns, such as the art of the insane and the art of the primitive. In fact, in the 1950s, she gifted Takiguchi with a glass painting, executed in a technique conventionally used in folk or naïve art. In her seminal article 'Ivan the Fool' from 1955, she wrote that she wanted her art to manifest the things that existed 'deep in the bottom of life' such as 'the tempests, buds, wounds, and genitalia that provoked my anxiety', and the 'hidden shadowy part of life on earth'.[53] Surrealism provided fertile ground for Kusama to explore the depths of the human psyche as a way to critique polite society.

A Gill

One work from the 1950s that Kusama particularly cared for is *A Gill*, from 1955 (no.27). After the destruction of her early oeuvre in 1956, Kusama went all the way from Matsumoto to Tokyo and borrowed two mixed-media works for her Seattle exhibition that she had previously given Takiguchi. They were *A Gill* and *Tempted Sun*. She eventually included only the former in the exhibition. For her, *A Gill* was a proud achievement of the 1950s that she wanted to present at her first solo exhibition in the United States.[54] The 'gill' of the work's title refers to the respiratory organ in aqueous animals. Without gills, fish cannot survive, which suggests Kusama's inseparable relationship with art during this time.

An awesome vista that again incorporates the mystical and the scientific, *A Gill* reveals the effects of chance. Using the technique of decalcomania, Kusama applied light blue gouache over a jet-black foundation built with *sumi*-ink. Over the central structure, she painted a world of minutiae, selecting certain colours to impart meanings related to the earth's basic elements. The blue in the central structure connotes an aqueous environment. The band of red oil paint that appears on the right-hand side evokes fire. A seepage of thin yellow paint applied over the decalcomania represents light and heat, whereas a spread of purple below symbolises shadow and cold temperature. A black lightning bolt in the yellow seepage refers to the discharge of electricity that accumulated in the mist generated by the transformation of water evaporation induced by temperature changes. The energy from the lightning gives life to countless red molecular figures.

From their varying sizes and movements, as animated in the painting, the tiny figures emerge first in the air in the painting's upper right-hand side with an explosive power, then spread around, and ultimately settle down on the bottom of the aquatic structure, colonising the ground. Some figures in the foreground are shooting white root-like projections downward, so they suggest a primeval state of life akin to plants or bacteria. Some of them are maturing in the air. The primordial universe of *A Gill* indicates Kusama's continuing interest in the life cycle and its mystery. Concomitantly, the work's fairly large format (61 × 72.5 cm) and assorted media point to her new interest in the Pacific Northwest School in Seattle, represented by Guy Anderson, Kenneth Callahan, Morris Graves and Mark Tobey, although their relationship to Kusama's work is one of resonance more than influence.

Kusama learned about their work through the US Information Service (USIS), which by the end of the Occupation era (1945–52) had opened twenty-three American Cultural Centers in key Japanese cities to actively facilitate cultural exchange between Japan and the United States. The American government's efforts resulted in a gradual shift of Japan's cultural orientation from Paris to the United States.[55] Among other things, they made US publications accessible to the Japanese public in the early 1950s when Japanese art magazines were still reluctant to promote American art. In the autumn of 1955, while visiting the 'exhibition of American Arts Books' at the USIS, Kusama requested Georgia O'Keeffe's contact information and immediately wrote a letter to her, explaining how she got the American artist's address.[56] She also obtained Callahan's address and wrote a letter to him as well. In doing so, she asked the two artists to explore the feasibilities of mounting her exhibitions in the United States, sending examples of her latest works to them by separate cover.[57]

O'Keeffe forwarded some of Kusama's works to New York dealer

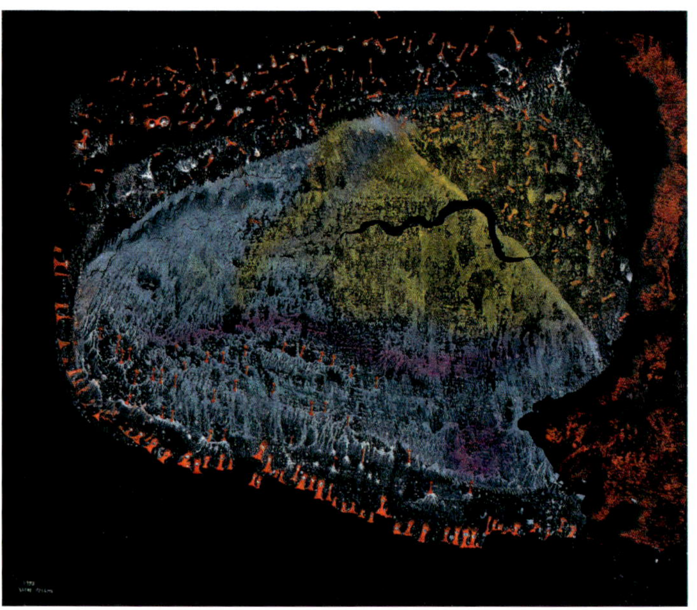

A Gill 1955
Gouache, India ink and oil on paper
61 × 72.5
Private collection

Betty Parsons, but Parsons declined them. Kusama's mixed media works significantly differed from the large oil paintings that graced the dealer's walls. For his part, Callahan brought the paintings to Zoe Dusanne, Seattle's first dealer to have specialised in modern art.[58] Dusanne's stable encompassed such notable Pacific Northwest figures as Anderson, Callahan, Graves and Tobey. She was familiar with the kind of sensibility present in Kusama's work – small, intricate, water-based mixed media. Known for her 'courageous eye', Dusanne promptly offered Kusama her first US solo exhibition.[59] The result was hardly surprising. The artist was certainly aware of the September 1953 article in *Life*, 'Mystic Painters of the Northwest', that featured a picture of Callahan's studio. In January 1956, Kusama wrote to Callahan's student Neil Meitzler: 'I found in "Life" [magazine], Mr. Callahan's work and himself in his studio.'[60] A persistent student, she sometimes hired translators to enable her to read the English books and articles, and became sympathetic to the Pacific Northwest artists' international approach, their political concerns and focus on the individual's interiority.[61]

The Seattle School was hardly a homogenous entity.[62] However, the lives of Anderson, Callahan, Graves and Tobey intersected from the late 1930s through the early 1940s when they acted upon their shared opposition to the Second World War and their serious concerns for humanity. Furthermore, due to the considerable presence of Asian and Native American populations, Seattle had a long history of communication with different cultures. Not only had Graves and Tobey travelled in Asia extensively, all four artists also appreciated the philosophical connections between Buddhism, Hinduism and Bahá'í.[63] Because of her *Nihonga* background, Kusama was also interested in the philosophical depths of ancient world cultures, which resulted in her intellectual dialogue with these artists.[64] In her 20 March 1956 letter to Meitzler she enthusiastically reported: 'I was interested [in] your *dessin* and the story of [American] Indian Dance which you saw in Seattle. Last year I saw also the Indian Dance in Tokyo.'[65] Her aspiration towards internationalism can also be related to her rejection of Japan's wartime xenophobia.

The Seattle group's attempts to convey the vastness of the universe through the smallest detail of nature, by perceiving 'an interconnectedness between humans and nature and microcosmic and macrocosmic aspects of the universe',[66] resonated with Kusama's art beginning with her wartime drawings of peonies. Her expanded use of materials, such as pastel, watercolour and oil from this period, parallelled Tobey's relatively small paintings rendered in tempera, pastel and watercolour on paper. Kusama herself explained in 1957 that it was through these artists 'dealing with mysticism born out of mechanical civilization' that 'I have been interested in Seattle'.[67]

The mysticism she mentioned here can be found in Tobey's Bahá'í faith, especially in his participation in an ascetic nineteen-day fast, or Graves's and Anderson's inspiration drawn from Swinomish tribal dancers' trance-like states during the course of their ceremonies. Similarly, in *A Gill*, Kusama pushed herself to an extreme degree of concentration on tiny details. By obsessively adding countless orange alien-looking organisms, each less than three millimetres long, she hoped to dislodge all control by reason. Her ambition can be further understood in the following statement in 'Ivan the Fool':

> The Devil is at once an enemy of art and an ally of art. It resides only in freedom. No sooner had something been established, he would leave it … Such devilish power is the power that provokes the earnest desire for spiritual freedom in eternity. A rising of that which is inexplicable allows people to see the world of yonder, wherein our spirit will be inspired to free itself. [68]

The Devil, according to her, is 'Mephistopheles', an epic hero prepared to destroy myths, traditional values and customary ways of life in order to build a brave new world.[69] As demonstrated by the excessive information control by the Japanese and US governments, that new world contained the dangerous possibility that individuals could be integrated into a world of totally administered thought and behaviour. Considering social conformity as modernity's paramount dilemma, Kusama advocated a sublime spiritual achievement that contained the potential for human liberation. Her focus on the irrational and mystical in art is reminiscent of how Walter Benjamin, an important theorist of modernity, ambivalently valued the writings of Franz Kafka, as works whose foci were determined by 'mystical experience (in particular, the experience of tradition) and … by the experience of the modern big-city dweller'.[70]

In works like *A Gill* Kusama endeavoured to embrace two irreconcilable ideas – modern rationalism and the mystical asceticism that she carried over from the idea of self-development in *Nihonga*. The critic Fukushima Tatsuo observed in 1955 that the most prominent feature of Kusama's 'metaphysical mysterious work is that she stands on rationalist grounds, yet shows a strong resistance to anti-humanism'.[71] It was her resistance to anti-humanism that would soon lead Kusama to her Infinity Net paintings in New York. Full of aspirations for the future, Kusama left Japan for Seattle on 18 November 1957.[72]

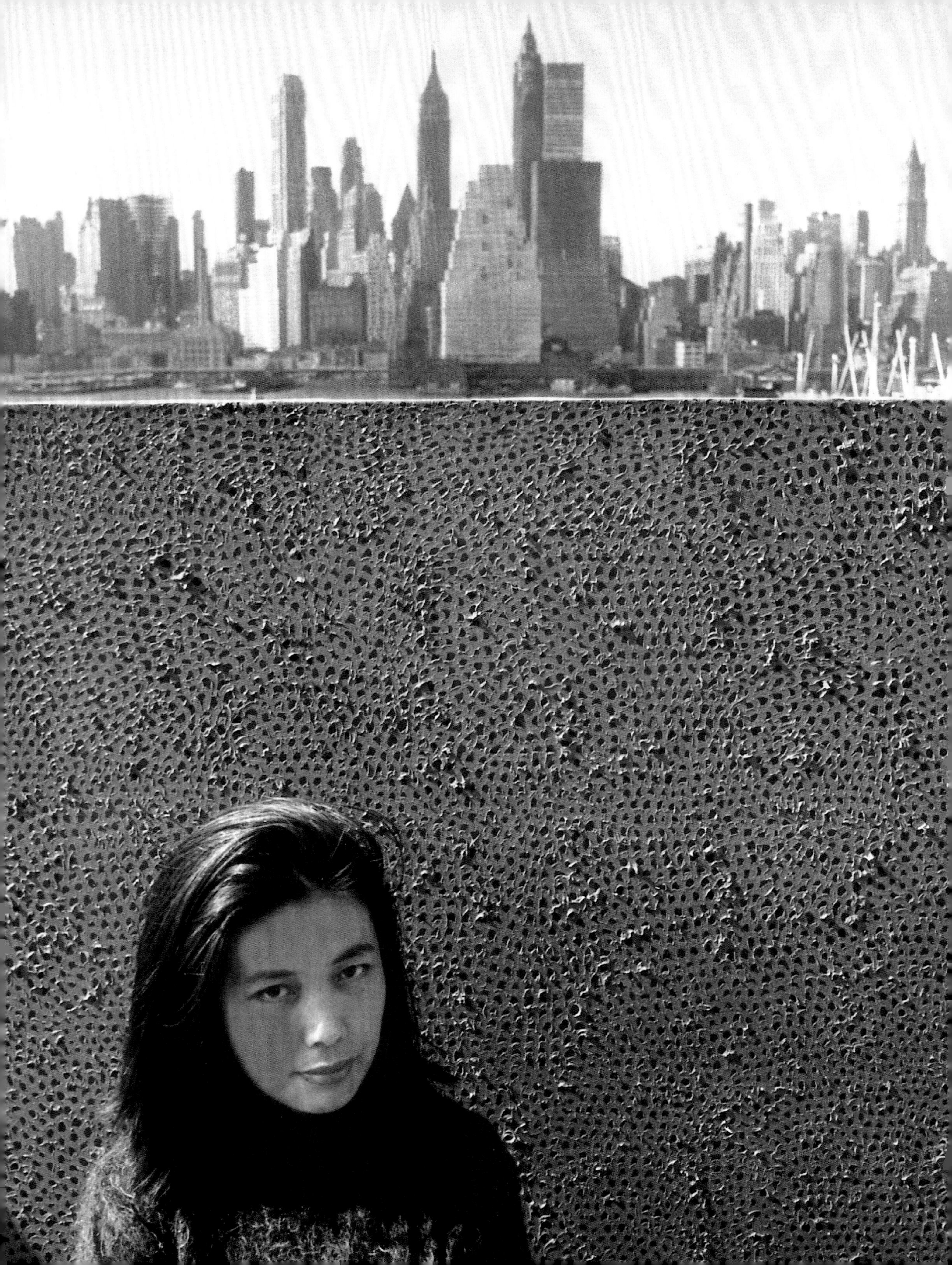

Kusama posing in front of an Infinity Net painting with the Manhattan skyline in the background, c.1961

Mignon Nixon

Infinity Politics

'Staying in Japan was out of the question. My parents, the house, the land, the shackles, the conventions, the prejudice ... For art like mine – art that does battle at the boundary between life and death, questioning what we are and what it means to live and die – this country was too small, too servile, too feudalistic, and too scornful of women. My art needed a more unlimited freedom, and a wider world.'[1]

In November 1957 Yayoi Kusama arrived in Seattle on a flight from Tokyo with a large sum in US dollars sewn into her dress and stuffed into the toes of her shoes, a letter from Georgia O'Keeffe tucked into her pocket, and a bundle of drawings crammed into her suitcase.[2]

Like many another artist émigré, Kusama had a plan, and it began, as such schemes often do, with what she was able to carry on her back, and sell: a cache of small works on paper, luminous drawings in gouache, ink and pastel.[3] A film of Kusama's New York years might find her peeling the sheets leaf by leaf from the luggage that accompanied her from Tokyo to Seattle to New York, offering them as calling cards and as barter. Early scenes might feature marathon sessions of solitary work as she painted her vast Infinity Nets, and nocturnal raids when she liberated discarded items from the street, and sat for hours with her neighbour Donald Judd stitching and stuffing cotton sacks to fashion the stiff phallic protuberances she would use to cover her Accumulation sculptures. Her prodigious energies would soon migrate to installations, happenings, body painting, film, fashion and 'sexual revolution'. She would protest the war in Vietnam with an 'Anatomic Explosion' on Wall Street. She would become a tabloid sensation.

By the time she left New York and returned to Japan for good in 1973, Kusama was, by popular account, 'as famous as Andy Warhol'.[4] But her appeal for the avant-garde had been exhausted, unlike his, by the machinery of self-promotion. Or so they say. Chroniclers of the scene deemed her return a retreat, whether under the banner of emotional breakdown or career meltdown. 'She wore herself out.' 'She overplayed her hand.' 'She sold out.' 'She lost her mind.' The explanations tend to arrive in the form of epithets.[5] And then there is another theory. She was sick and tired of war, burnt out on Vietnam, disillusioned by the failure of the era's utopian project of pacifism and liberation. Her departure was an act of political protest as much as of emotional surrender.

'Anxious blue eyes'

In November 1957 Yayoi Kusama arrived in Seattle on a flight from Tokyo with a large sum in US dollars sewn into her dress and stuffed into the toes of her shoes, a letter from Georgia O'Keeffe tucked into her pocket, and a bundle of drawings crammed into her suitcase.

By Kusama's own account, the early months in New York were a living hell.[6] She went hungry and shivered sleeplessly under a thin blanket in an unheated loft, isolated and afraid.[7] Similarly gritty details of precarious life in downtown New York can be found in many an artist's contemporary account.[8] But want, cold, and fear of 'a fierce and violent place' no doubt fell particularly heavily on someone who, at age twenty-nine, had survived a war and its toll of terror, isolation and deprivation, and who now also had to endure a lingering anti-Japanese prejudice in this mythic realm of 'unlimited freedom' that she had summoned all her resources to seek as the survivor's share.[9] Kusama, for one, seems to have considered her situation desolate by comparison to that of the friends who 'peered at me with anxious blue eyes', their very solicitousness seemingly intensifying her sense of separateness.[10]

O'Keeffe had warned her that it would be tough. 'In this country, the Artist has a hard time to make a living,' she cautioned in that first letter.[11] This grave reply from the legend in New Mexico seems only to have stiffened Kusama's resolve to leave Japan. In time, she would produce collages, or Accumulations, composed entirely of fields of airmail stickers, as if in tribute to the wonders of envelopes flung across the ocean and their magical paper contents, as well as to the post-war dream of internationalism.[12] A 'million yen' of family money illicitly exchanged for greenbacks and jammed into her shoes was sufficient to 'build several houses in Japan', or get a foothold in the art world in New York. But in her ambition, Kusama burned through the money fast. So for years her family in Japan secretly pressed yen into airmail envelopes and pitched them across the Pacific Ocean, like manna folded into paper planes.

One recurrent motif in Kusama's early gouaches is a glowing orb of colour, encircled by a bright aureole of white or red, pulsing at the centre of an opaque black ground, the effect an ecliptic image, something like a sun, or a planet, or a galaxy – or a cell. The ambiguity of scale between the infinitesimal and the infinite, it seems, was already present as a theme in her art.[13] By the autumn of 1959 she had translated this principle to the local idiom of all-over painting, and in the process realised the aim expressed to O'Keeffe in that first letter from Japan 'that my paintings be criticized in New York'.[14] Five large-scale white paintings inscribed with scintillating reticulated patterns formed Kusama's first solo show that October in New York, at the cooperative Brata Gallery. The 'Infinity Nets', as she would retrospectively call this vast, absorbing and still-ongoing body of work, attracted perceptive early reviews from the likes of Dore Ashton and the artist, critic and soon-to-be friend Donald Judd. Kusama had arrived. But she was already running out of time. Her visa was set to expire.[15]

Top: *Pacific Ocean* 1959
Watercolour and ink on paper
57 × 69.5
Above: *No.D* 1959
Oil on canvas
89.9 × 72.4
Private collection. Courtesy Paula Cooper Gallery, New York

'This was my "epic".'

In November 1957 Yayoi Kusama arrived in Seattle on a flight from Tokyo with a large sum in US dollars sewn into her dress and stuffed into the toes of her shoes, a letter from Georgia O'Keeffe tucked into her pocket, and a bundle of drawings crammed into her suitcase.

Pacific Ocean, a forerunner of the Infinity Nets, memorialises this voyage in a swirling pattern of tiny loops spread out like a voluminous fishing net beneath the canopy of the sky. Shimmering like the ocean as it might appear from the window of a plane on its way from Tokyo to Seattle, this small work encapsulates the 'wider world' that Kusama was hurrying to meet. Back in Japan, the artist recalls, she painted stones in the riverbed and the rivulets rushing around them. Some of the gouaches she brought to New York touch on that theme, but the journey across the Pacific enlarged the scope of her art and of her ambition. By 1959, her painting would be described by critics in oceanic terms: it was 'huge' in scale and composed of 'innumerable small arcs', like waves.

The five white-on-black canvases Kusama showed at the Brata Gallery, inaugurating a body of work that fifty years later seems almost to constitute an endless series, an infinity of Nets, attracted from its first critics a diversity of descriptions. 'The space is shallow, close to the surface, and achieved by innumerable small arcs imposed on a black ground overlain with a wash of white,' Judd reported.[16] 'The net is written over the surface in small, roughly rectangular movements,' Sidney Tillim remarked.[17] 'They are huge white canvases, lightly scored with gray dots and partly washed over again with a white film,' wrote Dore Ashton.[18] The paintings experimented freely with the medium of oil on canvas, still a relatively unfamiliar one to Kusama, whose formal training had been in the Japanese art of *Nihonga* painting, and whose early successes had come with intimate works in watercolour. Intent on having her painting 'criticized in New York', however, she moved quickly to confront the dominant mode of all-over painting, defined by large scale, expressive gesture and self-reflexive demonstrations of the medium itself.

'The layers of dry white paint, which result from a single touch of the brush repeated tirelessly over time, lend specificity to the infinity of space within an extraordinarily mundane visual field,' suggested one writer. This description is no critic's, but Kusama's own, conceived to emulate, but also to extend, the rhetoric of contemporary formalist criticism.[19] By highlighting 'dry white paint' and 'a single touch of the brush', she underlines the work's defiance of gestural abstraction. Then, by portraying the aesthetic effect of a 'tireless' repetition of a single mark, or touch, as 'an extraordinarily mundane visual field', Kusama recodes the affective economy of all-over painting from one of expressive plenitude to one of exhaustion. 'At first glance,' she recalls, 'the canvases, which were up to 14 ft in length, looked like nothing at all – just plain white surfaces.'[20] On close inspection, 'nothing at all', a blank, revealed a vertiginous complexity, the effect of an endless splitting.

The rhetoric of compulsive repetition that ultimately came to define the Nets in critical writing – partly as a result of the flattening effect of photography on large-scale works meticulously constructed to generate 'an extraordinarily mundane visual field' – has tended to diminish, if not negate, their aesthetic complexity and intense sensuality. The early Nets, which engage in vigorous tactile experiment, illuminate the process by which Kusama ultimately arrived at a means to 'lend specificity to an infinity of space'. In *No. D* (p.178), a smallish piece from 1959 that once belonged to Judd, dense white impasto roils the surface, the paint cresting into low relief, like waves buffeted by the wind, or like the flying carpet of cloud as it might appear from the window of a plane racing over the ocean from Tokyo to Seattle. Thick, glistening *O*s, rendered roughly, as if by gripping the brush in a clenched fist, clot and scab the dark ground, sometimes collapsing on themselves like burst balloons. And from this congested surface, the grey ground pops out in ragged patches like would-be polka dots, or like the ocean's blue-black depths glimpsed through peepholes in a cloudy sky.

No. F (no.45), also of 1959, offers a more varied surface, with the thick, raised passages concentrated on the left-hand side, where the consistency of paint is akin to toothpaste, caulking, or masticated gum, chewed up and spat out. In places the paint looks squirted, extruded, or curdled. Elsewhere, it flattens out, appearing tamped down or smeared. The tactile shifts in the painting are more pronounced here, and a protocol becomes legible. Up close, the self-perpetuating logic of the Net is revealed: each ring forms the nucleus of an expanding cluster of circles, a proliferation arrested only by the limit of the frame. The Net is a screen, or better a membrane, the *O*s linking into chains that overspread the ground. On closer examination, that ground is itself revealed to be a screen. For at the centre of each ring lie rows of minute dots, pinpoints of darkness that emanate from the painting's thinly washed surface of white-stained black. Picking up the threads of the canvas that each ring encircles, the diluted paint of the ground reveals a net behind the net, even as, from up close, the thick *O*s themselves turn out to be concentric circles, the hairs of the brush delicately incising rings within rings.

The self-reflexivity of Kusama's invention is meticulous. She may have been a relative novice to the medium of oil painting when she embarked on the Infinity Nets, but she firmly grasped, and then boldly reimagined, its dominant large scale, all over mode, recoding it from a phallic performance of ecstatic gesture, exemplified in the legendary drip paintings of Jackson Pollock, to a feminine one of libidinal diffusion, in which energy pulses in waves across the work's expanse. So in *No. F*, the membrane covering the ground seems to pull away from, but also to grip, the taut surface below, showing how oil painting on canvas is a matter of doubling (of netting a net, or screening a screen), but also how this self-reflexivity can be, in Kusama's later phrase, self-obliterating. Where the paint is thick, loops close up, a sporadic event that dramatises the interplay between top and bottom as one occludes or suppresses, animates or contests, the other. For the white screen is not exclusively the dominant partner. It is also acted upon, as if tugged, ruffled, or teased from underneath. The thicker gobs of paint seem to adhere top to bottom, as if to imply that the two could split apart, the net float away or slip off, or the bottom gain the upper hand.

Veering from the symbiotic to the parasitic, from equilibrium to rivalry, from meshing to tearing, and from fusion to dispersal, the dynamic of the partners that are conventionally called figure and ground – here two libidinally entangled fields – generates a specific tension in each work. Faint ripples, rhythmic oscillations and wild shudders stir the Nets, which rival any Abstract Expressionist canvas for libidinal drama. That this body of work, with its pulsating waves of convulsive energy, could hardly be more erotically evocative, is a point Kusama herself underscores in her 1967 film, *Kusama's Self-Obliteration* (no.82), which uses pulsing sound and light to dramatise the Nets' libidinal rhythms.[21] By this time, Kusama's painting has floated free of any support and is no longer bounded by a frame. She paints naked bodies, leaves drifting on a stream, even the flowing water itself. Only film can catch this fluid, self-erasing gesture with its wry parody of the gestural mark as a performance of virility. Here, a brush loaded with paint enacts transience and dispersal, a letting go of a letting go of a letting go.

After the success of her debut at Brata, a small artists' cooperative gallery on Tenth Street, in 1961, Kusama upped the ante in response to the opportunity for a solo show at Stephen Radich's uptown space. Working ever more feverishly, she produced a thirty-three foot-long Infinity Net mural to announce the scale of her ambition, which was manifold: to trump the machismo of the New York School with a self-consciously feminine, and exoticised, artistic persona; to replace the expressive gesture with an exhaustive one, pushing painting to its limits of spatial extent and 'monotony'; and to obliterate the self, reconceiving contemporary painting from a subjective statement of individual consciousness to 'nothingness' on an epic scale. 'This was my "epic", summing up all I was,' Kusama has remarked. 'And the spell of the dots and the mesh enfolded me in a magical curtain of mysterious, invisible power.'[22]

The Nets had become, in part, an exercise in overdoing, their effect being to expose and to upstage the hyperbolic excesses of gestural painting as a mode of masculine display. Styling her painting and her artistic persona as symptoms of a cultural crisis in which the performance of virility through individualistic expression in painting masked and abetted gender conformity and assembly-line production in the wider culture, Kusama challenged the core myths of the New York School. In so doing, she rejected the examples of contemporary 'women artists' of the New York scene – figures such as Helen Frankenthaler, Joan Mitchell, Lee Krasner and Grace Hartigan, who had embraced abstract painting as a potential zone of exclusion from the rigid gender divisions of the 1950s – and modelled herself instead on Georgia O'Keeffe, whose work and artistic self-fashioning exemplified a resistant, feminine modernism.[23] Playing the 'other' woman in a still culturally homogeneous masculine art world was to be as pivotal to Kusama's career as the performance of masculinity had been to Pollock's.[24] Perhaps in emulation of her idol, sensuously photographed by Alfred Stieglitz, Kusama would soon commission photographs from the likes of Rudolph Burkhardt and Hal Reiff, posing nude with, or on, her work, defying objectification of the exoticised female body through travesty, much as she had outrivalled the excesses of gestural painting in the Infinity Nets. And, like O'Keeffe, Kusama devised a frank sexual imagery in her art that was both consonant with the dominant trend of abstraction in its time and intently subversive of its masculinist mythology.

No film of Kusama's New York years could, then, resist this vignette: the encounter with her idol in 1961, at 53 East Nineteenth Street, in a shared apartment crowded with Infinity Nets and beginning to harbour a new body of work, the Accumulation sculptures.[25] After phoning to announce she was on the way, leaving Kusama short of time even to pop out for a roll of film, O'Keeffe would appear, her deep wrinkles reminiscent of 'grooves on the soles of canvas shoes': 'I'm Georgia O'Keeffe,' she said, stepping into the room. 'You must be Yayoi. How's everything going?'[26]

'I make them and make them and keep on making them, until I bury myself in the process. I call this "obliteration".'

In November 1957 Yayoi Kusama arrived in Seattle on a flight from Tokyo with a large sum in US dollars sewn into her dress and stuffed into the toes of her shoes, a letter from Georgia O'Keeffe tucked into her pocket, and a bundle of drawings crammed into her suitcase.

In time, she would produce assemblages recollecting this journey, so-called Accumulation sculptures composed of articles of clothing and accessories – dresses, coats, high-heeled shoes, hats, handbags, valises – bristling with indecorously overstuffed wads of paint-stiffened cloth. Swollen, lumpy phallic protuberances, densely packed with cotton batting, all but bursting at their tightly stitched seams, similarly blanket items of furniture, utensils and domestic appliances that Kusama salvaged from the streets of New York and incorporated into her burgeoning, room-sized installations. A sofa, armchairs, a cabinet, a folding table, a ladder, an ironing board, a baby carriage, every surface phalli-studded or phalli-filled, extend the endlessness of Kusama's Infinity Nets to the object world. With the very stuff with which, as the philosopher Félix Guattari once remarked, 'the consumer society litters its wretched and disenchanted universe',[27] she furnished a parallel one of consumption in reverse, a universe in which everything is saved, and all is lost.

Kusama's work is defined by economies of excess both material and psychic, and the reciprocities between them. With one efficient hyperbolic gesture, repeated ad infinitum, the Accumulations encapsulate the phallic economy of gender and the superfluities of the culture of commodity fetishism and planned obsolescence celebrated in America and imposed on Japan through rapid post-war industrialisation. The Accumulations ironically cater for – furnish, equip, dress, accessorise – a society in which the devastations of fascist ultra-authoritarianism, war deprivation and even atomic obliteration were somehow to be rectified through the production and consumption of disposable goods and their corresponding stereotypes, where overdoing was a social obligation in the performance of gender, consumerism and geopolitics alike.

Kusama's concern with rampant overproduction and feverish overconsumption is not, of course, limited to the circuits of capital, even if her work does constantly expose the toxic twinning of waste and want. The psychic and sexual economy of her work pursues a corresponding trend. For the dynamic of desire it enacts is at once manic and melancholic, hyperbolically indiscriminate and depressively indifferent. Desire is everywhere and nowhere, an overwhelming presence and a diffuse effect. In Phalli's Field, as Kusama would later call the infinite regress of her art, desire of every kind succumbs to its own compulsive reiteration, and is lost.

'Like being carried on a conveyor belt without ending to my death' [28]

In November 1957 Yayoi Kusama arrived in Seattle on a flight from Tokyo with a large sum in US dollars sewn into her dress and stuffed into the toes of her shoes, a letter from Georgia O'Keeffe tucked into her pocket, and a bundle of drawings crammed into her suitcase.

Like 'being carried on a conveyor belt without ending to my death,' she described her new life, referring to the marathon sessions during which she painted Infinity Nets, and later stitched the Accumulation sculptures.[29] As an adolescent in Matsumoto City, Kusama had been conscripted for labour in a parachute factory during the Second World War, enduring harsh and arduous conditions. Now, the deprivations of New York, where she was often 'down and out', renewed her determination to survive, but also stimulated a reprise of the debilitating labour she had once been forced to perform, and which had helped to cultivate the resistance to authority, regimentation and convention to which she consecrated her anti-authoritarian, anti-conformist, anti-patriarchal, anti-capitalist, anti-war art.

This seeming paradox of self-liberation through a slavish dedication to task is relieved in part by the artistic discipline Kusama acquired in her subsequent artistic studies, which nurtured sustained concentration over long periods, a capacity she exploited to the full in the Infinity Nets.[30] As a riposte to 'action painting', which Kusama criticised as a vacuous cliché by the late 1950s, the Infinity Nets dilated time and deferred action, meting out gesture in regular increments, using the 'single touch of the brush repeated tirelessly over time' to mark its passage.[31] Yet, the Infinity Nets are not only a meditative response to the rhetoric of 'action' as a false myth of individual creative agency in the margins of a culture of conformity and automation. They also attest to the consumer culture's hypnotic power, to the morbid appeal of being carried on a conveyor belt without ending to one's death.

Kusama's recourse to 'compulsive repetition' is a symptom of trauma, critics have argued, with the encouragement of the artist herself. This suffering is most often traced to a troubled family life. The effects of the war on her art have been less intensively explored. But it is clear that Kusama's art was conceived in rebellion against repression in every form: 'my parents, the house, the land, the shackles, the conventions, the prejudice'. What is traumatic in her art is its reflexive reiteration of that position, its continual protest against external control, which became intolerable in any measure precisely because of its overwhelming effects in the past. 'The militarism was inescapable. I suffered. It killed my mind' is her own comment on the matter.[32] As an art of epic excess, Kusama's work dramatises the scale of patriarchal totalitarianism's insult to the subject, its arrogation of prerogative over every dimension of life. Kusama's resistance to authority, the defining trend in her art, is traumatic to the extent that it is boundless, a repetition without end.[33]

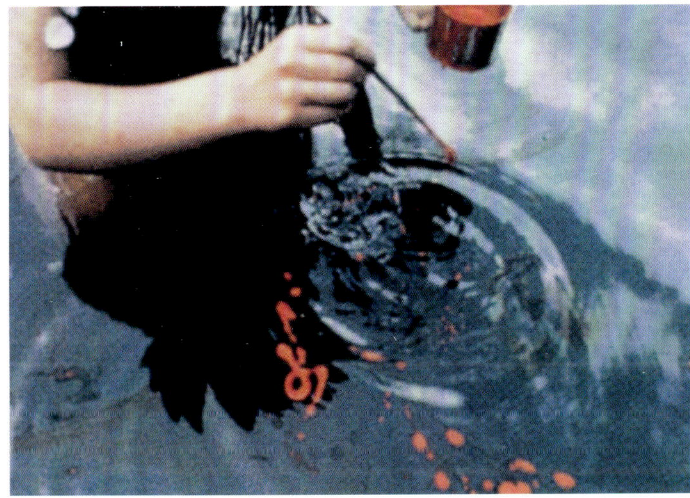

Top: Kusama posing in front of a 33-foot Infinity Net
Above: Detail from *Kusama's Self-Obliteration* 1968

And so, for example, Kusama has continued to produce Infinity Nets until the present day, implying that the series itself has the self-perpetuating momentum of a conveyor belt – that it can only end with death for the very reason that it is endless, a tautological formation that encapsulates the post-traumatic predicament of a subject, or a society, estranged from history and unable to lay to rest shadows of the past. With the Infinity Nets, Kusama enacts this predicament, exiling narrative in preference to the temporality of enactment, each brushstroke marking a moment of time passing, but not past. This labour-intensive technique tested the artist's endurance to its limits as surely as it tests those of the viewer and of painting itself. Even in their making, the Nets embodied the hardships of war and the trauma of repression, but also, and crucially, Kusama's 'endless' resistance to conformity, a kind of cosmic-orgasmic defiance of authoritarian control.

'All around the boat, on the ceiling and walls, were 999 black-and-white poster-size photos of it. When you stood in this room, the thousand boats would begin to spin around you, leaving you seasick and hallucinating.'

In November 1957 Yayoi Kusama arrived in Seattle on a flight from Tokyo with a large sum in US dollars sewn into her dress and stuffed into the toes of her shoes, a letter from Georgia O'Keeffe tucked into her pocket, and a bundle of drawings crammed into her suitcase.

By the early 1960s her solitary studio life as a painter of Infinity Nets had taken a social turn, with a little help from her friends, and with transgressive implications for her art.[34] *Aggregation: One Thousand Boats Show* was Kusama's 1963 installation at the Gertrude Stein Gallery, its centrepiece a phalli-studded rowboat and oars, upholstered in three dimensions, set in a room wallpapered with 999 black-and-white photographs of the same rowboat, emphasising the phallic contour of its prow (no.65). A film of Kusama's years in New York might stage the nocturnal operation in which her upstairs neighbour, Donald Judd, helps her wheel the salvaged vessel along the streets aboard a dolly, and takes part in the painstaking labour of stitching and stuffing the innumerable sacks required to fill it.[35] It might show her posing nude in the installation, directing Rudy Burkhardt to make the famous photograph in which she turns her back to the camera as she stands at the far end of the boat, filling in the narrow space between the boat and the wall. Kusama would now expand the Accumulations from objects into tableaux, her ultimate aim being to produce a fully spatial *mise en abyme*, a new infinity effect.[36]

Although the first Accumulations, a sofa and armchair, had appeared in a group show at the Green Gallery in 1962, their fuller realisation came with the incorporation of photography. *Aggregation: One Thousand Boats Show* exploited photographic reproduction in an industrial form, wallpaper, in a parody of all-over painting's inexorable slide into decoration, and in a revival of the surrealist device of conjoining the bodily fragment, or part-object, with the industrial multiple, or readymade.[37] Above all, however, the show used photography to conjure a corporeal surround of infinite regress.[38]

Top: Kusama posing in *Aggregation: One Thousand Boats Show* 1963 installation view, Gertrude Stein Gallery, New York
Bottom: Accumulation sculptures in Kusama's studio, 1964
Opposite: *Accretion No.3* 1964 Photo collage 110.8 × 70.2

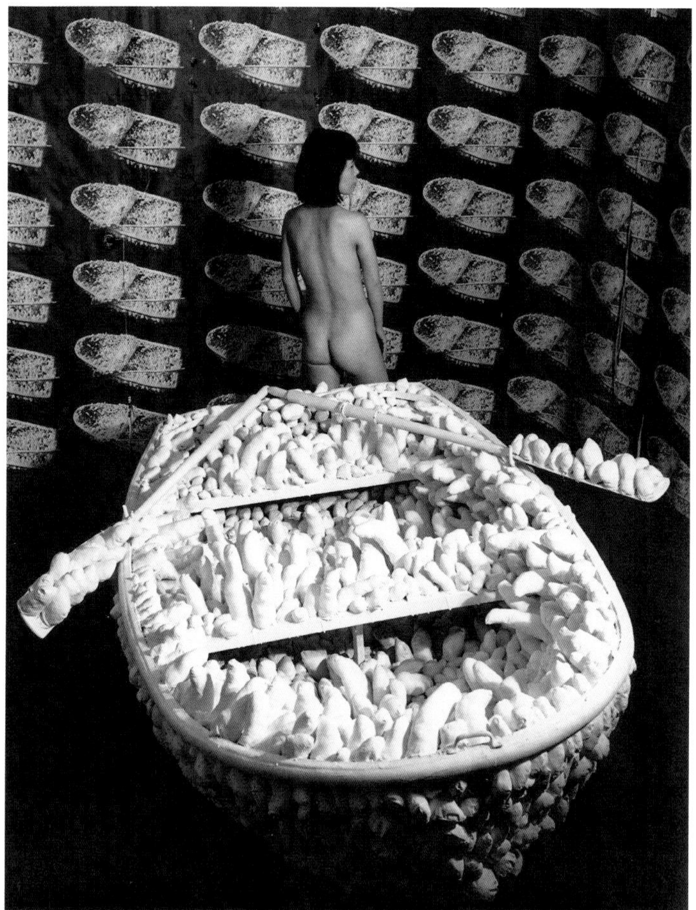

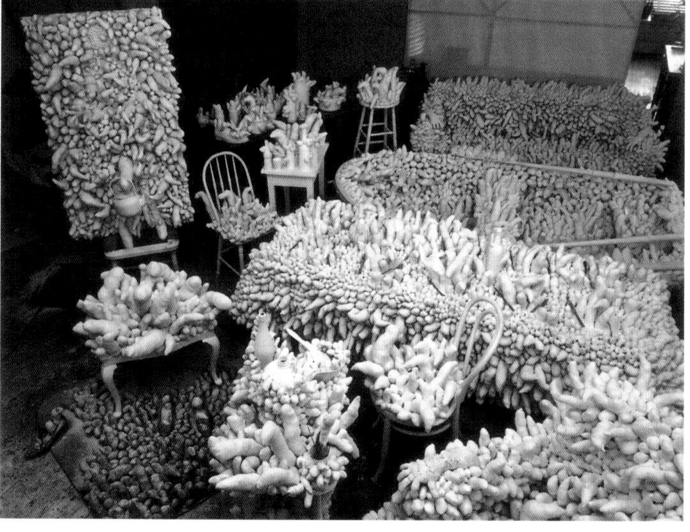

Infinite regress is a no-exit situation in which past, present and future converge at a single point. In the Infinity Mirror Rooms Kusama began to stage in 1965, that point is the viewer. *Aggregation: One Thousand Boats Show* anticipates the disorienting effect of mirrored rooms, in which perspective is, by definition, lost. The installation also highlights the latent seriality in Kusama's art. Through the relatively simple device of papering the walls, floor and ceiling with a gridded arrangement of photographs of the Accumulation rowboat, an object that was itself already fragmented through serial repetition, Kusama not only produced a *mise en abyme* but emphasised the way in which her Infinity Nets and Accumulation sculptures betrayed a 'serial attitude', as the artist and critic Mel Bochner described the emerging minimalist tendency.[39]

Kusama had already plotted this direction in a series of collages using black-and-white photographs of the Infinity Nets in a grid format. From a distance, these works, composed of immaculate silver-gelatin prints that yield a fine grey scale, anticipate Eva Hesse's later drawings made with washes of ink in her own tightly gridded works on paper. Hesse and Kusama are most often compared in terms of an 'obsessional' trend in the making of objects. But they are also bound together in the art of this time by a distinctive involvement with the psychic dynamics of seriality. The consistent protocol of the Infinity Nets, repeated 'tirelessly' over time, already implied seriality, but the reproductive potential of photography enabled Kusama to render exponentially increased complexity with greater efficiency, and with a diminished role for the artist's hand. Further, the technique of photocollage intensified the effects of splitting she had achieved in the Nets through the incorporation of a reproductive technology. Now Kusama could literally repeat, recycle, copy, crop, splice, enlarge, replicate, reduce, multiply and recombine the elements of her painting.[40]

If the gridded collages offered one take on seriality through an *Accumulation of Nets*, Kusama's title for these works, another set of photocollages, based on the Accumulation sculptures, abandoned the grid to release splitting over an unbounded field. By splicing together photographs of the surfaces of the Accumulations, from which all trace of the scaffoldings of furniture and clothing had been removed, Kusama constructed a terrain with the density and complexity of a coral reef. In works such as *Accretion No. 3* of 1964, object surrenders to mass, reviving the oceanic effect of the Infinity Nets, but now in a hyper-realistic mode. Exploiting the pristine clarity of the images precisely to compound the confusion arising from photographs that might equally be interpreted as magnifying a microscopic specimen or telescoping an expansive field, she exploited the potential of the medium to render its subject illegible and unreal, even if in minute detail. That the objective mode of photography particularly lends itself to uncanny effects is a lesson of surrealism that Kusama was quick to absorb and exploit, demonstrating that the Accumulations were not merely uncanny objects in themselves – *unheimlich* in Sigmund Freud's original term, or 'unhomely' – but could be deployed, through photographic splitting, in a kind of *mise en abyme* of the uncanny.[41]

For Freud, the *unheimlich* is precisely that which was once most homely, and from which one has become alienated through repression. The Accumulations turn domestic objects into uncanny doubles, making familiar things strange. In this they are classically, if hyperbolically, uncanny. Symptoms of repression are not far to seek, either, in the profusion of phalli that overwhelm these objects. If anything, the Accumulations burlesque the uncanny, spoofing its Freudian explanation – the male subject's repressed desire for his original home, the genitalia of the mother – by converting masculine anxiety into a feminine phallic obsession. Tropes of femininity are pervasively present in the boudoir armchairs and high-heeled slippers that ostentatiously lay claim to the uncanny, but also might be seen to banish adult sexuality altogether, or even to cast doubt on its plausibility. The profusion of phallic protuberances undermines the very proposition of phallic sexuality through excess, making the idea itself seem preposterous, bodying forth a child's wisdom about the absurdity of adult sexuality and its pretensions to tame the bodily drives.[42]

In a gallery setting, the Accumulations are unambiguously sculptural assemblages. Studio photographs of the objects 'at home' interpose them in a domestic milieu, which in turn makes them seem more *unheimlich* than the 'real thing'. These period photographs mediate between the Accumulation sculptures and the photocollages as a kind of stage (in the sense both of time

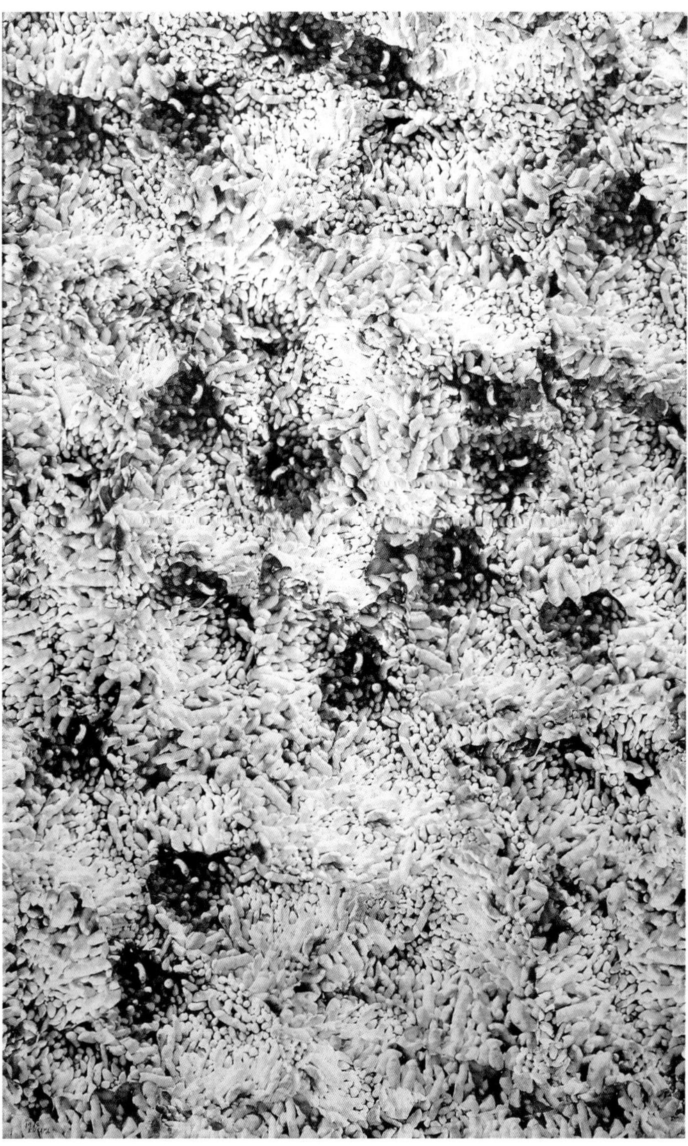

and setting) in a drama of regression. The photocollages Kusama produced using photographs of the Accumulation sculptures intensify and multiply the uncanny effects: the *unheimlich* migrates from the domestic object transformed into its unhomely double (the Accumulation sculpture or installation), to the photographic tableau, in which the objects are crowded together in an *unheimlich* home, to the photocollage, where the uncanny overwhelms the scene.

This process begins with photocollages in which Kusama herself appears – inserted, for example, in a pocket of space in a room crammed with Accumulation sculptures. By one interpretation, *Compulsion Furniture (Accumulation)* c.1964 (no.78), for example, shows the artist surveying a prodigious body of work. By another, the objects are closing in on her. Like a conjurer, her presence seems to hold the situation in check. Remove her, and the uncanny runs amok. Absent an armchair, a sofa, or a pair of high-heeled slippers to anchor the *unheimlich* to the world of objects, what remains is a boundless uncanny effect, a limitless alienation: an estrangement from the past through repression, and from time itself through infinite regress.

'We must have a sexual revolution, at all costs. In order to accomplish this I felt I would have to work like mad, and so that is just what I did.'

In November 1957 Yayoi Kusama arrived in Seattle on a flight from Tokyo with a large sum in US dollars sewn into her dress and stuffed into the toes of her shoes, a letter from Georgia O'Keeffe tucked into her pocket, and a bundle of drawings crammed into her suitcase.

What stands out in Kusama's autobiographical narrative of the 1960s, by comparison to others, is less the bone-cold loneliness, the visa woes, the gnawing ambition, the bitter pill of sexism, the strain of rivalry, or even the fear of going hungry or crazy, but the persistence of this word: war. Of the early years of the decade, Kusama writes, for example: 'this was at the beginning of a decline in America's fortunes ... the tremendous cost of the Vietnam War had set the country on a downward spiral'.[43] The account is retrospective, impossibly prescient, its narrative arc bent to the angle of later events, but nevertheless it is arresting for the sense of dark foreboding, rather than dawning possibility, that it casts over the New York scene at the beginning of the 1960s.

Writing in 1938, on the eve of the Second World War and in response to the rise of fascism, Virginia Woolf had observed: 'the public and private worlds are inseparably connected ... the tyrannies and servilities of one are the tyrannies and servilities of the other'.[44] The subject of Woolf's *Three Guineas* is the prevention of war. War begins at home, she warns, with the hierarchies and rivalries enacted in social rituals from education to dining to dress. The conditions Kusama enumerated as reasons for leaving Japan – 'my parents, the house, the land, the shackles, the conventions, the prejudice' of a country 'too servile, too feudalistic, and too scornful of women' for an 'art like mine' – all find echoes in *Three Guineas* and its withering indictment of Woolf's own class. The prevention of war, Woolf asserts, depends on social transformation, beginning with women from 'good families' gaining their freedom from 'the education of the private house'. Yayoi Kusama, youngest child of a well-to-do family, war survivor, refugee from totalitarianism, emerged from it all intent on self-liberation. Finding herself in New York as another war loomed, the Vietnam War, she responded by calling for sexual revolution.[45]

In 1966 Kusama stunned Venice with her *Narcissus Garden*, an installation of 1,500 plastic mirror balls filling the lawn of the Italian Pavilion at the Biennale (p.110). 'Your Narcissism for Sale' proclaimed a simple placard propped against a tree. For the advertised price of two dollars, a passer-by received a gleaming orb from the hands of the diminutive artist herself, resplendent in a gold and silver kimono. The Biennale organisers soon shut her down. Apparently inspired by the episode, which attracted wide attention, Kusama turned increasingly to protest performance, targeting the institutional hierarchies of the art world, most famously through a nude protest in the sculpture garden of the Museum of Modern Art in New York, but also the government and the economic establishment for prosecuting the war in Vietnam. She was to have regular skirmishes with the police in the years to come as she took her body-painting festivals, nude happenings, and anti-war protests into museums, parks, streets and the mass media.[46] In 1968, at the height of the war in Vietnam, she staged a series of Anatomic Explosions at sites including the United Nations, the Statue of Liberty, the Board of Election and the New York Stock Exchange, where she directed four naked professional dancers, two men and two women, accompanied by a bongo drummer, to perform near the statue of George Washington while the artist spray-painted their bodies with polka dots. 'The money made with this stock is enabling the war to continue' proclaimed her press release. 'We protest this cruel, greedy instrument of the war establishment.'[47]

Kusama actively embraced protest culture. A protest artist to the core, she was in her element with the advent of the counterculture, a groundswell of anti-authoritarian utopian energy in open rebellion against the establishment. This is where comparisons to Andy Warhol, who in other respects is her closest peer on the New York scene, falter. Both artists experimented with designating the workshop a kind of factory and exploited serial production, underlining the exhaustion of expressionism, and the affective resonance of exhaustion. Both, with evident irony, adopted commercial models of distribution, Kusama branching out into film and fashion enterprises to finance her performance and protest activities. Both expertly manipulated the machinery of the mass media, tacking between the commercial world of popular culture and a bohemian underground. Both courted and exploited fame as a means by which to operate in the wider culture. But Kusama ultimately 'failed' where Warhol prospered precisely because hers was a protest art. Remaining aloof from the contradictions his art exposed, Warhol could hardly be held responsible for them. He did not escape the 1960s unscathed, but he did emerge untarnished, and seemingly unmoved, by the failure of the utopian aspirations of youth culture. Kusama's fate was the contrary. When the dystopian turn from the era of pacifism and liberation struggles drew a backlash against the alternative political culture of that decade, it brought disillusionment to many, despair to some. Kusama left New York.

'Kusama must have realized herself that her subject was used up, that her time was over,' Alexandra Munroe has speculated.[48] Munroe is one of Kusama's most sympathetic critics. Significantly

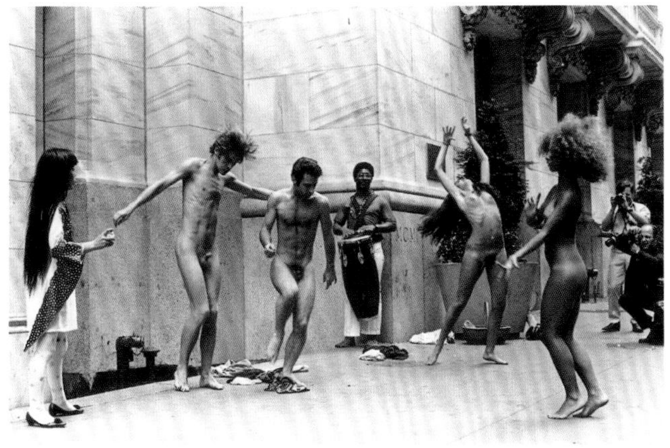

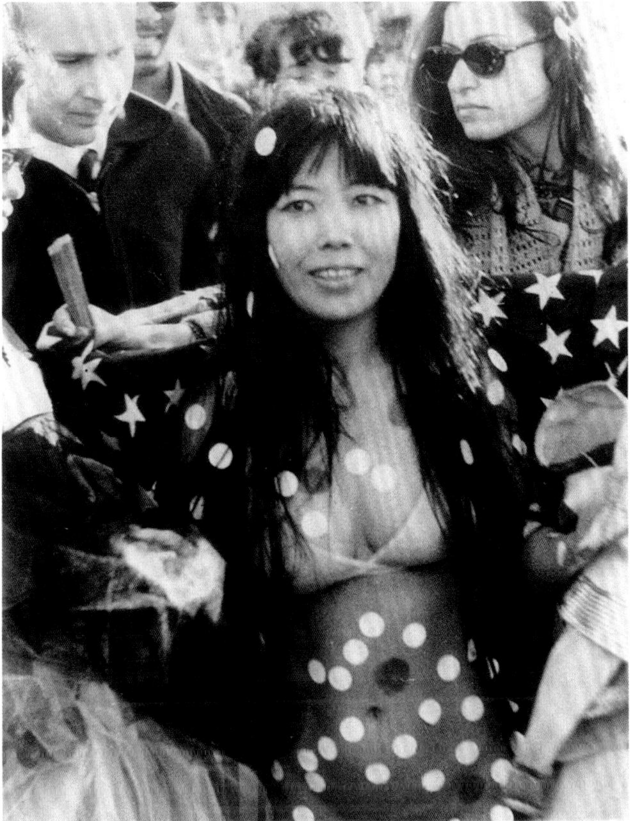

Top: *Anatomic Explosion on Wall Street* 1968
Above: Kusama at *Bust Out* happening, Sheep Meadow, Central Park, New York, 6 April 1969

responsible for reviving critical interest in Kusama's art as, precisely, a compelling body of protest work driven by anti-establishment 'outrage', Munroe conceives it as an avant-garde project subject to a definite historical limit, in keeping with revolutionary narratives. By this account, Kusama left New York to draw a line, or to underscore, in her own hand, the line that was being drawn for her by others. Kusama is, without doubt, a sophisticated student of avant-garde history, and Munroe is surely correct to say that she recognised when the scene she had worked tirelessly to galvanise was 'over'. Yet, the transgressive trend of Kusama's art as an enactment of perpetual protest also suggests that this withdrawal, like her earlier flight from Japan, was an act of defiance in itself. Less a retreat than a return, her move to Japan marked a critical turning point in post-war history as much as in Kusama's own work. It was one more act of political protest, and the one that was to have the most severe consequences for the artist herself, whose memory was all but expunged from histories of the time.

Even now, the political significance of Kusama's work in New York is largely ignored. Its burlesque of compulsive commodity fetishism through pandemic sexual fetishism; its exhaustion of trends in manic overproduction and frantic erotomania; its epic feats of outdoing and overdoing; its exposure of the art world's naked commercialism in stereotypic pin-up poses and hysterical orgies of hype – all have been subsumed in an overarching narrative of private obsession. Some observers accord her a *succès de scandale*. Fewer subscribe to infinity politics. The reasons for this are obvious. Kusama does not behave like a 'political' artist. The complex persona she cultivated of relentless striving, unrepentant fame-chasing, sexual magnetism and entrepreneurial flair, all sustained under the sway of hallucinatory visions, does not correspond to any available image of politics in art, though of course this is also precisely the point of the performance: to question what might signify as a political response to an atomic spectacle culture that is itself mad, in which reality itself is ever increasingly detached from reality.

As a structure to crystallise that hallucinatory or 'depersonalised' situation, why not a *mise en abyme*, or a kaleidoscopic chamber, as Kusama's Infinity Mirror Rooms and Floor Shows propose?[49] Why not an infinite-regress orgy? Mobilising – by borrowing (from friends) as well as lending (her own) – individual pathologies to expose social ones, Kusama's art does not project her symptoms and fantasies onto the world – the usual reading – so much as the reverse. It absorbs and concentrates external excess. Infinity Nets, Accumulations, Compulsion Furniture, Anatomic Explosions, Phalli Fields and festivals of Self-Obliteration consume the manic energies of totalitarian repression and the atomic consumer age and distill them in protest. So where her art enlarges and proliferates, it also reduces. This is the psycho-political geometry of the polka dot.

Kusama's technique of exposing the vicious circles of capitalism, the stereotype and war through overdoing – of expounding by compounding – was all too easily confused with an opportunistic embrace of commodity fetishism, celebrity narcissism and anti-war activism by an audience that was itself captive to the very splitting her art aimed to expose and to dramatise. The irony of Kusama's politics was lost in the infinite regress that is her art: a perpetual protest against the hall of mirrors of the so-called real world.

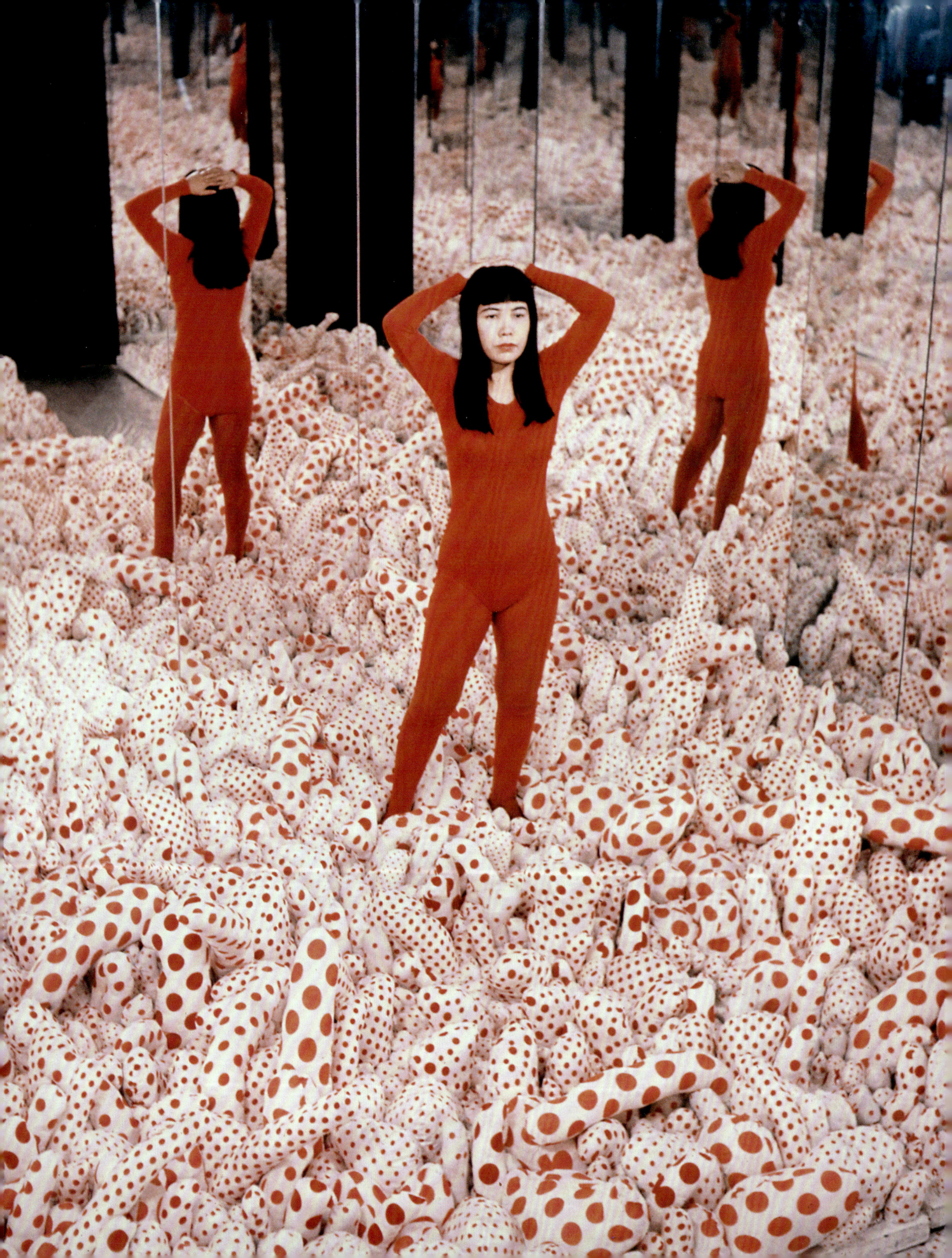

Infinity Mirror Room – Phalli's Field
1965, installation view, *Floor Show*,
Castellane Gallery, New York

Imagine yourself entering a darkened room in which every available surface, wall and object is caught in a web of dots. The ostensibly ordinary domestic room and its contents – animate viewers and inanimate work alike – come together in one collective plane of experience, united by hundreds of polka-dot glow-in-the-dark spots that have been stuck on every object and surface in the installation. Cut loose from the usual order of things, participants in this work find themselves centre stage in a disorienting and decidedly unfamiliar setting. This work seems to require something from its visitors – whether it be their presence, or their participation in an otherwise unscripted scenario. It forces a series of questions: Should you enter the room alone or with a crowd of other people? Is this an environment in which the viewing subject is trapped or set free? Is this a liberating, undifferentiated space of open-ended possibilities and freedom or, as most accounts would have it, an ominous and destabilising environment marked by dislocation and discomfort, in which one is set adrift, lost in the repetition of the spots, alienated and alone within a private psychological world? Either way the question remains: How are you supposed to act in such a space?

Yayoi Kusama has been creating environments or 'worlds' such as *I'm Here, but Nothing* 2000 (no.96) since the early 1960s, when she was one of the first installation artists of the post-war period who made the environmental conditions of her artwork central to her practice.[1] One of Kusama's first installations, *Infinity Mirror Room – Phalli's Field*, was shown at the Castellane Gallery in New York in 1965. Upon entering the room along a narrow section of red polka-dot painted floor, viewers found themselves reflected endlessly in the mirrored walls. The surrounding floor space was populated with a thick carpet of red and white spotted fabric forms, huddled together as though a field of straining and animated tubers. The room produced a dizzying and confusing visual experience in which the viewer and polka dots were mirrored, as the title of the work suggests, to 'infinity'.

Kusama's relationship to her own lived environment has been hard won, and in 1977 she elected to move into a psychiatric hospital in Tokyo, from where she continues voluntarily to live today. For all Kusama's successes on the New York art scene during the 1960s, her time in the city was far from easy as she

Jo Applin

I'm Here, but Nothing: Yayoi Kusama's Environments

struggled financially and emotionally. She felt a deep frustration with the alienating and macho art scene of a city that, for a Japanese woman with minimal English, was almost impossible to penetrate fully.[2] As early as 1963 Kusama articulated this sense of estrangement in terms of her environment, claiming 'I find myself being put into a uniform environment, one which is strangely mechanised and standardised. I feel this strongly in highly civilised America and particularly in New York. In the gap between people and the strange jungle of civilised society lie many psychosomatic problems.'[3] Kusama sought to capture something of this 'strangeness' in her installations that both exploit and resist precisely the experience of standardisation and uniformity the artist challenged in her daily life.

From her early abstract Infinity Net oil paintings (which Kusama described as 'without composition – without beginning, end or centre'[4]) to her sculptural objects and room environments, Kusama's artistic project has been characterised by 'an attempt to create a world'.[5] Minimalist artist and critic Donald Judd wrote favourably about Kusama's work in the 1960s, noting in an early review of her large near-monochrome Infinity Net paintings that they contained within their expansive scale an intimate concentration of formal connections, principally the 'small, dense arcs' which, Judd wrote, set up a series of 'relationships' that are 'subtle and depend on the surrounding area'.[6] While Judd meant to emphasise the cohesiveness of Kusama's work as a singular 'specific' object, his description also serves as a useful way of imagining the wider effect of Kusama's art as similarly establishing a series of 'subtle' and interdependent relationships, proliferating between her clusters of phallic forms, endless fields of polka dots, and the viewers who encounter them.[7] Describing Kusama's insistence that viewers see her works 'collectively' before they are seen 'individually', Judd noted in his review of *Driving Image Show* from 1964 that 'the collective impression is the more important anyway'.[8]

Kusama has always included elements in her installations that crowd and disrupt the boundaries between subject and object, forcing each into a relationship with the other. This can be seen, for instance, in the series of squashed yellow pumpkins that push up against their matching yellow spot-decorated environment in *Mirror Room (Pumpkin)* 1991, or the giant inflatable dot-covered balloons in her *Dots Obsession* series started in 1997, which, only lightly tethered, bob gently, adding to the sense of precariousness that troubles the terrain in which they are situated and complicates the spectator's task of inhabiting the same space (p.189). Kusama frequently poses for photographs alongside or inside her environments, donning outfits matching the surface patterns of the pumpkins, balloons and other objects so that her bodily outline is perfectly hidden against its background, artist and environment becoming indistinguishable from one another. A similar strategy of subsuming the body in the work is discernible in her series of open-fronted box forms such as *Leftover Snow in the Dream* 1982 (no.88), which Kusama stacks against the wall and from which snake bulbous organic and vital forms, pushing away from the wall into the space of the room, seeking companionship perhaps, or at least the viewer's touch. For Kusama, her environments function as a formal articulation of the psychological disorder she has suffered

Top, this page, and opposite: *Mirror Room (Pumpkin)* 1991
Mirror, iron, wood, plaster, styrofoam, acrylic
200 × 200 × 200
Hara Museum of Contemporary Art, Tokyo
Bottom: *Dots Obsession* 1998
Vinyl balloons, mirror
Dimensions variable
Les Abattoirs, Toulouse

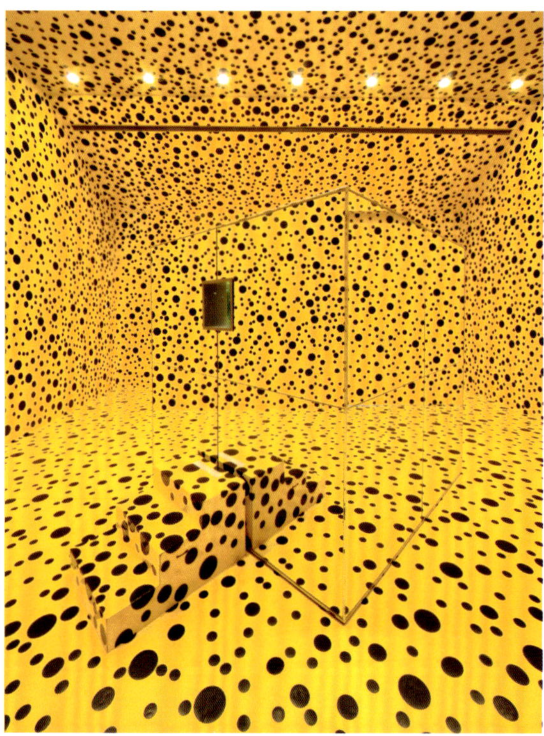

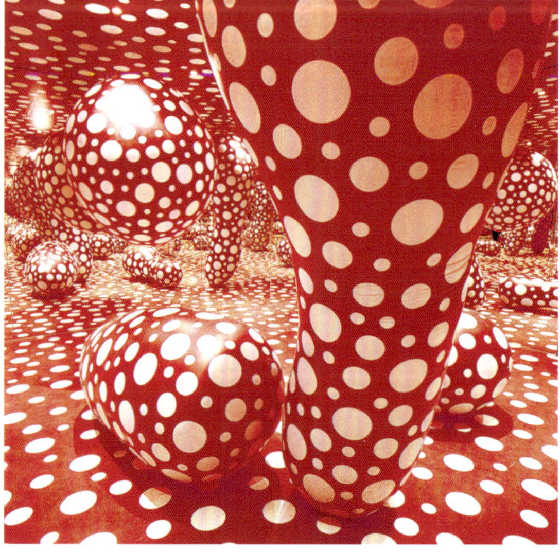

from since childhood, in which she feels herself under threat of dissolution or psychic breakdown, causing her to experience her entire environment as enveloped in an infinite web of polka dots. During these episodes Kusama describes how, through a form of psychic camouflage with her surroundings, she experiences a sense of 'self-obliteration' in which she feels her concept of self 'dissolving and accumulating, proliferating and separating'.[9]

Making Worlds

Kusama's exhibition *Aggregation: One Thousand Boats Show*, held at the Gertrude Stein Gallery, New York in 1963, was an early installation by the artist that featured a single rowing boat. The boat was covered in white stuffed protuberant forms and placed in a room, the walls of which were papered with 999 black and white photographs of the boat. This work is caught somewhere between the contemporary minimalist investment in sameness and repetition, and an uncanny scenario in which the boundaries between what is real and what is not are thrown into doubt. In a photograph of the exhibition Kusama posed naked, standing between the boat and walls with her back turned to the camera (see p.182). This photograph has been interpreted as an erotic performance, a reading supported by the phallic nature of the white protruding forms covering the boat, although Kusama's backward stance also suggests less a rejection of the viewing gaze than an invitation to follow her lead, to join in and take part. This theme was continued in Kusama's exhibition *Driving Image Show* held one year later at the Castellane Gallery, New York. This exhibition was a riot of colour compared to the minimal monochrome of *Aggregation*, although the corporeal references and crammed space spoke once again to Kusama's interest in filling rooms with bodily substitutes.

The show was comprised of two rooms, the first of which contained a chaotic mix of macaroni-covered shop mannequins and a dresser table, which were placed on a carpet of loosely strewn macaroni that cracked and crunched underfoot in an unsettling and noisy manner (Kusama recounted how at the opening of the exhibition she arranged for two 'macaroni-coated dogs' to be set loose, their 'frantic barking' startling viewers who were not expecting these disruptive additional participants.)[10] The second room housed a number of Kusama's recent Accumulation objects including the rowing boat from the previous year and several examples of Compulsion Furniture, amongst which was a protuberant covered armchair that sat among other stuffed and studded items of furniture. The pumpkins, phallic tubers, winding tendrils and ubiquitous polka dots to which Kusama returns time and time again function for the artist as both talisman and causal root of her anxiety – it seems she has to make them, so that she can escape them. By the mid-1960s the psychological aspect of Kusama's work dominated critical readings, from the disparaging description of her 'phallus-barnacled easy chair' as 'psychotic art' to the artist's own frequently cited accounts of her psychological illness.[11] Aside from the palliative or even potentially reparative aspect of her working process there are, however, other ways in which Kusama's environments might speak to a different kind of 'world building', extending beyond the psychological interiority of the artist to address a wider and culturally shared set of symptoms

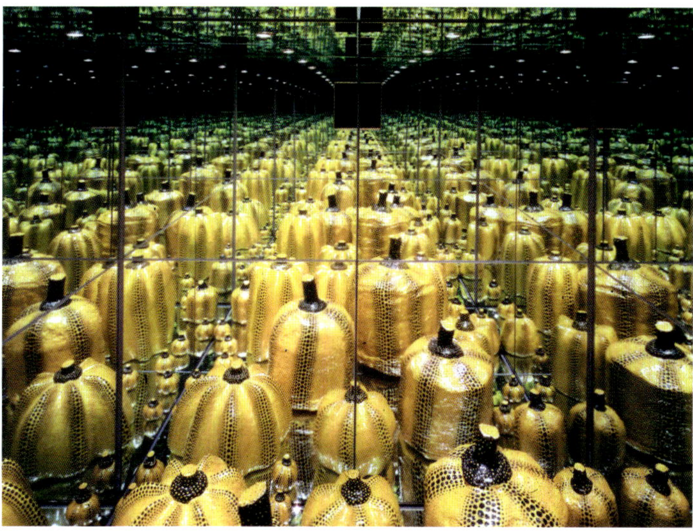

and drives. In recent years several nuanced psychoanalytic readings of Kusama's work have reconsidered it less as the output of a psychologically ill subject than in terms of its strategic production of a psychically charged encounter that is no longer irreducibly linked to the artist's own psychological state.[12]

In a number of photographs of the artist with her works, particularly those in which Kusama is represented reclining, snug as a bug, across the upright phallic forms of *Infinity Mirror Room – Phalli's Field* 1965, or photographs of *My Flower Bed* 1962, in which she poses curled up 'asleep' at the base of a sculpture made of hundreds of stuffed and red dip-dyed gloves (p.191), Kusama presents her work as a site of support and safety rather than alienation and psychic dissolution. This doubling of affect is seen in Kusama's recent Infinity Mirror Room environments in which mirrored rooms are pinpricked with hundreds of shimmering reflected lights. Viewers entering these rooms are enveloped in a magical scene in which obliteration and psychic rupture seem less the order of the day than a calmer, potentially more liberating experience that counters the endless fracture and confusion caused by her earlier environments.

Participation

I want to suggest that Kusama's environmental works represent another kind of fantasy distinct from their association with psychological disorder and breakdown, for in their invitation to participate they speak to a shared public sphere rather than an individual private world, which is more in tune with Kusama's later 'happenings' and 'body festivals' from 1967–9 than the kind of 'psychotic art' with which her earlier work is more commonly aligned. Kusama's Happenings, such as 'Naked Event at the New York Stock Exchange' 1968, have been somewhat sidelined within the history of 1960s Happenings and actions, dismissed, it seems, because of their lack of formal innovation in comparison to her other works. Although Kusama's happenings and performances are distinct from the kinds of environments offered by her room installations, they share a desire to bring together diverse subjects as onlookers, participants or collaborators within a scenario whose narratives and limits have been only loosely scripted by Kusama herself.[13]

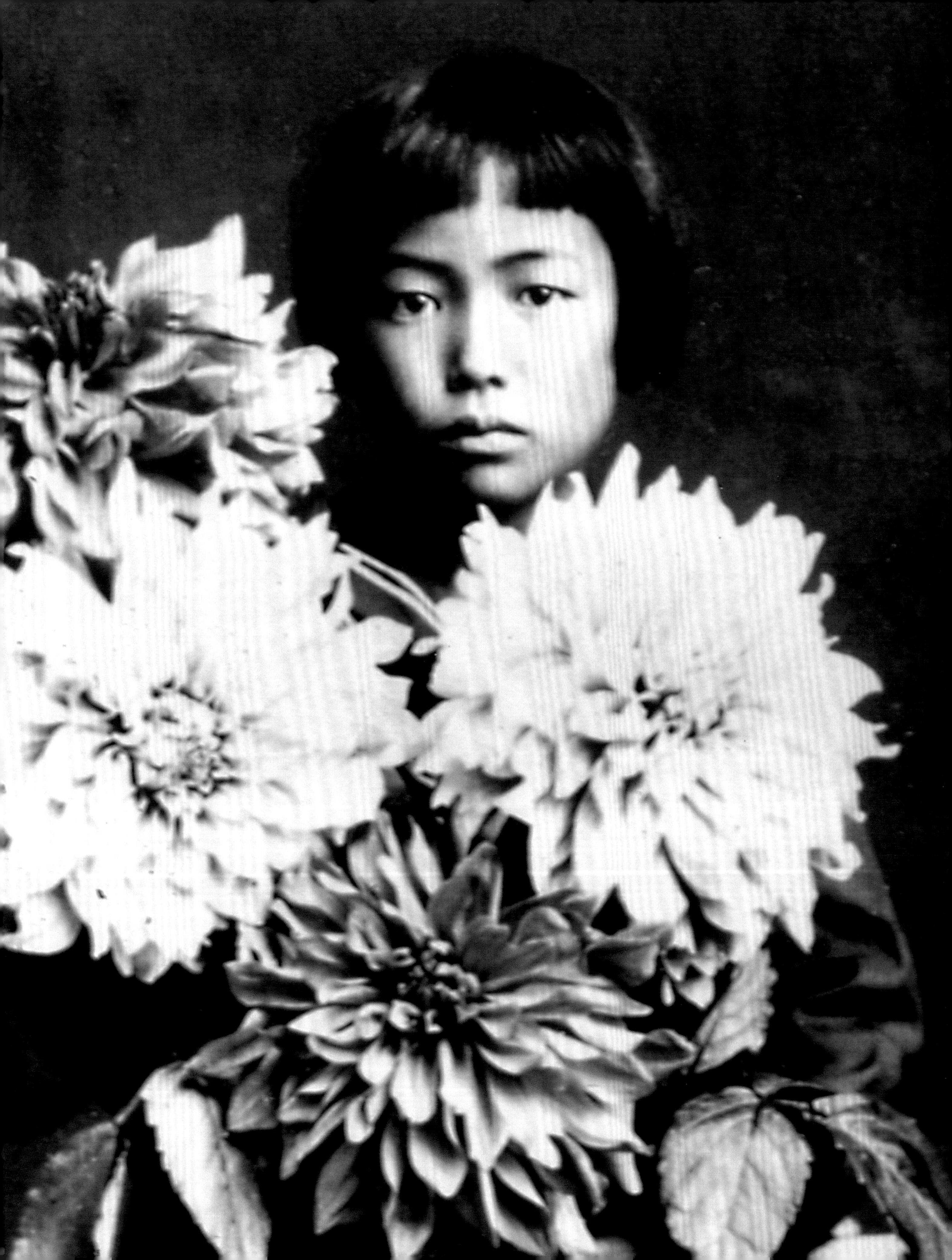

Kusama at the age of ten, 1939

Juliet Mitchell

Portrait of the Artist as a Young Flower

Yayoi Kusama is a Japanese artist, I am a British psychoanalyst. Some key features of our human condition are understood very differently by our two cultures and two disciplines; can our distinct trainings and practices shed any light on each other? In this brief essay I shall ask whether my understanding of hallucinosis adds anything to our appreciation of Kusama's artworks and whether, in turn, her artistic rendering of hallucinatory ways of perceiving the world tells us something new about the psychological process. Borrowed from biology, 'hallucinosis' indicates the state of hallucinating, much as one talks of neurosis or psychosis. We all hallucinate, for instance in our dreams; but 'hallucinosis' indicates a more general condition.

Kusama has always put her ability to hallucinate at the centre of what she is trying to depict. In her autobiographical narratives she gives pride of place to her experience of becoming a flower while sitting at table as a child: looking at the pattern of red flowers on the tablecloth, suddenly she became one of them; they started to chase her, so she flew upstairs to escape them but the stairs collapsed behind her and she fell, spraining her ankle. This is recounted many times; it becomes a poem and a book of poetry (*Violet Obsession* 1997), a sculpture (*Violet Obsession* 1994/2010) and a general motif through much of her work. At other times violets talk and she talks to them. She wants us to see her hallucinotic world: 'I am now determined to create a "Kusama world" which no-one has ever done and trodden into.'[1]

I suggest that being a flower offers a framework for Kusama's sense of self. In an early *Self-Portrait* 1950 (p.194) the centre of her face is an outline of a sunflower (like those in *Lingering Dream* 1949, no.1), with a faint circle around it and lips the only prominent human feature – sealed lips that have talked. To me it looks like a Cyclops-eye sad sunflower superimposed at the centre of a wavy, shadowy face, and then within the sunflower there is a faint echo of the lips from the outer face that is superimposed in its turn on the centre of the flower. Which is which?

Hallucinogenic images are identical with each other. Hence they cannot attain the status of a symbol that requires a point of difference from the object to which it refers. In her experience as a flower, Kusama *is* a flower. If one thing is the same as the other thing, what 'should' have become the symbol of the object becomes the real (the Kusama-flower), and the real (either the real child Kusama or the real tablecloth flower) is eradicated. The flower is now the real Kusama and the child Kusama is obliterated, or a tablecloth flower becomes a walking, talking botanical flower, and a botanical flower becomes a fairy which, in turn, the child becomes.

From within this framing flower self, Kusama looks at the world from an hallucinatory perspective – she plays with the millions of protuberances in or on her body that frighten and fascinate; she looks at the black holes into which one might fall, through webs of nets that keep things at a safe but disquieting, dissociated distance.

Kusama's many 'Infinity Nets' paintings suggest that nets can provide protection from black holes. Entering into a Kusama world is to see both together. In order to join her way of seeing, one needs to be able to shift what psychoanalyst Wilfred Bion called 'the vertex' – the perspective from which one looks. Disagreeing in part with an observation of Sigmund Freud's, Bion wrote: 'I suggest that the patient did not have a phobia of socks, but could see that what Freud thought were socks, were a lot of holes knitted together …' Most of us, most of the time think socks are socks – but we can look differently. We all somewhere dread and yearn for the void. It can be very frightening and simultaneously exciting to realise that the socks you put on in the morning, rather than the comforting, containing knitting that we imagined would protect our feet, are hundreds of holes into which, multiplied infinitely, one might fall forever. Likewise a tennis net can be a gathering of string 'knitted or knotted together' that stops a ball or a mass of holes which would meld into the larger void that awaits us.[2] Kusama knew both how to dread the also exciting void and how to protect herself through distancing – making things that are close up turn very small and far away or alternatively casting a massive veil or a spread of knitting or knotting over the emptiness. Art, the experience of the psychoanalytic clinic and the state of hallucinosis give us different ways of seeing double – holes and nets.

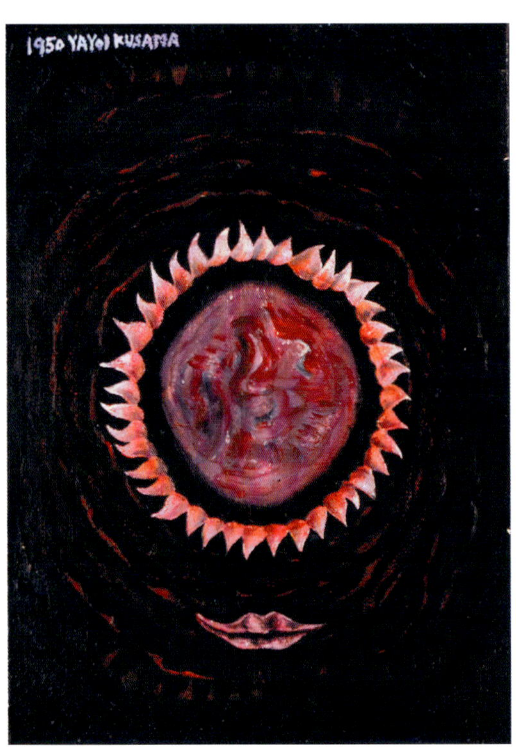

Of Kusama's hallucinations, Alexandra Munroe wrote: 'Hallucinatory experience is not disabling but emancipatory; it opens consciousness up to realms beyond banal and cruel existence.'[3] However, although positive hallucinations provide anyone with the feeling of pleasure that is otherwise missing, these positive hallucinations also depend on negative hallucinations which are frightening and painful. The result of these is not transcendence but anger, even the need to be 'evil' as we see in the suggestion of an 'evil eye' in some of Kusama's pictorial self-portraits and her latest flower sculptures. Many of Kusama's works get their strength from her knowledge of this further double dynamic.

To become a beautiful flower instead of a miserable child involves psychically eradicating the child. Kusama's artworks show the oscillation, or even simultaneity, of her insistent, excessive presence either as herself as only an image of herself (often a photograph) or as some other object or image – an animal or a plant – and her obliteration of herself as a person: in the first staging of *I'm Here, but Nothing* in 2000, only five chairs were around that family table designed for six, which was the size of her childhood family. Kusama depicts what happens when the child vanishes into a flower; it is wonderful and terrifying. As Munroe emphasises elsewhere, it is the art, not the hallucination, that is emancipatory. Kusama states this clearly: 'It is not my hallucinations, it is my will',[4] by which she is surely referring to her determination to depict her world (which can also be ours) for us. The story of the traumatic conditions that necessitated the hallucinatory vertex is part of the process in which the narrative Kusama tells, or the 'construction' she makes, indicates the psychical reality behind the use that she, as artist, makes of her hallucinations.[5]

The point is not to attempt any long-distance 'diagnosis' or wild analysis, but to consider the narratives Kusama herself uses to create her history. In brief, she presents herself as an interesting and gifted child with a creative and uncertain grip on reality, which manifested itself in what were sometimes hallucinations and at other times a child's imaginative identifications with animate and inanimate objects; the latter she would also sometimes smash to frightening, and fascinating, smithereens. According to Kusama, her mother was uncomprehending to the point of abuse of this, her fourth and last child. Her father was very kind to his youngest daughter but ruthlessly unfaithful to his wife, who tried to involve her daughter in the misery produced by his behaviour.

It seems that Kusama's autobiographical narrative comes closest to what the French psychoanalyst André Green claimed was the experience of a 'Dead Mother'. This is a mother whose maternal joy in her baby is suddenly and catastrophically cut short by her falling into a cataclysmic depression with which the baby then identifies. Green lists a number of likely causes for the origin of this 'dead mother complex', from the death of another child to the infidelity of the husband at the precise point where the mother should be supported by the father in her maternal pleasure – the case of Kusama's mother. (There will almost certainly be other factors, but I am referring only to the features of her history that Kusama herself selects.)[6]

Green makes this a very early trauma that occurs at a time when positive hallucination is a dominant mode of perception.

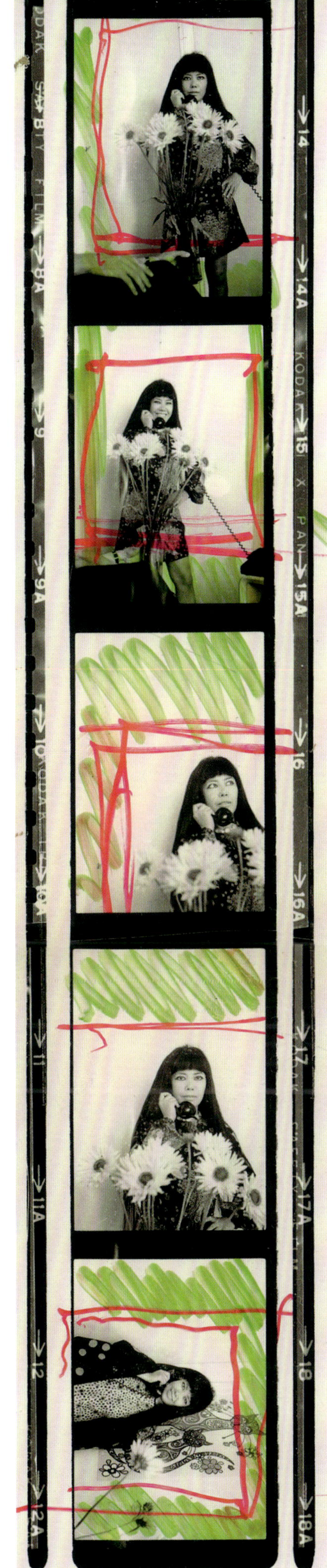

Right: Kusama with a bunch of flowers c.1970
Opposite: *Self-Portrait* 1950
Oil on canvas
34 × 24

Instead of the hallucinations being helped to become realistic perceptions through the internalisation of the good mother as a framing imago of someone who has acknowledged and loved her baby, the traumatised infant has only its own collapse and survival through its total identification with a non-loving, and therefore malign, 'dead' mother. Some of Kusama's outline drawings of female heads in profile certainly suggest portraits of 'dead' mothers; her own fascination with suicide, which seems as though in some sense it has taken place, bear out Green's observations. As Donald Winnicott noted, the catastrophe that is dreaded is the catastrophe that has already happened – it happened in infancy before it could be known about.

Thinking about Kusama's work, there would seem to be two stages to negative hallucinations. First there is the deathly unconscious eradication or scotomisation (the deliberate but total failure to see) of an image of a live person that should be there: a patient who introduced Winnicott to Jacques Lacan's theory of the imaginary 'mirror stage' (see below) added that it would be terrible for a child if it looked in the mirror and saw nothing. There is nothing where there should be something. Then there is a second stage. In states of emptiness, as Green comments, there will be a compensatory flooding in of bad and frightening objects. In a paper entitled 'On Being Empty of Oneself' the analyst Enid Balint, described her patient preferring the terrifying, raging wolves she 'saw' to the experience of nothing.[7]

With 'emptiness' we immediately come upon a cultural divergence. The state of emptiness for Western patients is the scene (or non-scene), the inner void that can only be *a-voided* by the proliferation of negative hallucinations. The person has scotomised the representation of themselves – there is no one in the mirror. The Dead Mother cannot perceive the baby and the baby has become totally identified with the unseeing mother. Anything is better than this emptiness.

In Japanese life and art, however, in and beyond Zen Buddhism, emptiness has a positive valence. In Western iconography, an empty mirror signifies that the person who is looking in is dead – a ghoul or a ghost. In the Orient an empty mirror signifies that symbols have no referents, nothing to clutter the spirit. A symbol without a referent is of course empty and we can start again from nothing. But just as Kusama adds a bright blue Western pigment to her depiction of perfect Japanese empty space (see Midori Yamamura on *Lingering Dream*, no.1, in this volume), so her mirrors echo each other in a beautiful kaleidoscopic dance of a million points of light or relay the artist's reflection repeated to infinity. Kusama is not there, but she would seem to be having her emptiness in both Eastern and Western ways.

What does Kusama show us when she looks at herself in a mirror? It seems possible she sometimes see nothing. Frontal images early in her career depict the point of merging between her vanished self and the object she became – particularly the flower. Later this would become a clearer transformation into a humanoid cat or monkey face. However, profile portraits increasingly feature in her work. It is impossible to see one's own complete profile in a mirror: her profile self-portraits, therefore, would suggest that she is not looking in a mirror but envisaging herself as the imaginary 'other'.

In 1973 Kusama made *Flowers and Self-Portrait* (no.85), a lovely segmented collage with an image of a simple flower beside a larger profile of a girl with caterpillar eyebrow and butterflies, fish and moths playing in and out of her hair. In 1977 the frontal portrait *Me* featured a profile bust on the chest. These particular profiles are benign but prefigure images of women in her most recent paintings which, perhaps because they are profiles and 'other', allow her to introduce malign aspects into her paintings.

The 2009 *Self-Portrait* has a sinister eye and a mouth halfway between frontal and profile; the surrounding painting has two near 'evil eyes' but the portrait is echoed and normalised (eyes and mouths) as it is repeated in the many profiles around it. As in many other paintings, these are linear to the point of resembling imaginary Arabic script. This profile perhaps indicates that Kusama has filled a frightening emptiness with a negative hallucination of herself in the form of her mother-as-wicked-witch or gypsy at the same time as she is representing that this is also not herself. In 2008 she finally paints a frontal *Self-Portrait* of herself as an ageless girl. If she has seen only an empty mirror, then it may be she has learnt that she is/was this person through her use of photographs.

From her early years, Kusama has used photographs of herself in her installations, in her happenings, with her paintings and in photo collages. Bryony Fer describes how the photograph's stillness relates to the movement around it.[8] Here I only want to suggest that where Kusama's self-image is concerned, the photograph takes the place of the mirror. Lacan famously described the uncoordinated infant captured in fascination by its still image in the mirror; the photograph substitutes for this moment and allows Kusama to see herself.

In 2009 Kusama produced *Flowers That Bloom at Midnight* (p.149), several huge sculptures reminiscent of one-time children's television programme *Bill and Ben the Flowerpot Men*. These are not explicitly self-portraits, but I want to treat them as commentaries on the flower-as-self motif in her work. A 2009 photograph of these sculptures shows the artist as she is in the present with orange hair, dotted orange dress; familiar orange sealed lips pick up the orange outline of the sculpture's flower-head, which in its turn has at its centre the evil eye (part orange and dotted) of the earlier profile portraits. Utterly fantastic, these sculptures and their photographs have the reality of illustrated folk tales. Flower and artist are finally the same but different, related but not identical. Negative and positive hallucinations have come together in what may signal the limit to the use of hallucinosis for Kusama's self-portraits.

The 'Kusama world' was never only a hallucinotic world; in using hallucinosis deliberately in order to portray her world, she necessarily changed it. In her use of sexuality Kusama takes us beyond the hallucinations that are also a prominent feature of its presentation. The other side to the stillness of the mirror/photograph is movement, as Fer describes. All the different modes of artistic production in which Kusama engages move. This is particularly noticeable after she goes to New York: the Infinity Nets undulate, heave and wriggle; the still dots shimmer, the holes grow deeper, the flowers breathe and talk, high-heeled shoes climb the ladders; in 'Happenings' people dance, gyrate and act. The phallic fields and their later versions as primeval aquatic growths flop flaccidly, writhe and grow erect. What Kusama has brought

Top: *The Moment of Regeneration*
2004
Mixed media
Middle: *Self-Portrait* 2009
Acrylic on canvas
Bottom: *Aftermath of Obliteration of Eternity* 2009
Mixed media
415 × 415 × 287.4
Opposite: *Flower Obsession* 2000
Sunflower performance, Ibaraki

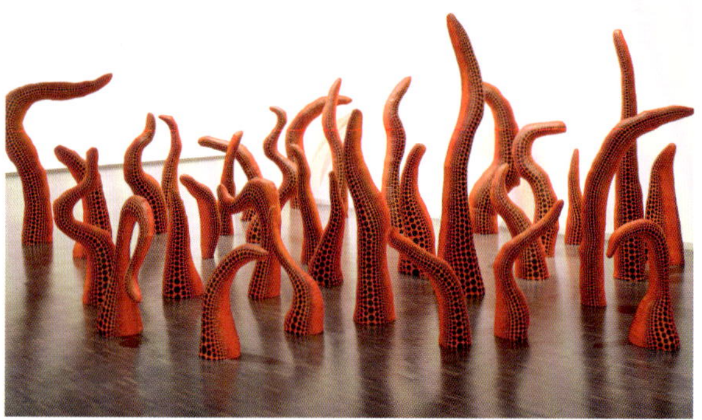

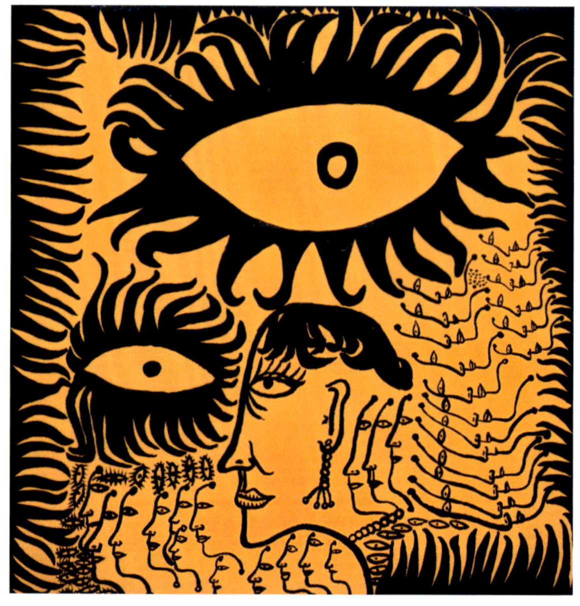

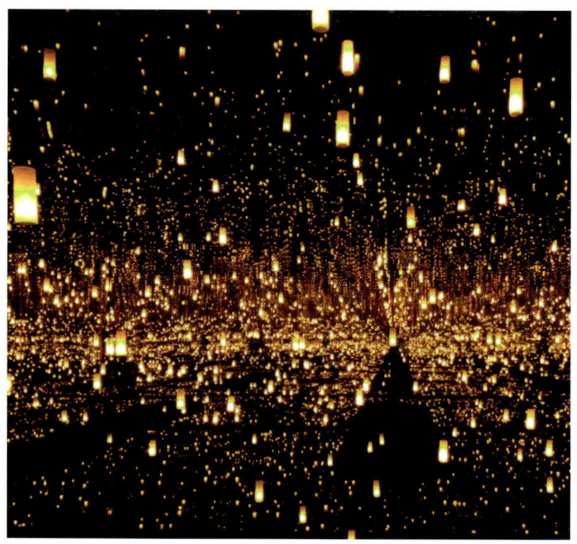

to counteract the deadness of the Dead Mother is the vibrancy of sexuality, which is the force at the centre of the 'life-drive'. It is also murderous as in rape and annihilatory as in the 'death-drive' (see *Desire for Death* 1976, or *I Who Committed Suicide* 1977, no.86).

As Winnicott would have appreciated, Kusama has introduced the polyvalence of sexuality through playfulness. The artist has frequently stated that she has been 'obsessed' as much as frightened by sexuality. Sexuality – its ecstatic pleasures and dangers – thus offers a homologue to the positive and negative hallucinations of the facial portraits: it too is her – and us.

The hat that bursts with hand-sewn penises in all stages of excitement is another ego or 'I'.[9] These are bisexual phalli belonging to girls no less than to boys. Before the prohibition of the Oedipus complex, girls and boys have the same phallic excitement. This is not the phallus of reproduction and sexual difference ('I am too busy with myself to worry about a male-woman problem'[10]). It is auto-erotic but, more importantly here, it is the fun-phallus that passes between children as they play their games of derring-do, of fear and pleasure.

There is very little in Kusama's work about reproduction, maternity or childbirth; 'the feminine mystique',[11] to which women and girls must submit, is parodied. Second-wave feminism of the late 1960s and early 1970s, particularly in New York, floridly advocated clitoral over vaginal sexuality. Kusama is not appropriating the male organ so much as saying 'I have got one too' and it is everywhere. In late infancy girls have a phallus (it may need to grow or it may be hidden) just as boys can be pregnant and give birth. Or so they both think. Sometimes the penis/clitoris is flaccid, having a rest, sometimes it is erect, excited and ready to go. The excitement can be had anywhere – on sofas, in boats, in shoes that fetishise, on chairs, dressers, ladders, in kitchens – the venues are limitless. The infinite multiplication of phallic forms refers to the infinite pleasure they can bring. If the girl as flower frames her existence, the lively sexual excess gives it content. The traumatised young child (or its revival in the unhappy adult) often manifests an over-excited over-sexualisation of pleasure. Turned into art, the superabundance of phalli is a witty representation of this.

What is normally emphasised with regard to the proliferation of phalli, the numerous Infinity Nets, holes and dots that have risen from holes, is their repetition. Compulsive repetition marks a traumatic experience: the trauma has permeated the psychological protective barrier and exploded inside with an 'unbound' energy; what fragment is left of the shattered ego repeatedly tries to get hold of this wild energy and bind it. Kusama's personal obsessions may be what she refers to as 'the stereotyped repetition of my illness' – but this is not the case with her art. Here depicting the same problematic issues over and over again in ways that nevertheless always differ, is a portrayal not of repetition but of superabundance.

The famous instance that underpins our expectation of compulsive repetition is Freud's observation of his grandchild mastering his mother's absence by obsessively throwing and retrieving a cotton-reel that represents her (the '*fort/da*' game). But Kusama's work does not know punctuation. There is no loss and regaining. The macaroni strewn on the floor may be crunched up and broken into pieces by the feet of visitors to the gallery, but this is like the windowpanes she claims to have shattered as a child.

Smashing to fragments is a homologue to feeling oneself fragmented and in pieces ('I went to pieces') – there is an equation between the broken-up object and the broken-up subject. Some traumatic reactions only elicit an unpunctuated stream that is also witnessed in addiction. Kusama has said she wants to drink endless cups of coffee, eat endless amounts of spaghetti, for fifty hours at a time to paint endless nets and dots; that life and death are a continuum in such a way that there is no real distinction between them. The point about infinity is that it is infinite and therefore needs Infinity Nets if one is not to fall off the edge of the world.

By the time of Kusama's latest work the phalli have also morphed into sea beasts, primitive plants rising from the depths or staying there as a tangled mass, creatures suggesting sexuality as the place of growth and energy, which can be 'agglomerated', 'accumulated' or 'aggregated'.[12] The excitement transformed into such images can produce a matching pleasure and anxiety in the viewer. Suicide can be painted, obliteration staged, so that the artistic representation itself becomes the symbol of what it depicts; playfulness can enter into the annihilation of the self and make it only an absence from which a presence – the artwork – can be born.

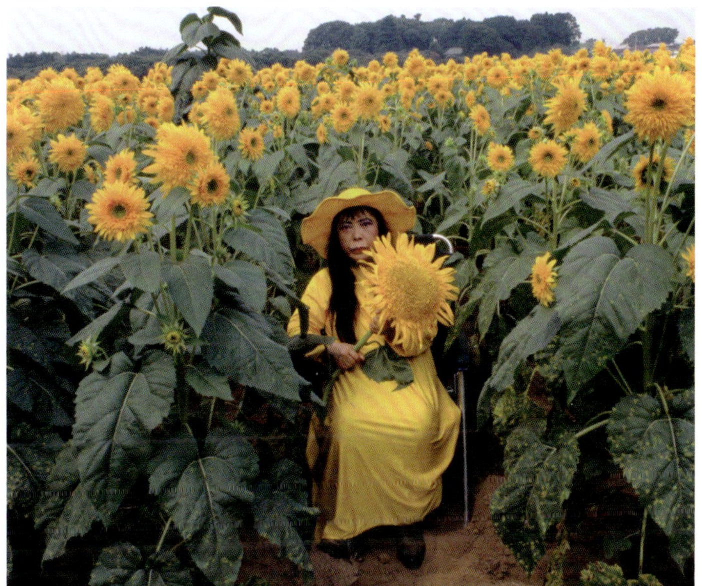

Notes

Introduction
Frances Morris

1 Yayoi Kusama, interview with Akira Tatehata in *Yayoi Kusama*, London 2000, pp.10–11.
2 Yayoi Kusama, 'Pipuru' ['People'], *Geijutsu Shinchō*, June 1959, p.31.
3 Yayoi Kusama, 'Onna hitori kokusai gadan o yuko' ['A lone woman goes in the international art world'], *Geijustsu Shinchō*, May 1961, pp.127–9.

Section Introductions
Rachel Taylor

Early Years 1929–1957

1 Masao Tsuruoka, 'Solo Exhibition of Yayoi Kusama', *Mizue*, May 1954, p.62.
2 Kenjirō Okamoto, 'New Faces: Yayoi Kusama', *Geijutsu Shinchō*, May 1955, p.14.
3 Yayoi Kusama, *Infinity Net: The Autobiography of Yayoi Kusama*, trans. Ralph McCarthy, London 2011, p.93.
4 Yayoi Kusama, quoted in Alexandra Munroe, 'Obsession, Fantasy and Outrage: The Art of Yayoi Kusama', *Yayoi Kusama: A Retrospective*, exh. cat., Center for International Contemporary Arts, New York 1989, p.12.

Coming to America: Infinity Net Paintings 1957–1961

1 Kusama, *Infinity Net*, p.20.
2 Ibid., p.21.
3 Ibid., p.23.
4 Stuart Preston, 'Twentieth-Century Sense and Sensibility', *New York Times*, 7 May 1961.

Accumulation Sculptures and Collages 1961–1965

1 Brian O'Doherty, 'Exhibitions Playing a Wide Field: International Selections of Painting and Sculpture in Local Galleries', *New York Times*, 29 December 1963.
2 Kusama, *Infinity Net*, p.47.

Walking Piece, Narcissus Garden and Self-Portraiture 1966

1 Bhupendra Karia, 'Biographical Notes', *Yayoi Kusama: A Retrospective*, exh. cat., Center for International Contemporary Arts, New York 1989, p.87.

Kusama's Self-Obliteration and the Rise of Happenings 1967–1973

1 Press release, June 1967.
2 *Village Voice*, 28 November 1968.

Experiments in Sculpture and Painting 1980s and 1990s

1 Bhupendra Karia, 'Biographical Notes', *Yayoi Kusama: A Retrospective*, exh. cat., Center for International Contemporary Arts, New York 1989, p.104.

Rising from Totalitarianism: Yayoi Kusama 1945–1955
Midori Yamamura

1 Kusama, *Infinity Net*, p.84; Digital recording of Kusama, interview by the author, Tokyo, 28 July 2006.
2 Hibino Kakei, letter to Harada Heisaku, 24 April 1989, Blanton Museum of Art Archives, University of Texas, Austin; Saeki Izumi (née Matsumoto), interview by Akie Terai based on the author's questions, 15 March 2007.
3 Yayoi Kusama, fax to the author, 1 March 2007.
4 Harada Katsumasa et al., *Shōwa niman'nichi no zenkiroku: Shōwa Day by Day* [*The Complete Record of Shōwa's 20,000 Days*], Tokyo 1990, vol.6, pp.50, 206.
5 Ibid., p.206.
6 Kazu Kaidō, 'Reconstruction: The Role of the Avant-Garde in Post-War Japan', *Reconstructions: Avant-Garde Art in Japan 1945–1965*, exh. cat., Museum of Modern Art, Oxford 1985, p.14.
7 Terai Akie, email to the author, 23 June 2010.
8 Yayoi Kusama, interview by Yōko Kawasaki based on the author's questions, 11 May 2007.
9 Kusama, fax to the author, 1 March 2007.
10 *Shōwa Day by Day*, pp.294–5.
11 Hamano Takiko, 'Watashi no taiken' ['My Experience'], *Nagano-ken hyakunen-shi* [*One Hundred Years of Nagano Prefecture*], Matsumoto 1984, p.62.
12 Kusama, fax to the author, 1 March 2007.
13 Yayoi Kusama, interview by Bhupendra Karia and Alexandra Munroe, Tokyo, 17 December 1988, the Fine Arts Library, University of Texas, Austin, CICA/ATT/001.06.
14 Narai Osamu, *The Modern Japanese Economy*, Tokyo 1984, p.11.
15 Hamano 1984, p.62.
16 Kusama, interview by Karia and Munroe, 17 December 1988.
17 *One Hundred Years of Nagano Prefecture*, pp.6, 10–11.
18 Kaidō 1985, p.14.
19 The Meiji Restoration was the beginning of Japan's transition from the feudal warlord polities to a modern nation-state.
20 For more on *Nihonga*, see Victoria Weston, *Japanese Painting and National Identity: Okakura Tenshin and His Circle*, Ann Arbor 2004.
21 *Nihonga* painters first make studies from life. They then make a composition based on their sketches. A satisfactory design will be made into a cartoon and transferred to a tableau base. Colouring follows to complete it.
22 Kawakita Michiaki, *Hayami Gyoshū sono hito to geijutsu* [*Gyoshū Hayami: His Art and Personality*], Tokyo 1977, p.10.
23 Tape No.16, Origin FAB 4169, Magnetic Recording Library, Library of Congress, Washington, D.C.
24 Andrew Gordon, *A Modern History of Japan: From Tokugawa Times to the Present*, New York and Oxford 2003, p.200.
25 Yayoi Kusama, interview by Bhupendra Karia and Alexandra Munroe, Tokyo, 16–18 December 1988.
26 Yayoi Kusama, 'Onna hitori kokusai gadan wo yuku' ['A lone woman goes into the international art world'], *Geijutsu Shinchō* [*New Current in Art*], May 1961, p.128.
27 Kusama, fax to the author, 1 March 2007.
28 Yayoi Kusama, 'Tobei o mae ni shite' ['On the Eve of Departure for the US'], [unidentified magazine, probably 1957], Kusama Papers, Kusama Studio, Tokyo.
29 Akira Tatehata, 'Spontaneous Surrealism', *Love Forever: Yayoi Kusama, 1958–1968*, exh. cat., Los Angeles County Museum of Art, 1998, p.62.
30 Uemura Takachiyo, 'Bijutsu to kagaku' ['Art and Science'], *Atorie* [*Atelier*], September 1947; 'Chūshō kaiga no mondai' ['The Issues in Abstract Art'], *Mizue*, November 1947.
31 Kusama, 'On the Eve of Departure'.
32 Tatehata 1998, p.62.
33 Kawakita 1977, pp.16–17.
34 Rupert Cox, *The Zen Arts: An Anthropological Study of the Culture of Aesthetic Form*, London and New York 2003, pp.48–69.
35 Kawakita 1977, pp.94–5.
36 Kusama, *Infinity Net*, p.76.
37 Seki Naoko, 'Taidan, Miura Kiyohiro/Kusama Yayoi' ['A Dialogue between Kiyohiro Miura and Yayoi Kusama'], *In Full Bloom: Yayoi Kusama, Years in Japan*, exh. cat., Tokyo 1999, p.24.
38 Ueshima Chōken, 'Bijutsukai kotoshi no momegoto' ['Art World's Scandals This Year'], *Bijutsu techō* [Art notebook], no.12, December 1948, p.41.
39 Mikami Makoto et al., 'Panreal Manifesto', *Genesis of Panreal Exhibition*, exh. cat., Nishinomiya 1998, p.3.
40 Yayoi Kusama, letter to Georgia O'Keeffe, 13 December 1955, Kusama Papers.
41 Yayoi Kusama, 'Invitation, First Solo Exhibition', 18–19 March 1952, Kusama Papers.
42 Mikami Makoto et al., 1998, p.3.
43 Nakai Yasuyuki, '"Panreal Art Association" Circa Establishment', ibid., p.14.
44 Yayoi Kusama, Fujimoto Tokuji, Ibe Masataka, 'Kusama joshi o kakonde "Geijutsukendan (Jō)"' ['With Miss Kusama'], *Shinano ōrai*, October 1978, p.18.
45 Between 1950 and 1952 Kusama also experimented with oil painting. See Midori Yamamura, 'Re-Viewing Kusama, 1950–1975: Biography of Things', *Yayoi Kusama, Mirrored Years*, Franck Gautherot (ed.), exh. cat., Dijon 2009, pp.63–76.
46 Anon., 'Kotoshi no hōpu, joryū gaka Kusama Yayoi' ['This Year's Hope, a Woman Artist Yayoi Kusama'], *Chūbu keizai shinbun*, 12 January 1955, Kusama Papers.
47 Anon., 'Kusama Yayoi Ten' ['Yayoi Kusama Exhibition'], Matsumoto 1952, Kusama Papers, n.p.
48 Nishimaru Shihō, *Hōkōki: Kyōki o ninatte* [*Records of Wandering: Taking on Insanity*], Tokyo 1991, pp.65–9.
49 Yayoi Kusama, interview by Alexandra Munroe, 14 December 1988, CICA/ATT/001.01.
50 For details, see Midori Yamamura, 'Kusama Yayoi's Early Years in New York: A Critical Biography', *Making A Home*, Eric C. Shiner and Reiko Tomii (ed.), exh. cat., New York 2007, pp.54–5.
51 Takiguchi Shūzō, 'Yōsei yo eien ni' ['Eternal Fairy'], *Yohaku ni kaku (2)* [*Marginalia, 2*], Tokyo 1982, p.305.
52 The Surrealist decalcomania technique was invented to achieve an accidental image by placing a blot of ink or a dab of paint onto a piece of paper, which is pressed against another sheet, creating two contingent patterns.
53 Yayoi Kusama, 'Iwan no baka' ['Ivan the Fool'], *Geijutsu Shinchō* [*New Current in Art*], May 1955, pp.164–5.

54 Three of Kusama's works were included in the *18th International Watercolor Exhibition* at the Brooklyn Museum, New York, in 1955.
55 'General Fact Sheet, American Cultural Centers in Japan', The National Archives, College Park, MD, B. 7359, Department of State Decimal File RG 59, 250, p.2.
56 Yayoi Kusama, letter to Georgia O'Keeffe, 15 November 1955.
57 Yayoi Kusama, letter to Neil Meitzler, 17 December 1955, Neil Meitzler Papers, University of Washington, Seattle.
58 Sarah Truax Albert, 'The Story of an Art Gallery', *Tribute to Zoe Dusanne: Modern Art Pavilion of the Seattle Art Museum*, exh. brochure, Seattle Center, Seattle 1977, n.p.
59 Zoe Dusanne, letter to Yayoi Kusama, 14 January 1956, Zoe Dusanne Papers, University of Washington, Seattle.
60 Yayoi Kusama, letter to Neil Meitzler, 11 January 1956.
61 Yayoi Kusama, letter to Neil Meitzler, 31 May 1956.
62 Cheryl Conkelton and Laura Landau, *Northwest Mythologies: The Interactions of Mark Tobey, Morris Graves, Kenneth Callahan, and Guy Anderson*, exh. cat., Seattle and London 2003, p.15.
63 Bahá'í is a Persian universalistic faith in which various manifestations of God throughout history contribute to human progress.
64 Anon., 'Kihin ni afurete iru' ['Full of Gracefulness'], *Asahi shinbun*, 28 December 1957, Kusama Papers.
65 Yayoi Kusama, letter to Neil Meitzler, 20 March 1956.
66 Conkelton and Landau 2003, p.22.
67 Anon., 'Kodoku no gaka Kusama Yayoi raishi' ['Solitary Artist Yayoi Kusama Visits Seattle'], *Hokubei Hōchi*, 2 December 1957, p.5.
68 Kusama, 'Ivan the Fool', pp.164–5
69 Ibid., p.165.
70 Benjamin wrote that it was 'the purity and beauty of a failure' that made Kafka's writings work. Walter Benjamin, 'Some Reflections on Kafka', *Illuminations*, Harry Zohn (trans.), Hannah Arendt (ed.), New York 1969, pp.141–5.
71 Fukushima Tatsuo, 'Shinpifū na sakuhin, chūmoku sareru Kusama Yayoi no koten' ['Mysterious Work, Remarkable Exhibition of Yayoi Kusama'], unknown newspaper, 6 April 1955, Kusama Papers.
72 Yayoi Kusama, letter to Neil Meitzler, 17 November 1956.

Infinity Politics

Mignon Nixon

1 All the italicised epigrams, except where indicated otherwise, are from Yayoi Kusama, *Infinity Net*, London 2011: pp.93, 20, 23, 47, 39, 137.
2 Ibid., p.14. Kusama records that 'To help cover travel expenses, I changed a million yen into dollars . . . This was of course against the law. In those days, a million yen was enough money to build several houses. I smuggled those few thousand dollars out of the country by sewing some of the bills into my dress and stuffing others into the toes of my shoes.' Kusama had tracked down O'Keeffe's address from Tokyo and wrote to her, enclosing several watercolours.
3 Ibid., p.11. She recalls that she hoped to sell the drawings and some fine kimonos she had also brought from Japan.
4 This comparison is repeated constantly in the reviews and interviews that accompanied Kusama's curatorial resurrection in the United States in the 1990s. For example, Andrew Solomon records that 'By 1968, Kusama was as famous as it gets. It is alleged that she received more mentions in the New York press than even Warhol.' Andrew Solomon, 'Dot Dot Dot', *Artforum*, February 1997, p.100.
5 *Village Voice*, for example, published this comment in its 28 November 1968 issue: 'Kusama is definitely suffering from over-exposure of over-exposure.' Quoted in Alexandra Munroe, 'Obsession, Fantasy and Outrage: The Art of Yayoi Kusama', in Bhupendra Karia (ed.), *Yayoi Kusama: A Retrospective*, exh. cat., Center for International Contemporary Arts, New York 1989.
6 Kusama, *Infinity Net*, p.17.
7 Ibid. 'New York was in every way a fierce and violent place… Compared to Seattle, this city was hell on earth. Spending all my time on my work and studies, I soon burned through what dollars I had getting enough food to make it through the day; scraping together cash for canvas and paints; problems with Immigration about my visa; illness…'
8 Two particularly evocative memoirs of the era, and artists' living conditions, are Yvonne Rainer's *Feelings Are Facts: A Life*, Cambridge, MA, 2006, and Patti Smith's *Just Kids*, New York 2010.
9 For an account of Kusama's wartime experience and its influence on her art, see Midori Yamamura, 'Rising from Totalitarianism: Yayoi Kusama, 1945–1955', in this volume.
10 Kusama, *Infinity Net*, p.20.
11 Extract of letter quoted in ibid., p.83.
12 For an excellent account of Kusama's early career in New York and her ties to Japan during this time, see Midori Yamamura, 'Kusama Yayoi's Early Years in New York: A Critical Biography', *Making A Home*, Eric C. Shiner and Reiko Tomii (eds.), exh. cat., New York 2007. According to Yamamura, Kusama's parents sent her money monthly, 'secretly hiding Japanese yen in airmail envelopes' (p.59).
13 Yamamura has observed that 'the Seattle group's attempts to convey the vastness of the universe through the smallest detail of nature' made this a receptive milieu for Kusama's work. See 'Rising from Totalitarianism'.
14 From a letter of 1957 to O'Keeffe, excerpted in Karia, *Yayoi Kusama: A Retrospective*, p.73.
15 According to Yamamura, Kusama's visa expired in 1959, and she was forced to switch to a student visa, which she fulfilled by enrolling at the Art Students League in 1960. Yamamura, 'Yayoi Kusama's Early Years', p.59.
16 Donald Judd, 'Reviews and Previews: New Names This Month', *Artnews* 58, no.6 (October 1959), p.17.
17 Sidney Tillim, 'In the Galleries', *Arts* 34, no.1 (October 1959), p.56.
18 Dore Ashton, 'Art: Tenth Street View', *New York Times*, 23 October 1959.
19 Kusama, *Infinity Net*, p.26.
20 Ibid., p.29.
21 Kusama made *Self-Obliteration* in the summer of 1967 with the collaboration of Jud Yalkut. For a contemporary discussion of the filming, and the naked happenings and demonstrations that inspired and are incorporated in it, see Jud Yalkut, 'The Polka-Dot Way of Life (Conversation with Yayoi Kusama)', *New York Free Press* 1, no.8 (15 February 1968), pp.8–9.
22 Kusama, *Infinity Net*, p.23.
23 On the question of abstraction and the 'woman artist', see Anne Middleton Wagner, *Three Artists (Three Women): Modernism and the Art of Hesse, Krasner and O'Keeffe*, Berkeley 1996.
24 On gestural painting and gender performance in the 1950s, see Griselda Pollock, 'Killing Men and Dying Women: A Woman's Touch in the Cold Zone of American Painting in the 1950s', in Fred Orton and Griselda Pollock: *Avant-Gardes and Partisans Reviewed*, Manchester 1996.
25 The apartment belonged to the architect George Matsuda. Contemporary photographs show the space largely taken up with Kusama's prolific production.
26 Kusama, *Infinity Net*, p.158.
27 Félix Guattari, 'Les Riches Affects de Madame Yayoï Kusama', *Yayoi Kusama: Infinity Explosion*, exh. cat., Fuji Television Gallery, Tokyo 1986, p.17, translated in Kusama, *Infinity Net*, p.141.
28 Kusama quoted in Yalkut, 'The Polka-Dot Way of Life', p.8.
29 Ibid. Kusama also compares her artistic process to 'continuing to drink thousands of cups of coffee or eating thousands of feet of macaroni'.
30 See Yamamura, 'Rising from Totalitarianism'.
31 Kusama, *Infinity Net*, p.26.
32 Kusama quoted in Andrew Soloman, 'Dot, Dot, Dot', *Artforum*, February 1997, p.66.
33 Juliet Mitchell has observed that 'Repetition is a response to trauma. As with replication, seriality is the symbolization of the repetition of trauma.' Tamar Garb and Mignon Nixon, 'A Conversation with Juliet Mitchell', *October* 113 (Summer 2005), p.20. This formulation might provide a useful way of thinking about how Kusama's art sustains a tension between repetition-as-trauma and seriality as the symbolic representation of it.
34 Kusama is reported to have been a Beatles fan.
35 Karia, *Yayoi Kusama: A Retrospective*, p.79.
36 Briony Fer offers an elegant analysis of *Aggregation: One Thousand Boats Show* and the relationship between photography and the tableau in *The Infinite Line: Re-Making Art After Modernism*, New Haven and London 2004, pp.91–4.
37 I discuss this conjuncture of the part-object (object of the drive) and the readymade in Kusama's art in 'o+x', *October* 119 (Winter 2007), pp.6–20.
38 The point that the photographs in the installation produce the effect of a *mise en abyme* was first made by J.F. Rodenbeck in 'Yayoi Kusama: Surface Stitch Skin', in *Inside the Visible: An Elliptical Traverse of 20th-Century Art in, of and from the Feminine*, ed. M. Catherine de Zegher, Cambridge, Mass., 1996, p.151.
39 Mel Bochner, 'The Serial Attitude', *Artforum* 16, no.4 (December 1967), pp.28–33. Midori Yamamura discusses the Infinity Nets in terms of seriality in 'Transforming Infinity: Yayoi Kusama's Net Paintings', in *Yayoi Kusama*, ed. Louise Neri (New York 2009), p.29.
40 Briony Fer's idea of 'partial repetitions' is suggestive here. See Fer, *The Infinite Line*, p.94.
41 Sigmund Freud, 'The Uncanny' (1919), in *The Standard Edition of the Complete Psychological Works of Sigmund Freud*, ed. and trans. James Strachey, London 1955, vol.17, pp.219–56.
42 For a discussion of infantile sexuality in Kusama's work as a mode of resistance to phallocentrism, see my *Fantastic Reality: Louise Bourgeois and a Story of Modern Art*, Cambridge, MA, 2005, pp.261–4.
43 Kusama, *Infinity Net*, p.17.
44 Virginia Woolf, *Three Guineas* (1938), in *A Room of One's Own/Three Guineas*, ed. Michèle Barrett, London 1993, p.270.
45 Recounting an episode in October 1967, when she staged a performance at the opening of an exhibition in Amsterdam, daubing the skin of the naked participants with fluorescent paint, Kusama recalls that she remonstrated with the audience, when it reacted angrily to the work, 'that the suppression of sex was directly related to war' (*Infinity Net*, p.115). Elsewhere in her autobiography, Kusama writes: 'My name was in the tabloids day after day, magazines carried stories about me, and the public was fascinated by my activities and movements. This said a lot about where people's real interests lay and proved how starved they were for Love and Peace.' In April 1969, Kusama recalls, 'the artist Louis Abolafia and I conducted a Happening to kick off our campaign for mayor of New York City on the Love and Nudity platform' (ibid., p.139).
46 According to Alexandra Munroe, Kusama staged some seventy-five happenings between 1967 and 1970, most of them in New York. Munroe, 'Obsession, Fantasy and Outrage,' p.29. Laura Hoptman puts the number closer to two hundred. Hoptman, 'The Princess of the Polka Dot', *Bazaar* (March 1998), p.388.
47 Kusama, 'Press Release for Naked Protest on Wall Street, New York, 10.30 a.m., Sunday 16 October, 1968', in Laura Hoptman, Akira Tatahata and Udo Kultermann, *Yayoi Kusama*, London 2000, p.107. The press release advertises a second event at the site. Photographs document Kusama with the four naked dancers at the Stock Exchange on 14 July 1968.
48 Munroe, 'Obsession, Fantasy and Outrage', p.30.
49 Hallucination and depersonalisation are terms often invoked by Kusama and her critics to describe the artist's subjective experience.

I'm Here, but Nothing: Yayoi Kusama's Environments

Jo Applin

1 Yayoi Kusama interviewed by Glenn Scott Wright, *Yayoi Kusama*, exh. cat., Victoria Miro Gallery, London 2008, n.p.
2 See Laura Hoptman, 'Yayoi Kusama: A Reckoning', *Yayoi Kusama*, London 2000, pp.32–83.
3 Yayoi Kusama interviewed by Gordon Brown, 1964, reprinted in Laura Hoptman, Akira Tatehata and Udo Kultermann, *Yayoi Kusama*, London and New York 2000, p.104.
4 Yayoi Kusama in Hoptman et al. 2000, p.103. See also my 'Resisting Infinity', in *Yayoi Kusama*, exh. cat., Victoria Miro Gallery, London 2008, n.p.
5 Yayoi Kusama interviewed by Glenn Scott Wright, 2008.
6 Donald Judd, 'Reviews and Previews: New Names this Month', *Art News*, October 1959, in *Donald Judd: The Complete Writings 1959–1975*, Halifax and New York 1975, p.2.
7 Ibid. Judd also included references to Kusama in his essay 'Specific Objects', in *Arts Yearbook 8: Contemporary Sculpture*, introduction by William Seitz, New York 1965, pp.74–83.
8 Judd, 'Yayoi Kusama' [1964], in *Donald Judd: The Complete Writings*, p.134.
9 Yayoi Kusama, quoted by Akira Tatehata in 'Magnificent Obsession', Pavilion, XLV Venice Biennale, *Yayoi Kusama*, Tokyo 1993, as cited in Hoptman, 2000, p.37.
10 Yayoi Kusama, artist's statement, 1964, as quoted in Udo Kulterman, '*Driving Image, Essen*', in Hoptman et al. 2000, p.89.
11 Edward T. Kelly, 'Neo-Dada: A Critique of Pop Art', *Art Journal*, vol.23, no.3, Spring 1964, pp.192–201, p.200.
12 See, for example, Mignon Nixon, 'Posing the Phallus', *October*, no.92, Spring 2000, pp.98–127, and Briony Fer, 'Objects Beyond Objecthood', *Oxford Art Journal*, vol.22, no.2, 1999, pp.25–36.
13 See Diedrich Diederson, 'Obsession as Revolution: Yayoi Kusama Follows Up a Hallucination with the Social Reality', in *Yayoi Kusama: Mirrored Years*, Rotterdam and Dijon 2008, pp.111–22.
14 Yayoi Kusama in Hoptman et al. 2000, p.104.
15 Ibid., p.119.
16 Ibid.
17 Hannah Arendt, *The Human Condition* [1958], Chicago 1998, p.199.
18 Ibid., p.52.
19 Ibid., p.52. See also Linda M.G. Zerilli, *Feminism and the Abyss of Freedom*, Chicago 2005, pp.19 and 199.
20 For recent literature on the idea of 'community' in relation to contemporary art, see *Communities of Sense: Rethinking Aesthetics and Politics*, ed. Beth Hinderliter, William Kaizen, Vered Maimon, Jaleh Mansoor and Seth McCormick, Durham and London 2009.
21 Hannah Arendt, 'What is Freedom?', in *Between Past and Future: Eight Exercises in Political Thought*, New York 1954, p.160.
22 Arendt [1958] 1998, p.183.
23 Zerilli argues that Arendt's 'space of appearances' is helpful in imagining a specifically feminist space of action and participation in which a model of collective freedom replaces the usual formulation of the 'subject question' in feminism as rooted in individual agency. Although Kusama resists feminist readings of her work, Zerilli's account of freedom and feminism offers a striking model through which to consider her environments. See Zerilli 2005.
24 See Hoptman et al. 2000.
25 'Take a Subway Ride from Jail to Paradise'. Press release for Happening on the Canarsie Line MBT 14th SW, New York, Sunday 12 noon, 17 November 1968, reprinted in Hoptman et al. 2000, p.114.

Portrait of the Artist as a Young Flower

Juliet Mitchell

1 Yayoi Kusama, 'A Process to Creation', in *Yayoi Kusama*, exh. cat., National Museum of Modern Art, Tokyo 2004.
2 W.R. Bion, *Brazilian Lectures*, vol.1, ed. Jayme Salomão, Rio de Janeiro, Brazil 1974, pp.38–9. Bion differentiates between the construction of hallucinations and illusions/delusions. He also introduced the term 'hallucinosis' for psychological sensory hallucinations. In this essay I am indebted particularly to his late work, some of which could have been written with Yayoi Kusama in mind, just as her work could have helped him formulate his ideas on moving the 'vertex' from the psychoanalytic clinic to the art world.
3 Alexandra Munroe, 'Between Heaven and Earth: The Literary Art of Yayoi Kusama', in *Love Forever: Yayoi Kusama 1958–1968*, Los Angeles 1998, pp.70–87.
4 Interview, 'Akira Tatehata in conversation with Yayoi Kusama', in Laura Hoptman, Akira Tatehata, and Udo Kultermann, *Yayoi Kusama*, London and New York 2000, p.16.
5 Sigmund Freud, 'Constructions in Analysis', in J. Strachey, ed., *The Complete Psychological Works of Sigmund Freud*, vol.XXIII, London 1937, pp.255–70.
6 André Green, 'The Dead Mother', in *On Private Madness*, London 1983/86, pp. 142–74. Green generalises from what I would see as 'accidental' occurrences – what falls to one's particular, individual lot. I myself would point to what befalls any child in the following circumstances: when the next baby arrives, the toddler, who until this moment was the baby, feels its emerging ego is annihilated. The accidental experience in the case of this, the 'sibling trauma' (see J. Mitchell, *Siblings: Sex and Violence*, Cambridge 2003), is that for the only or last child such as Kusama, the expected baby does not arrive and the toddler is left with the anxiety that in its jealousy it has killed it. Any trauma in later life resurrects an earlier trauma such as this key one. There is an element of this general situation in the important way in which Kusama was able to transmute her jealousy of fellow male artists into useful competition with them, particularly during her period in New York. However, the details of Green's thesis and the intricacies of his portrait fit the extremity of Kusama's narrative of her particular experience very well.
7 E. Balint, 'On Being Empty of Oneself', in *Before I Was I: Psychoanalysis and the Imagination*, ed. J. Mitchell and M. Parsons, London 1993, pp.37–56.
8 Bryony Fer, 'Objects beyond Objecthood', in *Oxford Art Journal*, 1999, vol.22, no.2, p.35, and *The Infinite Line: Re-Making Art after Modernism*, New Haven and London 2004, pp.85–99. Fer also applies Green's argument about negative hallucination to Kusama's work.
9 J. Mitchell, 'The Letter "I"', Freud Memorial Lecture. University College London 1986.
10 J. Mitchell, 'Procreative Mothers (Sexual Difference) and Child-Free Sisters (Gender)', in J. Browne, ed., *The Future of Gender*, Cambridge 2007, pp.163–89.
11 B. Friedan, *The Feminine Mystique*, New York 1964.
12 W.R. Bion, 'On Hallucination' [1958], in *Second Thoughts*, London 1967, pp.65–93.

Select Bibliography

Writings and Films by the Artist

Writings

'Iwan no baka' ['Ivan the fool'], *Geijutsu Shinchō* [*New Currents in Art*], May 1955, pp.164–5

'Watashi no mita Amerika no inshō (ge)' ['An impression of the United States from my perspective (second-half)'], *Shinano chūbu maiyū shinbun* [*Nagano Central Evening Post*], 19 March 1958

'Pīpuru' ['People'], *Geijutsu Shinchō*, vol.10 no.6, June 1959, p.31

'Onna hitori kokusai gadan o yuku' ['A lone woman goes into the international art world'], *Geijutsu Shinchō*, May 1961, pp.127–30

'*Narushisusu Gāden* to geijutsu no jiyū to kaihō' ['*Narcissus Garden* and freedom and liberation of art'], unpublished manuscript, c.1966, Kusama Papers

'Nyūyōku gaitō de zen'ra pātī o yatta watashi' ['I hosted nudist parties on streets in New York'], *Gendai* [*Today*], December 1968, pp.288–97

'To the Editor', *The Village Voice*, 17 April 1969

The Story of Tokyo Lee: Dramatic Collage in 10 Parts, unpublished manuscript, c.1970, Kusama Papers

'Waga tamashii no henreki to tatakai' ['Odyssey of my struggling soul'], *Geijutsu seikatsu* [*Art life*], November 1975, pp.96–113

Manhattan jisatsu misui jōshūhan [*Manhattan suicide addict*], Tokyo 1978; repr. pocketbook ed., Tokyo 1984; French ed. Isabelle Charrier (trans.), Dijon 2005. [Fiction]

Kurisutofā danshōkutsu [*Hustler's grotto*], Tokyo 1984; repr. Tokyo 1989; English ed. Ralph F. McCarthy (trans.), Berkeley 1998; Chinese ed. Jiazhen Wu and Yupei Lin (trans.), Taipei 1999. [Fiction]

Mugen no ami: Kusama Yayoi jiden [*Infinity Net: The autobiography of Yayoi Kusama*], Tokyo 2002; English ed. Ralph F. McCarthy (trans.), London 2011

Films

Kusama's Self-Obliteration, art dir. Jud Yalkut, cinematography and editing Shady Film Productions, New York 1967

Love-In Festival, Central Park, New York 1968

Flower Orgy, Yayoi Kusama Studio, New York 1968

Kusama's Room, Yayoi Kusama Studio, Tokyo 1999

Song of Manhattan Suicide Addict, Yayoi Kusama Studio, Tokyo 1999

Flower Obsession Gerbera, Yayoi Kusama Studio, Tokyo 1999

Flower Obsession Sunflower, Ibaraki 2000

Solo Exhibition Catalogues

Dai nikai Kusama Yayoi shinsaku ten [*The second Yayoi Kusama new works' exhibition*], The First Community Centre, Matsumoto 1952. Texts by Nobuya Abe, Yayoi Kusama, Chōichirō Majima, Yutaka Matsuzawa, Shūzō Takiguchi and Kieko Yamazaki

Frick, Thomas (ed.). *Love Forever: Yayoi Kusama, 1958–1968*, Los Angeles County Museum of Art, 1998. Texts by Laura Hoptman, Alexandra Munroe, Akira Tatehata and Lynn Zelevansky; selected exhibition history by Julie Joyce and Kristine C. Kuramitsu

Gautherot, Franck (ed.). *Yayoi Kusama: Performance and Environment, 1962–2000*, Le Consortium, Dijon 2001. Interview by Seung-duk Kim; texts by Xavier Douroux, Franck Gautherot, Robert Nickas, Vincent Pécoil and Éric Troncy

———. *Yayoi Kusama: The Mirrored Years*, Museum Boijmans Van Beuningen, Rotterdam 2009. Introduction by Franck Gautherot, Jaap Guldemond and Seung-duk Kim; texts by Diedrich Diederichsen, Franck Gautherot, Seung-duk Kim, Lily van der Stokker and Midori Yamamura

In Full Bloom: Yayoi Kusama, Years in Japan, Museum of Contemporary Art, Tokyo 1999. Conversation with Kiyohiro Miura; text by Hiroko Seki

Karia, Bhupendra (ed.). *Yayoi Kusama: A Retrospective*, Center for International Contemporary Arts, New York 1989. Introduction and bibliographical notes by Bhupendra Karia; text by Alexandra Munroe; comprehensive bibliography by Reiko Tomii

Kusama Yayoi ten [*Yayoi Kusama exhibition*], Fuji Television Gallery, Tokyo 1984. Texts by Yusuke Nakahara and Pierre Restany

Kusama Yayoi ten [*Yayoi Kusama exhibition*], Kitakyūshū Municipal Museum of Art, 1987. Texts by Yayoi Kusama, Toshiaki Minemura, Jun'ichi Nakajima, Shin'ichi Nakazawa and Herbert Read; chronology by Jun'ichi Nakajima

Kusama Yayoi ten: Hajikeru Uchū [*Yayoi Kusama exhibition: Bursting galaxies*], Sōgetsu Art Museum, Tokyo 1992. Texts by Kiichirō Hayashi, Hakuko Kajiwara, Naoko Kanda, Alexandra Munroe and Tetsuo Tani

Kusama Yayoi: Kusamatrix, Mori Art Museum, Tokyo 2004. Texts by Takashi Azumaya, David Elliott, Yayoi Kusama, Kou Machida, Fumio Nanjō and Ryūichi Sakamoto; chronology by Yayoi Kojima and Mayumi Uchida

Neri, Louise (ed.). *Yayoi Kusama*, Gagosian Gallery, New York 2009. Texts by Louise Neri, Robert Nickas and Midori Yamamura

Obsession: Yayoi Kusama, Fuji Television Gallery, Tokyo 1982. Texts by Gordon Brown, Udo Kultermann, Yūsuke Nakahara and Herbert Read; chronology by Shigeo Chiba

Yayoi Kusama: Infinity Explosion, Fuji Television Gallery, Tokyo 1986. Texts by Félix Guattari and Yayoi Kusama

Yayoi Kusama, 45th Venice Biennale, 1993. Texts by Yayoi Kusama and Akira Tatehata

Yayoi Kusama: Obsessional Vision, Arts Club of Chicago, 1997. Text by Judith Russi Kirshner

Yayoi Kusama Now, Robert Miller Gallery, New York 1998. Interview by Damien Hirst

Yayoi Kusama, Serpentine Gallery, London 2000. Texts by Laura Hoptman and Julia Peyton-Jones

Yayoi Kusama, National Museum of Modern Art, Tokyo 2004. Texts by Hitoshi Dehara, Yayoi Kusama, Tohru Matsumoto, Hiroshi Minamishima and Akira Shibutami; comprehensive bibliography by Hitoshi Dehara

Yayoi Kusama, Victoria Miro Gallery, London 2008. Interview with Glenn Scott Wright; text by Jo Applin; complete list of books by the artist

Books and Group Exhibition Catalogues

Armando, Henk Peeters, Hans Sleutelaar, Cornelis Bastiaan Vaandrager and Hans Verhagen (eds.), *De nieuwe stijl* [*The new style*], vol.1, Amsterdam 1965

Fer, Briony, *The Infinite Line: Re-Making Art After Modernism*, New Haven and London 2004

Forum voor architectuur en daarmee verbonden kunsten, vol.20, no.3, June 1967

Grunenberg, Christoph (ed.), *Summer of Love, Art of the Psychedelic Era*, exh. cat., Tate Liverpool, 2005

Jones, Amelia, *Body Art: Performing the Subject*, Minneapolis 1998

Kaprow, Allan, *Assemblage, Environment & Happenings*, New York 1966

Katz, Jonathan D. and David C. Ward (eds.), *Hide/Seek: Difference and Desire in American Portraiture*, exh. cat., National Portrait Gallery, Washington D.C. 2010

Lippard, Lucy, *Pop Art*, New York 1966

Minioudaki, Kalliopi and Sid Sachs (eds.), *Seductive Subversions: Women Pop Artists, 1958-1968*, exh. cat., University of the Arts, Philadelphia 2010

Molesworth, Helen (ed.), *Part Object, Part Sculpture*, exh. cat., Wexner Center for the Arts, Ohio 2005

Monochrome Malerei, exh. cat., Städtisches Museum Leverkusen Schloss Morsbroich, 1960

Munroe, Alexandra (ed.), *Japanese Art After 1945: Scream Against the Sky*, exh. cat., Solomon R. Guggenheim Museum, New York 1994

Nakajima, Izumi, 'Yayoi Kusama between Abstraction and Pathology', Griselda Pollock (ed.), *Psychoanalysis and the Image*, London 2006, pp.127–60

ZERO, Avant-garde Internationale des années 1950–1960 [*ZERO, International avant-garde, the years 1950–1960*], exh. cat., Museum Kunst Palast, Düsseldorf 2006

Posner, Helaine, 'Negotiating Boundaries in the Art of Yayoi Kusama, Ana Mendieta and Francesca Woodman', *Mirror Images: Women, Surrealism, and Self-Representation*, exh. cat., MIT List Visual Arts Center, Cambridge, Mass. 1998, pp.156–71

Rodenbeck, J. F., 'Yayoi Kusama: Surface, Stitch, Skin', C. deZegher (ed.), *Inside the Visible: An Elliptical Traverse of 20th Century Art: In, Of, and From the Feminine*, exh. cat., Institute of Contemporary Art, Boston 1994, pp.149–55

Schimmel, Paul (ed.), *Out of Actions: Between Performance and the Objects, 1949–1979*, exh. cat., Museum of Contemporary Arts, Los Angeles 1998

Yayoi Kusama, London 2000

Yamamura, Midori, 'Kusama Yayoi's Early Years in New York: A Critical Biography', *Making A Home*, Eric C. Shiner and Reiko Tomii (ed.), exh. cat., *Japan Society*, New York 2007, pp.52–64

Yoshimoto, Midori, 'Performing the Self: Yayoi Kusama and Her Ever-Expanding Universe', *Into Performance: Japanese Women Artists in New York*, New Brunswick 2005, pp. 45–77

Articles and Reviews in Periodicals

Anon.,'Watching Girl in Long Underwear Play Artist', *East Village Other*, vol.3, no.14, 8–14 March 1968, pp.6, 15

Ashton, Dore, 'Art: Tenth Street View', *New York Times*, 23 October 1959, p.58

Benedict, Michael, 'New York Letters', *Art International*, January 1966, p.98

Brown, Godron, 'Obsessional Painting', *Art Voices*, March 1964, pp.29–31

Camhi, Leslie, 'Woman on the Verge', *Village Voice*, vol. 43, issue 28, 14 July 1998, p.37

Carl, Alfred, 'Call Her Dotty', *Sunday News*, 13 August 1967, pp.10, 31

Celant, Germano, 'Yayoi Kusama', *Interview*, June 2005, pp.76–80

Fer, Briony, 'Objects Beyond Objecthood', *Oxford Art Journal*, vol.22, no.2, 1999, pp.25–36

Friis-Hansen, Dana, 'Yayoi Kusama's Feminism', *Art + Text*, no.49, September 1994, pp.48–55

Fukushima, Tatsuo, 'Kusama Yayoi no geijutsu (jō)' ['The art of Yayoi Kusama (part one)'], *Shin'yō Shinbun*, 22 November 1956

Hoptman, Laura, 'The Princess of the Polka Dot', *Harper's Bazaar*, March 1998, pp.381–2, 288

———. 'The Return of Yayoi Kusama', *MoMA*, July/August, pp.6–9

Ishikawa, Hiroyoshi, 'Jicchi ni mitekita amerika no sei kaihou buri' ['The firsthand account of sexual liberation in the United States'], *Hōseki* [Gem], December 1969, pp.314–17

Judd, Donald, 'Reviews and Previews: New Names This Month—Yayoi Kusama', *Art News*, vol.58, no.6, October 1959, p.17

———. 'In the Galleries: Yayoi Kusama', *Arts*, vol.38, no.10, September 1964, pp.68–9

———. 'Specific Objects', *Arts Yearbook*, vol.8, 1965, pp.74–83

Kelly, Edward T, 'Neo Dada: A Critique of Pop Art', *Art Journal*, vol.23, no.3, Spring 1964, pp.192–201

'Kotoshi no hōpu, joryū gaka Kusama Yayoi' ['This year's hope, a woman artist Yayoi Kusama'], *Chūbu keizai shinbun*, 12 January 1955

Koplos, Janet, 'The Phoenix Returns', *Art in America*, vol.87, no.2, February 1999, pp.92–8

Kroll, Jack, 'Yayoi Kusama', *Artnews*, vol.60, no.3, May 1960, p.15

Kultermann, Udo, 'The Art of Kusama Unveils Female Worldview', *Sculpture*, vol.16, no.1, January 1997, pp.26–31

Levin, Kim, 'Odd Woman Out', *Village Voice*, vol.34, issue 44, 31 October 1989, p.109

Lippard, Lucy, 'Eccentric Abstraction', *Art International*, vol.10, no.9, November 1966, pp.28, 34–40

Mikami, Mariko, 'Kusama Yayoi to Minimarizumu—kanshōsha to jikan' ['Yayoi Kusama and Minimalism—viewer and time'], *Bigaku* [*Aesthetic*], vol.55, no.4, Spring 2005

Nixon, Mignon, 'Posing the Phallus', *October*, no.92, Spring 2000, pp.98–127

———. 'o + x', *October*, no.119, Winter 2007, pp.6–20

'Nyūyōku doman'nakade sekkusu o enshutsu suru Nihon josei' ['A Japanese woman who directs sex in the middle of New York City'], *Heibon Panchi* [*Heibon punch*], vol.6, no.44, 10 November 1969, pp.130–3

O'Doherty, Brian, 'Season's End: Abstractions and Distractions', *New York Times*, 17 June 1962, p.103

Pollock, Griselda, 'Three Thoughts on Femininity, Creativity and Elapsed Time', *Parkett*, vol.59, 2000, pp.107–13

Preston, Stuart, 'Twentieth-Century Sense and Sensibility', *New York Times*, 7 May 1961

Sakagami, Keiko, '1960 nendai Nyūyōku ni okeru nihonjin ātisuto tachi—Kusama Yayoi to Ono Yoko no baai' ['Japanese artists in the 1960s New York—in the cases of Yayoi Kusama and Yoko Ono'], *Bijutsushi kenkyū* [*Research in art history*], no. 44, 2006

Shull, Leo, 'City Desk on B'Way', *Show Business*, 19 April 1969, pp.1, 17

Smith, Roberta, 'Intense Personal Visions of a Fragile Japanese Artist', *New York Times*, 20 October 1989

———. '60's Minimalism, Looking Handmade', *New York Times*, 24 May 1996

Solomon, Andrew, 'Dot Dot Dot', *Artforum*, vol.35, February 1997, pp.66–77

Sommers, Ed, 'Letter from Germany: Yayoi Kusama at the Galerie M.E. Thelen, Essen (May)', *Art International*, vol.10, no.8, October 1966, p.46

Tanikawa, Atsushi, 'Zōshoku no genma', ['Phantom of multiplication'], *Bijutsu techō*, vol.45, no.671, June 1993, pp.65–77

Tillim, Sidney, 'In the Galleries', *Arts*, vol.34, no.1, October 1959, p.56

Tomkins, Calvin, 'On the Edge', *New Yorker*, 7 October 1996, pp.100–3

Turner, Grady, 'Yayoi Kusama', *Bomb*, Winter 1999, pp.62–9

Uno, Kuni'ichi, 'Kyosei to uchū: Kusama Yayoi ten' ['Castration and cosmos: Yayoi Kusama exhibition'], *Bijutsu techō*, vol.40, no.599, September 1998, pp.117–27

Van Starrex, Al, 'Some Far-out Fashion With and Without Clothes', *Mr.*, vol.13, no.8, July 1969, pp.38–9, 41

Worth, Alexi, 'Kusama Dot Com', *New York Times Style Magazine*, 24 February 2008

Yalkut, Jud, 'The Polka-Dot Way of Life (Conversation with Yayoi Kusama)', *New York Free Press*, vol.1, no.8, 15 February 1968, pp.8–9

Zelevansky, Lynn, 'Flying Deeper and Farther: Kusama in 2005', *Afterall*, Spring/Summer 2006, pp.54–62

Archives

Blanton Museum of Art Archives and Fine Arts Library (audio recording listed in 'I. Oral Documentation', *Yayoi Kusama*, 1989), University of Texas, Austin

'Neil Meitzler Papers' (no. 2761), 'Zoe Dusanne Papers' (no.2430–4), Special Collection Division, University of Washington Library, Seattle

Yayoi Kusama Papers, Kusama Yayoi Studio, Tokyo

Films

Metamorphoses: L'École de New York, dir. Jean Antoine, Radio Télévision Belge de la Communauté Française, Brussels 1965

Body Festival ('Naked Happenings' from Orez Gallery, Novum Jazz, and the Balans Art Fair), Carrier no. V 24977, *Kunstprogramma KPI*, 16 November 1967, Netherlands Instituut voor Beeld en Geluid

Yayoi Kusama: I Adore Myself, dir. Takako Matsumoto, B.B.B. Inc., Tokyo 2008 [North American version entitled *Yayoi Kusama: I Love Me*]

World is Longing for Me: Yayoi Kusama – Avant-Garde Artist, Full Throttle, dir. Takako Matsumoto, NKH 16 July 2011

Works Exhibited at Tate Modern in 2012

Bold numbers at the end of entries refer to illustrations. Measurements of artworks are given in centimetres, height before width and depth. Information is correct at the time of going to press.

Lingering Dream 1949
Pigment on paper
136.5 × 151.7
Yayoi Kusama
1

Accumulation of the Corpses (Prisoner Surrounded by the Curtain of Depersonalization) 1950
Oil and enamel on seed sack
72.3 × 91.5
The National Museum of Modern Art, Tokyo
3

Corpses 1950
Oil on canvas
61 × 72.7
Yayoi Kusama
2

Earth of Accumulation 1950
Oil and enamel on seed sack
72.5 × 91
The Museum of Contemporary Art, Tokyo
5

On the Table 1950
Oil and mixed media on canvas
80.4 × 65.5
Yayoi Kusama
4

Self-Portrait 1950
Oil on canvas
34 × 24
Yayoi Kusama
p.194

Phosphoresce in the Daytime c.1950
Ink and pastel on paper
25.2 × 17.5
Yayoi Kusama
20

Untitled 1950s
Ink and pastel on paper
27 × 18.7
Yayoi Kusama
38

Heart 1951
Oil on canvas
31.8 × 41
Yayoi Kusama
7

Inside the Forest 1951
Oil on canvas
32 × 41.1
Yayoi Kusama
6

An Animal 1952
Ink, watercolour and pastel on paper
27 × 18.7
Yayoi Kusama
14

A Flower 1952
Ink on paper
27 × 18.7
Yayoi Kusama
10

Flower Bud 1952
Pastel and watercolour on paper
27 × 18.7
Yayoi Kusama
19

Flower Bud No.6 1952
Ink and pastel on paper
35.8 × 25.2
Yayoi Kusama
16

The Germ 1952
Ink and pastel on paper
24.7 × 18
Yayoi Kusama
9

The Parting 1952
Ink, watercolour, string and collage on silk mounted on paper
45 × 53
Yayoi Kusama
12

Rain in a City 1952
Ink and pastel on paper
35.6 × 25.2
Matsumoto City Museum of Art, Japan
18

The Stem 1952
Ink and watercolour on paper
25 × 18
Yayoi Kusama
17

Tree 1952
Gouache and pastel on paper
25.5 × 18
Yayoi Kusama
15

Untitled 1952
Ink and pastel on paper
26.2 × 18.8
Yayoi Kusama
11

Ancient Fire 1953
Gouache and ink on paper
29 × 22
Yayoi Kusama
29

Dots on the Sun 1953
Watercolour and pastel on paper
25.4 × 26.2
Museum of Contemporary Art, Tokyo
22

An Eye 1953
Pastel and watercolour on paper
27.5 × 20.3
Yayoi Kusama
30

Fern Kingdom 1953
Ink and gouache on paper
25 × 17.5
Collection of Sachie Gocho
37

Fish 1953
Ink, watercolour and pastel on paper
22.5 × 29.5
Yayoi Kusama
31

Fleeing Eye 1953
Ink and watercolour on paper
22.5 × 29.7
Yayoi Kusama
36

Flying People 1953
Ink and pastel on paper
27.2 × 20.2
Yayoi Kusama
28

'Girden' (Festival) 1953
Gouache and pastel on paper
35 × 24.5
Yayoi Kusama
34

Inward Vision No.1 1953
Pastel, watercolour and ink on paper
41.2 × 33.3
Blanton Museum of Art, The University of Texas at Austin. Gift of the Center for International Contemporary Arts; Emanuel and Charlotte Levine Collection, 1992
33

Inward Vision No.4 1953
Pastel, ink, watercolour and tempera on paper
33 × 40.6
Collection of Carla Emil and Rich Silverstein
32

Island No.7 1953
Watercolour and pastel on paper
30.5 × 26.5
Museum of Contemporary Art, Tokyo
21

The Sky 1953
Ink on paper
28.6 × 21.6
Private collection
35

The Woman 1953
Pastel, aqueous tempera and acrylic on paper
45.4 × 38.2
Blanton Museum of Art, The University of Texas at Austin. Gift of the Center for International Contemporary Arts; Emanuel and Charlotte Levine Collection, 1992
25

The Woman (33) 1953
Watercolour on paper
38.5 × 32.5
The National Museum of Modern Art, Tokyo
26

The Coral Reef in the Sea 1954
Ink and watercolour on paper
34.3 × 22.9
Collection of Marc Selwyn, Los Angeles
43

Dawn 1954
Watercolour on paper
66 × 54.6
Gertrude Stein

Flower Buds 1954
Ink, watercolour and pastel on paper
25 × 17.8
Yayoi Kusama
39

Heart 1954
Pastel and gouache on paper
34.9 × 24.8
Courtesy Peter Blum Gallery, New York
40

Leaves 1954
Goauche on paper
20.1 × 27.3
Yayoi Kusama
13

Untitled 1954
Gouache and pastel on paper
50.6 × 46.3
Yayoi Kusama
42

Untitled 1954
Gouache and ink on paper
46.7 × 51.2
Yayoi Kusama
41

A Gill 1955
Gouache, India ink and oil on paper
61 × 72.5
Private collection
27

God of the Wind 1955
Oil on canvas
51.5 × 64
Yayoi Kusama
8

No.19 H.S.W. 1956
Pastel and gouache on paper
59.7 × 45.7
The Museum of Modern Art, New York. Gift of Sally and Wynn Kramarsky, 1999
23

No. White A.Z. 1958–9
Oil on canvas
232 × 359
Shizuoka Prefectural Museum of Art
46

Dot Abstraction 1958–60
Oil on canvas
114.9 × 113
Private American collection. Courtesy Marc Selwyn Fine Art
44

No. A.B. 1959
Oil on canvas
210.3 × 414.4
Toyota Municipal Museum of Art
48

No. B White 1959
Oil on canvas
226.5 × 298
Chiba City Museum of Art
47

No.F 1959
Oil on canvas
105.4 × 132.1
The Museum of Modern Art, New York. Sid R. Bass Fund, 1997
45

Infinity Nets (White) 1959
Oil on canvas
131.1 × 117.5
Gayle and Paul Stoffel, Dallas. Courtesy Neal Meltzer Fine Art
49

Off-cut of Infinity Net painting 1960
Oil on canvas
36 × 990
Yayoi Kusama

Pacific Ocean 1960
Oil on canvas
183 × 183
Museum of Contemporary Art, Tokyo
50

Love Was Infinitely Shining 2010
Acrylic on canvas
194 × 194
Yayoi Kusama

Once the Abominable War is Over, Happiness Fills our Hearts 2010
Acrylic on canvas
194 × 194
Yayoi Kusama
102

Secret Moments 2010
Acrylic on canvas
162 × 162
Yayoi Kusama

Serene Mind 2010
Acrylic on canvas
162 × 162
Yayoi Kusama
104

The Silvery Universe 2010
Acrylic on canvas
194 × 194
Yayoi Kusama
105

Spring has Come 2010
Acrylic on canvas
194 × 194
Yayoi Kusama

Flowers That Bloom Tomorrow L 2011
Fiberglass Reinforced Plastic, metal, urethane paint
200 x 340 x 200
sculpture
Courtesy Victoria Miro Gallery, London; Ota Fine Arts, Tokyo and Yayoi Kusama Studio Inc.

Flowers That Bloom Tomorrow M 2011
Fiberglass Reinforced Plastic, metal, urethane paint
285 x 235 x 108
sculpture
Courtesy Victoria Miro Gallery, London; Ota Fine Arts, Tokyo and Yayoi Kusama Studio Inc.

Flowers That Bloom Tomorrow S 2011
Fiberglass Reinforced Plastic, metal, urethane paint
190 x 165 x 180
sculpture
Courtesy Victoria Miro Gallery, London; Ota Fine Arts, Tokyo and Yayoi Kusama Studio Inc.

Infinity Mirrored Room – Filled with the Brilliance of Life 2011
Wood, mirror, plastic, acrylic, LED lights, aluminium
300 × 617.5 × 645.5
Yayoi Kusama
107

Joseph Cornell 1903–1972
Untitled 1967
Collage on paper
47.5 × 28.7
Yayoi Kusama

Untitled c.1967
Collage on paper
28.2 × 33.2
Yayoi Kusama

Untitled c.1967
Collage on paper
36.2 × 24
Yayoi Kusama

Illustrated in the plate sections but not exhibited

No.8 H.A.P. 1956
Pastel, gouache and acrylic on paper
58.4 × 45.7
Los Angeles County Museum of Art. Purchased with funds provided by the Modern and Contemporary Art Council, Robert and Mary Looker, Robert H. Halff, The Hillcrest Foundation, the Audrey and Sydney Irmas Charitable Foundation, Blake Byrne, Helen N. Lewis and Marvin B. Meyer, Barry and Julie Smooke, Bob Crewe, Sharleen Cooper Cohen, and Robert W. Conn
24

No. T.W.3 1961
Oil on canvas
174 × 125.4
Suzanne Deal Booth and David Booth Collection, Austin, Texas
51

Lenders

Public collections
Akron Art Museum
Blanton Museum of Art, Austin
Chiba City Museum of Art
Des Moines Art Center
Forever Museum of Contemporary Art, Akita
Hiroshima City Museum of Contemporary Art
Hirshhorn Museum and Sculpture Garden, Washington
Hood Museum of Art, Hanover
Matsumoto City Museum of Art
Mudima Foundation, Milan
Museum of Contemporary Art, Tokyo
The Museum of Modern Art, New York
Museum Moderner Kunst, Stiftung Ludwig, Wien
The National Museum of Modern Art, Tokyo
Ota Fine Arts, Tokyo
Paula Cooper Gallery, New York
Peter Blum Gallery, New York
Shizuoka Prefectural Museum of Art
Stedelijk Museum, Amsterdam
Toyota Municipal Museum of Art
Walker Art Center, Minneapolis
Whitney Museum of American Art, New York
Victoria Miro Gallery, London

Private collections
Glenn and Debbie August
Collection of Barbara Bertozzi Castelli
Collection Caroline de Westenholz
Collection of Carla Emil and Rich Silverstein
Collection of Sachie Gocho
Amy Gold and Brett Gorvy
Collection of Judith and Richard Greer
Yayoi Kusama
Beatrice and Hart Perry Family Collection
Collection of Marc Selwyn, Los Angeles
Gertrude Stein
Collection of Jerome L. and Ellen Stern
Gayle and Paul Stoffel, Dallas. Courtesy Neal Meltzer Fine Art
Takahashi Collection
Private American collection. Courtesy Marc Selwyn Fine Art
Private collection
Private collection
Private collection, Berlin
Private collection, New York. Courtesy D'Amelio Terras
Private collection, Switzerland
Private collection. Courtesy Robert Miller Gallery, New York

Copyright

Photo Credits

All images © Yayoi Kusama Studio Inc. unless listed below.

© Shigeo Anzai, Benesse Art Site Naoshima p.149 top
© Bungeishunju p.124 top
© Sheldan C. Collins no.69
Fuji Television Gallery, Tokyo 1982 © ANZAÏ p.132 left
© Rick Hall no.25
© Yukio Hijikata p.125 right
© Eikoh Hosoe front cover, no. 81 (24 images in total)
© Doug Kuntz no.57
© Norman R.C. MacGrath p.73 left
© Antonio Maniscalco no.58
© 2010. Digital image, The Museum of Modern Art, New York / Scala, Florence nos.23, 24, 68, 71
© The Museum of Modern Art, New York. Photographic Archive. The Museum of Modern Art Archives, New York © 2011. Digital Image, The Museum of Modern Art, New York / Scala, Florence, Photo: Thomas Griesel no.65
© Paula Cooper Gallery, New York nos.35, 66
© Tom Powel no.61
© Adam Reich no.32
© Hal Reiff p.9, p.72 bottom
© Bob Sabin p.118 top right
© Sadamu Saito p.188 top
© Lee Stalsworth no.60
© Tate Photography, 2011, Dave Lambert no.63
© Tate Photography, 2011, Marcus Leith and Andrew Dunkley nos.1, 31, 33, 37, 38, 39, 44, 45, 48, 49, 50, 53, 54, 55, 62, 64, 84, 85, 86, 90, 91, 92, 93, 94, 95, 107
© Yoshitaka UCHIDA no.46
Kenneth Van Sickle p.10
© Robert Wedemeyer no.43
© Yasuhiko Yoshida (contact: 4-22-35 Nanko, Chigasaki-City, Kanagawa Prefecture, Japan) p.173 top

Index

Page numbers in *italic* type refer to illustrations.